CAMPING *guide to* WESTERN AUSTRALIA

Cathy Savage and Craig Lewis

www.boilingbilly.com.au

Boiling Billy, a licensed imprint of
Woodslane Press Pty Ltd
10 Apollo Street
Warriewood NSW 2102 Australia
Email: info@woodslane.com.au
Tel: 02 8445 2300
www.woodslane.com.au

This fully revised 3rd edition 2012

ISBN 9781921606168 (pbk.)

Design and Layout: Erica McIntyre
Cartography: Laurie Whiddon - Map Illustrations, Chris Crook - Country Cartographics, Pablo Canadia - A1 Cartography

Please be aware that conditions constantly change. Campsites are subject to closure without notice and camping fees may rise. It is the responsibility of individuals to enquire about the status of areas they wish to visit prior to departure.

Author: Savage, Cathy.
Title: Camping guide to Western Australia: the bestselling colour guide to over 450 campsites / Cathy Savage, Craig Lewis.
Edition: 3rd ed.
ISBN: 9781921606168 (pbk.)
Notes: Includes index.
Subjects: Camp sites, facilities, etc.—Western Australia—Directories.
Camping—Western Australia--Guidebooks.
Western Australia--Description and travel.
Other Authors/Contributors: Lewis, Craig (Craig William), 1966-
Dewey Number: 796.5409941

Your Help Please

Boiling Billy Publications welcomes feedback from readers. If you find things are different than what is stated in this guide, or you know of a suitable campsite that we can update in subsequent editions, then please write or e-mail us at

Boiling Billy Publications
Nimmitabel NSW 2631
Tel: 02 6454 6162
E-mail: info@boilingbilly.com.au
Web: www.boilingbilly.com.au
www.facebook.com/boillingbilly

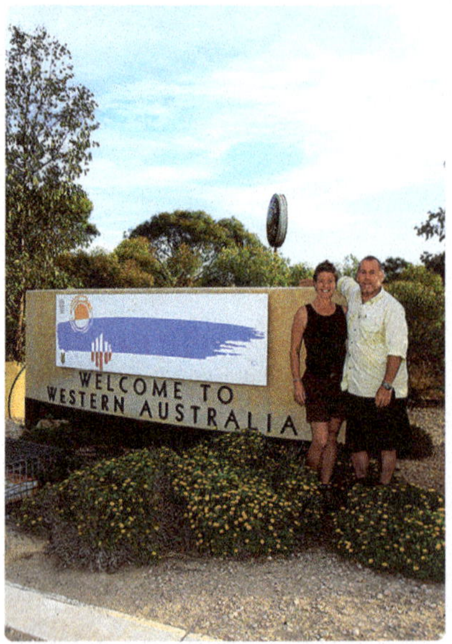

ABOUT the authors

Cathy Savage and Craig Lewis have been on an almost endless walkabout through Australia's backblocks for the past 18 years. As full-time authors and photographers, they both travel to write and write to travel, often spending up to 100 nights each year camped out in their quest to bring readers the best information in upcoming titles. They generally favour secluded bush campsites, far from the maddening crowds. This is by far their favourite style of camping.

When not on the road travelling their home base is a secluded farm tucked away high up on the coastal escarpment in the Monaro region of south-eastern New South Wales. From here they oversee a growing list of outdoor titles for their publishing company, Boiling Billy Publications, which they established in 1995. The view from their office window looks out over the pristine Brogo Wilderness in Wadbilliga National Park.

Cathy and Craig's website can be found at www.boilingbilly.com.au or you can keep up to date with the latest happenings or log your feedback on their Facebook page at www.facebook.com/boilingbilly

Contents

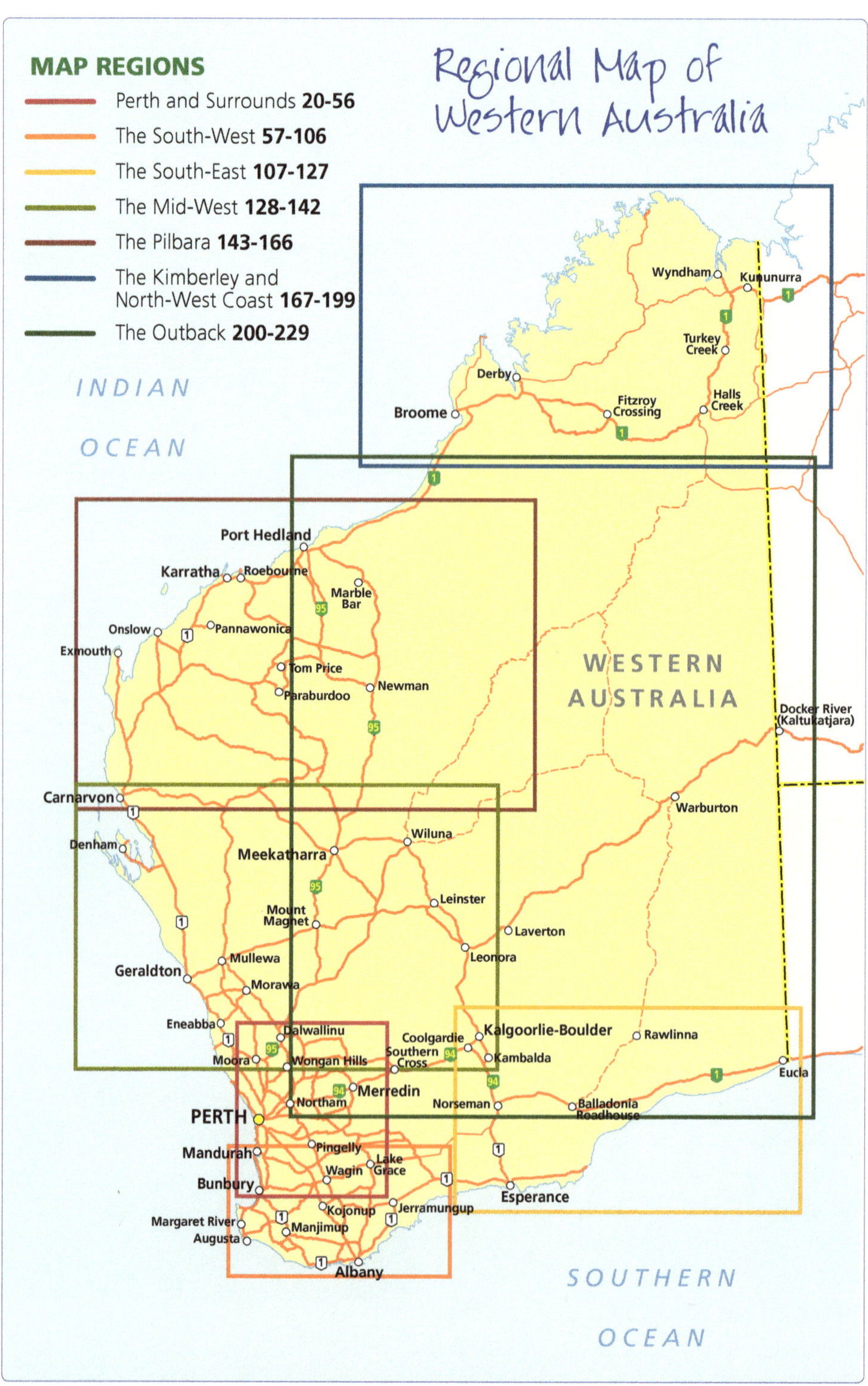

MAP REGIONS
Perth and Surrounds 20-56
The South-West 57-106
The South-East 107-127
The Mid-West 128-142
The Pilbara 143-166
The Kimberley and North-West Coast 167-199
The Outback 200-229
Regional Map of Western Australia
INDIAN OCEAN
SOUTHERN OCEAN
WESTERN AUSTRALIA
Wyndham
Kununurra
Turkey Creek
Derby
Fitzroy Crossing
Halls Creek
Broome
Port Hedland
Karratha
Roebourne
Marble Bar
Onslow
Pannawonica
Exmouth
Tom Price
Paraburdoo
Newman
Docker River (Kaltukatjara)
Carnarvon
Warburton
Denham
Wiluna
Meekatharra
Leinster
Mount Magnet
Laverton
Leonora
Mullewa
Geraldton
Morawa
Eneabba
Dalwallinu
Coolgardie
Kalgoorlie-Boulder
Rawlinna
Moora
Wongan Hills
Southern Cross
Kambalda
Eucla
Merredin
Northam
Norseman
Balladonia Roadhouse
PERTH
Mandurah
Pingelly
Lake Grace
Wagin
Bunbury
Esperance
Kojonup
Jerramungup
Margaret River
Manjimup
Augusta
Albany

Camping in Western Australia

Western Australia is a huge state. Covering more than 2 500 000 sq km, it boasts 12 500 km of stunning coastline and spans 2 400km from north to south. This vast landmass occupies a third of the continent.

This all equates to a lot of opportunities to pitch your tent and one of the best ways to experience the 'West's' natural beauty is to spend a night under the stars camping. The state's national parks, conservation areas, forests and reserves offer numerous places to enjoy for those who delight in the great outdoors. From the magnificent towering karri forests of the south-west to the beautiful deep gorges of the Kimberley to the vast desert areas of the outback, there are parks and reserves which cater for all styles of camping in a range of beautiful and diverse landscapes.

In the south of the state are numerous national park areas protecting some of Australia's most spectacular coastline. Here you can pitch your tent right beside the ocean. Watch for whales as they pass by the southern coastline, canoe some of the state's beautiful rivers and waterways or try your luck for a feed of marron while visiting this area. Further north in the Mid-West region, the vibrant colours of seasonal wildflowers are a major drawcard for both interstate travellers and locals alike while adventerous campers will find secluded campsites along some of the country's best known and remote outback roads. In the north of the state explore the magnificent Bungle Bungle ranges, enjoy the peace and solitude of a deserted beach in Cape Range National Park or go mud crabbing with a local at Kalumburu. Campers visiting the parks and reserves of Western Australia will be surrounded by natural beauty, be delighted by the local wildlife and become absorbed by the history of this ancient landscape.

Along with discovering the unique beauty of Western Australia, you can experience spectacular mountainscapes, such as those of the Stirling Range where you'll find a bewildering array of plants and wildlife in their natural environment. All this and more is available in the 170 parks and reserves within this guide. And if all this activity sounds too exhausting, then there are plenty of campsites throughout Western Australia where you can set up your camp and simply relax, whether it's for a weekend or a month.

Without doubt one of the best things about camping is that it is fun and in Western Australia there's something to suit everyone, whether you're a once-a-year camper, a long-term traveller, an avid adventurer, fisherman or diver, a bushwalker or a four-wheel drive tourer. No matter what type of camping you prefer, be it a secluded walk-in campsite, car-based camping beside a river or the ocean, or with your van at a campground with amenities, you will be sure to find an ideal campsite to suit your needs amongst the 450 plus sites in this guide.

Now's the time pack your tent and sleeping bag, grab some tucker and head out for a camping adventure in one of Western Australia's great camping areas listed in this guide. What are you waiting for?

Happy Camping

Craig Lewis and Cathy Savage
Kybeyan NSW

How to use this Guide

Camping Guide to Western Australia is designed in an easy-to-use format which makes finding a perfect campsite simple. The guide has been broken into different chapters covering the major tourism regions throughout Western Australia.

In this book, each park, forest or reserve throughout the state which allows camping has its own entry. You can locate their approximate positions on the regional maps at the beginning of each chapter. These maps provide an overview of the region covered in the chapter and provide a starting reference point. There are also a number of more detailed maps for some of the national parks, forests and reserves throughout the guide. The grey boxes on the regional maps at the start of each region show the area covered by these maps in that region.

Each entry, whether it be a national park, forest reserve or riverside area, has detailed information relating to that site including access details, map references (MR) and many include GPS coordinates. These map references refer to the Touring Maps section and can be used for locating the campsite. For example, MR: Map 55 E3 refers to Touring Map 55 and the grid reference is E3 – this is the location of Neds Camp in Cape Range National Park.

We use symbols to detail the facilities and activities at each site.

We have also included Further Information boxes for each park or reserve listing which provides a contact point for making enquiries or bookings, along with prices and other details that apply to the campsites.

Although all care has been taken when compiling this guide and all information is correct at the time of going to print, please be aware that conditions at many campsites are constantly changing. Camping fees may be introduced to previously free areas or may be increased from what is listed at the time of going to print. Some areas may also be closed from time to time. Fire and flood, for example, can have a marked effect on an area literally overnight.

Note for GPS users: A substantial number of campsites in this guide have coordinates (latitude and longitude) which can be utilised by those with GPS receivers as an additional means of navigating to the campsite. The coordinates were acquired during field research using GDA 94 map datum and are in HDDD MM.MMM format.

Remember

After you have chosen your campsite we strongly recommend that you contact the park, forest or reserve office prior to your departure to obtain advice on current and upcoming conditions. For sites where a camping/entry fee is payable we recommend that you contact the land managers to obtain the current fee schedule before arrival. Be aware that some sites may require advance bookings, especially during the peak tourist periods of December/January and Easter in the South-East regions, and during the dry season of May through to September in the far north. Booking requirements are detailed for these sites in the guide, however we also recommend you make your own enquiries prior to arrival to avoid disappointment.

Map Legend

Manning Gorge •	Campsite Name
Prison Boab Tree •	Point of Interest Name
	Campsite
	Picnic Area
	Lookout
	Nature Walk
	Information
	Boat Launching Area
Albany ○	Town
Lake Jasper ●	Locality
Mt Ragged ▲	Mountain Peak
Mammoth Cave •	Physical Feature
Gibb River Rd	Road Name
NATIONAL PARK	Park / Reserve Name
Gibb River	Lake / River Name
	Freeway
	Principal Road
	Secondary Road
	Minor Road
	Vehicular Track
	Walking Track
	State Border
	Railway
	Dam Wall
	Cliff
	Major River
	Minor River
	State Forest
	National Park / Reserve
	Recreation Reserve
	Orchard / Plantation
	Perennial Waterbody
	Non-perennial Waterbody
	Land Subject to Inundation
	Built-up Area

Campsite Symbols

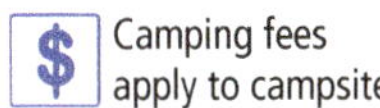
Camping fees apply to campsite

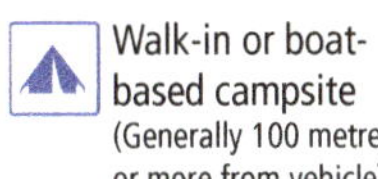
Walk-in or boat-based campsite (Generally 100 metres or more from vehicle)

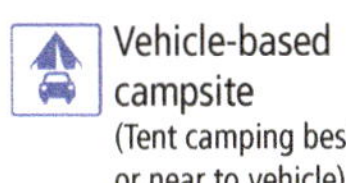
Vehicle-based campsite (Tent camping beside or near to vehicle)

Camper trailer accessible campsite

Caravan accessible campsite (including campervans - motorhomes check first)

4WD vehicle-only accessible site

Information centre/ board

Ranger/staff on site

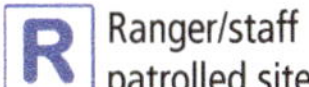
Ranger/staff patrolled site

Toilets

Wheelchair access to toilets

Picnic tables

Covered picnic tables/shelter

Wood fireplace/ BBQ

Electric/gas BBQ

Fires prohibited

Drinking water

Hot showers

Cold showers

No rubbish disposal at site

Public Telephone available

Graded walking tracks nearby

Bushwalking

Signposted nature walk

Signposted forest drive

Lookout/scenic area

Swimming nearby to campsite

Swimming not recommended

Crocodiles

Fishing nearby to campsite

Canoeing nearby

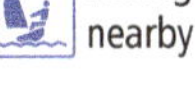
Sailing nearby

Water-skiing nearby

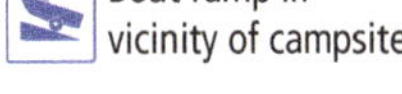
Boat ramp in vicinity of campsite

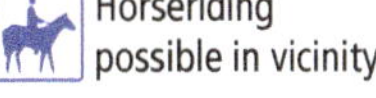
Horseriding possible in vicinity

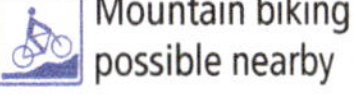
Mountain biking possible nearby

Bird watching

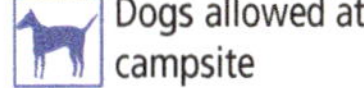
Dogs allowed at campsite

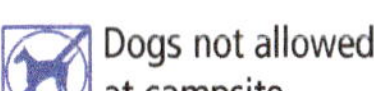
Dogs not allowed at campsite

Planning

If you're an old hand at camping, travelling in a campervan or towing a caravan, you probably already have everything for a camping trip. However, if you're a camping novice or simply just rusty – that is, you're planning to go camping but it's not something you do regularly – then the following tips may be helpful.

Like many experienced campers, we've found over the years the key to hassle-free camping is to follow the KIS principle – Keep It Simple. It's all about getting back to basics. Wander around any of the larger camping stores and you'll find a plethora of odds and ends which are claimed to make camp life easier and more comfortable. Stick to the basics. Travel light. We're pretty certain you'll enjoy your camping experience more by following this simple philosophy.

Your camping holiday will be much more enjoyable with the right gear. If you are setting up a camping outfit then buy the best gear you can afford. Quality gear will serve you well over a long period if looked after.

The warmer summer season is the most popular time to camp in the south-west and south-east regions of Western Australia while the northern 'dry season', from around May through to September, is the best time for camping in the Pilbara and Kimberley and North-West Coast. During the dry season days are generally warm and nights mild. The cooler months are also the most comfortable time to venture into Western Australia's outback areas with pleasant days and cool nights. The outback can experience extreme temperatures during summer and is best avoided at this time. Late autumn, early and late winter and spring are the best times to visit here. Remember to always pack a warm jumper and long pants.

Camping during the northern 'wet season' from December to February is both restrictive, due to many areas being closed and/or roads impassable, and uncomfortable, due to the high humidity

Biting insects such as spiders, bees, wasps, ants, ticks or mosquitoes can turn a dream camping holiday into a nightmare. To help protect yourself from these unwelcome visitors wear long pants, long-sleeved shirts and shoes and don't forget insect repellant. Mosquitoes and sand flies in particular can be a nuisance in the tropical areas of far north of Western Australia along the coastal fringes. They are generally at their worst around dusk, so be sure to cover up and use a DEET-based insect repellent to help avoid their irritating bites.

Never pitch your tent directly under large trees. Those large, shady trees lining our inland rivers might looking like inviting campsites but they have a habit of dropping branches without warning.

When planning your camping trip, don't head off without:

- Good maps. See 'Maps, Park Passes, Camping Fees and Permits' in this section. If you plan on venturing off the beaten track, be it bushwalking, vehicle touring or fishing, be sure to carry a detailed map of the area you plan to visit.
- A gas/liquid fuel stove. If the campsite you want to visit doesn't allow you to light a fire or provide cooking facilities, then you will need to take your own. A small single burner gas stove is fine for 2-3 people; two-burner stoves are needed for families.
- Insect repellent and a first aid kit. Mosquitoes, sand flies and bugs can be a nuisance while a good first aid kit is a necessity.
- Plenty of fresh drinking water. Don't rely on tank water or rivers/creeks at campsites for fresh drinking water. Although there may be water at the campsite it may be contaminated, making it undrinkable.
- Ample food supplies. If you are camping in remote areas well away from shops or supplies be sure to take enough food with you, and always pack enough tucker for an extra day or two in case inclement weather holds you up. When you're out in the fresh air, you often have a bigger appetite, especially if you combine some swimming, bike riding or bushwalking. Kids especially get very hungry on camping trips, so make sure you include plenty of healthy nibbles.

For a detailed equipment checklist see the Equipment Checklist section.

WE COULDN'T live without...

A comfortable folding chair is one luxury that we always pack. Sitting around camp with your drink of choice after a busy day enjoying the outdoors is just a whole lot more fun in a comfy chair.

A folding table, either the type with a hard top and folding legs or the newer aluminium slat type which pulls apart and rolls onto a bag, make camp life easier. We use both types, mostly the hard top but opt for the aluminum slat table when space is at a premium. Don't rely on campsites to have picnic tables.

Under Cover

There is a bewildering choice of camping accommodation available today, be it a tent, camper trailer, caravan, swag or roof top tent. Your choice of camping accommodation really depends on things such as the time you'll spend using it, your budget, available vehicle space (whether it is to be stowed in the vehicle, on a roof rack or towed), the number of people to accommodate and the environment it will be used in.

Now with the increasing use of four-wheel drives as towing vehicles, caravans and camper trailers are gaining in popularity at an amazing pace, especially the more rugged off-road units. These set ups are often favoured by long-term travellers who frequently venture off the beaten track and families who camp out regularly. Advantages of caravans and camper trailers include extra storage space, comfortable sleeping areas and extra shade and weather cover. Remember though that some destinations are out of bounds or just not practical if you are towing a caravan or trailer. Becoming increasingly more common are the number of national park campsites throughout the state which are not caravan or trailer friendly. These sites are ringed by bollards, providing a small vehicle parking space. You carry your camping gear over these to the grassed campsite.

Sleep Easy

Self-inflating camp mattresses are by far the best choice for tent-based campers and offer a comfortable night's sleep. Mattresses range from ultra-light three-quarter length models for bushwalkers through to heavier and more bulky double models which are perfect for vehicle-based campers. We use a double self-inflating mattress as our tent mattress and it also doubles as our swag mattress. Self-inflating mattresses roll up to form a compact cylinder which can easily be stowed in your vehicle or on a roof rack. Although they rarely leak, don't forget a puncture repair kit just in case. Comfortable bedding is also a must. Winter nights in Western Australia's southern outback can fall below freezing. A good, zero-degree rated sleeping bag will cover most camping scenarios. We use sleeping bags when bushwalking but prefer sheets and a doona when vehicle-based camping. And don't forget your pillow.

Now I See the Light

The quality and choice of camp lighting has improved a lot in recent years. While gas (LPG or butane) lanterns are still popular, we have found the portable 12-volt fluorescent lights to be the best all-round camp lighting. These units throw out good light with minimal current draw from your vehicle's battery. Rechargeable lanterns are another option (they can be recharged via your vehicles cigarette lighter socket) while a rechargeable torch or two takes up little room. We also take with us a good quality headlamp which is indispensable for cooking and other late night camp chores.

Let's Cook

An increasing number of national park campgrounds no longer permit camp fires of any type, a trend that is on the increase right across Australia. If a camping area has a wood fireplace and you'd like a camp fire, then please use it — don't create a new one – and keep your cooking fire small. Be sure to bring firewood with you as firewood is either scarce or non-existent at many campsites. A folding grate for the fire and a BBQ plate (some camping areas provide these), frying pan, a few pots with lids and a couple of billies and maybe a camp oven is all that's required for camp cooking. A pair of sturdy leather gloves and shovel are also handy.

Increasing, many national parks and council camping reserves have gas/electric barbeques for visitor use. However, our advice is to always bring along a gas/fuel stove on your camping adventures. This allows you to be self sufficient in all weather (except on days of total fire bans).

MAPS, PARK PASSES, CAMPING FEES AND PERMITS

Maps

All campsites in this guide are referenced to the Touring Map section in the back of the book (abbreviated to MR in campsite descriptions). This road atlas, which covers all of Western Australia, is used to locate campsites along with the regional maps and national park/forest maps in this guide.

Detailed maps for many of Western Australia's national park areas are available through visitor information centres as well as through specialist map retailers.

A NOTE on camping fees

A note on camping fees: The camping fees indicated in the Further Information box are correct at the time of printing and generally reflect the low season fee. Peak season fees may be higher than those listed. Camping fees may rise or be introduced to areas which may have previously been free of charge. We recommend that you enquire with the land managers about the status of areas they wish to visit, including current fees, prior to departure.

Park Passes

Visitor fees apply to many parks within Western Australia. The Department of Environment and Conservation (DEC) provide a range of Park Passes for visitors which cover park entry fees. Please note that Park Passes do not cover camping fees. The different Park Passes available are:

Day Pass valid for one day only. Entry to any national park on that same day. Available from DEC offices, rangers and park entry stations.

Holiday Pass valid up to four weeks. Unlimited entry to any national park. Available from DEC offices.

Annual Local Park Pass valid for 12 months. Unlimited entry to one chosen national park or a group of local parks. Available from DEC offices.

Annual All Parks Pass valid for 12 months. Unlimited entry to all national parks. Available from DEC offices.

For further information or for details of your nearest park pass outlet or to purchase park passes contact any DEC office, to purchase over the phone dial 08 9219 8000 or visit the DEC website at www.dec.wa.gov.au

For safety purposes, some remote walk-in sites or canoe access sites may require visitors to register their intentions with the land managers.

Travel Permits

To travel through some Aboriginal Lands in Western Australia a travel permit may be required. For details on areas and roads where permits apply contact the Department of Indigenous Affairs on 1300 651 077or visit their website at www.dia.wa.gov.au Please note that permits must be obtained prior to travelling on or through Aboriginal Lands. Remember, if you intend travelling from the Northern Territory you must first obtain your permits prior to entering Western Australia.

Quarantine

When travelling into Western Australia it is important to remember that fresh fruit and vegetables, as well as certain fruit, vegetable and animal based products including honey cannot be carried over the border into Western Australia from either South Australia or the Northern Territory. If you have prohibited items with you either eat them beforehand or surrender fresh fruit and vegetables to officers at Quarantine Stations. Fines do not apply if you hand in fruit and vegetables at the Quarantine Stations, however, hefty fines do apply if fresh fruit and vegetables are carried into Western Australia. Mobile random spot checks do occur at border crossings without permanent, staffed quarantine stations.

Fishing

In Western Australia all marine fishing is managed in four broad biological regions (bioregions), each with its own set of recreational fishing regulations. In addition, there are a number of recreational fisheries and fishing activities throughout Western Australia with their own specific set of rules and which require a licence including freshwater angling, net fishing and fishing for abalone, rock lobster or marron. Details of the four bioregions, regulations and licences can be found at www.fish.wa.gov.au or contact the Department of Fisheries Western Australia on 08 9482 7333.

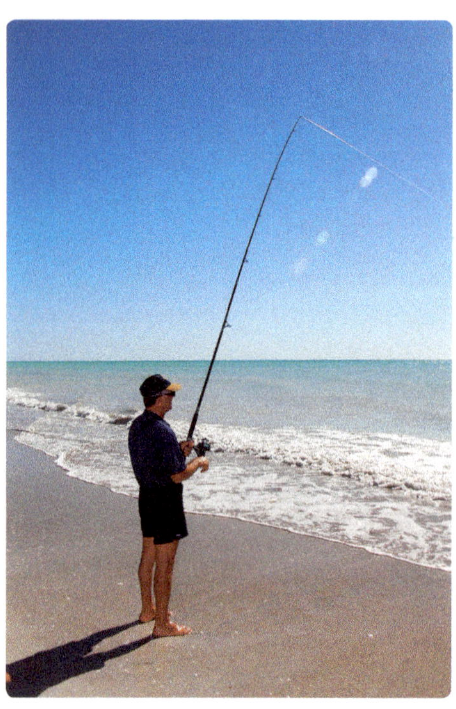

Boating Permits

In Western Australia every skipper of a registrable, recreational vessel, powered by a motor greater than 4.5kwp (6 hp) (RST vessel) is required to hold a Recreational Skipper's Ticket. Interstate visitors to Western Australia who hold a valid/current interstate skipper's ticket will be taken that they hold a recreational skipper's ticket for a period of three months. Go to www.transport.wa.gov.au/ and navigate your way to the marine page for details or call Transport WA Recreational Skippers Ticket (RST) information line on 08 9216 8966

Prospecting and Fossicking

In Western Australia a Miner's Right allows the holder to prospect on Crown land and take and keep samples and specimens of any ore or material up to 20 kilograms. A Miner's Right may be obtained for a fee from The Department of Mines and Petroleum, Mineral House, 100 Plain Street, East Perth, or at any Mining Registrar's Office. Details can be found at the Department of Mines and Petroleum website dmp.wa.gov.au or tel: 08 9222 3333.

CROCODILE AND MARINE STINGERS WARNING

Two species of crocodile occur in Western Australia: the estuarine (saltwater or 'salties') crocodile and the freshwater (or 'freshies') crocodile. Both species are found extensively throughout northern Australia, with the estuarine crocodile's Western Australian habitat extending south to near Port Hedland. Many of the rivers, creeks, waterholes and wetland/mangrove areas of The Kimberley and North-West Coast and parts of the Pilbara coast, along with the surrounding ocean, are inhabited by saltwater crocodiles. These creatures are dangerous and caution is required when camping or undertaking recreational activities such as boating, canoeing or fishing in areas that are known crocodile habitats. The crocodile warning symbol used throughout this book is to be seen as a guide only and is not intended to replace caution and common sense! Please obey any warning signs in the areas you are travelling through. The absence of a warning sign does not necessarily imply that an area is safe for water-based activities. Remember, when you enter the Kimberley or Pilbara regions you are entering crocodile country. Seek local advice or contact the local DEC office and be crocodile wise.

Freshwater crocodiles are relatively common in the north of Western Australia, with the state having probably the largest population due to a wide range of suitable habitats such as the massive Argyle and Kununurra lakes created by the Ord River dam system. 'Freshies' can be seen throughout the Kimberley in gorges and freshwater billabongs. Early morning and in the afternoon are the best times to see them as they bask in the sun or float in the shallows searching for food.

Compared with the saltwater crocodile, 'freshies' are generally smaller, being rarely longer than three metres and are not considered as aggressive.

The flyer Crocodiles produced by DEC offers advice on how to be 'crocodile wise' and is an excellent resource to have on hand when travelling in these areas. It is available at DEC offices or can be downloaded at www.dec.wa.gov.au/pdf/plants_animals/living_with_wildlife/crocodiles.pdf

Marine stingers, such as the potentially deadly Box Jellyfish and Irukandji, occur in the coastal waters of Western Australia from Geraldton north. These stingers are usually active between October and April and swimming is definitely not recommended during these times. There are however some coastal towns and resorts which have stinger nets to enclose a safe swimming area. It is recommended to always check with local authorities prior to swimming. Further information on Australia's marine stinger can be found at www.marinestingers.com.au

CAMPING WITH YOUR DOG

Dogs are not permitted in the national parks, conservation parks and nature reserves of Western Australia. There are a number of state forest and council reserve camping areas that allow dogs restrained on a leash. Every campsite in this guide details if dogs are allowed.

Please note that extensive 1080 fox baiting is undertaken throughout Western Australia by land managers and farmers, and in some cases these can be close to areas where camping is allowed. All baited areas are signposted, however, baits can be carried out of signposted areas by birds or animals. If travelling and camping with your pet in areas that are baited it is advisable that your pet be muzzled to prevent it taking a bait. Contact the land managers in the areas you intend travelling through for up-to-date information on baiting programs.

FIRE WARNINGS AND RESTRICTIONS

At times fire bans and/or restrictions may be in force throughout Western Australia. It is vital to always confirm fire ban dates and restrictions with local authorities such as Fire and Emergency Services Authority of Western Australia (FESA), land managers, council, police and information centres prior to lighting any camp fire. Fire ban information can be obtained at any time by phoning the Total Fire Ban information line on 1800 709 355, or by visiting www.fesa.wa.gov.au

On days declared total fire bans you're not allowed to have any fire in the open, including solid fuel fires, gas cookers or barbeques. Total fire bans are generally broadcast on local radio stations and it's your responsibility to be aware of these. On days of high-fire danger it may be prudent to refrain from having open fires; use gas or fuel-cooking appliances instead.

To protect the natural environment and the local wildlife a number of national parks and reserves listed in this guide do not permit camp fires. For these parks and reserves it is essential that you carry your own gas/fuel stove for cooking.

Camp Fires

Firewood

Firewood is becoming scarce, or sometimes non-existent, at popular camping areas. Apart from firewood, fallen and dead timber also provides habitats for the local wildlife. If you're camping where camp fires are permitted, it is advisable to either bring with you from home, purchase or collect your wood prior to arrival to the campsite. Some parks prohibit the collection of firewood within the park and some parks may have signposted firewood collection points outside the park boundary. Please do not cut down any vegetation, either living or dead, and do not collect or use wood that may have habitat holes. Also, to help protect the spread of exotic weeds and pests, some national parks and reserves request that collected firewood from outside the immediate area is not to be taken into the parks. We strongly recommend that you always carry a gas/fuel stove for cooking, even if camp fires are permitted at your intended campsite.

Camp Fire Safety

If you use a camp fire you must ensure that all combustible material is clear for four metres in all directions, never leave your camp fire unattended and always put your camp fire out with water (never with sand or dirt). Never throw cans or glass into your camp fire. Remember the average-sized camp fire. . .

- is capable of generating over 500 degrees of heat after burning for only three hours when extinguished with sand or dirt, retains up to 100 degrees of heat for eight hours — always use water instead
- when extinguished with a bucket of water retains little or no heat after of period of 10 minutes. If it's safe to touch, it's safe to leave.

FURTHER Information

Fire and Emergency Services Authority WA (total fireban updates and bushfire updates)
Tel: 1800 709 355
Website: www.fesa.wa.gov.au
All fire emergencies dial 000

TREADING SOFTLY ON WESTERN AUSTRALIA

Queensland's parks and reserves are some of the state's most precious and at the same time sensitive recreational resources. When enjoying these areas, whether it be camping, walking, canoeing, cycling, car touring, 4WDing or just going bush, it's important to tread lighting on the environment.

Minimal impact camping is the way to go.

When setting up camp there are a few simple guidelines, which if followed, will help ensure that Queensland's parks and reserves are preserved for everyone to enjoy in the future.

Minimal impact camping guidelines:

Be prepared: Plan your trip carefully and make sure your gear is in good order (for good gear tips, see 'Planning' in this section). Have an alternative plan in case of wet weather, road closures, fire bans etc.

Camp fire safety: Use fireplaces where provided and observe any fire bans. Clear combustible material four metres away from the fire. Be sure the fire is out before leaving (for more, see the section 'Fire Warnings and Restrictions'). Be sure to pack a gas/fuel stove for cooking.

Protect plants and animals: If possible, make your camp to avoid trampling plants or disturbing animals. Do not feed wildlife as 'human food' can cause illness and disease to animals. Pack food away when not at camp and at night to discourage wildlife.

Waterway care: Don't pollute waterways. Don't use soap or detergents in or close to waterways. Wash at least 100 metres from waterways.

Toilet time: Use toilets if provided. If not, bury wastes at least 100 metres away from campsites and watercourses, in a hole at least 15cm deep. If possible (make sure there is no additional combustible material nearby) burn toilet paper before covering the hole.

Use rubbish bins if provided or take your rubbish with you when you leave. Don't bury rubbish – animals will most likely dig it up. Leave campsites in better condition than you found them.

Neighbours: Be considerate of others when camping nearby. Keep noise to a minimum and observe campsite quiet times (usually 10pm to 7am).

OUTBACK AND REMOTE AREA TRAVEL

When travelling in the outback and remote northern regions of Western Australia it is recommended for safety purposes that you leave your travel plans and details with a family member or friend. Check ins and follow ups should then be made with them at regular intervals.

When travelling in outback regions always stay on public access roads and tracks. Never venture off onto unmarked or non-signposted tracks — these could be station tracks on private property and you could be trespassing. Permission must be gained from land owners prior to any travel on private property. Remember, just because there is no fence it does not mean it is not private property.

When travelling Western Australia's remote and outback regions please remember at all times to:

- Stay on public main roads and designated access roads/tracks.
- Do not travel on closed roads—heavy penalties apply.
- If travel permits are required for the route you intend to travel make sure you obtain these prior to departure.
- After rain or flooding always check road conditions before travelling. The local police or council who administer the area you are travelling to can advise you on the current road conditions.
- Always leave gates as found.
- Never camp beside a stock watering point —it discourages stock from coming to the water to drink.
- Watch out for livestock on roads and never approach livestock.
- Do not use livestock water troughs as baths or wash tubs.
- Never make your camp in a dry creek bed—flash flooding can occur.
- Bury human waste and burn toilet paper.

Do not bury garbage—take it out with you as it will inevitably be dug up by animals.

- Always check local fire ban conditions.
- Use a gas/fuel stove. Collection of wood in many national parks is not allowed. Please observe any regulations regarding collection of firewood.
- If travelling with a pet keep it with you at all times and always on a lead. Never leave it unattended—territorial dingoes and wild dogs may attack and kill your pet or the area may be baited.
- Always carry plenty of water and spare fuel. Although some places may have drinking water available, outback areas rely on rain, bores and springs for their water needs.

WHAT TO PACK

Camping Equipment

- ❑ Bucket
- ❑ Chairs
- ❑ Dust pan & brush
- ❑ First Aid Kit
- ❑ Fluro light
- ❑ Ground sheet
- ❑ Head torch
- ❑ Mattress/s
- ❑ Mattress pump
- ❑ Pillows and cases
- ❑ Screen/mesh tent
- ❑ Sleeping bag
- ❑ Spare rope
- ❑ Swag
- ❑ Table
- ❑ Tent
- ❑ Tent pegs
- ❑ Tent poles
- ❑ Tent rope
- ❑ Torch
- ❑ Torch batteries
- ❑ Water container

Cooking Equipment

- ❑ Matches and/or lighter
- ❑ Firelighters
- ❑ Two burner gas stove and gas bottle
- ❑ BBQ plate
- ❑ Grill or grate
- ❑ 2 saucepans with lids
- ❑ Frying pan
- ❑ Camp oven
- ❑ Trivet - to fit camp oven
- ❑ Billy
- ❑ Tripod hanger and hooks
- ❑ Pie dish - to fit camp oven
- ❑ Pizza tray - to fit camp oven
- ❑ Camp oven lifters
- ❑ Shovel - long handled
- ❑ Leather gloves

Miscellaneous Cooking Items

- ❑ Roll of aluminium foil
- ❑ Roll of cling wrap
- ❑ Paper towel
- ❑ Plastic bottle for milk
- ❑ Plastic bottle for cordial
- ❑ Plastic bottle for extra water
- ❑ Storage containers with lids
- ❑ Zip lock bags

Personal Eating Equipment - 1 per person

- ❑ Bowl
- ❑ Fork
- ❑ Knife
- ❑ Mug
- ❑ Plate
- ❑ Spoon
- ❑ Steak Knife
- ❑ Tea spoon

Cooking Utensils

- ❑ Mixing bowls

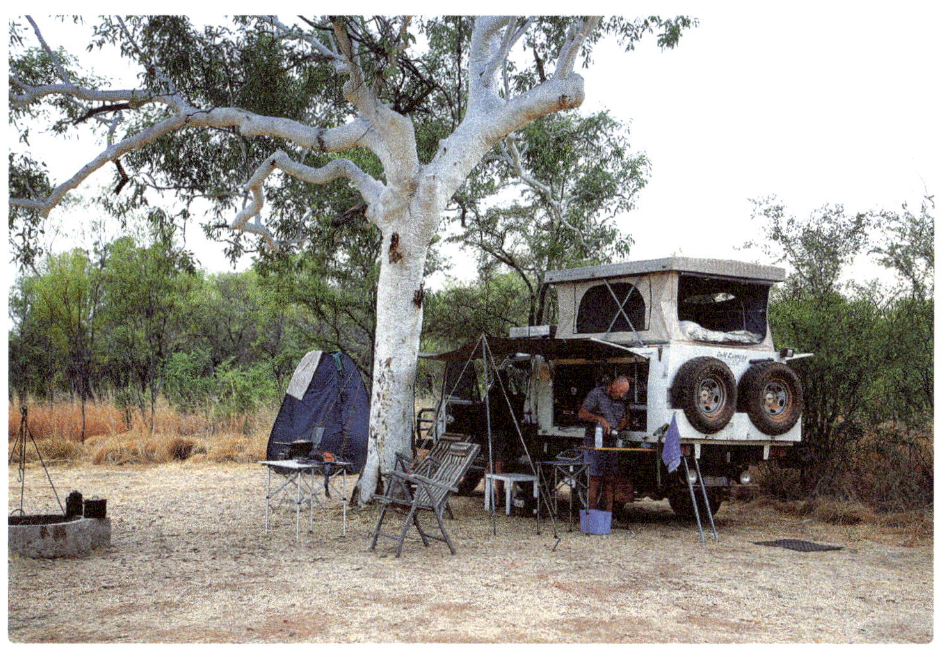

- ❑ Measuring jug
- ❑ Tongs - short or long
- ❑ Bar-B-Q Mate/scraper
- ❑ Basting brush
- ❑ Serving spoon
- ❑ Slotted serving spoon
- ❑ Peelers
- ❑ Egg flip
- ❑ Flat grater
- ❑ Can opener with bottle opener
- ❑ Swiss Army Knife
- ❑ Flat Strainer
- ❑ Egg rings
- ❑ Large sharp knife
- ❑ Bread/Serrated edge knife
- ❑ Wooden spoons
- ❑ Cutting board
- ❑ Mesh toaster
- ❑ Measuring spoon and/or tablespoon
- ❑ Extra plate and bowl for serving
- ❑ General purpose scissors

Washing/Cleaning Equipment

- ❑ Cloth
- ❑ Clothesline and pegs
- ❑ Detergent
- ❑ Dish brush
- ❑ Garbage bags
- ❑ Scourer
- ❑ Scrubbing brush
- ❑ Sponge
- ❑ Tea towel/s
- ❑ Wash up bucket
- ❑ Washing powder for clothes

Personal Items

- ❑ Comb and/or brush
- ❑ Toothbrush
- ❑ Toothpaste
- ❑ Towel
- ❑ Face Washer
- ❑ Soap and container
- ❑ Shampoo and Conditioner
- ❑ Deodorant
- ❑ Sunblock
- ❑ Toilet paper
- ❑ Insect repellent

USEFUL RESOURCES AND CONTACTS

Department of Environment and Conservation (DEC) – Campground Bookings
Tel: 08 6467 5000
Web: www.dec.wa.gov.au/campgrounds

Department of Environment and Conservation (DEC) – General Enquiries
Tel: 08 9334 0333
Web: www.dec.wa.gov.au

Department of Indigenous Affairs
Tel: 1300 651 077
Web: www.dia.wa.gov.au

Department of Fisheries Western Australia
Head Office –
Tel: 08 9482 7333
Web: www.fish.wa.gov.au

Department of Mines and Petroleum
Miners Rights –
Tel: 08 9222 3333
Web: www.dmp.wa.gov.au

Fire and Emergency Services Authority
FESA public information line –
Tel: 1300 657 209
Total Fire Ban Information Line –
Tel: 1800 709 355
Web: fesa.wa.gov.au

Main Roads Western Australia
Tel: 138 138
Web: www.mainroads.wa.gov.au

RAC
Road Service **Tel:** 131 111
Web: www.rac.com.au

Western Australian Visitor Centre
Tel: 1800 812 808 or 08 9483 1111
Web: www.westernaustralia.com or www.bestofwa.com.au

Regional Visitor Information Centres
For other accredited information centres visit the Western Australian Visitor Centre website at www.westernaustralia.com

Albany
Tel: 08 9841 9290
Web: www.amazingalbany.com

Broome
Tel: 08 9195 2200
Web: www.broomevisitorcentre.com.au

Carnarvon
Tel: 08 9941 1146
Web: www.carnarvon.org.au

Cervantes
Tel: 08 9652 7672
Web: www.visitpinnaclescountry.com.au

Denham
Tel: 08 9948 1590
Web: www.sharkbayvisit.com

Denmark
Tel: 08 9848 2055
Web: www.denmark.com.au

Derby
Tel: 08 9191 1426
Web: www.derbytourism.com.au

Dwellingup
Tel: 08 9538 1108
Web: www.murray.wa.gov.au

Esperance
Tel: 08 9083 1555
Web: www.visitesperance.com Exmouth
Tel: 08 9949 1176
Web: www.exmouthwa.com.au

Geraldton
Tel: 08 9921 3999
Web: www.geraldtontourist.com.au

Halls Creek
Tel: 08 9168 6262
Web: www.hallscreek.wa.gov.au

Hyden
Tel: 08 9880 5200
Web: www.waverock.com.au

Kalgoorlie
Tel: 08 9021 1966
Web: www.kalgoorlietourism.com

Karratha
Tel: 08 9144 4600
Web: www.pilbaracoast.com

Kununurra
Tel: 08 9168 1177
Web: www.kununurratourism.com

Lancelin
Tel: 08 9655 1100
Web: www.gingin.wa.gov.au

Leonora
Tel: 08 9037 7016
Web: www.leonora.wa.gov.au

Mandurah
Tel: 08 9550 3999
Web: www.visitmandurah.com

Margaret River
Tel: 08 9780 5911
Web: www.margaretriver.com

Nannup
Tel: 08 9756 1211
Web: www.nannupwa.com

New Norcia
Tel: 08 9654 8056
Web: www.newnorcia.wa.edu.au

Newman
Tel: 08 9175 2888
Web: www.newman-wa.org

Norseman
Tel: 08 9039 1071
Web: www.norseman.info

Pemberton
Tel: 08 9776 1133
Web: www.pembertonvisitor.com.au

Port Hedland
Tel: 08 9173 1711
Web: www.phvc.com.au

Rottnest Island
Tel: 08 9372 9732
Web: www.rottnestisland.com

Tom Price
Tel: 08 9188 1112
Web: www.tompricewa.com.au

Bureau of Meterology
Recorded Information Line –
Tel: 1300 659 213
Web: www.bom.gov.au

Perth and Surrounds

ENCOMPASSING AREAS WITHIN A COUPLE of hours drive from the the city, this picturesque region takes in some diverse and beautifully scenic landscapes. If you are looking to spend a few nights under canvas you'll be sure to find a great selection of campsites to choose from.

Close to the city itself is the Perth Hills National Parks Centre where you will find a well set-up camping area with good facilities, making this a top spot for first-time tent-based campers and groups. Also west of the city are popular campsites set in Avon Valley National Park. If you're a keen walker or cyclist the long distance Bibbulmun walking track and the Munda Biddi cycle trail both offer fabulous camping opportunities. If an island campsite appeals then only a short ferry ride away is Rottnest Island with the delightful Allison camping area.

In the south of the region is the scenic Lane Poole Reserve beside the Murray River, with great camping and recreational opportunities. There are nine separate camping areas scattered throughout the reserve where you can pitch your tent. Lake Brockman also offers good camping and is a popular destination for water-based activities.

To the south is Yalgorup National Park with the pretty Martin's Tank Lake campground, ideal for tent-based campers while caravanners find Herron Point camping area on the Peel-Harvey estuary a comfortable stopover.

Colourful spring wildflowers are just one of the many features in the north-east of the region with camping and caravanning options available in many of the country towns.

It is possible to enjoy this region all-year round, however the popular holiday periods of Christmas, Easter and most long weekends do make some areas very busy and advance bookings may be necessary.

BEST Campsites!

 **Baden Powell Campground**
Lane Poole Reserve

 **Homestead campsite**
Avon Valley National Park

 **Martin's Tank Lake campground**
Yalgorup National Park

 **Allison camping area**
Rottnest Island

 **Perth Hills National Parks Centre campsite**
Beelu National Park

N
0
100km
Wubin
Dalwallinu
Hwy
Kalannie
Beacon
Burakin
Moora
Northern
Great
Brand
Wongan
Hills
Koorda
Mukinbudin
Bullfinch
Nulla Nulla
Highway
Wyalkatchem
Dowerin
Goomalling
Road
Merredin
Gingin
Wanneroo
Hwy
Yanchep
Toodyay
Toodyay
Great
Eastern
Kellerberrin
Cunderdin
Northam
Bruce Rock
York
Road
Chidlow
Quairading
Narembeen
PERTH
Beverley
Great
Fremantle
Armadale
Highway
Corrigin
Hyden
Kwinana
Kwinana
Brookton
Brookton
Kondinin
Rockingham
Mundijong
Freeway
Pingelly
Old
Hwy
Albany
Kulin
Mandurah
Southern
Wickepin
Pinjarra
Dwellingup
Boddington
Narrogin
Waroona
Coast
Lake Grace
Williams
Highway
Western
Harvey
Hwy
South
Dumbleyung
Wagin
Darkan
Road
Hwy
Coalfields
Bunbury
Collie
Dardanup
1 Avon Valley National Park
2 Ballidu
3 Beacon Area
4 Beelu National Park
5 Bencubbin Area
6 Beverley
7 Bibbulmun Track - Northern Section
8 Boddington
9 Brookton
10 Bruce Rock
11 Calingiri
12 Coastal Plain Walk Trail
13 Corrigin
14 Dalwallinu
15 Dandaragan
16 Dryandra Woodland
17 Dwellingup
18 Guilderton
19 Heron Point Reserve
20 Hoffman Mill
21 Jurien Bay
22 Kalannie
23 Kellerberrin
24 Kokerbin Nature Reserve
25 Kondinin
26 Koorda
27 Kulin
28 Lake Brockman (Logue Brook Dam)
29 Lake Leschenaultia
30 Lake Yealering
31 Lane Poole Reserve
32 Miling
33 Moora
34 Mukinbudin
35 Munda Biddi Trail
36 Narembeen
37 Narrogin
38 Pinjarra
39 Rottnest Island
40 Sandy Cape Recreation Park
41 Trayning
42 Walyunga National Park
43 Wandering
44 Waroona Dam
45 Wave Rock, Hyden
46 Westonia
47 Wickepin
48 Wyalkatchem
49 Yalgorup National Park

1

Avon Valley National Park

Located 45km north-east of Midland, the park features granite outcrops, forests and views over the Avon Valley and River. With over 90 bird species identified within the park, it is a popular spot for bird watching. From Midland proceed north-east towards Toodyay for 40km to the signposted Morangup Road, which leads 5.3km to the signposted Quarry Road and entrance station to the national park. To access the section of park on the northern side of Avon River, take Plunkett Road, which is accessed off Harper Road from Toodyay.

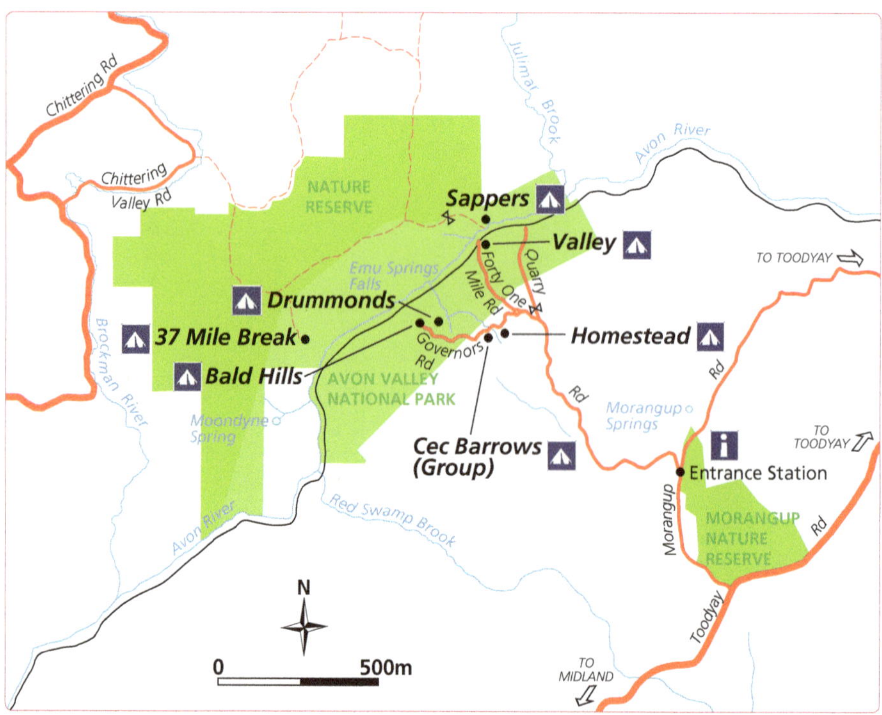

Homestead campsite

From park entrance station follow Quarry Road in north-westerly direction for 8.8km to Y-junction. At this junction keep left for 550m to the next Y-junction. At this junction keep left along Governors Drive and follow this for 1.5km to the signposted access into the camping area. Free form, shaded camping area beside creek with 4 to 5 sites. Bring drinking water and firewood.

GPS S:31 36.510 E:116 14.800

MR: Map 8 G8

Homestead campsite

PERTH AND SURROUNDS

Cec Barrow Group Camping Area

Signposted access along Governors Drive 250m west of Homestead CS access track. Large area for groups, with hot water shower donkey. Bring firewood.

GPS S:31 36.564 E:116 14.639
MR: Map 8 G8

Drummonds campsite

Signposted access along Governors Drive, 2.5km west of Homestead CS access track. Then drive in 400m to the small camping area with limited camper trailer space. Suitable for camper trailers with 4WD tow vehicle due to steep access. Bring drinking water and firewood.

GPS S:31 36.357 E:116 13.736
MR: Map 8 G8

Bald Hill campsite

Signposted access along Governors Drive, 2.5km west of Homestead CS access track. Then drive in 200m to the open camping area with free form camping and some shade. Some tank water. Bring firewood.

GPS S:31 36.370 E:116 13.423
MR: Map 8 G8

Bald Hill campsite

Valley campsite

From park entrance station follow Quarry Road in north-westerly direction for 8.8km to Y-junction. At this junction keep left for 550m to the next Y-junction. At this junction keep right along the signposted 41 Mile Rd. This leads 1.5km to the camping area. Some tank water. Bring firewood.

GPS S:31 35.296 E:116 14.550
MR: Map 8 G8

Sappers campsite

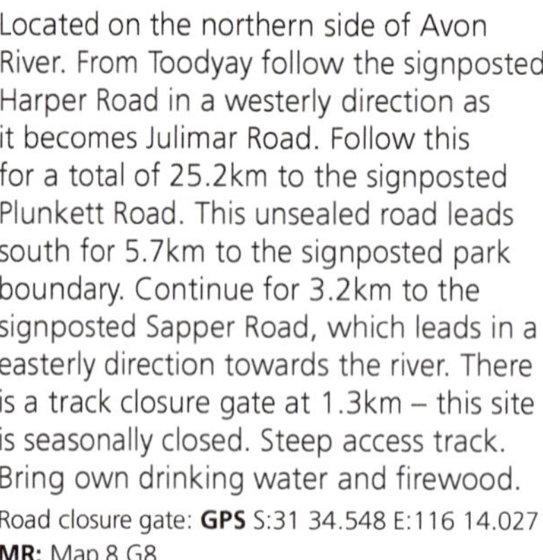

Located on the northern side of Avon River. From Toodyay follow the signposted Harper Road in a westerly direction as it becomes Julimar Road. Follow this for a total of 25.2km to the signposted Plunkett Road. This unsealed road leads south for 5.7km to the signposted park boundary. Continue for 3.2km to the signposted Sapper Road, which leads in a easterly direction towards the river. There is a track closure gate at 1.3km – this site is seasonally closed. Steep access track. Bring own drinking water and firewood.

Road closure gate: **GPS** S:31 34.548 E:116 14.027
MR: Map 8 G8

37 Mile Break campsite

Located on the northern side of Avon River. Follow directions as for Sappers campsite. From Sappers Road continue in a south-westerly direction for a further 5km to a track on the left. Take this track and follow it in a southerly direction for 2.5km to a track on left which then leads in 60m to the bush camping area. Bring drinking water and firewood.

GPS S:31 36.688 E:116 11.062
MR: Map 7 F8

37 Mile Break campsite

FURTHER *Information*

Avon Valley National Park

Tel: 08 9295 9100. Bookings are necessary for Cec Barrow Group Camping Area.
Park entrance fee: $11.00 per vehicle. Park entrance fee and camping fees payable at park entrance stations on Quarry Road and Plunket Road.
Camping fees: From $7.00 per adult/night and $2.00 per child (under 16)/night.
NB: No camping during fire season, generally 1 December to 30 April. However dates may change from year to year, check with national park office.

2 Ballidu

Ballidu was originally settled in 1909, to the east of the present townsite, and services the surrounding grain and sheep farms. Located 240km north-east of Perth along the Northam-Pithara Road, 25km south of the Great Northern Highway. Wildflower area.

Ballidu Caravan Park

Located on Wallis Street in Ballidu, close to all town facilities. Laundry facilities. Bring firewood.

MR: Map 8 I1

FURTHER *Information*

Ballidu Tavern

Tel: 08 9674 1213
Camping fees: Tent sites from $5.00 per site/night up to 2 people. Unpowered sites from $10.00 per site/night up to 2 people. Powered sites from $15.00 per site/night up to 2 people. Fees payable at on-site honesty box.

3 Beacon Area

Beacon is situated in the north-east wheat belt, 315km north-east of Perth and 48km north of Bencubbin. The region is popular with birdwatchers and wildflower lovers.

Beacon Caravan Park

Located on Lucas Street in Beacon, close to all town facilities. Gas/fuel stove only. Laundry facilities.

MR: Map 31 C7

FURTHER Information

Beacon Caravan Park Manager
Tel: 0488 025 853
Beacon Visitor Information Centre
Tel: 08 9686 1014
Web: www.beacon.wa.tc
Camping fees: Tent sites from $5.50 per site/night. Powered caravan sites from $16.50 per site/night. Fees collected daily by ranger.

Biliburning Rock camping area

Located 34km north of Beacon. From the eastern end of town take the signposted Ingleton Road and follow this north. Unmarked walks up the rock. Bring drinking water and firewood.

MR: Map 31 C8

FURTHER Information

Beacon Visitor Information Centre
Tel: 08 9686 1014
Web: www.beacon.wa.tc
Shire of Mount Marshall
Tel: 08 9685 1202
Web: www.mtmarshall.wa.gov.au
Before lighting camp or cooking fires, enquire at shire office for fire restrictions.

PERTH AND SURROUNDS

4 Beelu National Park

A range of nature based activities are run throughout the year through DEC's Nearer to Nature program at the Perth Hills National Parks Centre. Activities include bush crafts, guided walks, discovering Nyoongar culture, animal encounters, and during the warmer months an outdoor cinema. Alternatively, visitors can enjoy one of the scenic walks through the national park, even a section of the Bibbulmun Track or enjoy the views over Mundaring Weir. Access to Beelu National Park and Perth Hills National Parks Centre is signposted from Mundaring via Mundaring Weir Road.

Perth Hills National Parks Centre campsite

From Mundaring take the signposted Mundaring Weir Road and follow this for 6.1km to the signposted Allen Road. Allen Road leads 500m to the information centre, car park and campsite. Carry gear from car park into camping area with 12 sites in shaded location. Camp kitchen. Firewood supplied. Popular area for school groups and the like.

GPS S:31 57.239 E:116 10.623

MR: Map 11 F3

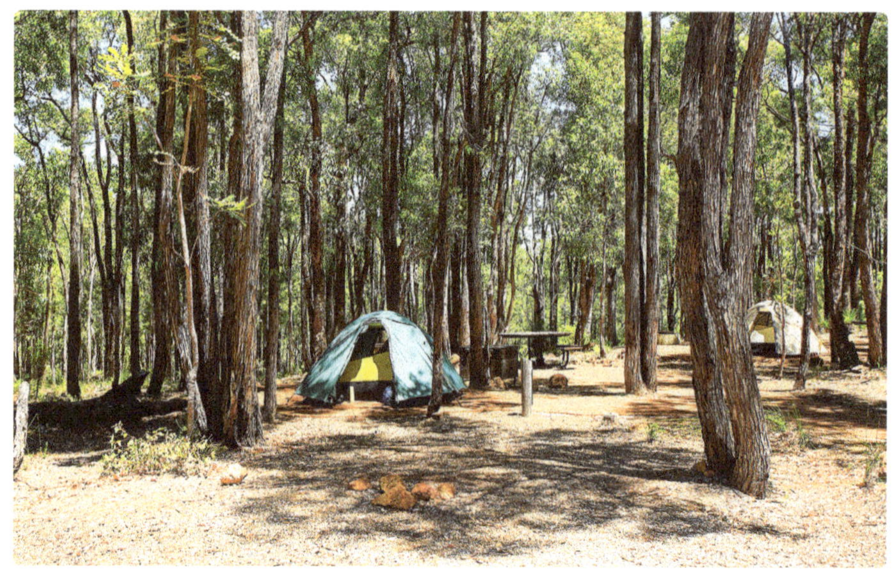

Perth Hills National Parks Centre campsite

Patens Brook campsite

     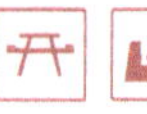 

Located 3km from the Perth Hills National Parks Centre. Walk-in site on Patens Brook Trail. Limited water supply, best to take own. Firewood supplied. Gas/fuel stove preferred.

MR: Map 11 F3

FURTHER Information

Perth Hills National Parks Centre

Tel: 08 9295 2244. Bookings essential for both sites.

Web: www.dec.wa.gov.au/n2n

Camping fees: Perth Hills National Parks Centre Campsite: From $8.80 per adult/night and $6.60 per child (16 and under)/night. Patens Brook campsite: From $5.00 per person/night.

5 Bencubbin Area

Bencubbin is the centre of the north-eastern wheatbelt and is 273km north-east of Perth. The area has a rich grain, wheat and sheep farming history. A large variety of wildflowers can be seen during the wildflower season from June to October.

Bencubbin Caravan Park

Located at the southern end of town on the Bencubbin-Trayning Road. Laundry facilities.

MR: Map 9 D2

FURTHER Information

Shire of Mount Marshall

Tel: 08 9685 1202

Web: www.mtmarshall.wa.gov.au

Camping fees: Tent site from $5.50 per site/night. Caravan site from $16.50 per site/night. Fees payable at council office: 80 Monger Street, Bencubbin, 8.30am to 4.30pm weekdays.

Marshall Rock camping area

Located 10km south-east of Bencubbin. Signposted access on Marshall Rock South Road off the Mukinbudin road. Bring drinking water and firewood. Gas/fuel stove preferred.

MR: Map 9 D2

FURTHER *information*

Shire of Mount Marshall
Tel: 08 9685 1202
Web: www.mtmarshall.wa.gov.au
Before lighting camp or cooking fires, enquire at shire office for fire restrictions.

6 Beverley

Beverley was established in 1838 and is located 135km east of Perth in the central wheatbelt region on the banks of the Avon River.

Beverley Caravan and Camping Ground

Situated on Council Road in Beverley, behind the council chambers, within walking distance to town facilities. Gas/fuel stove only. Laundry facilities.

MR: Map 12 K3

FURTHER *information*

Beverley Shire Office
Tel: 08 9646 1200
Web: www.beverley.wa.gov.au
Camping fees: Tent site from $10.00 per person/night. Powered site from $25.00 per site/night for 2 people. Fees payable at council office at 136 Vincent Street, open 8.30am to 4pm weekdays. Weekends: fees payable at on-site honesty box.

7 Bibbulmun Track – Northern Section

The Bibbulmun Track is Western Australia's longest walking track. The track starts from the Perth suburb of Kalamunda and finishes at Albany on the south coast, totalling 963km. Marked the full length, the track was originally designed for urban people to go bush. The northern section of the Bibbulmun Track is from Kalamunda to Donnelly River Village. Bibbulmun Track walkers will traverse some of the south-west's most beautiful and scenic regions and experience a variety of forest types. The track can be tackled in one go for those with the time and energy or can be done in sections with numerous vehicle access points along the track. All walkers should be well prepared and self-sufficient. The purchase of the excellent Bibbulmun Track Guides and maps are recommended.

Bibbulmun Track camping areas

Walk-in access via the Bibbulmun Track. Water may not always be reliable, always carry extra. Gas/fuel stoves preferred. **NB:** No fires at Yourdamung and Blackwood campsites or in the Lane Poole Special Conservation Zone. Fire restrictions occur from October to May, please contact local authorities to obtain current details. Carry copy of maps and guides.

Trackhead: Kalamunda

MR: Map 11 F3

Hewett's Hill Campsite 10.3km from Kalamunda
Ball Creek Campsite 10.6km from Hewett's Hill
Helena Campsite 8.6km from Ball Creek
Waalegh Campsite 9.5km from Helena
Beraking Campsite 8.5km from Waalegh
Mt Dale Campsite 11.5km from Beraking
Brookton Campsite 8.3km from Mt Dale
Canning Campsite 11.1km from Brookton
Monadnocks Campsite 15.6km from Canning
Mt Cooke Campsite 12.7km from Monadnocks
Nerang Campsite 12.6km from Mt Cooke
Gringer Creek Campsite 16.6km from Nerang
White Horse Campsite 17.6km from Gringer Creek
Mt Wells Campsite 14.5km from White Horse Hills
Chadoora Campsite 14.8km from Mt Wells
Swamp Oak Campsite 32.4km from Chadoora
Murray Campsite 18.6km from Swamp Oak
Dookanelly Campsite 17.8km from Murray
Possum Springs Campsite 19.3km from Dookanelly
Yourdamung Campsite 18.7km from Possum Springs
Harris Dam Campsite 13.5km from Youdamung
Yabberup Campsite 41.0km from Harris Dam
Noggerup Campsite 17.7km from Yabberup
Grimwade Campsite 21.9km from Noggerup
Blackwood Campsite 40.1km from Grimwade
Gregory Brook Campsite 18.0km from Blackwood
Donnelly River Village 20.6km from Gregory Brook.
MR: Map 20 G1

FURTHER Information

DEC Recreation & Trails Unit
Tel: 08 9334 0265. Walking groups of eight or more must contact the Recreation & Trails Unit for a Notice of Intent form.
The Bibbulmun Track Foundation
Tel: 08 9481 0551
Web: www.bibbulmuntrack.org.au

PERTH AND SURROUNDS

8 Boddington

Located 123km south-east of Perth and to the west of the Albany Highway. The surrounding region is a mix of agricultural, forestry and mining industries. The Hotham River beside the caravan park offers fishing for redfin and perch.

Boddington Caravan Park

Located on Wuraming Avenue in town, close to town amenities and shops. Camp kitchen, laundry facilities. Gas/fuel stove only.
MR: Map 12 I8

FURTHER Information

Boddington Caravan Park
Tel: 08 9883 8018. Bookings recommended.
Camping fees: Tent sites from $20.00 per site/night for 2 people. Powered van sites from $28.00 per site/night for 2 people. Refundable key deposit for boom gate and amenities block.

9 Brookton

Brookton is an ideal spot to stay and take in the local attractions such as Nine Acre Rock and the Yenyenning Lakes and is located on the Brookton Highway, 138km south-east of Perth.

Brookton Caravan Park

Located on Brookton Highway in Brookton. Laundry facilities.

MR: Map 12 L5

FURTHER Information

Brookton Caravan Park
Tel: 08 9642 1434
Camping fees: Unpowered sites from $17.00 per person/night. Powered sites $23.00 per site/night up to 2 people.

10 Bruce Rock

Situated in the heart of the wheatbelt, Bruce Rock is 247km east of Perth. Visit the nearby historic Bruce's Rock, believed to be the site of the district's last Aboriginal Corroboree.

Bruce Rock Caravan & Camping Park

Situated on Dunstall Street in Bruce Rock, beside the town swimming pool. Camp kitchen, laundry facilities.

GPS S:31 52.451 E:118 09.101
MR: Map 9 F8

FURTHER Information

Bruce Rock Shire Council
Tel: 08 9061 1377
Web: www.brucerock.wa.gov.au
Camping fees: Tent sites from $7.20 per person/night. Powered sites from $18.50 per site/night. Fees payable to caretaker.

Bruce Rock Caravan and Camping Park

11 Calingiri

Calingiri is an ideal base for visiting the attractions within the Shire of Victoria Plains. These include the Benedictine Community, the Wyening Mission, historic buildings at Bolgart and the wildflowers in Piawaning and Gillingarra. The town is located 141km north-east of Perth.

Calingiri Caravan Park

Located on Cavell Street in Calingiri. Gravel surface not suitable for tents. Gas/fuel stove only.

MR: Map 8 G4

FURTHER Information

Shire of Victoria Plains
Tel: 08 9628 7004
Web: www.victoriaplains.wa.gov.au
Camping fees: Unpowered from $8.25 per site/night for 2 people. Powered from $16.50 per site/night for 2 people. Fees payable at council office at 28 Cavell Street, Calingiri.

12 Coastal Plain Walk Trail

The Coastal Plain Walk Trail traverses the Swan Coastal Plain from Yanchep National Park to Melaleuca Conservation Park. The plain has diverse flora and walkers will see coastal heath to jarrah forests, woodlands and wildflowers. Walkers need to be self-sufficient and carry own water, water at campsites is for emergency use only. The Coastal Plain Walk Trail map and the Wild About Walking brochure are available from DEC. Trail trackhead is at Ghost House Ruins 5km north of the McNess Visitors Centre in Yanchep National Park.

Shapcotts campsite

On the Coastal Plain Walk Trail, 300m from trackhead at Ghost House Ruins. Carry water. Gas/fuel stove preferred.

MR: Map 1 C2

Ridges campsite

On the Coastal Plain Walk Trail, 15.6km from Shapcotts campsite. Carry water. Gas/fuel stove preferred.

MR: Map 1 C2

Moitch campsite

On the Coastal Plain Walk Trail, 19.9km from Ridges campsite. Carry water. Gas/fuel stove preferred.

MR: Map 1 D3

Prickly Bark campsite

On the Coastal Plain Walk Trail, 17km from Moitch campsite and 3.2km from Cooper Road Trackhead. Carry water. Gas/fuel stove preferred.

MR: Map 1 D3

FURTHER Information

Yanchep National Park
Tel: 08 9405 0759
Park entrance fee: $11.00 per vehicle, applicable at Yanchep National Park.

13 Corrigin

Corrigin and surrounding region has many attractions including the Dog Cemetery and the Pioneer Museum as well as a profusion of wildflowers during the spring. It's 235km south-east of Perth on the Brookton Highway.

Corrigin Caravan Park

Located on the corner of Larke Crescent and Kirkwood Street in Corrigin. Close to all town facilities. Camp kitchen, laundry facilities.

MR: Map 13 E4

FURTHER Information

Corrigin Caravan Park
Tel: 08 9063 2515
Camping fees: Sites from $28.00 per site/night for 2 people. Power available.

14 Dalwallinu

The first town on Western Australia's famous Wildflower Way, Dalwallinu is 254km north-east of Perth on the Great Northern Highway. The town and its surrounding region offers numerous cultural and natural attractions for the visitor. Wildflower season is from July to October.

Dalwallinu Caravan Park

Located on Dowie Street in Dalwallinu. Gas/fuel stoves only. Laundry facilities.

MR: Map 30 L7

FURTHER Information

Dalwallinu Caravan Park
Tel: 08 9661 1253
Camping fees: Tent sites from $19.50 per site/night for 2 people. Powered sites from $22.00 per site/night for 2 people.

15 Dandaragan

The Shire owned and run Pioneer Park is situated in the Dandaragan township. Dandaragan is 180km north of Perth and to the east the Brand Highway.

Pioneer Park

Located on Dandaragan Road in Dandaragan.

MR: Map 7 C2

FURTHER Information

Shire of Dandaragan
Tel: 08 9651 4010
Web: www.dandaragan.wa.gov.au
Camping fees: Tent sites from $10.00 per tent/night. Van sites from $15.00 per van/night. Fees payable to shire office on Dandaragan Road, open 8am to 5pm. Shire office closed on Wednesday, fees payable at honesty box outside shire office.

16 Dryandra Woodland

Popular area for bushwalkers, wildlife spotters, picnickers, cyclists, horse riders and campers. Visitors will see a variety of flora from spring wildflowers to woodlands of white barked wandoo and powderbark, which can be viewed along one of the many walking trails. Drive the Dryandra Drive Trail, tune your vehicle's radio to the signposted frequency to learn about the region's history. Located 27km north of Williams via the York Williams Road and 24km north-west of Narrogin via the Wandering Narrogin Road. Access signposted from Narrogin and from North Bannister on the Albany Highway and Cuballing on the Great Southern Highway.

Congelin Campground

Signposted access off the York Williams Road, 27km north of Williams. Bring drinking water and firewood.

MR: Map 12 L7

FURTHER Information

DEC Narrogin District Office
Tel: 08 9881 9200
Camping fees: From $7.00 per adult/night and $2.00 per child (under 16)/night. Fees payable via self payment reply paid envelopes from the Information Station.

17 Dwellingup

Dwellingup is 110km south of Perth, and can be accessed from the north via Del Park Rd from North Dandalup on the South Western Highway, or from the west via the Pinjarra Williams road from Pinjarra on the South Western Highway.

Marrinup camping area

From Dwellingup travel west for 2.5km on the Pinjarra Rd, then turn right (north) into Grey Road. Follow Grey Road north for 2.4km to a crossing of the railway line. Once over the railway line at 100m is a track on the right signposted to the camping area, which leads in 200m to camping area with dispersed bush camping, with some shaded sites. Self sufficient campers. Bring drinking water and firewood.

GPS S:32 42.125 E:116 01.647
MR: Map 11 F7

Marrinup camping area

FURTHER Information

Dwellingup Tourist Information Centre
Tel: 08 9538 1108
Web: www.murray.wa.gov.au

18 Guilderton

This seaside village is situated at the mouth of the Moore River and safe swimming beaches, river and ocean fishing, and canoeing on the Moore River. Located 94km north of Perth access is via Guilderton Road off the Wanneroo Road.

Guilderton Caravan Park

Situated at the mouth of the Moore River on Dewar Street in Guilderton. Gas/fuel stoves only. Camp kitchen, laundry.

MR: Map 7 B7

FURTHER Information

Guilderton Caravan Park

Tel: 08 9577 1021. Bookings recommended.
Web: www.guildertoncaravanpark.com.au
Camping fees: Fees vary according to season, contact office for current fee schedule. Other accommodation available.

19 Herron Point Reserve

The reserve is situated on the Peel-Harvey Estuary and is an ideal site for fishing, prawning and walking. Abundant and varied birdlife can be found here. Located south-west of Pinjarra, access is via Herron Point Road signposted off the Forrest Highway 12.7km south of Greenlands Road, which leads 8km to Pinjarra.

Herron Point camping area

Located at end of Herron Point Road, 3.6km west of the Forrest Highway. Open camping area with 15 sites overlooking the estuary, has limited protection so is susceptible to onshore winds. Bring drinking water and firewood. **NB:** Area is baited, keep dogs on lead at all times.

GPS S:32 44.475 E:115 42.690
MR: Map 11 E8

FURTHER Information

Murray Shire Council

Tel: 08 9531 7777

Pinjarra Visitor Centre

Tel: 08 9531 1438
Web: www.pinjarravisitorcentre.com.au
Camping fees: From $10.00 per vehicle/night. Fees apply 1 November to 31 April only, no fees rest of year. Caretaker on site 1 November to 31 April.
NB: Solid fuel fire ban 1 November to 15 March inclusive. Use gas/fuel stove only during this period. Dates may change, check with local authorities prior to lighting a fire.
Maximum stay: 2 nights.

20 Hoffman Mill

Once the site of a thriving mill town, Hoffman Mill was establised in the early 1900s. Remains of the old mill can still be seen today. Located on Clarke Road 17km east of the South Western Highway. Access via Logue Brook Dam Road signposted off the South Western Highway, south of Yarloop and north of Harvey.

Hoffman Mill camping area

From the highway take the road signposted to Logue Brook Dam (this is 9km north of Harvey and 6km south of Yarloop) and follow this road east for 11.7km where the road becomes Clarke Road. Continue along Clarke Road for a further 6.1km to the camping area. A large area with free form camping with some good shade trees. Water from river, boil or treat first. Bring drinking water. Bring firewood. Gas/fuel stove preferred.

GPS S:33 00.220 E:116 05.119

MR: Map 16 G2

FURTHER Information

DEC Hoffman Block, South West

Tel: 08 9735 1988

Camping fees: From $7.00 per adult/night and $2.00 per child (under 16)/night. Fees collected by ranger.

NB: Closed to camping from the end of Easter to 1 November, each year.

NB: Solid fuel fire bans apply from 15 December to 14 March, check with local authorities for current times and dates.

Hoffman Mill camping area

21 Jurien Bay

The popular holiday town of Jurien is home to a large rock lobster fishing fleet. The region offers safe swimming, fishing, sailboarding and diving. Just 24km from town is the spectacular rock formations known as The Pinnacles. The town is situated on the coast, 266km north of Perth with access via Jurien Road off the Brand Highway.

The Pinnacles near Jurien Bay

PERTH AND SURROUNDS

Jurien Bay Tourist Park

Located on Roberts Road in Jurien Bay. Café, camp kitchen, laundry facilities, children's playground.

MR: Map 30 I7

FURTHER Information

Jurien Bay Tourist Park

Tel: 08 9652 1595. Bookings recommended.
Web: www.jurienbaytouristpark.com.au
Camping fees: Fees vary according to season, contact office for current fee schedule.
NB: Dogs are permitted in the off peak season, a dog bond applies.

22 Kalannie

Situated within the wildflower region, Kalannie is located 45km east of the Great Northern Highway. To the west of Kalannie is Petrudor Rock, a great spot for a day visit and a picnic.

Kalannie Caravan Park

Located on Roche Street north in Kalannie. Bring own gas/fuel stove. Laundry facilities.

MR: Map 31 A7

FURTHER Information

Kalannie Caravan Park
Tel: 08 9666 2068
Camping fees: Contact office for current fee structure. Fees collected by caretaker daily.

23 Kellerberrin

Kellerberrin is located 202km to the east of Perth along the Great Eastern Highway. The small Kellerberrin Caravan Park is located at the sportsgrounds.

Kellerberrin Caravan Park

Located 1.3km north of the highway. From the highway at the western end of town, take the signposted West Crossing Road and then turn onto Hinckley Street. Follow Hinckley Street and then take the signposted Connelly Street. Laundry facilities.

GPS S:31 37.657 E:117 42.672
MR: Map 9 C7

FURTHER Information

Kellerberrin Caravan Park Caretaker
Tel: 0428 138 474. Bookings recommended.
Kellerberrin Shire
Tel: 08 9045 4006
Camping fees: Unpowered sites from $18.00 per site/night for 2 people. Powered sites from $25.00 per site/night for 2 people. Fees collected by caretaker daily.

24 Kokerbin Nature Reserve

The reserve surrounds the large granite outcrop of Kokerbin Rock, which offers panoramic views of the surrounding countryside. Visitors will find caves and rock formations to explore, walking trails and wildflowers. Located 10km north of Kwolyin, access is signposted along the Bruce Rock Quairading Road.

Kokerbin Rock camping area

From the Bruce Rock Quairading Road, 39km west of Bruce Rock, take the road signposted to Kokerbin Rock, this leads north for 8.7km to crossroads. Turn onto signposted O'Grady Road and after 500m is access track signposted to Kokerbin. This leads in 600m to the camping and picnic area. Bring firewood. Gas/fuel stove preferred.

GPS S:31 53.237 E:117 42.580

MR: Map 13 D1

FURTHER Information

DEC Merebin

Tel: 08 9041 6000

Bruce Rock Shire

Tel: 08 9061 1377

Web: www.brucerock.wa.gov.au

NB: Solid fuel fire bans apply from October to March – check with local authorities for current dates.

NB: Camping is to be phased out from this area, please contact land managers prior to setting up camp for up-to-date conditions.

25 Kondinin

Kondinin is located 280km east of Perth and 60km west of Hyden and Wave Rock.

Kondinin Caravan Park

Located on Gordon Street in Kondinin. Camp kitchen, laundry facilities.

GPS S:32 29.725 E:118 15.842

MR: Map 14 G5

FURTHER Information

Kondinin Shire Office

Tel: 08 9889 1006

Web: www.kondinin.wa.gov.au

After hours contact: Kondinin Roadhouse **Tel:** 08 9889 1190 or Kondinin Hotel **Tel:** 08 9889 1009

Camping fees: Unpowered sites from $10.00 per site/night. Powered sites from $17.00 per site/night. Refundable key deposit required. Bookings and fees payable at above businesses.

Kondinin Caravan Park

26 Koorda

Koorda is located 235km north-east of Perth. This neat council caravan park is surrounded by natural bushland and hosts spectacular wildflowers in season.

Koorda Caravan Park

Located on Scott Street in Koorda. Limited grassed tent sites. Laundry facilities. Bring firewood.

MR: Map 31 B7

FURTHER Information

Koorda Shire
Tel: 08 9684 1219
Web: www.koorda.wa.gov.au
Camping fees: Tent sites from $5.00 per adult/night. Powered van sites from $24.20 per site/night. Fees payable to shire office on Allenby Street or at on-site honesty box.

27 Kulin

Kulin is situated 100km east of the Great Southern Highway and Narrogin.

Kulin Caravan Park

Located on Johnson Street in Kulin. Laundry facilities. Bring gas/fuel stove.

MR: Map 14 G6

FURTHER Information

Kulin Caravan Park
Tel: 08 9880 1053
Camping fees: Unpowered tent sites from $8.00 per person/night. Powered van sites from $25.00 per site/night for 2 people. Fees collected by caretaker.

28 Lake Brockman (Logue Brook Dam)

The lake is a popular swimming and recreation area and offers great fishing, with trout often restocked. Located 6km east of the South Western Highway with access via the signposted Logue Brook Dam Road which leaves the highway 6km south of Yarloop and 9km north of Harvey.

Lake Brockman Tourist Park

Signposted access on Logue Brook Dam Road, 6.3km east of the highway. Located on the southern shores of the lake. Bring firewood or available for sale.

GPS S:33 00.199 E:115 58.384

MR: Map 15 F2

FURTHER Information

Lake Brockman Tourist Park

Tel: 08 9733 5402. Bookings recommended mid December to end January.

Camping fees: Unpowered sites from $10.00 per adult/night. Powered sites from $12.00 per adult/night.

Lake Brockman bush camping

From the South Western Highway take the signposted Logue Brook Dam Road, (this is 9km north of Harvey and 6km south of Yarloop) and follow this for 5.2km to the road that leads over the dam wall. Follow this road for 3km to the end of the road and the bush camping area overlooking the lake and situated within shady jarrah trees. This is the main camping area, there are a number of overflow camping areas which are only open when necessary during peak periods. Natural boat launch. Bring drinking water and firewood. Gas/fuel stove preferred.

GPS S:32 59.275 E:115 58.808

MR: Map 15 F2

FURTHER Information

DEC Collie

Tel: 08 9735 1988

Camping fees: From $7.00 per adult/night and $2.00 per child (under 16)/night. Fees collected by ranger daily.

29 Lake Leschenaultia

The lake was built in 1897 by the Western Australian Government Railway to replenish steam engines travelling to Northam, York and beyond. Today's visitors can enjoy water activities of swimming, fishing and canoeing as well as bird and wildlife spotting. In season the lake is surrounded by beautiful wildflowers. Located 2km north-west of Chidlow, access is signposted along Rosedale Road.

Lake Leschenaultia

PERTH AND SURROUNDS

Lake Leschenaultia campsite

At Chidlow take the signposted Thomas Street and follow this for 300m to the signposted Rosedale Road. Rosedale Road leads 2.2km to the signposted access to the lake. The access road leads in 300m to the sheltered camping area best suited for tents (with flat tent pads) and camper trailers. Kiosk/café, laundry facilities, canoe hire. Firewood available for purchase.

GPS S:31 51.075 E:116 15.273
MR: Map 12 G2

FURTHER Information

Lake Leschenaultia Ranger's Office
Tel: 08 9572 4248. Advance bookings required. A one off booking fee of $7.00 applies to all sites.
Web: www.mundaring.wa.gov.au
Camping fees: From $8.00 per person/night. Gates locked at night, times vary throughout the year. A key system is available, a refundable deposit is required for key.

Lake Leschenaultia campsite

30 Lake Yealering

The lake is popular for water activities such as water skiing, fishing, canoeing and swimming. Located to the east of Yealering, access is via the Wickepin Corrigin Road.

Lake Yealering Caravan Park

Located on the Wickepin-Corrigin Road in Yealering. Key for amenities block. Firewood supplied.

MR: Map 13 D6

FURTHER Information

Lake Yealering Caravan Park

Tel: 08 9888 7014. Bookings recommended.
Camping fees: Contact office for current fee structure. Fees collected by caretaker daily.

CAMPING with your dog

If you own a well behaved and well socialised dog you may wish to take your 'best friend' along camping with you. Dogs are usually welcome in state forests and some reserves, but are not permitted in national parks. Each listing in this guide indicates whether you can bring your dog with you.

31 Lane Poole Reserve

Lane Poole Reserve covers nearly 55,000 hectares. The Murray River runs through the reserve and is ideal for swimming, fishing and canoeing. Bushwalking, picnicking and camping are other popular activities in the reserve. Visitors to Lane Poole Reserve will find forests of jarrah, blackbutt and marri, and in spring colourful wildflower displays. Abundant wildlife, including the chuditch and quokka, can be seen along with numerous bird and reptile species. Located 7.5km south of Dwellingup, access is suitable for conventional vehicles. From Dwellingup proceed east towards Wellington for 800m to the signposted Nanga Road. Access is signposted 6.3km along Nanga Road. All roads within the reserve are gravel roads.

Baden Powell Campground

Signposted access along Park Road, 1.8km south-east of the park entrance station. Very large area on the northern banks of the Murray River with free form camping among pine trees. Limited drinking water, bring own. Bring firewood.

GPS S:32 46.216 E:116 05.189
MR: Map 12 G8

Baden Powell Campground

Charlie's Flat Campground

Signposted access along River Road, 4.7km south-east of Baden Powell CG and 1.7km south of Bobs Crossing (the causeway crossing of Murray River). Camping area located above the river on the eastern banks, with 16 individual campsites best suited for tent based camping, 2 sites suitable for small camper trailer or small caravan. Bring drinking water and firewood.

GPS S:32 46.810 E:116 06.456
MR: Map 12 G8

Tony's Bend Campground

Signposted access along River Road, 2.6km south of Charlie's Flat CG. Located on the eastern banks of the river. Well shaded camping area with 13 individually numbered tent sites. Bring drinking water and firewood.

GPS S:32 47.709 E:116 06.431
MR: Map 12 G8

Tony's Bend Campground

PERTH AND SURROUNDS

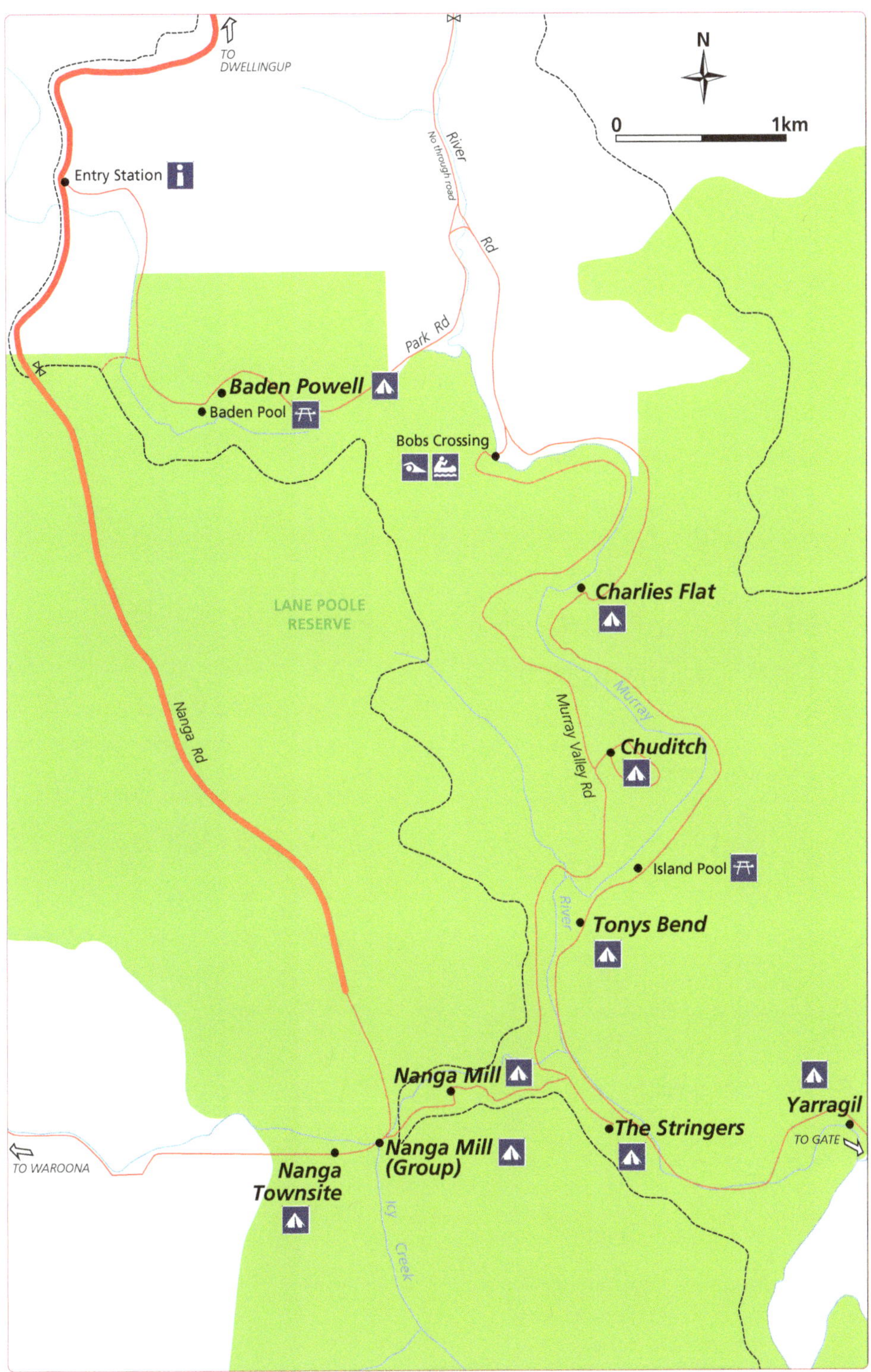

TO DWELLINGUP
N
0
1km
Entry Station
River
No through road
Rd
Park Rd
Baden Powell
Baden Pool
Bobs Crossing
LANE POOLE RESERVE
Charlies Flat
Murray
Murray Valley Rd
Nanga Rd
Chuditch
Island Pool
River
Tonys Bend
Nanga Mill
Yarragil
TO GATE
The Stringers
TO WAROONA
Nanga Mill (Group)
Nanga Townsite
Icy Creek

PERTH AND SURROUNDS

Yarragil Campground

Signposted access along River Road, 2.9km south of Tony's Bend CG. Located on the eastern side of the river on the northern banks of a bend in the river. Small area with 2 tent based sites, carry gear over bollards to sites. Bring drinking water and firewood.

GPS S:32 48.302 E:116 07.495
MR: Map 12 G8

Yarragil Campground

Chuditch Camping Area

Signposted access along Murray Valley Road on the western banks of the river, 3.4km south of the western end of Bobs Crossing (causeway crossing over the Murray River). Then drive in to the large camping area with 24 individually numbered campsites, some sites carry-in tent based sites, 6 sites suitable for camper trailers, smaller caravans and campervans (trailers and vans will require unhitching, although 2 sites are drive through sites). Located on the western banks of the river. Camp kitchen. Limited tank water, boil or treat first. Bring own drinking water. Gas/fuel stove only.

GPS S:32 47.238 E:116 06.541
MR: Map 12 G8

Stringers Campground

Signposted access along Murray Valley Road, 2km south of Chuditch CA. Then drive in 400m to the small tent based camping area with 6 individually numbered sites, carry gear in over bollards to tent pads. Located on western banks of the river. Bring drinking water and firewood.

GPS S:32 48.259 E:116 06.517
MR: Map 12 G8

Stringers Campground

Nanga Mill Campground

Signposted access along Murray Valley Road, 400m west of the Stringers CG access track. Very large area among the pine trees providing good shelter. Short walk to the river. Untreated water, boil or treat first. Bring own drinking water. Bring firewood.

GPS S:32 48.159 E:116 05.966
MR: Map 12 G8

PERTH AND SURROUNDS

Nanga Mill Campground

Nanga Townsite Campground

Nanga Mill Group camping area

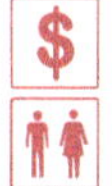        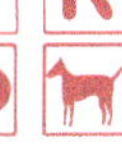

Signposted access along Murray Valley Road, 500m west of Nanga Mill CG. Shaded camping area among pines on the southern side of the road. Bring drinking water and firewood.

GPS S:32 48.297 E:116 05.703
MR: Map 12 G8

Nanga Townsite Campground

     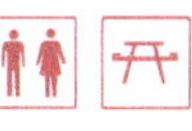   

Signposted access along Nanga Road, 300m west of Nanga Mill Group CA. Shaded camping area beside the road. Short walk to carry gear in from the car park. Bring drinking water and firewood.

GPS S:32 48.326 E:116 05.543
MR: Map 12 G8

FURTHER Information

DEC Dwellingup

Tel: 08 9538 1078. Online advance bookings are required for Charlies Flat, Tonys Bend, Yarragil, Chuditch, Stringers and Nanga Mill Group camping areas. Other areas: Baden Powell, Nanga Mill and Nanga Townsite camping areas pay at entry station on Park Road or to Ranger.
Camping fees: From $7.00 per adult/night and $2.00 per child (under 16)/night.
Maximum stay: 14 consecutive days during school holidays.
NB: Solid fuel fire ban from 15 December to 15 March inclusive, bring own gas/fuel stove during this period. Check dates with local DEC office before lighting a fire.
Collection of firewood within the reserve is not permitted, please bring own from home or purchase from local distributors.
Please keep dogs on leash at all times as fox baiting is carried out in the reserve.

WHO WAS Lane-Poole?

Charles Edward Lane-Poole was a devoted conservationist and Western Australia's first conservator of forests. Prior to 1918 before the Forests Act, there was no legislation regarding how much timber could be cut, where and how it could be cut nor were there any regeneration plans in place. In 1918 when Lane-Poole saw the devastating effect of 70 years of uncontrolled tree felling he set out to devise a forest management plan to reduce the number of felling operations to a level that forests could withstand. For his plan to work it was necessary that an Act of Parliament be passed, and all remaining forests be declared areas of State Forest. Lane-Poole had strong oppostion from commercial and sawmilling industries, however his push for legislation has become the foundation for forest management practices that conserve forests, rather than the uncontrolled exploitation of them.

32 Miling

Miling is located 60km north-east of Moora on the Great Northern Highway. The township is surrounded by sweeping wheat fields and sheep grazing farmland.

Miling Sports Reserve Rest Area

Located on Miling East Road, to the east of the Great Northern Highway, at the sports reserve in Miling.

MR: Map 7 F1

FURTHER Information

Miling Travel Stop

Tel: 08 9654 1013. Open Monday to Friday 8am to 6pm and Saturday 8am to 12 noon. Must check in and pay fees at Miling Travel Stop to receive access to the site.

Camping fees: From $10.00 per site/night. Power available.

33 Moora

A popular stop for those travelling the wildflower trail, Moora is situated on the picturesque Moore River and is located 172km north of Perth.

Shire of Moora Caravan Park

Located on Dandaragan Street in Moora, adjacent to the town swimming pool. Short walk to all town facilities. Camp kitchen, laundry.

MR: Map 7 D2

FURTHER Information

Shire of Moora

Tel: 08 9651 0000

Web: www.moora.wa.gov.au

Camping fees: Unpowered tent sites from $19.00 per site/night for 2 people. Powered van sites from $26.00 per site/night for 2 people. Fees payable at council office at 34 Padbury Street or at honesty box.

Moora RV Short Stay site

Located at the far end of the Roberts Street car park, opposite IGA, in Moora. Suitable for self-contained units only, must have only toilet, shower and water holding facilities.

MR: Map 7 D2

FURTHER Information

Shire of Moora

Tel: 08 9651 0000

Web: www.moora.wa.gov.au

Maximum stay: 24 hours.

34 Mukinbudin

Mukinbudin is to the north-east of Perth and 82km north of Merredin, which is on the Great Eastern Highway.

Mukinbudin Caravan Park

Located on Cruickshank Road in Mukinbudin. Nearby to all town services. Laundry facilities.

MR: Map 9 F2

FURTHER Information

Mukinbudin Caravan Park Caretaker

Tel: 08 9047 1103. Bookings recommended for powered sites.

Camping fees: Unpowered sites from $7.50 per site/night for 2 people. Powered sites from $20.00 per site/night for 2 people.

35 Munda Biddi Trail

The Munda Biddi Trail is a long distance cycling trail which stretches from Mundaring, north-east of Perth, to Albany on the south coast. The trail is being built in three stages with Stage 1 Mundaring to Collie (332km) completed. Stage 2, Collie to Manjimup (250km) and Stage 3 from Manjimup to Albany, eventually making the trail a total of 1,000km. Winding through forests and national parks, the trail follows along bush tracks and old railway lines. To allow for restocking purposes and to offer a range of accommodation the trail passes through a town at least every second day. Campsites along the trail are located 35km to 40km apart and between towns or a day's ride. Each campsite is well equipped with flat tent sites, toilet, table, shelter, water tank and bike shelters. Camp fires are not permitted at all campsites, carry a gas/fuel stove. There are a range of good maps and guides for the trail, and the Munda Biddi Trail Foundation website is a great information resource.

Munda Biddi Trail campsites – Mundaring to Collie

Access along the Munda Biddi Trail. Water may not always be reliable - always carry extra. Gas/fuel stoves only. Carry copy of maps and guides.

Trackhead: Mundaring

MR: Map 11 F2

Carinyah Campsite 42km south of Mundaring

Wungong Campsite 35km south of Carinyah and 26km north of Jarrahdale

Dandalup Campsite 34km south of Jarrahdale and 44.9km north of Dwellingup

Bidjar Ngoulin Campsite 28.5km south of Dwellingup

Lake Brockman (see page 39) 32km south of of Bidjar Ngoulin

Yarri Campsite 46km south of Lake Brockman and 45km north of Collie

Collie 45km south of Yarri.

MR: Map 16 G4

FURTHER Information

DEC Recreation and Trails Unit
Tel: 08 9334 0265
Web: www.dec.wa.gov.au/content/view/159/793/
Email: recreationandtrails@dec.wa.gov.au

Munda Biddi Trail Foundation
Tel: 08 9481 2483
Web: www.mundabiddi.org.au

36 Narembeen

Narembeen's major industry is wheat and sheep. Visit Roe Lookout for views over the town and district or take some time to birdwatch at Roe Dam. The local reserves of Mt Walker Rock, Twine Reserve or Anderson Rock have unusual rock formations and wildflowers displays during the late winter and early spring. Narembeen is located 290km east of Perth,

Narembeen Caravan Park

Located on Currall Street in Narembeen, beside the swimming pool. Some shaded sites. Laundry, playground. Gas/fuel stove only.

GPS S:32 03.816 E:118 23.768
MR: Map 14 H2

FURTHER Information

Narembeen Shire
Tel: 08 9064 7308
Web: www.narembeen.wa.gov.au
Camping fees: Unpowered sites from $8.30 per site/nite. Powered sites from $21.00 per site/night. Fees payable at council office at 1 Longhurst Street between 8.30am and 5pm during week days, on weekends payable to on-site caretaker.

Narembeen Caravan Park

37 Narrogin

The rural community of Narrogin is situated 210km south-east of Perth on the Great Southern Highway.

Narrogin Caravan Park

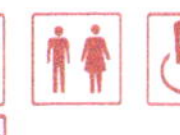

Located on Williams Road in Narrogin. Laundry facilities. Some firewood supplied.

MR: Map 13 A8

FURTHER Information

Narrogin Caravan Park

Tel: 08 9881 1260

Camping fees: Unpowered sites from $10.00 per person/night. Powered sites from $20.00 per night/site.

38 Pinjarra

Located on the South Western Highway 20km south-east of Mandurah, 16km south of North Dandalup and 25km north of Waroona.

Pinjarra 24 Hour Self Contained Unit Stop

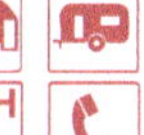

Rest area in the centre of town, with access signposted on the Pinjarra Williams Road. Situated close to the Pinjarra Heritage Train Station.

GPS S:32 37.783 E:115 52.744

MR: Map 6 G7

FURTHER Information

Pinjarra Visitor Centre

Tel: 08 9531 1438. Open Wednesday to Friday 9.30am to 4pm and on weekends 10am to 3pm.

Web: www.pinjarravisitorcentre.com.au

Maximum stay: Unpowered sites from $10.00 per person/night. Powered sites from $20.00 per night/site.

TOTAL Fire ban

On days that are declared a total fire ban it is illegal to light any fire in the open, in tents and in canvas camping trailers. This includes any naked flame (portable stoves, gas and solid fuel BBQ). It is your responsibility to be aware of which fire district your campsite falls under. Fire bans are usually broadcast on the local radio station.

39 Rottnest Island

Rottnest Island, just off the coast of Perth, has an interesting and varied history, and is well known for its recreation facilities. The island's beaches and bays are perfect for swimming, snorkelling, fishing, surfing and boating. Access to the island is via ferry services from Perth, Fremantle and Hillarys. Don't forget your camera, push bike and helmet as the island's roads make for delightful cycling.

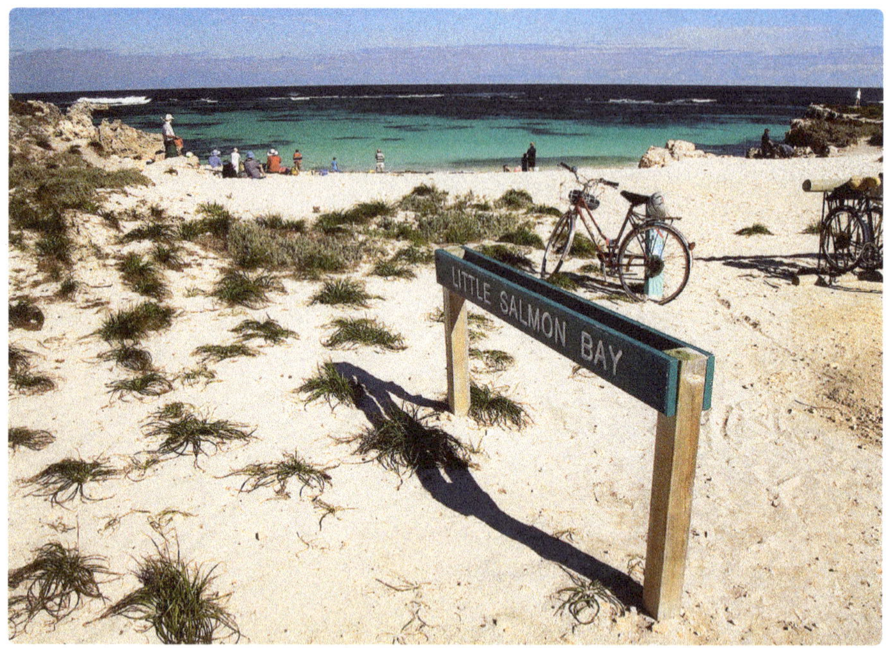

Rottnest Island

PERTH AND SURROUNDS

Allison camping area

Located at Thomson Bay on Rottnest Island. Gas/fuel stove only.

MR: Map 3 B3

FURTHER Information

Rottnest Island Authority

Tel: 08 9432 9111

Web: www.rottnestisland.com

Rottnest Island Visitor & Information Centre

Tel: 08 9372 9752. Pre-bookings are essential during all school and summer holidays. All campers must proceed to the Accommodation Centre at Rottnest Island Jetty prior to setting up camp.

Camping fees: From $12.00 per adult/night and $6.00 per child (up to 12)/night.

40 Sandy Cape Recreation Park

This scenic coastal park is an ideal destination with its excellent fishing, swimming and beach combing opportunities. Signposted access along the Indian Ocean Drive north of Jurien Bay.

Sandy Cape Recreation Park camping area

Signposted access along Indian Ocean Drive 13km north of Jurien Bay and then drive west for 6km on unsealed road to the information bay. Bring drinking water. Gas/fuel stove only. Ezy-dump facility.

MR: Map 30 I7

FURTHER Information

Shire of Dandaragan
Tel: 08 9652 0800
Web: www.dandaragan.wa.gov.au
Camping fees: From $15.00 per site/night, fees payable at honesty box at information bay.

41 Trayning

Trayning has a rich history dating back to the time when prospectors travelled through on their way to the Goldfields. Cereal crops and sheep are the region's main industries. Trayning is located 235km east-north-east of Perth and 61km north of Kellerberrin on the Great Eastern Highway.

Trayning Caravan Park

Located on Sutherland Street in Trayning, close to the town swimming pool. Gas/fuel stove only. Laundry facilities.

MR: Map 9 C4

FURTHER Information

Shire of Trayning
Tel: 08 9683 1001
Web: www.trayning.wa.gov.au
Camping fees: Unpowered tent sites from $11.50 per site/night for 2 people. Powered caravan/motorhome sites from $20.00 per site/night. Fees payable at shire office in Railway Street or at on-site honesty box after hours.

42 Walyunga National Park

Walyunga National Park is well known for its abundant native animals, birdlife, beautiful wildflowers during winter and spring, and its rugged valley scenery. The Avon River runs through the middle of the park, providing one of the country's best white water canoeing courses, and is part of the popular Avon Descent held each August. There are numerous walking trails of varying lengths and grades. Walyunga National Park is 40km north-east of Perth and is accessed via Walyunga Road signposted off the Great Northern Highway. Note: The park is locked each evening at 5pm, all campers must be in by that time and there is no camping from 1 December to 30 April.

Walyunga Pool

Walyunga camping area

Tent based camping only. Short walk from car park to campsites. From the Great Northern Highway, 17km north of Midland, take signposted Walyunga Road and follow this east for 1.7km to the park boundary gate. Then a further 1.6km to Walyunga Pool day use area access road, then a further 800m to the car park and walk to Boongarup Pool camping area. Bring drinking water. Some firewood supplied. Gas/fuel stove preferred.

Boongarup Pool: **GPS** S:31 43.918 E:116 04.449

MR: Map 2 J4

FURTHER Information

Walyunga National Park - Ranger

Tel: 08 9571 1371. Bookings essential, to be made with Walyunga National Park Ranger.

DEC Mundaring District Office

Tel: 08 9295 9100

Park entrance fee: $11.00 per vehicle.

Camping fees: From $7.00 per adult/night and $2.00 per child (under 16)/night.

43 Wandering

The town of Wandering is situated to the east of the Albany Highway and can be reached from the south via Crossman or from the north via North Bannister. The town has numerous historical buildings. Take a wildflower walk along the Wandering Road North or visit nearby Boyagin Rock.

Wandering Caravan Park

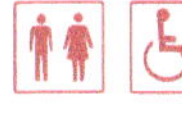

Located on Cheetaning Street in Wandering. Some firewood supplied, best to bring own.

MR: Map 12 J7

FURTHER Information

Shire of Wandering
Tel: 08 9884 1056
Web: www.wandering.wa.gov.au
Camping fees: From $10.00 per site/night for 2 people. Fees payable at shire office at 22 Watts Street.

44 Waroona Dam

Built as an irrigation dam, Waroona Dam was completed in 1968. Popular area for swimming, fishing, bushwalking, wildflowers, canoeing and water skiing. From Waroona on the South Western Highway take the signposted McDowell Street to the east for 5km following the signage to Lake Navarino.

Lake Navarino Forest Resort camping area

From Waroona take the signposted McDowell Street to the east and follow this as it becomes Nanga Brook Road for a total of 5km to the signposted Scarp Rd. Then follow Scarp Road for 1.8km to the signposted Invarell Road. This then leads 1.5km to the office and resort. Bring drinking water and firewood. Powered sites available, camp kitchen, laundry facilities.

GPS S:32 50.659 E:115 58.872
MR: Map 15 F1

Lake Navarino Forest Resort camping area

Navarino Lakeside Camping

From Lake Navarino Forest Resort office continue in a south-easterly direction for 2km to the signposted access to the camping area. This track then leads in 1.2km to the large free form camping area on the lake's southern foreshore.

Some good shade. Natural boat launch. Bring drinking water and firewood.

GPS S:32 51.015 E:115 59.965

MR: Map 15 F1

Navarino Lakeside camping

FURTHER Information

Lake Navarino Forest Resort

Tel: 08 9733 3000 or 1800 650 626. Advance bookings required for Lake Navarino Forest Resort camping area.

Web: www.navarino.com.au

Camping fees: Lake Navarino Forest Resort camping area: Unpowered sites from $24.00 per site/night for 2 people. Powered sites from $28.00 per site/night for 2 people. Navarino Lakeside Camping: From $8.00 per adult/night and $4.00 per child (3-16)/ night. Fees to be paid at office prior to setting up camp.

NB: $20.00 refundable dog bond. Solid fuel fire ban from 15 December to 30 April inclusive, gas/fuel stoves only during this period.

45 Wave Rock, Hyden

The granite outcrop known as Wave Rock is an impressive 110 metres long and 15 metres high. It was formed millions of years ago after being exposed to millennia of weathering and water erosion. Take a walk in the surrounding bushland, visit the cave of the Aboriginal outlaw Mulka, go bird spotting or simply enjoy the displays of spring wildflowers. Wave Rock is located close to the township of Hyden, 340km east of Perth via the Brookton Highway.

Wave Rock

Wave Rock Caravan Park

From Hyden proceed east for 2km and then take road signposted to Wave Rock and follow this north for 1km to the signposted access road. This access road leads 1.1km to the caravan park. Kiosk/store, camp kitchen, swimming pool, laundry facilities. Gas/fuel stove only.

GPS S:32 26.514 E:118 53.860

MR: Map 14 K4

FURTHER *Information*

Wave Rock Caravan Park
Tel: 08 9880 5022
Web: www.waverock.com.au
Camping fees: Unpowered sites from $28.00 per site/night for 2 people. Powered sites from $35.00 per site/night for 2 people.

46 Westonia

The region has a rich history of gold mining and sandalwood cutting. Visit the granite outcrops of Elachbutting Rock, Baladjie Rock, Sandford Rocks Nature Reserve and the Edna May Gold Mine just north of town. Westonia is located north of the Great Eastern Highway, 316km east of Perth and 52km east of Merredin.

Westonia Caravan Park

Located on Wolfram Street in Westonia. Gas/fuel stove only. Laundry facilities.

MR: Map 10 I4

FURTHER *Information*

Shire of Westonia
Tel: 08 9046 7063
Web: www.westonia.wa.gov.au
Camping fees: Unpowered tent sites from $11.00 per site/night. Powered van sites from $15.00 per site/night. Fees payable to on-site caretaker or at council office on Wolfram Street.

47 Wickepin

Wickepin is located south-east of Perth and 38km north-east of Narrogin on the Great Southern Highway.

Wickepin Caravan Park

Located on Wogolin Road in Wickepin. Firewood supplied. Laundry facilities.

MR: Map 13 C7

FURTHER *Information*

Wickepin Caravan Park
Tel: 08 9888 1089
Camping fees: Unpowered sites from $15.00 per site/night for 2 people. Powered sites from $20.00 per site/night for 2 people.

48 Wyalkatchem

Located in town are numerous National Trust and Heritage listed buildings. Wyalkatchem is a great spot to base yourself whilst exploring the surrounding nature reserves, lakes and wells. Wyalkatchem is 191km north-east of Perth via Toodyay and 115km north-west of Merredin.

Wyalkatchem Caravan Park

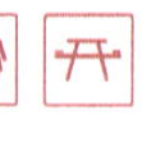

Located on the Goomalling-Merredin Road in Wyalkatchem. Camp kitchen, laundry facilities.

MR: Map 9 A4

FURTHER Information

Wyalkatchem Caravan Park
Tel: 0427 814 042
Camping fees: Tent sites from $10.00 per site/night for 2 people. Powered sites from $25.00 per site/night. Fees collected by caretaker.

49 Yalgorup National Park

Yalgorup National Park preserves the coastal vegetation of the Swan coastal plain. Within the park is a chain of 10 lakes, with Lake Clifton and Lake Preston being the largest, which provide shelter for migrating birds from the northern hemisphere as well as numerous local species. Visitors can view the algae growth structures of stromatolites and thrombolites at the northern end of Lake Clifton, as well as a number of walking trails. Located just south of Mandurah with the camping area in the southern section of the park near Preston Beach, and accessed off Old Coast Road 12km south of Old Bunbury Road.

Martin's Tank Lake campground

From the Old Coast Road, take the signposted road to Preston Beach. Follow this road west for 6.9km to the signposted access track to the national park. This unsealed and sometimes corrugated road leads 4.6km to the access track to the camping area. Then drive in a south-easterly direction for 950m to the camping area with 13 individually numbered sites, well shaded and protected, on the western shores of Martin Tank Lake. Bring drinking water. Gas/fuel stove only.

GPS S:32 50.687 E:115 40.109
MR: Map 15 D1

FURTHER Information

DEC Mandurah
Tel: 08 9303 7750
Camping fees: From $7.00 per adult/night and $2.00 per child (under 16)/night. Fees collected by Ranger.

The South-West

MAGNIFICENT OLD GROWTH FORESTS, delightful freshwater rivers, spectacular coastlines, fabulous camping opportunities along with a great range of recreational activities are just some of the jewels that await campers to the picturesque south-west region. If heights are not a worry then you can attempt the climb to the lookout tower atop the Gloucester Tree at Pemberton; at 72 metres the world's tallest fire lookout tree. Take a walk through the tree tops east of Walpole, fish for your dinner from one of Albany's coastal beaches, paddle a canoe along a serene stretch of the Blackwood River, pack your four-wheel drive for an adventure through the remote D'Entrecasteaux National Park, stretch your legs along a section of the Bibbulmun Track or saddle up for a cycling jaunt on the Munda Biddi Trail. There sure is plenty to do in this region.

BEST Campsites!

Conto Campground
Leeuwin-Naturaliste National Park

Honeymoon Pool camping area
Wellington National Park

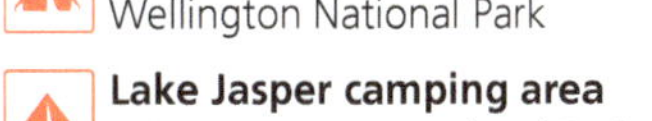

Lake Jasper camping area
D'Entrecasteaux National Park

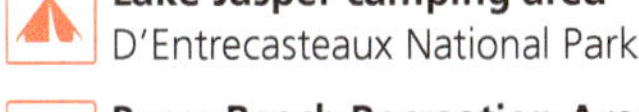

Parry Beach Recreation Area
Parry Beach

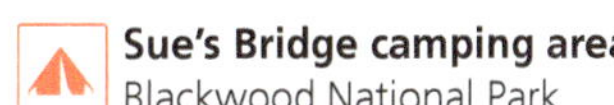

Sue's Bridge camping area
Blackwood National Park

Those who crave beach side camping should head for the coastal locations to the east and west of Albany, or in Fitzgerald River and D'Entrecasteaux national parks. A four-wheel drive vehicle is needed to get to some of the more remote sites. On the west coast is the spectacular Leeuwin-Naturaliste National Park with its delightful Conto Campground.

Wellington National Park has Honeymoon Pool camping area which is a lovely camp spot to the west of Bunbury while further south and north-east of Augusta is Sue's Bridge camping area on the Blackwood River, a popular destination for canoeists.

In the east of the region spring wildflowers are in abundance in Stirling Range National Park which has a small, but well-appointed camping area.

This region can be enjoyed by campers all-year round, although winter can be cold and wet. It is well patronized by both locals and visitors during the holiday seasons.

Mandurah
Pinjarra
Dwellingup
Bannister
Boddington
Marradong
Waroona
Narrogin
Williams
Wickepin
INDIAN
OCEAN
Lake Yalgorup
YALGORUP NATIONAL PARK
Lake Preston
Harvey
LANE POOLE CONSERVATION RESERVE
Darkan
Wagin
Dumbleyung Lake
Bunbury
Burekup
Collie
Coalfields
Dardanup
Boyanup
Stratham
Capel
Mumballup
Moodiarrup
Katanning
Donnybrook
Dunsborough
Busselton
Balingup
Boyup Brook
Kojonup
Mayanup
Bridgetown
Nannup
Margaret River
Prevelly
Manjimup
Brockman
LEEUWIN-NATURALISTE NATIONAL PARK
Augusta
Frankland
Muirs Highway
Lake Muir
SHANNON NATIONAL PARK
Shannon
Pemberton
D'ENTRECASTEAUX NATIONAL PARK
Northcliffe
MOUNT FRANKLAND NATIONAL PARK
D'ENTRECASTEAUX NATIONAL PARK
Windy Harbour
Broke Inlet
Walpole
Denmark
WALPOLE-NORNALUP NATIONAL PARK
Old Coast Road
South Western Hwy
Great Southern Highway
Albany Highway
Coalfields Road
Vasse Hwy
Bussell
Sues Road
South Western Highway
South Coast Highway
N
0
50km
51 Albany Area
52 Alexandra Bridge
53 Augusta
54 Balingup Area
55 Bibbulmun Track - Southern Section
56 Blackwood National Park
57 Bremer Bay Area
58 Bridgetown
59 Broomehill
60 Cape to Cape Track
61 D'Entrecasteaux National Park
62 Fitzgerald River National Park
63 Glen Mervyn Dam
64 Hopetoun Area
65 Ironstone Gully Falls
66 Lake King
67 Lake Poorrarecup
68 Lake Towerinning
69 Leeuwin-Naturaliste National Park
70 Leschenault Peninsula Conservation Park
71 Munda Biddi Trail
72 Mt Frankland South National Park
73 Nannup

74 Nyabing
75 One Tree Bridge Conservation Park
76 Pallinup Nature Reserve
77 Parry Beach
78 Pemberton Area
79 Pingrup
80 Rapids Conservation Park
81 Shannon National Park
82 St Johns Brook Conservation Park
83 Stirling Range National Park
84 Stockton Lake
85 Tambellup
86 Walpole-Nornalup National Park
87 Warren National Park
88 Waychinicup National Park
89 Wellington National Park
90 West Cape Howe National Park
91 Willow Springs

51 Albany Area

Albany is situated on the state's southern coast and is 408km from Perth via the Albany Highway. The City of Albany Council has established a number camping areas within the shire, set along its beautiful coastline. In addition to camping, the region features numerous historical sites, magnificent coastal scenery, nature reserves, rivers and mountains. Activities include boating, fishing, swimming, bushwalking, sightseeing plus much more. Fire restrictions apply to this region so it is wise to check with local authorities prior to lighting any fires.

Flood Gates camping area

Located to the west of Albany with signposted access along Torbay Inlet Road. From Albany proceed west along Princess Royal Drive to the signposted Lower Denmark Road. Follow Lower Denmark Road for 21km to the signposted Perkins Beach Road. This road leads south for 1.8km to the signposted Torbay Inlet Road, which in turn leads 2.1km to the small camping area with six sites suitable for tent based camping and one drive through camper trailer site. Well protected, shady, grassed area. It is possible to launch small boats via the natural boat launch. Self-sufficient campers. Bring drinking water. Gas/fuel stove only.

GPS S:35 02.375 E:117 40.802
MR: Map 21 F6

Cosy Corner East camping area

Located to the west of Albany with signposted access along Cosy Corner Road. From Albany head west along Princess Royal Drive to the signposted Lower Denmark Road. Follow Lower Denmark Road for 22.4km to the signposted Cosy Corner Rd. Cosy Corner Road leads south for 3.5km to the signposted access road to the camping area. This access road leads in 500m to the shaded camping area set back from the water. Bring drinking water. Gas/fuel stove only.

GPS S:35 03.575 E:117 38.774
MR: Map 21 F6

Normans Beach camping area

From Albany follow the South Coast Highway in a north-easterly direction for 37km to the signposted Homestead Road. Homestead Road (which becomes unsealed after 5km) leads south for

9.1km to the signposted Normans Beach Road, which in turn leads 2.2km to the small camping area on the inlet with some shaded sites. Limited facilities at this site so best suited for self-sufficient campers. Bring drinking water. Gas/fuel stove only.

GPS S:34 55.299 E:118 12.853
MR: Map 22 I5

Norman's Beach camping area

East Bay camping area

From Albany follow the South Coast Highway in a north-easterly direction for 37km to the signposted Homestead Road. Homestead Road (unsealed road, and once past Normans Beach Road is signposted as a winding road and is not suitable for caravans) leads south 12.1km to the signposted East Bay Road which leads 700m to the small camping area at the north-eastern end of Two Peoples Bay. Open area with no shade or protection from winds. Beach boat launch. Limited facilities at this site so best suited for self-sufficient campers. Bring drinking water. Gas/fuel stove only.

GPS S:34 56.281 E:118 10.788
MR: Map 22 I5

East Bay camping area

Bettys Beach camping area

From Albany follow the South Coast Highway in a north-easterly direction for 37km to the signposted Homestead Road. Homestead Road (unsealed road and once past Normans Beach Road is signposted as a winding road and not suitable for caravans) leads south 14.4km to Betty's Beach. Small area among a number of private shacks/huts. Open area with little protection from the prevailing

TO DENMARK
Hay River
Tudor
South Coast Hwy
Lower Denmark Rd
Torbay
Marbelup
Elleker
Cuthbert
Cosy Corner
Flood Gates
Shelley Beach
Torbay Head
Torbay Bay
WEST CAPE HOWE NATIONAL PARK
Little Chorkerup
TO MOUNT BARKER
Settlement Rd
Albany Hwy
Green Valley
King River
MILL BROOK NATURE RESERVE
Millbrook Rd
Yalingup Brook
Chester Pass Rd
Napier
Kalgan
Kalgan River
King River
Albany
Melville
Oyster Harbour
Little Grove
King George Sound
Michaelmas Island
Breaksea Island
Nanarup
Taylor Inlet
East Bay Road
TWO PEOPLES BAY NATURE RESERVE
Cape Vancouver
Many Peaks
Homestead Rd
Norman Beach
Betty Beac
TORNDIRRUP NATIONAL PARK
Cave Point
Bald Head
Eclipse Island

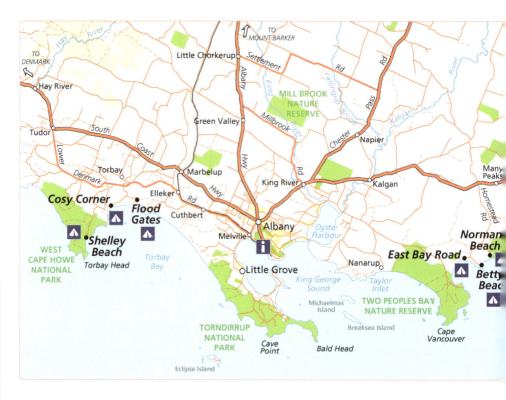

winds. Beach boat launch. Limited facilities at this site so best suited for self-sufficient campers. Bring drinking water and firewood.

GPS S:34 56.223 E:118 12.500

MR: Map 22 I5

Betty's Beach camping area

TO BREMER BAY
Pallinup River
Hwy
Mettler
Sandalwood Rd
Boat Harbour
Coast
South
BASIL ROAD NATURE RESERVE
Cheyne Bay
Cape Riche
Cape Riche
Cheyne Beach Rd
Hassell Beach
WAYCHINICUP NATIONAL PARK
Waychinicup Inlet
Cheyne Beach
N
Mermaid Point
Bald Island
SOUTHERN OCEAN
0 20Km

Boat Harbour camping area

From Albany follow the South Coast Highway in a north-easterly direction for 106km to the signposted road to Boat Harbour. Follow this road in a south-easterly direction for 12.8km to a T-intersection. Turn right (south) at the intersection and follow the road for a further 6.4km to the camping area. Access road has some steep sections along with soft sandy sections (this road can be seasonally closed so it's best to check road conditions first). Access for caravans is best suited using a 4WD tow vehicle. Dispersed camping along the creek and inlet. Short walk to beach. Bring drinking water. Gas/fuel stove only.

GPS S:34 30.696 E:118 48.212
MR: Map 22 L2

Boat Harbour camping area

FURTHER Information

Albany Visitor Centre
Tel: 08 9841 9290
Web: www.amazingalbany.com.au
Maximum stay: 7 days.

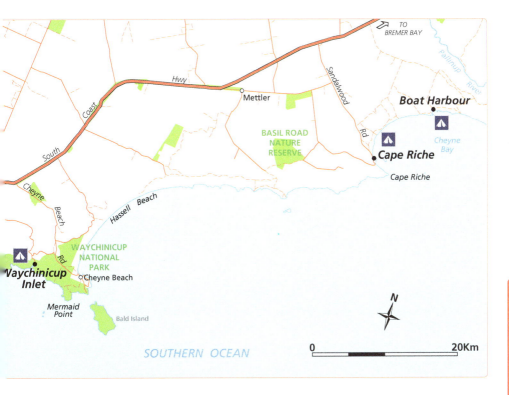

Cape Riche camping area

From Albany follow the South Coast Highway in a north-easterly direction for 97.8km to the signposted Sandalwood Road. The unsealed Sandalwood Road leads in a south-easterly direction for 18.2km to the camping area. Scenic area. Limited tank water. Bring drinking water and firewood. 4WD boat ramp.

Generators permitted at this site during certain hours so it's best to check with caretaker for times.

GPS S:34 35.861 E:118 44.981
MR: Map 22 L3

FURTHER Information

Cape Riche – Caretaker
Tel: 08 9847 3088
Camping fees: From $5.00 per person/night. Children under 16 free of charge.

52 Alexandra Bridge

The Blackwood River is one of the south-west's more popular destinations for fresh water fishing, canoeing, swimming and camping. Alexandra Bridge crosses the river along the Brockman Highway east of Karridale.

Alexandra Bridge Camping Ground

Signposted access off the Brockman Highway on the eastern side of Alexandra Bridge, 10km east of Karridale. Drive in 1.6km to the large and popular camping area beside the Blackwood River. Dispersed bush camping with shaded sites with sandy bases. Popular location for families with children. Picnic tables in the day use area. Outdoor cold showers. Some firewood is supplied but it is best to bring own if you plan on having a campfire.

GPS S:34 09.804 E:115 11.052
MR: Map 19 C2

Alexandra Bridge Camping Ground

FURTHER Information

Alexandra Bridge Caretaker
Tel: 08 9758 2244
Camping fees: From $7.00 per adult/night and $5.00 per school aged child/night. Fees collected by caretaker.

THE SOUTH-WEST

53 Augusta

Augusta is located on the south-west tip of the state and is popular for fishing, boating, swimming, surfing and sightseeing. There are numerous whale watching areas in the region where from June to December Humpback and Southern Right Whales migrate north and can often be seen close to shore. Situated at the mouth of the Blackwood River, Augusta is 330km south of Perth.

Turner Caravan Park

Signposted access along Blackwood Avenue at the southern end of town. Blackwood River frontage. Camp kitchen, laundry facilities, some firewood supplied.

GPS S:34 19.391 E:115 09.768

MR: Map 19 C3

FURTHER Information

Turner Caravan Park

Tel: 08 9758 1593. Bookings recommended during peak periods of December to May.

Web: www.turnerpark.com.au

Camping fees: Unpowered sites from $27.00 per site/night for 2 people. Powered sites from $32.00 per site/night for 2 people.

Flinders Bay Caravan Park

Located 3km south of Augusta, with access signposted along Albany Terrace. From Augusta, drive in a southerly direction along Blackwood Avenue, which becomes Leeuwin Road, then take the signposted Albany Terrace. Beach frontage. Laundry facilities. Some firewood supplied. Boat ramp nearby.

GPS S:34 20.402 E:115 10.003

MR: Map 19 C3

FURTHER Information

Flinders Bay Caravan Park

Tel: 08 9758 1380. Bookings recommended.

Web: www.flinderspark.com.au

Camping fees: Unpowered sites from $29.00 per site/night for 2 adults. Powered sites from $35.00 per site/night for 2 adults.

Dog bond: Refundable bond may apply.

NB: Park closed from 1 June to 1 September yearly.

Flinders Bay Caravan Park

54 Balingup Area

Known for its arts and crafts centre, wineries and specialty shops, Balingup is on the South Western Highway between Donnybrook and Bridgetown.

Balingup Transit Park

Located on Walter Road in Balingup. From the highway at the northern end of Balingup take the signposted Jayes Road and follow this for 250m to the signposted Walter Road which leads 80m to the park. Some firewood supplied.

GPS S:33 46.931 E:115 59.160

MR: Map 16 G7

FURTHER Information

Balingup General Store
Tel: 08 9764 1051
Camping fees: From $22.00 per site/night for 2 people. Fees payable at General Store.
NB: $10.00 refundable key deposit for amenities block.
Maximum stay: 3 nights.

Grimwade Townsite bush camp

Located 11km north-east of Balingup and 14km east of Kirup. From Balingup proceed north along the highway for 1km to the signposted Grimwade Road. Follow this road for 11.3km to a track on the left which leads in 150m to a dam where bush camping is possible in this vicinity. Popular trail bike area. The Bibbulmun Walking Track passes this site. If travelling from Kirup take the signposted road to Grimwade. This road is opposite the pub and leads 13.6km to the site. There are no facilities here, so it's best suited to self-sufficient campers. Bring drinking water and firewood. There is a solid fuel fire ban from December to March, so it's Gas/fuel stove only then.

GPS S:33 42.037 E:116 02.702

MR: Map 16 G6

FURTHER Information

DEC Kirup Local Office
Tel: 08 9731 6232

THE SOUTH-WEST

55 Bibbulmun Track – Southern Section

The Bibbulmun Track is Western Australia's premier long distance walking track. Totalling a length of 963km, the track runs from the Perth suburb of Kalamunda to Albany on the south coast and marked the full distance. The southern section of the Bibbulmun Track is from Donnelly River Village to Albany. Bibbulmun Track walkers traverse some of the south-west's most beautiful and scenic landscapes and forest types. The track can be tackled in one go for those with the time and energy or can be walked in sections with numerous vehicle drop-off access points to the track. All walkers should be well prepared and self-sufficient. The informative Bibbulmun Track Guides and maps are recommended.

Bibbulmun Track

THE SOUTH-WEST

Bibbulmun Track camping areas

Access via the Bibbulmun Track. Water may not always be reliable, always carry extra. Gas/fuel stove preferred. **NB:** No fires after Dog Pool campsite to Albany. Fire restrictions occur from October to May, please contact local authorities to obtain current details. Carry copy of maps and guides.

Trackhead: Donnelly River Village

MR: Map 20 G1

Tom Road Campsite 15.9km from Donnelly River Village

Boarding House Campsite 22.8km from Tom Road

Beavis Campsite 19.1km from Boarding House

Beedelup Campsite 19.5km from Beavis

Warren Campsite 45.4km from Beedelup

Schafer Campsite 21.1km from Warren

Gardner Campsite 29.1km from Schafer

Lake Maringup Campsite 15.9km from Gardner

Dog Pool Campsite 24.5km from Lake Maringup

Mt Chance Campsite 19.4km from Dog Pool

Woolbales Campsite 20.4km from Mt Chance

Long Point Campsite 17.2km from Woolbales

Mt Clare Campsite 12.2km from Long Point

Frankland Campsite 27.5km from Mt Clare

Giants Campsite 13.7km from Frankland River

Rame Head Campsite 15.6km from Giants

Boat Harbour Campsite 33.2km from Rame Head

William Bay Campsite 19.9mk from Boat Harbour

Nullaki Campsite 31.5km from William Bay

West Cape Howe Campsite 16.5km from Nullaki

Torbay Campsite 16.4km from West Cape Howe

Hidden Valley Campsite 17.5km from Torbay

Albany Trackhead 19.3km from Hidden Valley.

GPS S:35 01.667 E:117 53.132
MR: Map 22 G6

FURTHER Information

DEC Recreation & Trails Unit
Tel: 08 9334 0265. Walking groups of eight or more must contact the Recreation & Trails Unit for a Notice of Intent form.

The Bibbulmun Track Foundation
Tel: 08 9481 0551
Web: www.bibbulmuntrack.org.au

56 Blackwood National Park

The park encompasses stands of jarrah-marri forest along the Blackwood River. The river is Western Australia's longest river, stretching some 500km from its headwaters north-east of Balingup to the Southern Ocean at Augusta. The river is popular for swimming, canoeing and fishing. Access to Blackwood National Park is via Sues Road, which is signposted off the Brockman Highway, or via Warner Glen Road, which is signposted off the Bussell Highway.

Sues Bridge campground

From the Brockman Highway, 27km east of Karridale, take the signposted Sues Road. Sues Road proceeds north for 9.1km to the signposted access to the recreational area. This access road leads in 400m to the self-registration station and camping area. Large area with 25 individually numbered, well shaded sites. Fifteen tent sites, three camper trailer sites, five caravan sites, one group site and one area specifically set up for disabled campers. Camp kitchen. Canoe launching facility. Bring drinking water and firewood. Gas/fuel stove only during summer (high fire danger) season.

GPS S:34 04.618 E:115 23.302
MR: Map 19 D2

Chapman Pool camping area

Situated near the junction of the Blackwood River and Chapman Brook with signposted access on Warner Glen Road. From the Bussell Highway, 14km south of Margaret River, take the signposted Warner Glen Road and proceed east for 10.6km to the signposted access to the recreation area. This unsealed access road leads in 700m to the self-registration station and camping area. Twelve individually numbered campsites and one group camping area. Canoe launching facility. Bring drinking water and firewood. Fire restrictions apply during summer (high fire danger) season.

GPS S:34 05.495 E:115 12.501
MR: Map 19 C2

FURTHER Information

DEC Busselton District Office
Tel: 08 9752 5555
Camping fees: From $7.00 per adult/night and $2.00 per child (up to 16)/night. Fees payable at self-registration station.

57 Bremer Bay Area

Bremer Bay is located 183km north-east of Albany with access signposted off the South Coast Highway. The superb coastal scenery is one of the highlights of this region. Popular area for boating, fishing and scuba diving.

Millers Point Reserve

From Bremer Bay proceed west along the Borden-Bremer Bay Road for 47km to signposted Millers Point Road (this is 13km south-east of the South Coast Highway). This unsealed road (which can be corrugated) leads south for 6km to a T-intersection. Turn left at this junction and follow the track for 160m to the camping area on Beaufort Inlet. Dispersed bush camping among paper bark trees with some shaded sites. Bring drinking water and firewood.

GPS S:34 27.169 E:118 52.709
MR: Map 22 L2

FURTHER Information

Shire of Jerramungup
Tel: 08 9835 1022
Camping fees: From $7.00 per person/night. Fees payable to patrolling ranger.

Gordon Inlet camping area

From Bremer Bay proceed east along Bremer Bay Road for 1.7km to the signposted Beach Access. Proceed north along the beach access road and cross the sandbar (4WD vehicles only) to Gordon Inlet Road. Continue in northerly direction along Gordon Inlet Road for 8.4km to crossroads. At these crossroads proceed north for a further 9.2km to a Y-junction. Keep right for 300m to a small bush campsite nestled in vegetation beside the inlet. Narrow access track with overhanging vegetation and sandy sections. Self-sufficient campers. Recommended to take own portable toilet. Bring drinking water. Gas/fuel stove only.

GPS S:34 17.401 E:119 29.701
MR: Map 23 D7

House Beach camping area

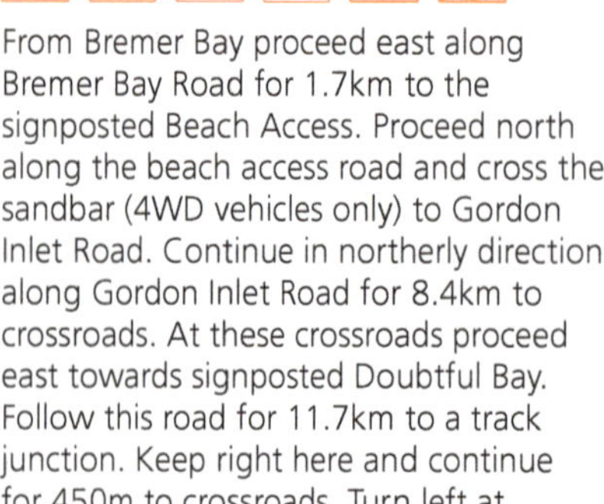

From Bremer Bay proceed east along Bremer Bay Road for 1.7km to the signposted Beach Access. Proceed north along the beach access road and cross the sandbar (4WD vehicles only) to Gordon Inlet Road. Continue in northerly direction along Gordon Inlet Road for 8.4km to crossroads. At these crossroads proceed east towards signposted Doubtful Bay. Follow this road for 11.7km to a track junction. Keep right here and continue for 450m to crossroads. Turn left at these crossroads and proceed in a north-easterly direction for 1.7km to a T-intersection. At this intersection turn left and proceed north for 440m to site of an old homestead (private property – do not enter). There are tracks to the left and right of the homestead which lead to areas of bush camping. Some sites to the east (right) of the homestead are shaded and protected. Sites to the west (left) of the homestead are located above the beach boat launch and close to the toilet. Recommended to bring own portable toilet. Limited facilities at this site so best suited for self-sufficient campers. Bring drinking water. Gas/fuel stove only.

GPS S:34 21.957 E:119 31.475
MR: Map 23 D7

House Beach camping area

FURTHER Information

Bremer Bay Community Resource Centre & Visitors Centre
Tel: 08 9837 4171
Web: www.bremerbaycrc.net.au

58 Bridgetown

Situated on the Blackwood River, Bridgetown is known for its beautiful countryside and surrounding jarrah forests. Bridgetown is 90km south-east of Bunbury on the South Western Highway.

Bridgetown Caravan Park

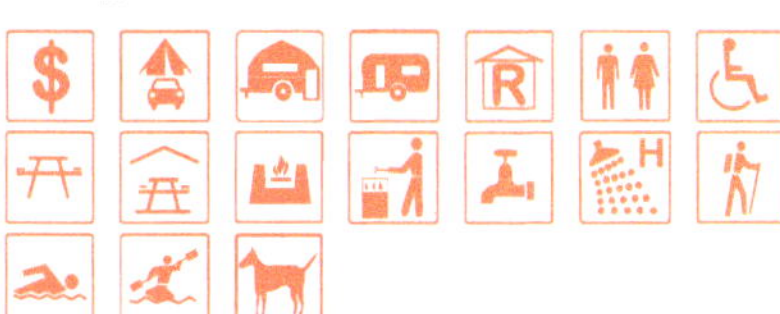

Located on the South Western Highway at the southern end of town beside the Blackwood River. Camp kitchen, laundry facilities. Some firewood supplied.

GPS S:33 58.312 E:116 08.153

MR: Map 16 H8

FURTHER Information

Bridgetown Visitor Information Centre

Tel: 08 9761 1740

Web: www.bridgetown.com.au

Camping fees: Unpowered site from $23.00 per site/night up to 2 people. Powered site from $25.00 per site/night up to 2 people. Fees payable at on-site honesty box or to Visitor Information Centre.

THE SOUTH-WEST

59 Broomehill

Visitors to Broomehill can take in the history of the town's Heritage Trail walking track. The village is located 160km north of Albany on the Great Southern Highway.

Broomehill Caravan Park

Located at the corner of Morgan Road and Journal Street in Broomehill. Laundry facilities. Gas/fuel stove only.

MR: Map 17 E6

FURTHER Information

Shire of Broomehill-Tambellup

Tel: 08 9825 3333

Web: www.shirebt.wa.gov.au

Camping fees: From $25.00 per site/night up to 2 people. Power available. Fees payable at shire office on the Great Southern Highway (Mon to Fri 8.30am to 3.30pm) or after hours to caretaker, **Tel:** 08 9824 1354.

60 Cape to Cape Track

Running between Cape Naturaliste and Cape Leeuwin, this walking track is 135 kilometres in length. The walk is signposted the whole way and passes along sections of soft sandy beaches, constructed pathways and old vehicle tracks through woodlands. Fit experienced walkers who like a challenge can undertake the track in one go over five to seven days of it can be covered in shorter day or overnight walks for those less enthusiastic.

Walk-in campsites: Mt Duckworth, Moses Rock, Ellensbrook & Deepdene

Walk-in sites along the track. Water from tanks, can be limited, may need to boil or treat first. Gas/fuel stoves only.

MR: Map 15 B6/7/8 & 19 B1/2/3 & C3

FURTHER Information

Friends of Cape to Cape Track
Email: info@capetocapetrack.com.au
Web: www.capetocapetrack.com.au
DEC Busselton office
Tel: 08 9752 5555

THE SOUTH-WEST

61 D'Entrecasteaux National Park

Enjoy bushwalking, spectacular coastal scenery, beach combing, fishing, boating and canoeing in the rivers, lakes and isolated beach campsites within the vast expanses of D'Entrecasteaux National Park. The park stretches from Black Point in the north-west for 130km to the south-east near Walpole. Featuring a landscape of coastal limestone cliffs, basalt columns, swamps, lakes, pristine sandy beaches, shifting sand dunes and majestic jarrah and karri forests. A range of camping is available with some sites accessible by conventional vehicles and others by 4WD vehicles. All visitors travelling via 4WD through the park should contact DEC offices for up-to-date access information. Please exercise caution at all river fords.

SOUTH-EAST SECTION

Crystal Springs campground

Located on Mandalay Beach Road. Mandalay Beach Road is signposted off the South Western Highway, 13km west of Walpole. Then drive in 260m to the well shaded camping area with grassy sites. Boil or treat water first. Bring drinking water and firewood.

GPS S:34 59.023 E:116 36.347

MR: Map 20 L7

Crystal Springs campground

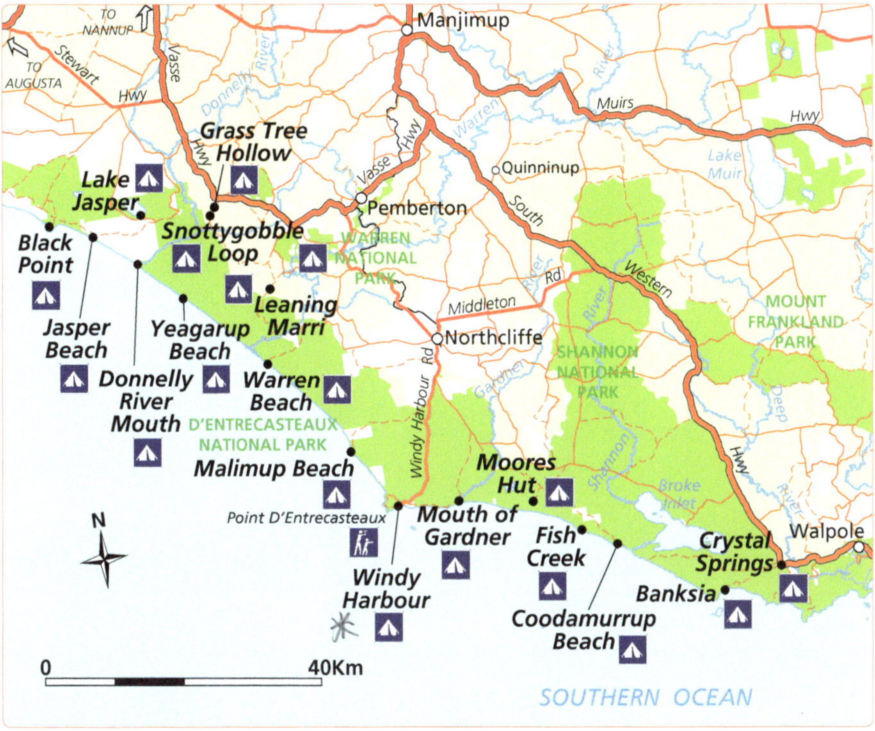

TO NANNUP
TO AUGUSTA
Stewart Hwy
Vasse Hwy
Donnelly River
Manjimup
Warren River
Muirs Hwy
Lake Muir
Quinninup
Grass Tree Hollow
Lake Jasper
Black Point
Jasper Beach
Snottygobble Loop
Pemberton
WARREN NATIONAL PARK
South Western Hwy
Leaning Marri
Yeagarup Beach
Donnelly River Mouth
Warren Beach
Middleton Rd
Northcliffe
MOUNT FRANKLAND PARK
SHANNON NATIONAL PARK
D'ENTRECASTEAUX NATIONAL PARK
Windy Harbour Rd
Gardner River
Shannon River
Deep River
Malimup Beach
Moores Hut
Broke Inlet
Point D'Entrecasteaux
Mouth of Gardner
Fish Creek
Crystal Springs
Walpole
Windy Harbour
Coodamurrup Beach
Banksia
N
0 40Km
SOUTHERN OCEAN

Banksia campsite

From Crystal Springs campground proceed in a south-westerly direction towards signposted Banksia Camp for 6.6km to track on the right. Turn right (west) and follow this track for 1km to a Y-junction. Keep left at Y-junction along signposted Banksia Track and follow it for 1.6km to track on left signposted to Banksia Camp. This track leads in 660m to the self-registration station and a further 40m to the camping area with seven individually numbered campsites/ camping nodes (node 1 is a group camping area). Shelter hut provides accommodation for up to 12 people (bookings are not necessary and is on a first come basis). A shower room is located beside the shelter where it is possible to hang your own shower/ solar shower bag. Soft sandy access tracks which will require lowering of tyre pressures. Popular surfing area. Bring drinking water. Gas/fuel stove only.

GPS S:35 00.262 E:116 30.714

MR: Map 20 K7

Banksia campsite

Broke Inlet camping area

Located on the southern shores of Broke Inlet and north-west of Banksia Camp. 4WD access via Fisherman's Track, which is seasonally closed. From Crystal Springs campground proceed in a south-westerly direction towards signposted Banksia Camp for 6.6km to track on the right. Turn right (west) and follow this track for 1km to a Y-junction. Keep left at Y-junction along signposted Banksia Track and follow it for 1.4km to track junction. At this junction continue straight ahead to the signposted Banksia Camp. Allow 1.5 hours travel time from the Banksia Camp turn-off off Mandalay Beach Road. Soft sandy access tracks. There are no facilities at this site so best suited for self-sufficient campers. Bring drinking water. Gas/fuel stove preferred.

MR: Map 20 K6

FURTHER Information

DEC Walpole District Office
Tel: 08 9840 0400
Park entrance fee: $11.00 per vehicle.
Camping fees: From $7.00 per adult/night and $2.00 per child (under 16)/night. Fees payable at self-registration station.

CENTRAL SECTION

Moores Hut camping area

Access from the south is via the signposted Broke Inlet Road off the South Western Highway, 26km north-west of Walpole. Follow Broke Inlet Road in a westerly direction for 8km to the signposted Chesapeake Road. Follow Chesapeake Road in a north-westerly direction for 20.6km to the signposted Moores Track. This leads in 3.9km to a T-intersection. Turn right (west) towards signposted Coodamurrup and follow this for 6.3km to the site of Moores Hut and camping area with sheltered and grassy sites, set 2km back from Coodamurrup Beach. Access from Northcliffe: take the signposted Boorara Road (following the signage to Chesapeake Road) and follow this as it becomes Gardner River Road to the signposted Chesapeake Road, which then leads 8.9km to Moores Track. Soft sandy access tracks. Bring drinking water and firewood.

GPS S:34 51.407 E:116 13.904
MR: Map 20 J6

Moores Hut camping area

Coodamurrup Beach camping area

Dispersed bush camping at Coodamurrup Beach. Sites along beach and behind dunes. Located 2km south-west of Moores Hut CA. Access via Moores Track, see Moores Hut camping area for access details. Bring drinking water. If you wish to have a fire please bring your own fire bin/bucket and firewood. Gas/fuel stove preferred.

MR: Map 20 J6

Fish Creek camping area

Access from the south is via the signposted Broke Inlet Road off the South Western Highway, 26km north-west of Walpole. Follow Broke Inlet Road in a westerly direction for 8km to the signposted Chesapeake Road. Follow Chesapeake Road in a north-westerly direction for 20.6km to the signposted Moores Track. This leads in 3.9km to a T-intersection. At this intersection turn left (east) to the signposted Fish Creek and follow the signage to the camping area, set back from the coast. Bring drinking water. If you wish to have a fire please bring your own fire bin/bucket and firewood. Gas/fuel stove preferred.

MR: Map 20 J6

Malimup Beach camping area

Located 25km south-west of Northcliffe. Access via Summertime Track off Windy Harbour Road. Best suited to self-sufficient campers only. Bring drinking water. If you wish to have a fire please bring your own fire bin/bucket and firewood. Gas/fuel stove preferred.

MR: Map 20 H5

Mouth of Gardner camping area

Dispersed bush camping behind dunes of Gardner Beach beside the Gardner River. Access from Windy Harbour Road, via seasonally closed track. Very soft sandy access tracks. No facilities at this site so best suited for self-sufficient campers. Bring drinking water. If you wish to have a fire please bring your own fire bin/bucket and firewood. Gas/fuel stove preferred.

MR: Map 20 I6

FURTHER Information

DEC Pemberton District Office

Tel: 08 9776 1207

Park entrance fee: $11.00 per vehicle.

Camping fees: From $7.00 per adult/night and $2.00 per child (under 16)/night. Fees payable at self-registration station.

NB: At the time of publication access to Fish Creek, Moores Hut and Coodamurrup Beach was not possible, however access was likely to be possible at a later date.

Windy Harbour Naturebase camping ground

Located 27km south of Northcliffe via Windy Harbour Road. Popular surfing area. Camp kitchen. Bring drinking water. Some firewood supplied.

MR: Map 20 H6

FURTHER Information

Windy Harbour – Caretaker

Tel: 08 9776 8398

Park entrance fee: Park pass not required.

Camping fees: From $11.50 per adult/night and $5.50 per child (under 15)/night. Family rate 2 adults/2 children (under 15) $30.00 per site/night. Fees payable to caretaker.

NORTH-WEST SECTION

Warren Beach camping area

Dispersed bush camping at Warren Beach and along access track. From Northcliffe travel towards Pemberton and then take the signposted Richardson Road, which proceeds in a westerly direction. Follow Richardson Road to its junction with Lewis Road, then take Lewis Road and follow this to Warren Beach Track. Use existing campsites only. Limited facilities at this site so best suited for self-sufficient campers. Bring drinking water. Bring drinking water. If you wish to have a fire bring own fire bin/bucket and firewood. Gas/fuel stove preferred.

MR: Map 20 G5

Leaning Marri campsite

From the Vasse Highway, 9km west of Pemberton, turn onto the signposted Old Vasse Road and follow this for 50m to the signposted Ritter Road. Ritter Road leads south for 11.2km to the signposted access track to the camping area. This track leads in 170m to the camping area with eight individually numbered campsites, two of which are group tent based campsites with carry gear into sites. Lake Yeagarup is a short walk, where water based activities can be undertaken. Bring drinking water. Fireplaces are located at the group camping areas, bring firewood. Gas/fuel stove only at individual sites.

GPS S:34 32.336 E:115 52.486

MR: Map 20 G4

Leaning Marri campsite

Yeagarup Beach camping area

Dispersed bush camping at Yeagarup Beach. Access via Ritter Road off Old Vasse Road, see Leaning Marri campsite for access to Ritter Road. Self-sufficient campers only. Bring drinking water. If you wish to have a fire bring own fire bin/bucket and firewood. Gas/fuel stove preferred.

MR: Map 20 G4

Grass Tree Hollow camping area

     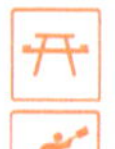  

Signposted access 1.4km along Boat Landing Road, which is accessed off the Vasse Highway 21.2km west of Pemberton. Camping area has seven individually numbered campsites, each with level a level tent pad, table and fireplace. Located on the banks of the

Donnelly River with walking tracks along the river. Bring drinking water and firewood. Gas/fuel stove preferred.
GPS S:34 25.550 E:115 48.354
MR: Map 20 G4

Snottygobble Loop camping area

Signposted access 2.6km along Boat Landing Road, which is accessed off the Vasse Highway 21.2km west of Pemberton. Camping area has 11 individually numbered campsites, each with level a level tent pad. Sites suitable for small campervans (campervans that have wheel base similar to a car). Located on the banks of the Donnelly River with walking tracks along the river. Bring drinking water and firewood. Gas/fuel stove preferred.
GPS S:34 26.118 E:115 47.854
MR: Map 20 G4

Donnelly River Mouth camping area

Self-sufficient bush camping at mouth of the Donnelly River with boat access only to this site via the Donnelly River. Boat ramp located at end of Boat Landing Road, 3km south of Snottygobble Loop CA. Bring drinking water. If you wish to have a fire bring own fire bin/bucket and firewood. Gas/fuel stove preferred.

Donnelly River boat ramp:
GPS S:34 26.914 E:115 46.586
MR: Map 19 F4

Lake Jasper camping area

Access is from the north-west via Black Point Road. Follow directions to the crossroads with Wapet Track 2km north of Black Point CA. From the crossroads proceed in a south-easterly direction for 8km to a T-intersection. Turn left here onto the road signposted to Lake Jasper and follow this for 10.6km to a T-intersection. At this junction the road to the left (north-west) leads 3.3km to the camping area with three sites on the southern shores of the lake. Bring drinking water. Gas/fuel stove only.
GPS S:34 25.266 E:115 41.505
MR: Map 19 F4

Jasper Beach camping area

Access is from the north-west via Black Point Road. Follow directions for Black Point CA to the crossroads with Wapet Track 2km north of Black Point CA. From the crossroads proceed in a south-easterly direction along Wapet Track for 8km to a T-intersection. Turn right towards signposted Jasper Beach for 800m to the dispersed bush camping behind the beach dunes. There are no facilities at this site so best suited for self-sufficient campers. Bring drinking water. Gas/fuel stove only.

Jasper Beach entrance track:
GPS S:34 26.510 E:115 36.724
MR: Map 19 F4

Lake Jasper

Black Point Recreation Site

Access is from the north-west via Black Point Road. From the Vasse Highway take the signposted Stewart Road to the west and follow this for 6.7km to the signposted Black Point Road. Black Point Road then leads in a south-westerly direction for 4.9km to its junction with Fouracres Road. At this junction the Black Point Road continues in a southerly direction (this is a seasonally closed road) to meet at a set of crossroads, with Wapet Track, 2km north of the camping area. Alternative route is to turn onto Fouracres Road and follow for 20.6km, then turn left onto Milyeannup Coast Road follow for 8.2km, then turn left onto Woodaburrup Road and follow it for 22.3km to a set of crossroads, with Wapet Track. At crossroads track on right leads 2km to the camping area where there are 15 sheltered sites among coastal heath. Access roads are soft sandy tracks. Popular surfing area. Bring drinking water. Gas/fuel stove only.

GPS S:34 25.006 E:115 32.746
MR: Map 19 E4

Black Point

FURTHER Information

DEC Pemberton District Office

Tel: 08 9776 1207
Park entrance fee: $11.00 per vehicle.
Camping fees: From $7.00 per adult/night and $2.00 per child (under 16)/night. Fees payable at self-registration station.
NB: At the time of publication access to Lake Jasper via Scott Road off the Vasse Highway was not possible due to bridge collapse, however access via this route may be possible at a later date.

62 Fitzgerald River National Park

Covering an area of 329 039ha, Fitzgerald River National Park features a diverse landscape ranging from rugged coastal cliffs to protected beaches to river valleys. An array of wildflowers bloom throughout spring, and from August to November whales can be seen as they move along the coast. Fishing and bushwalking are other popular activities. Situated between the towns of Bremer Bay in the west and Hopetoun in the east, there is conventional vehicle access to the eastern side of the park from Hopetoun via Hamersley Drive. In the west conventional vehicle access is via Point Ann Road off Collets Road.

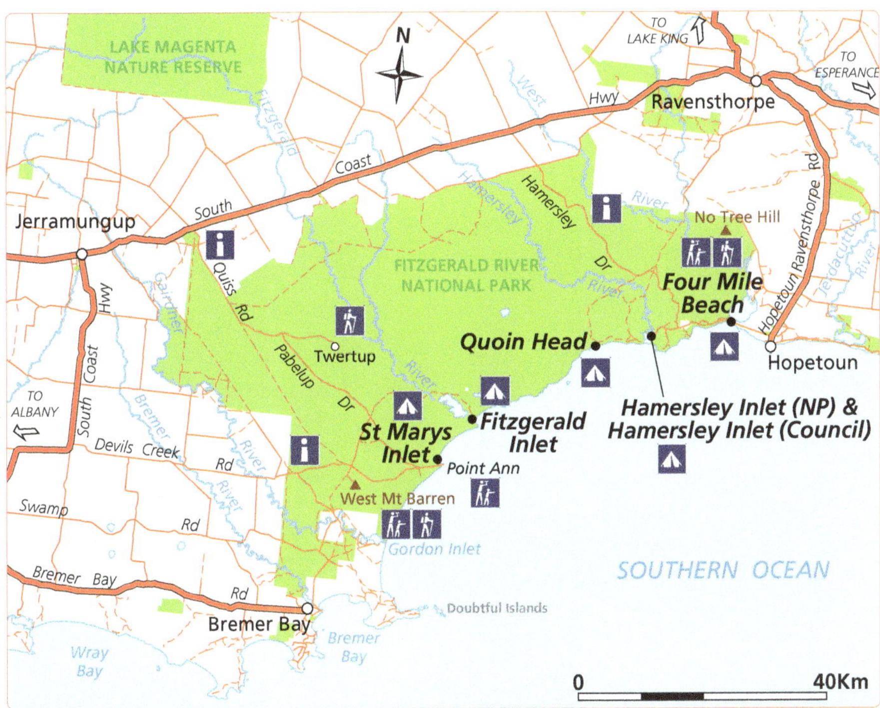

WEST SIDE

St Marys Inlet camping ground

From the South Coast Highway take the signposted access road to the park, signposted as Quiss Road. This is 19km east of Jerramungup and 94km west of Ravensthorpe. Follow Quiss Road in a south-easterly direction for 48.3km to the signposted access road to Pt Ann. Turn left and head towards Pt Ann for 16km to the signposted access to St Marys Inlet Camping Ground. This leads into the camping area with 13 individually numbered campsites. Most are well sheltered from the coastal winds. Limited sites suitable for camper trailer and small caravans. Bring drinking water. Gas/fuel stove only.

GPS S:34 09.878 E:119 34.601
MR: Map 23 D6

St Marys Inlet camping ground

FURTHER Information

West Side: Fitzgerald River National Park – Ranger
Tel: 08 9837 1022
Fitzgerald River National Park – Ranger In Charge
Tel: 08 9835 5043.
Park entrance fee: $11.00 per vehicle.
Camping fees: From $7.00 per adult/night and $2.00 per child (under 16)/night. Fees payable at self-registration stations at park entry stations.

EAST SIDE

Hamersley Inlet camping area

From Ravensthorpe proceed in a westerly direction along the South Coast Highway for 41.6km to the signposted Hamersley Drive/West River Rd. Hamersley Drive proceeds south for 46.7km to the signposted access road on the right (this is 21km west of Hopetoun via Hamersley Drive which is signposted 1.4km north of Hopetoun). This road leads 3.7km to the camping area access track, which is signposted with a tent symbol, and leads in 100m to the small camping area with dispersed bush camping. Access track can be washed out, dry weather access only. Bring drinking water. Gas/fuel stove only.
GPS S:33 56.938 E:119 55.579
MR: Map 23 F4

Quoin Head camping area

From Ravensthorpe proceed in a westerly direction along the South Coast Highway for 41.6km to the signposted Hamersley Drive/West River Rd. Hamersley Drive proceeds south for 33.1km to the signposted access track on right to Quoin Head (this is 26km west of Hopetoun via Hamersley Drive which is signposted 1.4km north of Hopetoun). Follow this track in a south-westerly direction to the coast and the camping area. Dry weather access only as the road is closed during wet weather. Steep access track suitable only for 4WD vehicles. Bring drinking water. Gas/fuel stove only.
Quoin Head access track: **GPS** S:33 52.558 E:119 52.858
MR: Map 23 F4

Four Mile Beach camping area

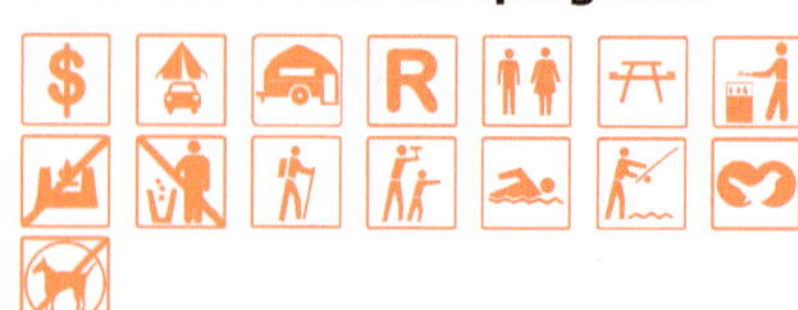

Signposted access along Hamersley Drive, 12km west of Hopetoun. Hamersley Drive is signposted along the Hopetoun-Ravensthorpe road 1.4km north of Hopetoun. Best suited for tent based camping and small campervans. Bring drinking water. Gas/fuel stove only.
MR: Map 24 G4

FURTHER Information

East Side: Fitzgerald River National Park – Ranger
Tel: 08 9838 3060
Fitzgerald River National Park – Ranger In Charge
Tel: 08 9835 5043.
Park entrance fee: $11.00 per vehicle.
Camping fees: From $7.00 per adult/night and $2.00 per child (under 16)/night. Fees payable at self-registration stations at park entry stations.
NB: At time of publication Quoin Head camping area was closed to camping, however open for day visits. This site may reopen at a later date for camping.

62 Glen Mervyn Dam

Popular waterskiing, swimming and fishing location. The dam is located south of Collie and accessed off the Collie-Mumballup Road.

Glen Mervyn Dam bush camping

Dispersed bush camping on the western shores of the dam. From Collie proceed south along the Collie-Mumballup Road for 17km to signposted Best Road on the west (this is 540m north of the boat ramp access road and 4.8km north of Mumballup). Best Road leads west for 1km to a gravel track (the first track), which then leads south for 800m to the western shores and numerous tracks that lead to bush camping areas. Access track can be rough and rutted with washouts. Limited facilities at this bush campsite so it's best suited for self-sufficient campers. Bring drinking water. Gas/fuel stove only.

GPS S:33 29.909 E:116 05.851
MR: Map 16 H5

FURTHER Information

Collie Visitor Information Centre
Tel: 08 9734 2051
Web: www.collierivervalley.org.au

THE SOUTH-WEST

Glen Mervyn Dam bush camping

64 Hopetoun Area

Hopetoun is situated on the shores of the Southern Ocean, 50km south of Ravensthorpe. Within the council's boundaries are a number of camping areas which provide excellent boating, fishing and swimming opportunities. There is conventional vehicle access to all sites.

Hamersley Inlet Reserve camping area

Located within Fitzgerald River National Park, park entrance fee applies. From Ravensthorpe proceed in a westerly direction along the South Coast Highway for 41.6km to the signposted Hamersley Drive/West River Rd. Hamersley Drive proceeds south for 46.7km to the signposted access road on the right (this junction is 21km west of Hopetoun via Hamersley Drive which is signposted along the Hopetoun-Ravensthorpe road 1.4km north of Hopetoun). The access road leads 6.3km to the open camping area with no shade and limited level tent sites. Best suited to camper trailers and campervans. Shower cubicle suitable to hang own solar shower/shower bag. Bring drinking water. Gas/fuel stove only.

GPS S:33 57.505 E:119 54.890

MR: Map 24 F4

Mason Bay Camping & Recreation Grounds

Signposted access to Mason Bay along Southern Ocean East Road, 33km east of Hopetoun. Then drive in southerly direction for 1.4km to the camping area. Terraced camping area, some sites with ocean frontage while other sites are set well back from the beach. Beach boat launch. Bring drinking water. Some firewood supplied.

GPS S:33 57.287 E:120 28.756

MR: Map 24 I4

Mason Bay Camping and Recreation Grounds

Starvation Bay (Powell Point) camping area

From Hopetoun take the signposted Southern Ocean East Road for 43km to the signposted access to Starvation Bay. (Southern Ocean East Road becomes

Springdale Road east of the access road.) Then drive in 100m to the camping area with dispersed bush camping and good shelter among trees. Shower cubicle suitable to hang own solar shower/ shower bag in. Electric barbecue in day use area in the boat ramp car park. Beach boat launch. Bring drinking water. Some firewood supplied. There is also a second area which is accessed 50m further north along Springdale Road and leads in 360m to an open camping area overlooking the ocean. This access track is narrow with overhanging vegetation which could cause damage to vehicle paintwork.

GPS S:33 55.156 E:120 33.344

2nd camping area: **GPS** S:33 55.022 E:120 33.290

MR: Map 24 J4

Starvation Bay camping area

Kundip Rest Area

Signposted access 30km north of Hopetoun along the Hopetoun-Ravensthorpe Road. Large rest area on the west side of the road with dispersed bush camping and some shade. **NB:** Take note of any signage regarding maximum stays. Take a stroll along the Heritage Walking Trail. Bring drinking water and firewood.

GPS S:33 41.423 E:120 11.142

MR: Map 24 G2

FURTHER Information

Shire of Ravensthorpe
Tel: 08 9839 0000

Ravensthorpe & Hopetoun District Visitors Centre
Tel: 08 9838 1277

Camping fees: From $7.00 per site/night. Fees payable at on-site honesty box.

65 Ironstone Gully Falls

At nine metres in height, these falls are most picturesque after recent rain falls, whilst colourful wildflower displays can be found in the surrounding countryside from August to October. Access to the falls and campsite is along Goodwood Road, south-east of Capel and south-west of Donnybrook.

Ironstone Gully Falls camping area

Signposted access along Goodwood Road, 11km south-east of Capel and 18km south-west of Donnybrook. Dispersed bush camping among trees set back from the falls. Bring drinking water and firewood.

GPS S:33 39.085 E:115 42.291

MR: Map 15 E6

FURTHER Information

Shire of Capel
Tel: 08 9727 0222
Web: www.capel.wa.gov.au

Donnybrook Visitors Centre
Tel: 08 9731 1720
Web: www.donnybrookwa.com.au
Maximum stay: 24 hours.

66 Lake King

Walk the Roe Heritage Trail and retrace part of the historic journey taken by surveyor General Roe in 1848. Check out the Lake King saltwater lake and picnic at Mount Madden Cairn. Or travel east to the Rabbit Proof Fence for magnificent displays of wildflowers during the spring. Lake King is 117km east of Lake Grace on the Newdegate Ravensthorpe Road.

Lake King Caravan Park

Located on Critchley Avenue in Lake King. Camp kitchen, laundry facilities.

MR: Map 27 B4

FURTHER Information

Lake King Tavern
Tel: 08 9874 4048
Camping fees: Unpowered tent sites from $8.00 per adult/night. Powered van sites from $25.00 per site/night for 2 people. Fees payable at Lake King Tavern.

67 Lake Poorrarecup

A popular water based activities destination, Lake Poorrarecup is located west of the Albany Highway and east of the town of Frankland. The camping area is located at the northern edge of the lake. Signposted access is off Poorrarecup Road, 33km west of Cranbrook and 13km east of Frankland on the Frankland-Cranbrook Road. Unsealed access road.

Lake Poorrarecup camping area

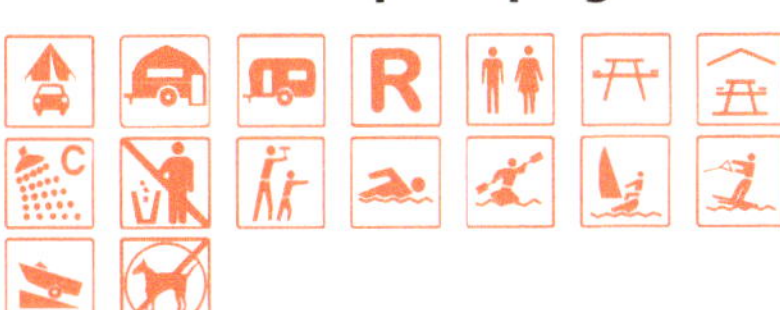

Signposted access 10km along Poorrarecup Road. Poorrarecup Road proceeds in a southerly direction off the Frankland-Cranbrook Road and is signposted 12km east of Frankland and 34km west of Cranbrook. Natural boat ramp. Childrens playground. Bring drinking water and firewood. Gas/fuel stove preferred.

MR: Map 21 C2

FURTHER Information

Shire of Cranbrook

Tel: 08 9826 1008

Web: www.cranbrook.wa.gov.au

NB: A solid fuel fire ban exists from October to May each year – gas/fuel stove only during this period. Please check with local authorities prior to lighting any fire.

68 Lake Towerinning

This large lake is surrounded by farmland and is a haven for waterbirds, making it a popular destination for bird watchers as well as for water based activities. Access to the lake is off Darkan Road South, 2km north of the Boyup Brook Arthur Road and 7km south of Duranillin.

Lakeside Camping Area

Signposted access along Darkan Road South, 2km north of the Arthur River Boyup Brook road and 7km south of Duranillin. Kiosk, camp kitchen, laundry. Limited tank water available so it's best to bring your own drinking water. Bring firewood or purchase on site.

MR: Map 16 K5

FURTHER Information

Lakeside Camping Area

Tel: 08 9863 1040. Bookings necessary during long weekends and holiday periods.

Web: www.lakesidecamping.com.au

Camping fees: Unpowered sites from $20.00 per site/night for 2 people. Powered sites from $25.00 per site/night for 2 people.

69 Leeuwin–Naturaliste National Park

This popular park features magnificent coastal scenery, beautiful surfing beaches, walking trails, caves, scenic drives and towering Karri forests. Two caves in the park, Calgardup and Giants Caves, offer self-guided tours whilst guided tours are available for Ngilgi, Lake, Mammoth, Jewel and Moodyne Caves. The park is also popular for swimming, fishing and whale watching. Covering 20,000ha, Leeuwin-Naturaliste National Park stretches from Cape Naturaliste in the north to Cape Leeuwin in the south, with lighthouses at each cape which are open to visitors. Numerous access points along the coast lead to many of the park's visitor areas.

Cape Leeuwin Lighthouse

THE SOUTH-WEST

Hamelin Bay Caravan Park & Camping Area

Signposted access 2.3km along Hamelin Bay Road. Hamelin Bay Road is signposted off Caves Road. Caves Road is signposted off the Bussell Highway 3km north of Augusta, then travel for 13.3km to Hamelin Bay Road. Alternatively from Karridale (on the Bussell Highway) take the signposted Bushby Road to the west for 2km to Caves Road, then turn left (south) for 3km. Kiosk, laundry, playground. Some firewood supplied.

GPS S:34 13.312 E:115 01.974

MR: Map 19 B3

Hamelin Bay Caravan Park and Camping Area

FURTHER *Information*

Hamelin Bay Caravan Park

Tel: 08 9758 5540. Bookings necessary during school and public holidays and long weekends.

Camping fees: Unpowered sites from $20.00 per site/night up to 2 people. Powered sites from $25.00 per site/night up to 2 people.

Conto Campground

Signposted access 1.7km along Conto Road, west of Caves Road, then drive in 230m to the campground access. Conto Road is signposted off Caves Road 1.2km south of the signposted Forrest Grove Road (which leads 6.7km to the Bussell Highway 13.2km south of Margaret River) and 3km north of the northern signposted access to Boranup Drive. Very large area with five separate camping areas: Davies Drive with 12 sites (2 suitable for small caravans), Hamelin Hollow with 22 sites including a camp kitchen (7 sites suitable for small caravans and 1 site suitable for disabled access), Isaacs with 13 sites (1 site suitable for small caravan) – this is a campfire prohibited area, Whaler's Cove with 11 sites (3 suitable for small caravans), Whistlers Way with 14 sites (11 are suitable for small caravans) along with and camp kitchen. Limited tank water, boil or treat first or bring own drinking water. Bring own firewood or available for purchase on site.

GPS S:34 04.826 E:115 00.965

MR: Map 19 B2

Conto Campground

Boranup Forest campground

Signposted access along Boranup Drive, 1.5km west of Caves Road from the southern entrance of Boranup Drive. The southern entrance of Boranup Drive is signposted off Caves Road, 3.3km north of Bushby Road to Karridale (on the Bussell Highway) and is 10.6km south of the northern entrance of Boranup Drive. The northern entrance of Boranup Drive is 3km south of the signposted Conto Road. The drive is a total of 14km. Campground has seven individually numbered sites. One-way access track through the campground is narrow and tight. Bring drinking water. Some firewood supplied.

GPS S:34 10.690 E:115 04.075

MR: Map 19 B3

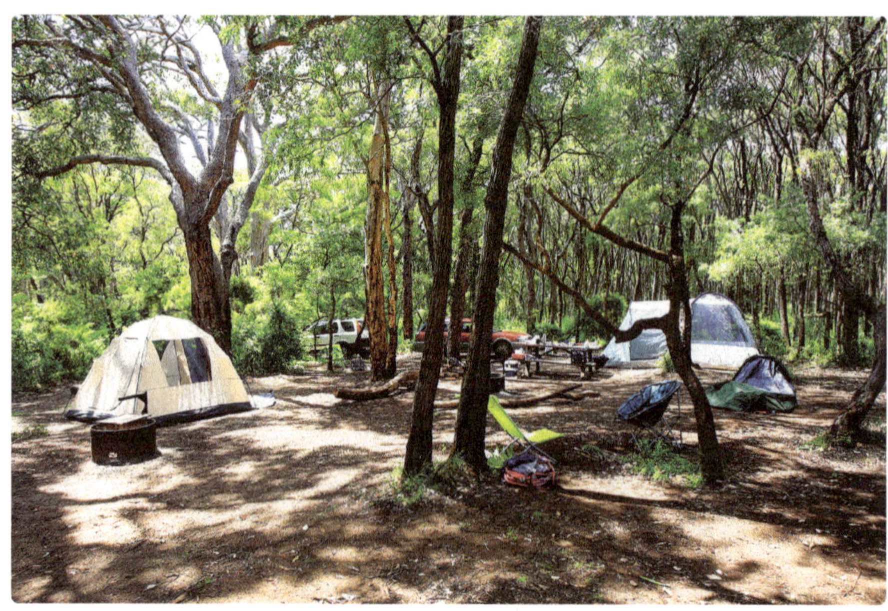

Boranup Forest campground

Point Road campground

Located 4km along Point Road. Point Road is accessed off Boranup Drive and is 130m to the west of the park information boards at the northern end of Boranup Drive. The northern end of Boranup Drive is 3km south of the signposted Conto Road. Access track is suitable for high clearance AWD, there are a number of larger rocks along/in the track so careful wheel positioning would be required. Close to fishing and surfing beach. Bring drinking water. Some firewood supplied.

GPS S:34 05.556 E:115 01.028

MR: Map 19 B2

Point Road campground

FURTHER Information

DEC Busselton District Office

Tel: 08 9752 5555

Conto Campground

Tel: 08 9757 7025

Camping fees: From $7.00 per adult/night and $2.00 per child/ night. Fees collected by Rangers or payable at self-registration stations.

NB: Conto Campground is signposted as 'An Alcohol Free Campground'.

70 Leschenault Peninsula Conservation Park

The peninsula separates the Leschenault Estuary from the Indian Ocean, and is located to the west of Australind. The park is well-known for its white sandy beaches which are perfect for swimming and fishing. The park's peppermint and tuart woodlands are home to brushtail and ringtail possums. Access to Leschenault Peninsula Conservation Park is via Buffalo Road off Old Coast Road, 10km north of Australind. Caravanners should check road conditions first. Mosquitos can be thick at times so have good mosquito protection when visiting.

Belvidere Camping Ground

From the Old Coast Road take the signposted Buffalo Road, 9.8km north of Australind. Buffalo Road proceeds in a westerly direction for 2.8km from here the road becomes gravel and turns south, then continues for a further 4.4km to the camping area. Here you'll find 10 individually numbered campsites with sandy bases and some shaded sites. Two sites are suitable for caravans and three sites are for groups. Walking access to the beach and estuary. Bring drinking water. Some firewood supplied.

GPS S:33 14.092 E:115 41.837

MR: Map 15 E4

Belvidere Camping Ground

The Cut camping area

Walk-in, cycle or boat access only. Located at end of the peninsula, 8.5km south of Belvidere. Bring drinking water and firewood.

MR: Map 15 E4

FURTHER Information

DEC Wellington District Office

Tel: 08 9735 1988

Camping fees: From $7.00 per adult/night and $2.00 per child/ night. Fees collected by Ranger.

THE SOUTH-WEST

71 Munda Biddi Trail

The Munda Biddi Trail is a long distance cycling trail which stretches from Mundaring, north-east of Perth, to Albany on the south coast. The trail is being constructed in three stages, and when completed the trail will be a total of 1,000km of mountain bike touring. Winding through forests and national parks, the trail follows bush tracks and old railway lines. For restocking purposes and accommodation options the trail passes through a town at least every second day. Campsites along the trail are located 35km to 40km apart between towns or a day's ride. Each campsite is well equipped with flat tent sites, toilet, table, shelter, water tank and bike shelters. Camp fires are not permitted at campsites so carry a gas/fuel stove. There are a range of detailed maps and guides for the trail and the Munda Biddi Trail Foundation website is a great information resource.

Munda Biddi Trail campsites – Collie to Manjimup

Access along the Munda Biddi Trail. Water may not always be reliable, always carry extra. Gas/fuel stoves only. Carry copy of maps and guides.

Trackhead: Collie

MR: Map 16 G4

Nglang Boodja Campsite 46.5km south of Collie and 48km north of Donnybrook

Nala Mia Campsite 44.6km south-west of Donnybrook and 27km north of Nannup

Karta Burnu Campsite 24km south of Donnelly Mill and 23km north of Manjimup

Manjimup 23km south of Karta Burnu.

MR: Map 20 I2

Munda Biddi Trail campsites – Denmark to Albany (75km)

Access along the Munda Biddi Trail. Water may not always be reliable, always carry extra. Gas/fuel stoves only. Carry copy of maps and guides. Camping in this section is available at Flood Gates CA and Cosy Corner East, refer to Albany Area page 60.

Trackhead: Denmark

MR: Map 21 D6

Trackhead: Albany Visitor Information Centre

GPS S:35 01.667 E:117 53.132

MR: Map 22 G6

FURTHER Information

Munda Biddi Trail Foundation
Tel: 08 9481 2483
Web: www.mundabiddi.org.au

DEC Munda Biddi Trail Coordinator
Tel: 08 9334 0265

72 Mt Frankland South National Park

Established in 2004, the park is one of seven that make up the Walpole Wilderness Area. Within the park is the popular Fernhook Falls, accessed off the South Western Highway, north-west of Walpole. To the north of Walpole is the Swarbrick Walpole Wilderness Discovery site which is home to forest art and some magnificent old growth karri forest and is accessed off the North Walpole Road.

Fernhook Falls camping area

From Walpole proceed in a westerly direction along the South Western Highway for 34km to the signposted Beardmore Road (this is 85km south-east of Manjimup). Beardmore Road proceeds in an easterly direction for 5.9km to the signposted access into Fernhook Falls. This then leads in 150m to the self-registration station and camping area with nine individually numbered sites located above Deep River. Two sites are suitable for camper trailers, and two sites have shelter huts. Bring drinking water. Some firewood supplied.

GPS S:34 49.139 E:116 35.499
MR: Map 20 L5

Centre Road camping area

From Walpole proceed in a westerly direction along the South Western Highway for 20km to the signposted Centre Road. This unsealed road leads east for 4.9km to a hut and a small camping area below the hut suitable for two campsites. Located on the western banks of Deep River. Some firewood supplied.

GPS S:34 54.587 E:116 37.343
MR: Map 20 L6

FURTHER Information

DEC Walpole District Office
Tel: 08 9840 0400
Camping fees: From $7.00 per adult/night and $2.00 per child (under 16)/night. Fees payable at self-registration station.
Maximum stay: 3 nights for hut stays.

73 Nannup

The charming town of Nannup is surrounded by delightful jarrah forests and lush farmlands. Take a walk along the Blackwood River, fish or canoe or take a scenic drive through the region and visit local food producers. Keep your eye out for the 'Nannup Tiger', an elusive Thylacine (Tasmanian Tiger) which is firmly entrenched in the town's folklore. Centrally located in the south-west of the state, Nannup is 60km south-east of Busselton via the Vasse Highway.

Brockman Caravan & Camping Ground

Located on Brockman Street in Nannup beside the Visitor Centre. Situated beside the Blackwood River there are a number of well shaded sites, camp kitchen, laundry, playground. Bring drinking water and firewood.

GPS S:33 58.555 E:115 45.871

MR: Map 19 F1

FURTHER Information

Nannup Visitor Centre

Tel: 08 9756 1211

Web: www.nannupwa.com.au

Camping fees: Unpowered from $25.00 per site/night for 2 people. Powered from $30.00 per site/night for 2 people. Fees payable to visitor centre.

74 Nyabing

Nyabing and the surrounding areas were first settled by sandlewood cutters during the 1800s and now serves the region's agricultural enterprises. Nyabing is located 65km east of Katanning.

Nyabing Caravan Parking Facility

Located at the Nyabing Recreation Grounds on Martin Street in Nyabing. Campfires are permitted but remember to bring your own fire bin/bucket and firewood.

MR: Map 18 G4

FURTHER Information

Shire of Kent

Tel: 08 9829 1051

Web: www.kent.wa.gov.au

Camping fees: From $15.00 per site/night for up to 2 people. Fees payable at shire office in Richmond Street, Nyabing. Office hours Mon to Fri 8.30am to 4.30pm, outside these hours fees payable at honesty box at council office.

75 One Tree Bridge Conservation Park

Home to One Tree Bridge, the impressive 'Four Aces' — four enormous Karri trees that are thought to be over four hundred years old — and Green's Island, originally the Green family farm dating from the 1921 settlement scheme. Access is signposted off Donnelly Drive which is signposted off Graphite Road, 26km west of Manjimup.

Green's Island camping area

From the northern end of Manjimup take the signposted Graphite Road, which is also the Nannup Road, and follow this in a westerly direction for 22.3km to the signposted Donnelly Drive. The unsealed Donnelly Drive leads north for 1.5km to the signposted turn to the camping area, which in turn leads 2.1km to the camping area with six camping bays surrounding a large grassed area. Tent based campers can carry gear into the central grassed area while caravans can park around the perimeter. Bring drinking water. Firewood supplied.

GPS S:34 11.957 E:115 56.717
MR: Map 20 G2

FURTHER Information

DEC Pemberton District Office
Tel: 08 9776 1207
Manjimup Tourist Bureau
Tel: 08 9771 1831

76 Pallinup Nature Reserve

This small nature reserve is located on the southern banks of the Pallinup River. Access is along the South Coast Highway, south of the Bremer Bay turn-off.

Pallinup Nature Reserve Rest Area

Rest area located on the southern side of the bridge crossing the river and on the western side of the road. Signposted access along the South Coast Highway 5km south of the signposted Bremer Bay Road and 65km south of Jerramungup, and 114km north-east of Albany. Bring drinking water and firewood.

GPS S:34 24.391 E:118 43.658
MR: Map 22 K1

FURTHER Information

Shire of Jerramungup
Tel: 08 9835 1022
Maximum stay: May apply, take heed of any signage.

77 Parry Beach

Situated on picturesque William Bay, the beach offers excellent swimming, fishing and boating. Located 29km west of Denmark with access signposted off the South Coast Highway. Conventional vehicle access.

Parry Beach Recreation Area

From Denmark proceed west along the South Coast Highway for 22.6km to the signposted Parry Beach Road. This leads south for 5.9km to the signposted access road to the camping area, which leads in 500m. Large camping area with shaded, dispersed free form camping which is well protected with sites back from the beach. Showers are solar hot water showers so they may not always be hot! Beach boat launch. Boil or treat tap water, bring drinking water. Bring firewood.

GPS S:35 02.360 E:117 09.583

MR: Map 21 C6

FURTHER Information

Shire of Denmark
Tel: 08 9848 0300
Web: www.denmark.wa.gov.au

Denmark Tourist Bureau
Tel: 08 9848 2055
Web: www.denmark.com.au

Camping fees: From $10.00 per site/night for 2 people. Fees payable to on-site caretaker.

NB: There is a vehicle height restriction of 2.4 metres for the area.

THE SOUTH-WEST

78 Pemberton Area

Pemberton and its surrounds boast numerous natural attractions for visitors including the Gloucester Tree and the Dave Evans Bicentennial Tree, both fire lookout trees which visitors can climb. Why not take a dip, fish or picnic at Big Brook Dam or enjoy the many delicacies on offer from local food producers, including some of Western Australia's best wines. Pemberton is 76km south of Nannup on the Vasse Highway

Big Brook Arboretum

From the northern end of town take the signposted Golf Links Road and follow this for 1.7km to the signposted Mullineaux Road. Mullineaux Road leads for 6.8km to the signposted access to the Arboretum, which leads in 530m to the small camping area located close to the arboretum. Bring drinking water and there is firewood supplied.

GPS S:34 24.253 E:116 00 214

MR: Map 20 H3

Big Brook Arboretum

Moons Crossing camping and picnic area

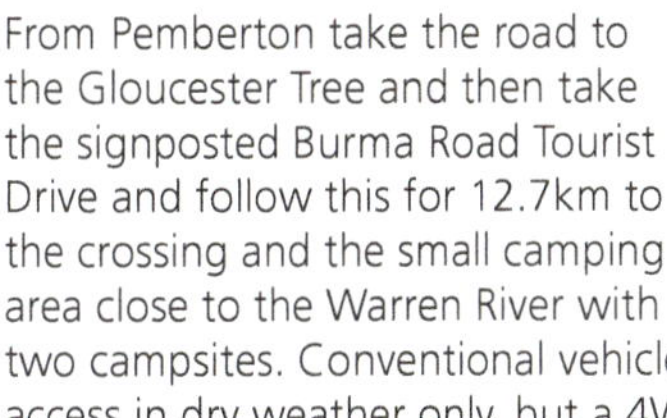

From Pemberton take the road to the Gloucester Tree and then take the signposted Burma Road Tourist Drive and follow this for 12.7km to the crossing and the small camping area close to the Warren River with two campsites. Conventional vehicle access in dry weather only, but a 4WD vehicle is recommended, especially if using the crossing (the campsite is on the Pemberton side of the river). Bring drinking water and firewood.

GPS S:34 30.417 E:116 08.643
MR: Map 20 I4

Moons Crossing camping and picnic area

FURTHER Information

DEC Pemberton District Office
Tel: 08 9776 1207

Pemberton Visitor & Tourist Centre
Tel: 08 9776 1133
Web: www.pembertonvisitor.com.au
Camping fees: From $7.00 per adult/night and $2.00 per child (under 16)/night. Fees payable at self registration stations.
Maximum stay: 3 nights at Big Brook Arboretum.

79 Pingrup

The region has many historical and natural sites to visit which include the Shearer's Monument – a giant sized replica of a shearer's handpiece, located in town and the impressive Pink Lakes, between Pingrup and Nyabing. Pingrup is 38km east of Nyabing and 50km south of Lake Grace.

Pingrup Caravan Park

Located on Sanderson Street in Pingrup. Power available.

MR: Map 18 I3

FURTHER Information

Pingrup Community Resource Centre
Tel: 08 9820 1101
Web: www.pingrup.crc.net.au
Camping fees: From $20.00 per site/night for up to 2 people. Refundable deposit for amenities key required. Fees payable to Pingrup Community Resource Centre, open Monday to Friday 9am to 4.30pm, outside these hours see Pingrup Sailors Arm Hotel, **Tel:** 08 9820 1041.

80 Rapids Conservation Park

Canebrake Pool, on the Margaret River, is within the newly proclaimed Rapids Conservation Park and offers visitors the opportunity for swimming, fishing and canoeing. Campsites are beside the river. Cranebrake Pool is located 25km north-east of Margaret River township and is accessed via unsealed roads suitable for conventional vehicles. Check road conditions first if towing a caravan.

Canebrake Pool camping and picnic area

From Margaret River proceed north along the Bussell Highway for 4km to the signposted Osmington Road and follow this in an easterly direction for 15.7km to the signposted Canebrake Road. Canebrake Road leads north for 5.7km to the signposted access to Canebrake Pool and leads in 150m to the self-registration and camping area with nine individually numbered campsites. Best suited for smaller caravans. Bring drinking water. Firewood supplied.

GPS S:33 52.826 E:115 16.926
MR: Map 15 C8

FURTHER Information

DEC Busselton District Office
Tel: 08 9752 5555
Camping fees: From $7.00 per adult/night and $2.00 per child (under 16)/night. Fees payable at self-registration station.

THE SOUTH-WEST

81 Shannon National Park

The Shannon campground is located at the old Shannon town site which once boasted businesses such as a general store and butcher along with a church and a school. The park itself covers 53,500ha and protects Karri, Jarrah and Marri forests. Visitors can enjoy the park's wildflowers, one several walks or the self-guided Great Forest Trees Drive. Access to the campground is signposted off the South Western Highway, 32km east of Northcliffe and 53km south of Manjimup.

Shannon Campground

From Northcliffe head north for 2.4km and then turn right (east) onto the signposted Middleton Road which leads 25.5km to the South Western Highway. Turn right (south-east) on the highway and follow for 3.3km to the signposted access to the camping area. This unsealed road leads in 650m to the large camping area with 28 individually numbered campsites among pine trees. On-site information board details campsite suitability. Camp kitchen and two shelter huts. Donkey hot water system. Boil or treat tap water first. Bring drinking water. Firewood supplied.

GPS S:34 35.679 E:116 24.706
MR: Map 20 J4

FURTHER Information

DEC Pemberton District Office
Tel: 08 9776 1207
Park entrance fee: $11.00 per vehicle.
Camping fees: From $7.00 per adult/night and $2.00 per child (under 16)/night. Fees payable at self-registration station.

Shannon Campground

82 St Johns Brook Conservation Park

Enjoy a refreshing swim in St Johns Brook or take in the area's logging history along the Old Timberline Walking Trail in this secluded park near Nannup. Beware of the Nannup Tiger, part of the area's folk history! Access is via the signposted Mowen Road, which is signposted off the Vasse Highway north of Nannup. Access road is unsealed but suitable for conventional vehicles.

Workmans Pool camping area

From Nannup proceed north along the Vasse Highway for 1.4km to the signposted Mowen Road. Follow Mowen Road in a westerly direction for 6.7km to the signposted Barrabup Pool Road. This leads north for 900m to the signposted access, which leads 340m to the camping area with six individually numbered campsites, three are suitable for tent based camping only. Bring drinking water. Some firewood supplied.

GPS S:34 57.244 E:116 41.278
MR: Map 15 F8

Barrabup Pool camping area

Signposted access 2.5km north of Workmans Pool along Barrabup Pool Road. Track on right just prior to the day use area leads into the camping area with five tent based campsites, carry gear into sites. Boil or treat water first or bring drinking water with you. Some firewood is supplied.

MR: Map 15 F8

Sleep Hewer's Hut

Walk-in or cycle along the Old Timberline Trail 4km north of Barrabup Pool. Boil or treat water first. Gas/fuel stove only.

MR: Map 15 F8

FURTHER Information

DEC Kirup Local Office
Tel: 08 9731 6232
Camping fees: From $7.00 per adult/night and $2.00 per child (under 16)/night. Fees payable at self-registration station.

83 Stirling Range National Park

The rugged Stirling Range stretches for 65km and rises abruptly from the flat plains of the surrounding farmland. Home to a large and diverse array of plants and animals, the park is popular with visitors during the main wildflower season which runs from September to November. A number of walking tracks of varying grades leave from the camping area. Access to the park is signposted off Chester Pass Road, 76km north-east of Albany.

Moingup Springs Camping Area

From Albany proceed north along the South Coast Highway for 12km to Bakers Junction, then proceed along the signposted Chester Pass Road for a further 64km to the signposted access to the camping area. Access road leads in 100m to the grassed and shaded camping area, best suited for tent based camping as the site has limited spaces for camper trailers. Gas/fuel stove only.

GPS S:34 24.067 E:118 06.137
MR: Map 22 H2

FURTHER Information

DEC Albany Regional Office
Tel: 08 9842 4500
Park entrance fee: $11.00 per vehicle.
Camping fees: From $7.00 per adult/night and $2.00 per child (under 16)/night. Fees collected by ranger.

Moingup Springs Camping Area

84 Stockton Lake

Located 8km east of Collie is the old Stockton open cut mine. Now filled with water, the mine is an artificial lake popular for water activities. Access to Stockton Lake is via Piavanini Road off the Coalfields Highway.

Stockton Lake camping area

From Collie proceed east towards Darkan and Arthur River for 6.4km to the signposted Piavanini Road, which leads 1.4km to the signposted Western Entrance to Stockton Lake. This entrance leads in 200m to the lake with dispersed bush camping around the lake's southern shores. Alternatively the eastern entrance is signposted off the Darkan/Arthur River road 700m east of Piavanini Road, and leads in 1.5km to the lake and camping areas. Bring drinking water and firewood.

GPS S:33 23.088 E:116 13.696

MR: Map 16 H4

FURTHER Information

DEC Collie District Office
Tel: 08 9735 1988

THE SOUTH-WEST

85 Tambellup

The village of Tambellup is situated along the Great Southern Highway, 35km north of Cranbrook and 23km south of Broomehill. The Tambellup Heritage Trail showcases to visitors the history of the town's early settlement and is centered along the Gordon River.

Tambellup Caravan Park

Located on Norrish Street in town. Laundry facilities.

MR: Map 17 E7

FURTHER Information

Shire of Broomehill-Tambellup
Tel: 08 9825 3555
Web: www.shirebt.wa.gov.au
Camping fees: From $16.50 per site/night up to 2 people. Refundable key bond. Fees payable at shire office on the Norrish Street (Monday to Friday 8.30am to 4.30pm) or contact caretaker 0488 012 172.

86 Walpole–Nornalup National Park

Surrounding Walpole and Nornalup Inlets, the park is home to the Giant Tingle tree, pristine bushland and limestone cliffs. Enjoy scenic drives, bushwalking, swimming, canoeing and four-wheel driving. The park is known for the Valley of the Giants Tree Top Walk, the Valley of the Giants Ancient Empire Walk and the Hilltop Giant Tingle Tree Trail. Coastal walks include the easy Conspicuous Cliff Walks and the harder 6km Coalmine Beach Heritage Trail. Although there is no camping within the park there are two caravan parks situated on the boundaries of the national park.

Coalmine Beach Holiday Park

From Walpole proceed east along the South Coast Highway for 2.5km to the signposted Coalmine Beach Road, which leads 1.3km to the large well shaded caravan park on the shores of Nornalup Intlet. Popular surfing spot. Shop, camp kitchen, laundry, playground. Some firewood supplied or bring your own.

GPS S:34 59.402 E:116 44.321

MR: Map 21 A7

FURTHER Information

Coalmine Beach Holiday Park

Tel: 1800 670 026. Bookings essential for Christmas and New Year holidays.

Web: www.coalminebeach.com.au

Camping fees: Unpowered sites from $27.00 per site/night for 2 people. Powered sites from $31.00 per site/night for 2 people. Park has low, mid and high season rates.

Peaceful Bay Caravan Park

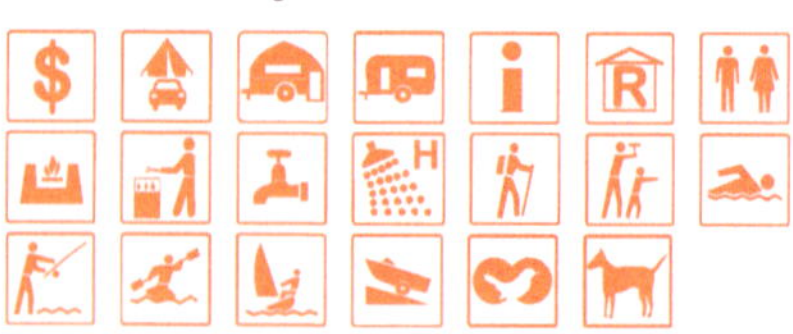

This grassed park with scattered trees provides good shade and shelter for campers and is a popular surfing spot. For fisherfolk a beach boat launch is located nearby. From Nornalup proceed in an easterly direction for 14.3km to the signposted road to Peaceful Bay. This road leads south for 7.8km to road signposted to the caravan park, which leads 1km to the park office and entrance. Shop, camp kitchen, laundry. Some firewood supplied or bring your own if planning a campfire.

GPS S:35 02.417 E:116 55.683

MR: Map 21 B7

FURTHER Information

Peaceful Bay Caravan Park

Tel: 08 9840 8060. Bookings essential for Christmas, New Year and Easter holidays.

Web: www.peacefulbaywa.com.au

Camping fees: Unpowered sites from $23.00 per site/night for 2 people. Powered sites from $28.00 per site/night for 2 people.

87 Warren National Park

One of the many outstanding features of Warren National Park are the towering karri trees. The Warren River snakes its way through the park and is popular for fishing, swimming and canoeing. Take a stroll along the Heartbreak Walk Trail and visit the Dave Evans Bicentennial Tree and perhaps even climb it, but it's a long way to the top! Access to the park's camping areas is via the signposted Heartbreak Trail off Old Vasse Road which is signposted off the Vasse Highway, 12km south-west of Pemberton and off the Northcliffe Road, 8km south of Pemberton.

Drafty's Camp

Signposted access 3.9km along Heartbreak Trail which is signposted off the Old Vasse Road, 7.8km west of the Northcliffe Road and 3.8km east of the Vasse Highway. There are two camping areas/loops, both have a self-registration station: area/loop 1 has 16 individually numbered campsites and a camp kitchen while area/loop 2 has six individually numbered campsites. Bring drinking water. Firewood for cooking fires is supplied. Gas/fuel stove recommended.

Loop 1: **GPS** S:34 30.666 E:115 56.780
Loop 2: **GPS** S:34 30.662 E:115 56.852
MR: Map 20 H4

THE SOUTH-WEST

Warren Camp

Signposted access along Heartbreak Trail, 1.6km east of Drafty's Camp access. Then in short distance to the camping area with six individually numbered campsites and a group camping area. Sites 1 to 4 carry gear in from car park. Communal fireplaces and tables. Bring drinking water. Firewood for cooking fires is supplied. Gas/fuel stove recommended.

GPS S:34 30.560 E:115 57.685

MR: Map 20 H4

FURTHER Information

DEC Pemberton District Office

Tel: 08 9776 1207

Park entrance fee: $11.00 per vehicle.

Camping fees: From $7.00 per adult/night and $2.00 per child (under 16)/night. Fees payable at self-registration stations.

88 Waychinicup National Park

Waychinicup National Park showcases some of the south coast's most spectacular scenery and in spring is carpeted with colourful wildflowers, while the picturesque Waychinicup River is popular with canoeists and fisherfolk. The park stretches from Normans Beach in the west across Mt Manypeaks to Cheyne Beach in the east with access for conventional vehicles to the camping area off Cheyne Beach Road, which is signposted off the South Coast Highway.

Waychinicup Inlet camping area

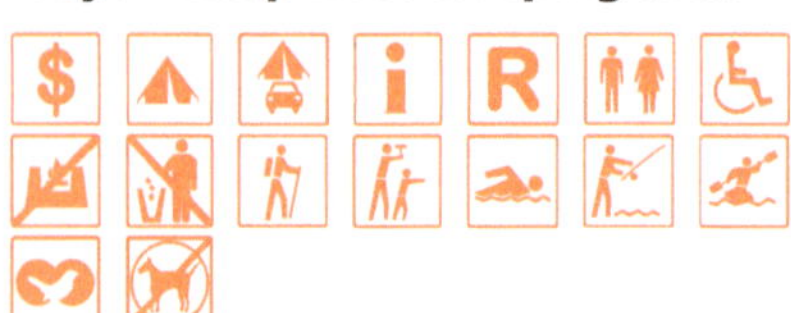

From Albany follow the South Coast Highway in a north-easterly direction for 48km to the signposted Cheyne Beach Road. This leads in a south-easterly direction for 13km to the signposted Waychinicup Rd. Follow Waychinicup Road in a westerly direction for 5.6km to the scenic camping area at the mouth of the Waychinicup River. This camping area is for tent camping only with nine individually numbered sites all with flat tent pads. Carry gear into sites. Sites 3 and 4 have tent pad close to car park. Bring drinking water. Gas/fuel stove only.

GPS S:34 53.575 E:118 20.011

MR: Map 22 J5

FURTHER Information

DEC Albany Regional Office

Tel: 08 9842 4500

Camping fees: From $7.00 per adult/night and $2.00 per child (under 16)/night. Fees payable at self-registration station or to patrolling ranger.

THE SOUTH-WEST

89 Wellington National Park

The park offers an array of activities for its visitors. Swim, cycle, bushwalk, fish, canoe, go rafting and in spring there are colourful wildflower displays. Within the park is the Collie River Valley along with magnificent Jarrah, Marri and Karri forests. Visit Wellington Dam and camp at Potter's Gorge or beside the Collie River at Honeymoon Pool. Access is via unsealed roads which are suitable for conventional vehicles. Signposted access is off the Coalfields Highway 18km west of Collie.

Potters Gorge camping area

From the Coalfields Highway proceed south along the Wellington Dam road for 8.7km to the signposted road to Potters Gorge. This is Tom Jones Drive. Follow this road in a south-easterly direction for 1.4km to the camping area. Large open, free form camping area on the edge of the dam with plenty of shade. Outdoor cold shower. Natural boat ramp. Boil or treat tap water or bring drinking water. Some firewood supplied.

GPS S:33 23.402 E:115 58.893
MR: Map 16 G4

Honeymoon Pool camping area

From the Coalfields Highway proceed south along the Wellington Dam road for 4.7km to road signposted to Honeymoon Pool. This road proceeds in south-westerly direction for 4.5km to the camping area with 20 individually numbered, well sheltered and protected campsites above the Collie River. Gas barbecue in day use area. Boil or treat tap water, or bring drinking water. If planning a campfire bring firewood.

GPS S:33 22.811 E:115 56.323
MR: Map 16 G4

Honeymoon Pool camping area

Stones Brook camping area

Located 100m west of Honeymoon Pool CA, access signposted at Honeymoon Pool. Best for tent based camping, some sites gear will need to carried in a short distance. Individually numbered sites. Camp kitchen. Boil or treat tap water or bring drinking water with you. Gas/fuel stove only.

GPS S:33 22.587 E:115 56.268
MR: Map 16 G4

Stones Brook camping area

Gel Coat Rapids camping area

Located 500m west of Stones Brook CA. Tent based camping only, carry gear in a short distance. Boil or treat tap water or bring drinking water. Gas/fuel stove only.

GPS S:33 22.666 E:115 56.053

MR: Map 16 G4

FURTHER Information

DEC Collie District Office

Tel: 08 9735 1988

Camping fees: From $7.00 per adult/night and $2.00 per child (under 16)/night. Fees payable at self-registration stations or collected by patrolling ranger.

THE SOUTH-WEST

90 West Cape Howe National Park

West Cape Howe National Park boasts a stunning coastline of dolerite cliffs framed against the Southern Ocean. A varied mix of vegetation types from Karri forest to low coastal heath to stands of Peppermint and colourful spring wildflowers can be found within the park. Visitors can enjoy swimming and scuba diving at Shelley Beach, but be aware of strong rips in this area. There is also four-wheel drive access to some of the remote scenic areas within the park. The park is located 40km west of Albany with access via Shelley Beach Road off Coombes Road which comes off Cosy Corner Road.

Shelley Beach camping area

This open, grassed area offers beach frontage but unfortunately has no shade or protection from onshore winds. Located to the west of Albany access is signposted along Cosy Corner Road. The access road down to the beach is unsealed, steep and winding and is not suitable for towing caravans or camper trailers. From Albany proceed west along Princess Royal Drive then take the signposted Lower Denmark Road. Follow Lower Denmark Road for 22.4km to the signposted Cosy Corner Rd. Cosy Corner Road leads south for 3km to the signposted Coombes Road/Shelley Beach. This road leads west for 2.2km to the signposted Shelley Beach Road, which in turn leads south for 5.5km to the camping area. Bring drinking water. Gas/fuel stove only.

GPS S:35 06.541 E:117 37.774
MR: Map 21 F7

FURTHER Information

DEC Albany Regional Office
Tel: 08 9842 4500
Camping fees: From $7.00 per adult/night and $2.00 per child (under 16)/night. Fees collected by patrolling Ranger.

THE SOUTH-WEST

Shelley Beach camping area

91 Willow Springs

This former forestry site is set amongst Jarrah forest along the Nannup Scenic Drive/Gold Gully Road between Nannup and Bridgetown. Keen walkers and cyclists can tackle parts of The Bibbulmun Track and Munda Biddi Trail which pass close by. Conventional vehicle access is off the Brockman Highway east of Nannup and west of Bridgetown.

Willow Springs camping area

From Nannup proceed east along the Brockman Highway for 22.2km to the signposted Gold Gully Road, this is 23km west of Bridgetown. This unsealed road leads south for 5.4km to the camping area, which has dispersed bush camping surrounded by tall shady trees. Limited facilities at this site so best suited for self-sufficient campers and it is recommended to bring your own portable toilet. Bring drinking water and firewood.

GPS S:34 02.780 E:115 55.524

MR: Map 20 G1

FURTHER Information

DEC Kirup Local Office
Tel: 08 9731 6232

THE SOUTH-WEST

Willow Springs camping area

The South-East

STRETCHING FROM THE ESPERANCE Highway east to the South Australian border, the rugged and relatively isolated south-east region offers visitors a range of camping opportunities from well appointed campgrounds through to remote bush campsites. Cape Le Grand National Park, east of Esperance, is one of the region's most popular destinations with its easy access and beautiful scenery. Within the park there are two camping areas with top facilities.

BEST Campsites!

Seal Creek camping area
Cape Arid National Park

Lucky Bay camping area
Cape Le Grand National Park

Skippy Rock camping area
Stokes National Park

The Breakaways camping area
Granite and Woodlands Discovery Trail

Thomas River camping area
Esperance Region

Further east is the isolated Cape Arid National Park boasting five camping areas, fabulous coastlines and in the north of the park are the peaks of Russell Range including Mt Ragged where there is a small campsite for walkers. Bush campsites at Balbinya and Deralinya ruins are further north of Mt Ragged and are reminders of pastoral activities of the late 1800s.

To the west of Esperance are a great selection of coastal camping reserves as well as the campsites in Stokes National Park. Only a short ferry trip away is the chance to camp overnight on Woody Island.

The unsealed Granite and Woodlands Discovery Trail between Hyden and Norseman offers the opportunity the explore the region's mallee woodlands and makes a great alternative from the well-travelled coastal route. There are a number of good campsites along this route to break your journey.

Interstate travellers will find dotted along the Eyre Highway between Norseman and the South Australian border numerous roadhouses and pastoral properties, as well as roadside rest areas, which provide camping.

Enjoy this wonderfully remote and rugged region all-year round, although the summer months are the most popular time for the coastal campsites while mid-winter can be cold, wet and windy at times.

QUEEN VICTORIA SPRING NATURE RESERVE
Lake Yindarlgooda
Cundeelee
Kalgoorlie-Boulder
Curtin
Karonie
Chifley
Zanthus
Kitchener
913 Mile
Coolgardie
Buningonia (Coonana)
Kambalda
Lake Lefroy
Coolgardie – Esperance
Higginsville
Eyre
96
95
Norseman
Balladonia Roadhouse
Highway
Lake Johnston
Lake Dundas
DUNDAS NATURE RESERVE
PEAK CHARLES NATIONAL PARK
98
Lake Tay
Salmon Gums
Lake Mends
Pyramid Lake
Highway
Truslove
94
NUYTSLAND NATURE RESERVE
97
CAPE ARID NATIONAL PARK
Boyatup
Condingup
South
Coast
Highway
Yerritup
Esperance
Wharton
92
99
CAPE LE GRAND NATIONAL PARK
93
100
RECHERCHE ARCHIPELAGO NATURE RESERVE
N
0
150km
THE SOUTH-EAST

- 92 Cape Arid National Park
- 93 Cape Le Grand National Park
- 94 Esperance Region
- 95 Granite & Woodlands Discovery Trail
- 96 Nullarbor Plain (Eyre Hwy)
- 97 Nuytsland Nature Reserve
- 98 Peak Charles National Park
- 99 Stokes National Park
- 100 Woody Island Nature Reserve

92 Cape Arid National Park

The isolated Cape Arid National Park is well-known for its beautiful sandy beaches and rocky headlands. Stunning displays of wildflowers can be seen during spring, summer and autumn while beach fishing and four-wheel driving are popular activities in the park, as is bushwalking. Cape Arid National Park is located 127km east of Esperance. Access to the different parts of the park can be made from Fisheries Road (4WD only east of Baring Road to Poison Creek) from Esperance or Merivale Road off Fisheries Road. Camping in the park is isolated and is best suited to self-sufficient campers. Carry sufficient water and a gas/fuel stove when visiting this park.

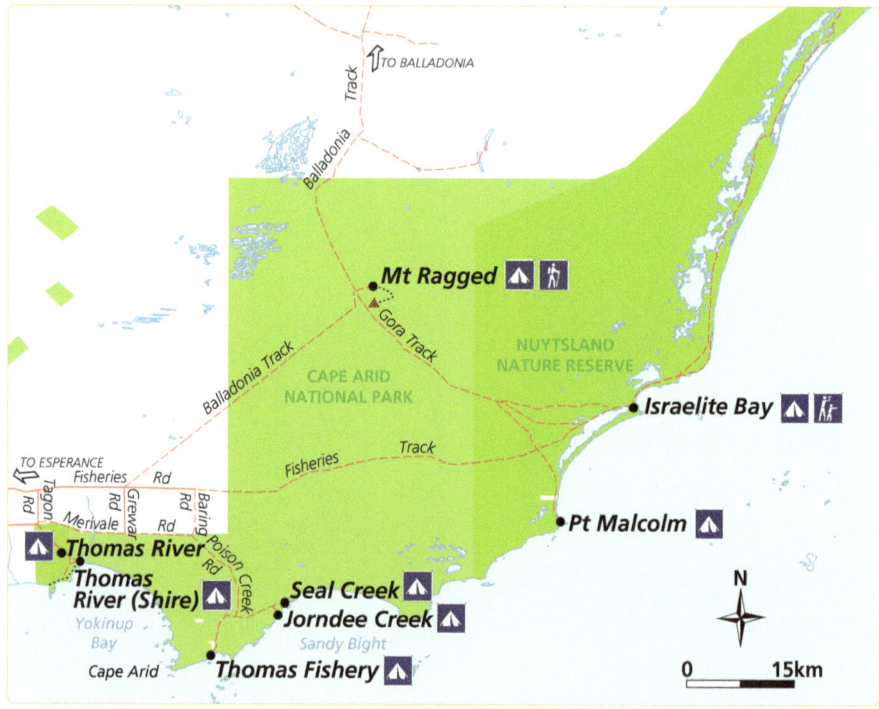

Thomas River camping area

Signposted access 8.5km along Thomas River Road, then drive in 240m to the self-registration station. Open camping area with little protection from winds with 17 individually numbered campsites all with flat areas. Thomas River Road is signposted off Merivale Road, 95.7km east of the junction of Fisheries and Merivale roads (5km north-east of Esperance). Bring drinking water. Gas/fuel stove only.

GPS S:33 51.251 E:123 00.7807

MR: Map 26 L5

View from Thomas River camping area

Jorndee Creek camping area

Signposted access along Poison Creek Road. From Fisheries Road take the signposted Baring Road, this is 123km east of Esperance and 23km east of the signposted Tagon Road. Follow Baring Road south for 7.7km to the signposted road to Poison Creek. Follow this road south for 17.7km to a T-intersection and then turn left towards Poison Creek. Follow this for 6.2km to the signposted access to Jorndee Creek. This access road leads 1.7km to the camping area with three small tent based sites which are well protected among banksia trees, although there's little shade. Suitable for AWD vehicles. Walk to beach. Bring drinking water. Gas/fuel stove only.

GPS S:33 55.929 E:123 19.390

MR: Map 28 H5

Jorndee Creek camping area

Seal Creek camping area

Signposted access along Poison Creek road, 2km east of Jorndee Creek CA access road. Then drive in 70m to the camping area with 13 well protected and shaded individual camping bays, 6 of which are suitable for camper trailers and caravans. Walk to beach and creek. If towing a caravan it is best to check road conditions first as Poison Creek Road can be corrugated. Bring drinking water. Gas/

fuel stove only.
GPS S:33 54.845 E:123 20.044
MR: Map 28 H5

Seal Creek camping area

Thomas Fishery camping area

Signposted access along Poison Creek Road. From Fisheries Road take the signposted Baring Road, this is 123km east of Esperance and 23km east of the signposted Tagon Road. Follow Baring Road south for 7.7km to the signposted road to Poison Creek. Follow this road south for 17.7km to a T-intersection and then turn right into the track signposted to Thomas Fishery. Follow this track for 8.9km to the small camping area with three small tent based campsites which are well protected, tucked away in the vegetation above the beach. Walk to beach. This site can be closed during wet conditions. Bring drinking water. Gas/fuel stove only.
GPS S:33 59.554 E:123 13.317
MR: Map 28 H5

Mt Ragged camping area

Signposted access along the Balladonia Road, 165km east of Esperance. The Balladonia Road is signposted along Fisheries Road, 15km east of the signposted Tagon Road. Then proceed in a north-easterly direction for 40km to the signposted access to Mt Ragged. Alternatively from the Eyre Highway, take the signposted 4WD only road, Balladonia Road (this is 200m east of Balladonia Roadhouse), and follow this south for 131km to the signposted access to Mt Ragged. This access track leads 3.3km in an easterly direction to the small, sheltered camping area, with 4 sites, at the southern end of the mountain range. Bring drinking water. Gas/fuel stove only.
GPS S:33 27.953 E:123 27.631
MR: Map 28 H4

FURTHER information

DEC Esperance District Office
Tel: 08 9083 2100
Park entrance fee: $11.00 per vehicle.
Camping fees: From $7.00 per adult/night and $2.00 per child (up to 16)/night. Fees payable at self-registration stations or on-site honesty boxes.

93 Cape Le Grand National Park

This scenic park boasts the beautiful beaches of Le Grand, Hellfire, Lucky Bay and Rossiter Bay and, along with its rocky headlands and magnificent rugged coastal scenery, makes it one of the state's most visited national parks. At Cape Le Grand National Park you can enjoy swimming, fishing and, in season, whale watching, while in spring and early summer the park is carpeted in colourful wildflowers. Access to Cape Le Grand National Park is signposted along Merivale Road, 30km east of Esperance.

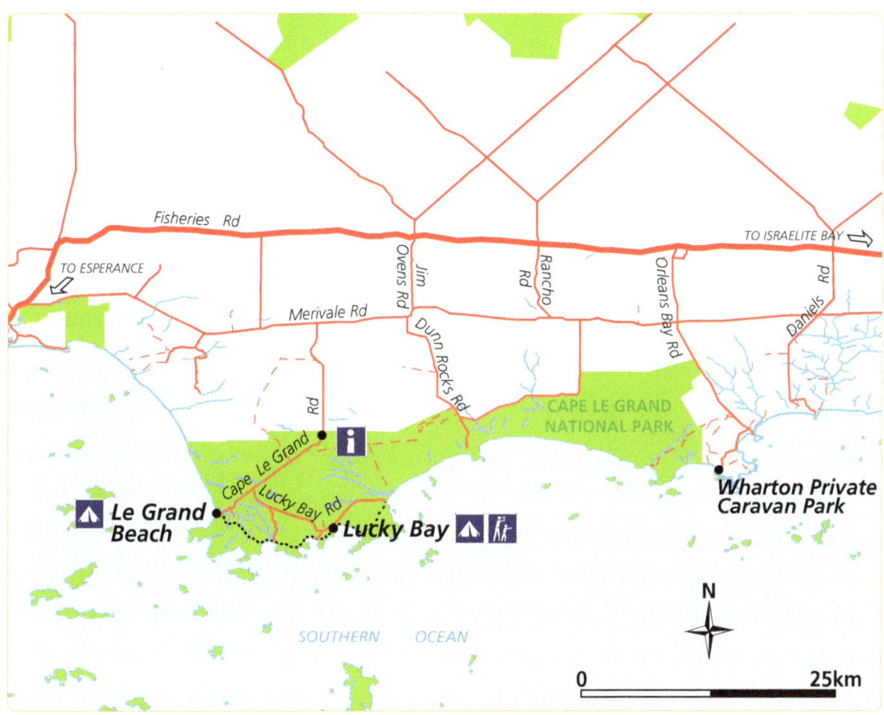

Lucky Bay camping area

From Merivale Road, 30km east of Esperance, take the signposted Cape Le Grand Road. This road leads south for 11.6km to the park entrance station and then leads a further 7.4km to a road junction. At this junction turn left and proceed in a south-easterly direction towards the signposted Lucky Bay for 8.4km to the signposted access to the camping area. There are two areas for campers. One is for tent based camping which offers well sheltered campsites located close to the camp kitchen. Gear needs to be carried into the camping area from the car park. The other area is for vehicle based camping which is suitable for camper trailers, caravans, motorhomes and campervans. This open area is located above the beach with 25 numbered sites. Camp kitchen. Solar hot showers. 4WD vehicle recommended if using the beach boat launch. Gas/fuel stove only.

Tent camping area: **GPS** S:33 59.466 E:122 13.214
Vehicle based camping area: **GPS** S:33 59.509 E:122 13.198
MR: Map 26 G6

Lucky Bay camping area

Le Grand Beach camping area

From Merivale Road, 30km east of Esperance, take the signposted Cape Le Grand Road. This road leads south for 11.6km to the park entrance station and then leads a further 7.4km to a road junction. At this junction proceed straight ahead towards the signposted Le Grand Beach for 4.1km to the camping area. Scenic camping area set back from the beach with 15 individually numbered sites surrounded by coastal heath. Camp kitchen. Solar hot showers. Gas/fuel stove only.

GPS S:33 58.743 E:122 07.184
MR: Map 26 G6

Le Grand Beach camping area

FURTHER Information

DEC Cape Le Grand National Park Office
Tel: 08 9075 9072
DEC Esperance District Office
Tel: 08 9083 2100
Park entrance fee: $11.00 per vehicle.
Camping fees: From $9.00 per adult/night and $2.00 per child (up to 16)/night. Fees payable at self-registration stations or to on-site Campground Hosts during peak periods.

94 Esperance Region

Esperance and its environs are well known for its spectacular natural beauty and hosts a number of great campsites. Why not visit beautiful beaches, which are perfect for summertime swimming, surfing, fishing, diving, snorkelling and sailboarding all with a backdrop of spectacular coastal scenery. The crystal clear waters of Esperance are renowned for whale spotting, along with commonly seen seals and dolphins. Take a drive along the scenic Great Ocean Drive; one of the best ways to view the region's wonderful attractions.

Munglinup Beach camping area

Access to this site can be had from Munglinup, 109km west of Esperance on the South Coast Highway by taking the signposted Doyle Road (west of Munglinup) or Fuss Road (east of Munglinup). Follow these roads south to the signposted Springdale Road and (proceed west for 6.3km if coming down Doyle Road or 9.8km if coming down Fuss Road) to the signposted Muglinup Beach Road. This leads south for 6.8km to the camping area with 14 individually numbered sites set back from the beach. 4WD beach boat launch. Boil or treat tap water first or bring drinking water. Fires are permitted in season, bring own firewood.

GPS S:33 51.842 E:120 47.863
MR: Map 24 K3

Munglinup Beach camping area

FURTHER Information

Esperance Visitor Centre
Tel: 08 9071 2330 or 1300 664 455
Web: www.visitesperance.com
Camping fees: From $10.00 per site/night. Fees collected by Caretaker.

Quagi Beach camping area

From Esperance proceed in a westerly direction along the South Coast Highway for 63km to the signposted Farrells Road. This unsealed road, which can be rough at times, leads south for 10.3km to the camping area, with 14 sites, some of which are well shaded and protected by the coastal vegetation. Tap water, boil or treat first or bring drinking water. Bring firewood for campfires.

GPS S:33 49.731 E:121 17.536
MR: Map 25 B6

Quagi Beach camping area

Membinup Beach camping area

From Esperance proceed east along Merivale Road for 75km to the signposted Daniels Road. This unsealed road, which can be rough in patches and is only suitable for 4WD vehicles, leads in a southerly direction for 12km to the camping area where dispersed bush camping is along tracks behind the beach among coastal heath. Some sites are accessed via narrow winding tracks that can have overhanging vegetation. Located close to beach and creek. Recommend that portable toilet is taken. Bring drinking water. Bring own fire drum/pot and firewood. If towing a caravan it would be best to check road conditions before travelling to this site.

GPS S:33 53.467 E:122 39.015
MR: Map 26 J5

Alexander Bay camping area

From Esperance proceed east along Merivale Road for 81km to the signposted Alexander Road. The unsealed Alexander Road, which can be corrugated, leads south for 10.6km to the camping area information board and a further 200m to the camping area with 13 individually numbered campsites set among the coastal heath, with some sites having picnic style shelters. Flat, gravel based sites best suited for camper trailers, campervans and caravans. Popular fishing spot. Bring drinking water and firewood.

GPS S:33 53.106 E:122 44.884
MR: Map 26 J5

Alexander Bay camping area

Kennedy Beach camping area

From Esperance proceed east along Merivale Road for 89.5km to the signposted Exchange Road. Exchange Road, which is a 4WD only access track and can be impassable in wet conditions, leads in a southerly direction for 14km to the small bush camping area located behind the sand dunes with one campsite, possibly two, among the coastal vegetation. Bring drinking water. Bring own fire drum/pot and firewood.

GPS S:33 53.444 E:122 53.861
MR: Map 26 K5

FURTHER Information

Esperance Visitor Centre
Tel: 08 9083 1555
Web: www.visitesperance.com

Shire of Esperance
Tel: 08 9071 0666
Web: www.esperance.wa.gov.au
Camping fees: From $2.00 per person/ night. Fees payable at on-site honesty boxes or to patrolling rangers.
NB: Solid fuel fire bans apply in this region. Check with local authorities prior to lighting any fire.

Balbinya Ruins bush camping area

Located 12.3km east of Mount Ragged Track. Access track is 12.4km south of the junction of Mount Ragged Track and Balladonia Road and 46km north of Mt Ragged camping area access track (see page 112). Dry weather, 4WD access only as access road can be rough. Camp on the grassed open area around the ruins or among the shaded treed sites on the edge of the clearing. Self-sufficient campers only as there are no facilities. Bring drinking water. Firewood in vicinity although the use of gas/fuel stove is preferred.

GPS S:33 05.301 E:123 34.008
MR: Map 28 H3

Balbinya Ruins

Juranda Rockhole bush camping area

Access track is 16km south of Balbinya Ruins access track (see above), then drive in a short distance to the bush camping beside the large rockhole. Some shaded sites. Self-sufficient campers only – no facilities. Bring drinking water. Gas/fuel stove preferred.

GPS S:33 13.023 E:123 27.150
MR: Map 28 H3

Deralinya Ruins bush camping area

Located 7km west of Mount Ragged Track and 250m west of Parmango (Esperance) Road. From Mount Ragged Track, access track is 12.4km south of the junction of Mount Ragged Track and Balladonia Road and 46km north of Mt Ragged camping area access track. Access track from Parmengo Road (**GPS** S:33 03.255 E:123 23.119) approx 7km south of Mount Ragged Track and Balladonia Road junction. 4WD recommended. The camping area is behind the homestead near the dam amongst trees. Self-sufficient campers only. Bring drinking water. Gas/fuel stove preferred.

GPS S:33 03.145 E:123 23.022
MR: Map 28 H3

FURTHER information

DEC Esperance District Office
Tel: 08 9083 2100
NB: Although these areas are not managed by DEC they can assist with general enquiries, ie: road conditions etc.

Deralinya Ruins, page 117

Thomas River camping area

Located 400m south of the national park's Thomas River CA in Cape Arid National Park. From Esperance take the signposted Merivale Road and follow this east for 95.7km to the signposted Thomas River Road. Thomas River Road leads south for 8.9km to the signposted access track, which leads in 170m to the camping area with 11 individually numbered campsites located close to the river and the beach. Bring drinking water. Campfires are permitted in season, bring own fire drum/bucket and firewood. Gas/fuel stove preferred.

GPS S:33 51.236 E:123 01.083
MR: Map 26 L5

Thomas River camping area (Shire)

FURTHER Information

Esperance Visitor Centre
Tel: 08 9071 2330 or 1300 664 455
Web: www.visitesperance.com

DEC Esperance District Office
Tel: 08 9083 2100
Park entrance fee: $11.00 per vehicle.
Camping fees: From $7.00 per adult/night and $2.00 per child (up to 16)/night. Fees payable at self-registration stations or to Ranger. Dogs are only permitted in the camping area. The surrounding areas of park and beaches are part of the national park, and dogs are not permitted.

95 Granite and Woodlands Discovery Trail

This interesting drive of around 300km between Hyden and Norseman traverses temperate woodland forests scattered with rocky granite outcrops. Located along the unsealed drive are 16 interpretive sites which allows visitors to stop and explore this remote region. A brochure of the Trail is available and details the trail's history, vegetation and landscape. Contact the information centres listed in the Further Information box for a copy. From Hyden take the road to the east signposted to Norseman. From Norseman take the road signposted to Hyden which is off the Norseman-Coolgardie Road 8km north of the Eyre Highway at Norseman.

The Breakaways camping area

From Wave Rock proceed in an easterly direction for 135km towards Norseman to the signposted access to the Breakaways, this is 55.2km west of McDermid Rock CA. This track leads in a southerly direction for 600m to the base of the breakaways. Bring drinking water and firewood. Fires permitted in season.

GPS S:32 16.665 E:120 15.772
MR: Map 27 C2

McDermid Rock camping area

Signposted access along the Hyden-Norseman Road, 55.2km east of The Breakaways CA, and 2.6km west of the signposted Victoria Rocks Road and 5.4km west of Lake Johnston CA. Then drive in a northerly direction for 1.5km to the sheltered camping area with dispersed bush camping among mallee woodlands. Bring drinking water and firewood. Fires permitted in season.

GPS S:32 01.312 E:120 44.336
MR: Map 27 C2

McDermid Rock camping area

Lake Johnston bush camping area

Signposted access along the Hyden-Norseman Road, 105km west of Hyden and 19.8km west of the signposted access to Disappointment Rock, and 5.4km east of McDermid Rock CA. Then drive in 150m to the small open camping area overlooking Lake Johnston. Camp only in the designated sites. There is space for about 4 or 5 camps. Bring drinking water and firewood. Fires permitted in season.

GPS S:32 00.613 E:120 47.358
MR: Map 27 C2

Lake Johnston bush camping area

FURTHER Information

Wave Rock Information Centre, Hyden
Tel: 08 9880 5182
Norseman Visitor Centre
Tel: 08 9039 1071
Main Roads WA – Road Conditions
Tel: 1800 013 314

96 Nullarbor Plain (Eyre Hwy)

The Nullarbor Plain is a massive lump of limestone which was formed over 50 million years ago. Millennia has weathered and sculptured the Nullarbor so today there's an amazing network of underground caves, blowholes and sinkholes which have formed by rain trickling down through the limestone. There are spectacular ocean views and whale watching vantage points in places where the Eyre Highway passes close to the Great Australian Bight. Historical memorials dotted along the route provides an insight in the region's early days. The Eyre Highway is one of Australia's great road trips. Roadhouses en-route can advise you of the local attractions and provide directions.

Nullarbor Plain

THE SOUTH-EAST

Ten Mile Rocks Rest Area

Designated 24 hour rest area. Signposted access along the Eyre Highway, 78km east of Norseman and 112km west of Balladonia. Located on the northern side of the highway. Bring drinking water and firewood.

GPS S:32 04.112 E:122 33.568
MR: Map 28 G1

Fraser Range Rest Area

Designated 24 hour rest area. Signposted access along the Eyre Highway, 3.3km east of Ten Mile Rocks RA 109km west of Balladonia. Located on the southern side of the highway. Bring drinking water and firewood.

GPS S:32 04.381 E:122 35.599
MR: Map 28 G1

FURTHER Information

Main Roads Western Australia
Tel: 138 138
Web: www.mainroads.wa.gov.au

Fraser Range Sheep Station

Signposted access along the Eyre Highway, 102km east of Norseman and 88km west of Balladonia, then drive in a southerly direction for 1.5km to the office. Store, camp kitchen, laundry, station tours, other accommodation available. Firewood for campfires is supplied.

GPS S:32 01.449 E:122 47.403
MR: Map 28 G1

FURTHER Information

Fraser Range Sheep Station
Tel: 08 9039 3210
Web: www.fraserrangestation.com.au
Camping fees: Unpowered sites from $22.00 per site/night for 2 people. Powered sites from $30.00 per site/night for 2 people.

Balladonia Roadhouse Caravan Park

Signposted access along the Eyre Highway at Balladonia, 190km east of Norseman and 181km west of Caiguna. Store, restaurant, fuel, camp kitchen. There is only limited rain water here so it is best to bring drinking water. Firewood is supplied.

GPS S:32 21.167 E:123 37.078
MR: Map 28 H2

FURTHER Information

Balladonia Hotel Motel
Tel: 08 9039 3453. Open from 6am to 10pm.
Camping fees: Unpowered sites from $18.00 per site/night for 2 people. Powered sites from $28.00 per site/night for 2 people.

Woorlba Rest Area

Designated 24 hour rest area. Signposted access along the Eyre Highway, 50km east of Balladonia and 131km west of Caiguna. On southern side of highway. Bring drinking water and firewood.

GPS S:32 26.187 E:124 06.282
MR: Map 33 B8

Baxter Rest Area

Designated 24 hour rest area. Signposted access along the Eyre Highway, 115km east of Balladonia and 67km west of Caiguna. On southern side of highway. Bring drinking water and firewood.

GPS S:32 21.372 E:124 47.191
MR: Map 33 C8

FURTHER Information

Main Roads Western Australia
Tel: 138 138
Web: www.mainroads.wa.gov.au

THE SOUTH-EAST

Caiguna Roadhouse

Signposted access on the Eyre Highway at Caiguna, 181km east of Balladonia and 65km west of Cocklebiddy. Bring firewood.

GPS S:32 16.237 E;125 29.305
MR: Map 33 D8

FURTHER Information

Caiguna Roadhouse
Tel: 08 9039 3459. Open 24 hours.
Camping fees: Unpowered sites from $20.00 per site/night for 2 adults. Powered sites from $25.00 per site/night for 2 adults.

Cocklebiddy Roadhouse

Signposted access along the Eyre Highway at Cocklebiddy, 65km east of Caiguna and 92km west of Madura. Open camping area with no shade.

GPS S:32 02.254 E:126 05.843
MR: Map 33 E7

FURTHER Information

Cocklebiddy Roadhouse
Tel: 08 9039 3462. Open from 6.30am to 9pm.
Camping fees: Unpowered sites from $20.00 per site/night for 2 adults. Powered sites from $25.00 per site/night for 2 adults.

Madura Pass Motel camping area

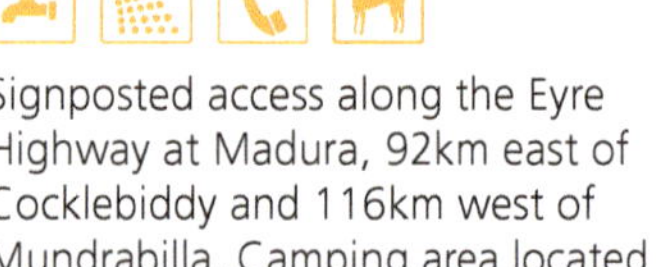

Signposted access along the Eyre Highway at Madura, 92km east of Cocklebiddy and 116km west of Mundrabilla. Camping area located behind the roadhouse and motel. Bring firewood for campfires.

GPS S:31 53.974 E:127 01.209
MR: Map 34 G7

FURTHER Information

Madura Pass Motel
Tel: 08 9039 3464. Open from 6.30am to 10pm (Monday to Saturday) and to 9pm (Sunday).
Camping fees: Unpowered sites from $15.00 per site/night for 2 adults. Powered sites from $25.00 per site/night for 2 adults. Key access to amenities block, refundable deposit.

Mundrabilla Roadhouse

Located on the Eyre Highway, 116km east of Madura and 66km west of Eucla.

GPS S:31 49.061 E:128 13.311

MR: Map 34 I6

FURTHER Information

Mundrabilla Roadhouse

Tel: 08 9039 3465. Open 6.30am to 9.30pm.

Camping fees: Unpowered sites from $15.00 per site/night for 2 adults. Powered sites from $20.00 per site/night for 2 adults. Refundable deposit for amenities key.

Eucla Pass Caravan Park

Located on the Eyre Highway at Eucla, 66km east of Mundrabilla Roadhouse and 12km west of the WA/SA border. Camp kitchen.

GPS S:31 40.702 E:128 52.914

MR: Map 34 J6

FURTHER Information

Eucla Pass Caravan Park

Tel: 08 9039 3468. Open 6.30am to 8.30pm.

Camping fees: Unpowered sites from $15.00 per site/night for 2 people. Powered sites from $20.00 per site/night for 2 people.

Eucla Pass Caravan Park

97 Nuytsland Nature Reserve

Incorporating the spectacular coastal cliffs of the Great Australian Bight along with a string of remote, windswept ocean beaches, Nuytsland Nature Reserve protects almost 500km of rugged coastline and stretches from Cape Arid National Park eastwards to Red Rock Point. The Eyre Bird Observatory and sections of the old Overland Telegraph Line constructed in 1876 are within the reserve and are worth a visit. Access to the west of the reserve is only by 4WD vehicles along Fisheries Road through Cape Arid National Park. This is a remote area which is recommended for self-sufficient campers only.

Point Malcolm camping area

Point Malcolm camping area

Signposted access along Fisheries Road (4WD access through Cape Arid National Park - Fisheries Road can be extremely corrugated), 52km east of the signposted Baring Road (which leads to Poison

Creek). Then drive 13.2km south to the small campsite close to the beach access track. Small shaded area with limited camper trailer space. Bring drinking water with you. Gas/fuel stove only.

GPS S:33 47.566 E:123 45.223

MR: Map 28 I5

FURTHER Information

DEC Esperance District Office
Tel: 08 9083 2100
Park entrance fee: $11.00 per vehicle.

Israelite Bay bush camping area

From Esperance proceed east along Fisheries Road for 123km to the signposted Baring Road, which leads to Cape Arid National Park and Poison Creek. From Baring Road continue in an easterly direction (road now becomes accessible only to 4WD vehicles and can be extremely corrugated), for a further 69km to the Telegraph Station ruins and the camping areas located among the shady trees to the east of the ruins. The use of a portable toilet at this site is recommended. Bring drinking water. Bring own fire drum/pot and firewood. Gas/fuel stove preferred.

GPS S:33 37.372 E:123 51.844

MR: Map 28 I4

FURTHER Information

DEC Esperance District Office
Tel: 08 9083 2100
Camping fees: From $2.00 per person/per night. Fees payable at on-site honesty box or to patrolling rangers.

Israelite Bay bush camping area

98 Peak Charles National Park

Visitors who are fit and agile can tackle the moderately demanding climb to the summit of Peak Charles for extensive views over the surrounding mallee woodlands and salt lakes to the east. During spring the park is ablaze with colour from the spectacular displays of wildflowers. Located south-west of Norseman, access is off the Lake King-Norseman Road, which is signposted off the Coolgardie-Esperance Highway, 54km south of Norseman. It's advisable to check road conditions prior to travelling to the park, especially after wet weather.

Peak Charles camping area

Signposted access along the Lake King-Norseman Road, 29km south-west of the Coolgardie-Esperance Highway, and then drive in a southerly direction for 22km to the camping area on the eastern side of Peak Charles. Suitable for small off-road camper trailers and caravans. Limited facilities, best suited for self-sufficient campers. Bring drinking water. Gas/fuel stove preferred.

MR: Map 27 D3

FURTHER Information

DEC Esperance District Office
Tel: 08 9083 2100

THE SOUTH-EAST

99 Stokes National Park

The picturesque Stokes Inlet is popular for fishing, canoeing and bird watching and is the centerpiece to this picturesque park. The coastal areas of Skippy Rock in the west and Fanny Cove and Shoal Cape in the east of the park offer spectacular coastal scenery. Those with a 4WD vehicle can access the historic Moir family homestead, the first family in the area to be granted a farming lease around Stokes Inlet in 1888. Access to Stokes Inlet is signposted off the South Coast Highway, 78km west of Esperance.

Benwenerup Campground

Benwenerup Campground

From the South Coast Highway, 78km west of Esperance, turn into the signposted Stokes Inlet Road. This road leads south for 5.6km to the signposted access to the camping area. Access road leads in 510m to the campground with 10 individually numbered and secluded campsites among the vegetation, all with flat, gravel based tent sites. A number of sites are suitable for groups. Camp kitchen. Boat ramp at nearby day use area. Bring drinking water. Gas/fuel stove only.

GPS S:33 51.505 E:121 02.305
MR: Map 25 A6

Fanny Cove camping area

From the South Coast Highway, 62km west of Esperance, take the signposted Farrells Road and follow this in a southerly direction for 6.7km to a track on the west. This track is not signposted. This unsealed, sandy track leads 3.3km to the national park boundary and then a further 10.8km to a T-intersection. At this intersection turn left (south) and follow this for a further 1.7km to the camping area with four open sites, with little shade and scant protection from the wind, although there are good views over the cover. Access track can have deep and/ or difficult sandy sections. Popular surfing and snorkelling spot. Table and shelter in the day use area. Bring drinking water. Gas/fuel stove only.

GPS S:33 51.353 E:121 11.565
MR: Map 25 B6

Fanny Cove camping area

Skippy Rock camping area

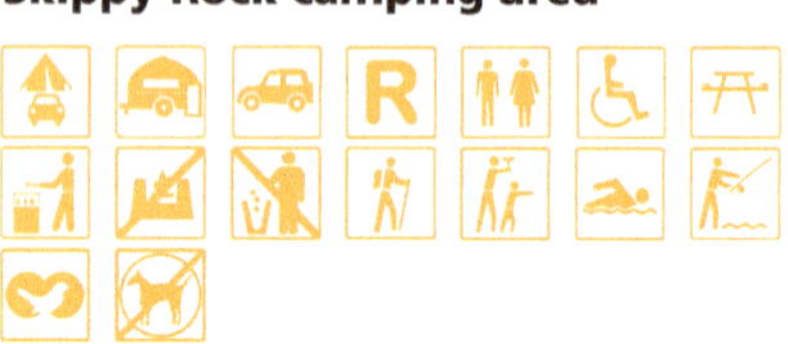

From the South Coast Highway, 88km west of Esperance, take the signposted Springdale Road. Follow Springdale Road in a southerly direction for 6.1km to the signposted Four Wheel Drive Only track. This track is just after the road turns west. The 4WD track proceeds in a southerly direction for 1.9km to the park boundary and then for a further 4.7km to the camping area with 9 individually numbered camping bays protected in among the vegetation. Popular surfing and snorkelling spot. Bring drinking water. Gas/fuel stove only.

GPS S:33 51.505 E:121 02.305
MR: Map 24 L3

FURTHER information

DEC Esperance District Office
Tel: 08 9083 2100
Park entrance fee: $11.00 per vehicle.
Camping fees: From $7.00 per adult/ night and $2.00 per child (up to 16)/night. Fees payable at self-registration station at Benwenerup Campground.

100 Woody Island Nature Reserve

Woody Island is one of a number of islands of the Archipelago of the Recherche. The archipelago has a rich history dating back to the time of whalers, sealers and even pirates! Woody Island Nature Reserve is a nature lover's paradise where activities include diving, snorkelling, bird watching, bushwalking, fishing and swimming. Access to Woody Island Nature Reserve is via a one and three quarter hour boat cruise from Esperance.

Woody Island Eco Stays

Located on Woody Island Nature Reserve. Camp kitchen with fridges. Campers can bring a gas/fuel stove or use facilities at the campground. Laundry facilities.

MR: Map 25 F6

FURTHER Information

MacKenzies Island Cruises

Tel: 08 9071 5757. Bookings necessary.
Web: www.woodyisland.com.au
Camping fees: Campers with own tent and sleeping equipment: From $25.00 a single/night, extra person $22.00 per night. Family rates from $71.00 per family (2 adults + 2 children)/night. Contact office for camping options and pricing using island supplied camping equipment.
Boat Cruise: From $60.00 per adult return.

THE SOUTH-EAST

The Mid-West

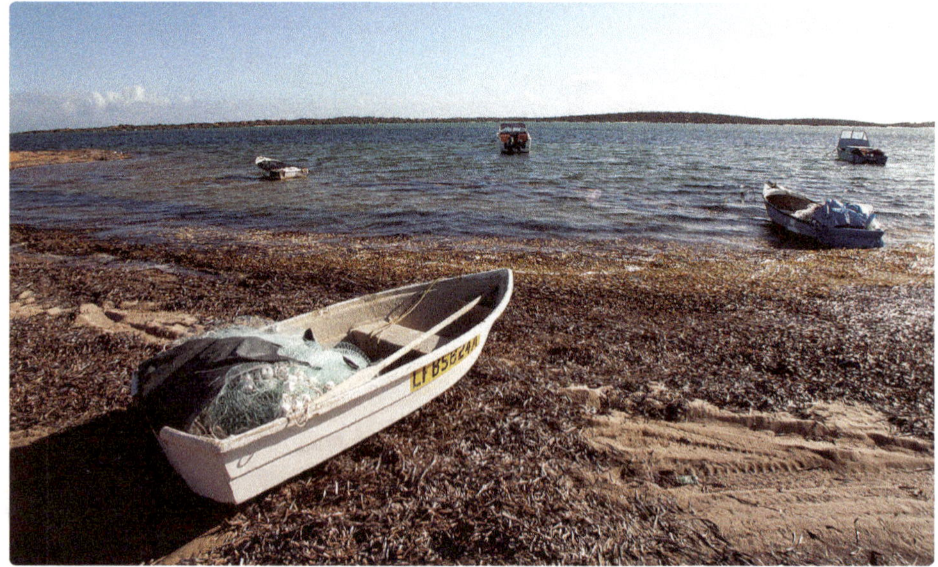

WESTERN AUSTRALIA'S MID-WEST region encompasses coastal stretches where beachside camping is popular, along with vast tracts of remote country to the east. The major population centres of Geraldton and Denham are in this region, along with the popular dolphin veiwing at Monkey Mia.

To the north of Geraldton and situated on the coast is the protected camping area at Coronation Beach. This beach is a popular site for surfing and windsurfing while to the east of Geraldton is Ellendale Pool, situated on the Greenough River. Here campers can try their luck at fishing or paddling their canoe along a peaceful stretch of the river.

Further to the north and located on the Peron Peninsula, the Denham area has four bush campsites situated along the peninsula's western shore while located at the tip of the peninsula is the large Francois Peron National Park. The national park offers a number of remote campsites, all of which are only accessible by four-wheel drive vehicles.

At the south-eastern end of the Peron Peninsula is Hamelin Pool where ancient stromatolite structures, or 'living fossils' can be easily viewed from a boardwalk. There is a caravan park located here.

In the far east of the region are the remote former pastoral stations of Lake Mason and Mt Elvire, which were once home to large numbers of sheep and are now managed by the Department of Environment and Conservation. Here you will find campsites located in the vicinity of the homesteads and shearer's quarters.

Visit this area in the cooler winter months if possible when days are mild and nights cool. Summer temperatures away from the coast are usually hot.

BEST Campsites!

Lake Mason camping area
Lake Mason

Gregories camping area
Francois Peron National Park

Coronation Beach camping area
Geraldton Area

Hamelin Pool Caravan Park
Hamelin Pool

Miners camp camping area
Coalseam Conservation Park

101 Bilyuin Pool

Bilyuin Pool is a permanent waterhole on the Murchison River. Located to the north-west of the Great Northern Highway, access is via the Ashburton Downs Road which leaves the highway 75km north of Meekatharra.

Bilyuin Pool camping area

From Meekatharra take the Great Northern Highway towards Newman for 75.8km to the signposted Ashburton Downs Road. Follow this road in a north-westerly direction for 14.3km to the Murchison River crossing. There are numerous tracks on the north side of the river that lead in 800m to bush campsites. It is advised that campsites be set well back from the river's banks to allow stock access to water. Camping is on the northern side of the river and on the western side of the road. Bush camping best suited for self-sufficient campers. Bring drinking water and firewood. This is cattle country so please do not interfere with stock.

GPS S:25 54.312 E:118 39.747
MR: Map 37 C5

FURTHER Information

Shire of Meekatharra
Tel: 08 9980 0600
Web: www.meekatharra.wa.gov.au

THE MID-WEST

102 Carnamah

Located on the Midlands Road, the town of Carnamah has a rich history. Many of its historical buildings from the early 1920s and 30s still stand, including MacPherson Homestead, built in 1869. Visitors will be rewarded with expansive views of the Yarra Yarra Lakes from the Lakes Lookout.

Carnamah Caravan Park

Located on King Street, which is signposted off McPherson Street in Carnamah. Gas/fuel stove only. Laundry facilities.
MR: Map 30 J6

FURTHER Information

Carnamah Caravan Park Caretaker
Tel: 08 9951 1785
Camping fees: Unpowered sites from $17.00 per site/night for 2 people. Powered sites from $24.50 per site/night per 2 people. Fees payable to on-site caretaker.

103 Coalseam Conservation Park

Coalseam Conservation Park was the site of Western Australia's first coal mine. Coal was discovered in 1846 by the Gregory brothers along the banks of the Irwin River and today visitors can view old mine shafts, coal seams and fossils along with diverse variety of indigenous flora. From August to October the park is carpeted with everlasting daisies which provides a spectacular highlight to the landscape. The park is located 32km north of Mingenew and 51km south of Mullewa with access via Coalseam Road, which is signposted off the Mingenew-Mullewa Road. Please take care when exploring around mine shafts within the park. Camping permitted from mid-July to mid-October during wildflower season.

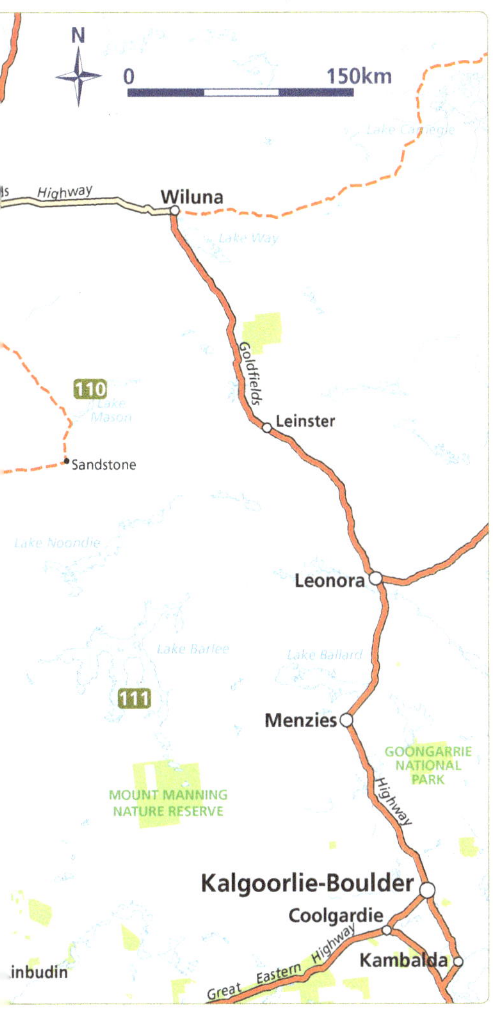

Miners Camp camping area

Located 36km north of Mingenew. From Mingenew follow Coalseam Road to the park's southern boundary. Continue north for 5km to the signposted access to the camping area then follow signage to the open camping area on the eastern banks of the Irwin River South. Bring drinking water and firewood.

MR: Map 30 J4

Breakaway camping area

Located 35km north of Mingenew. From Mingenew head north on Coalseam Road and once over the Irwin River the road turns to the west. Continue along Coalseam Road to the signposted access to the camping area and then drive in a southerly direction for a short distance to the open camping area with little shade. Limited facilities at this site which is best suited for self-sufficient campers. Bring drinking water. Gas/fuel stove only.

MR: Map 30 J4

FURTHER Information

DEC Geraldton Regional Office

Tel: 08 9921 5955

Camping fees: From $7.00 per adult/night and $2.00 per child (under 16)/night. Fees collected daily by campground hosts.

104 Denham Area

Located on the southern edge of the Peron Peninsula, the Shire of Shark Bay has a number of bush campsites set aside for campers. Denham offers safe swimming beaches, rugged coastal cliffs as well as scenic drives. Visitors can enjoy the World Heritage listed Shark Bay Marine Park and the dolphins at Monkey Mia, view living fossils at Hamelin Pool, boating, fishing or just relax in the beautiful surrounds. Conventional vehicle access to all sites off Shark Bay Road.

Denham

Eagle Bluff camping area

Signposted access on Eagle Bluff Road off Shark Bay Road, 18km south-east of Denham. Campsites located on the bluff or at the nearby lagoon. Popular site for bird watching, fishing and snorkelling. Bring drinking water. Gas/fuel stove only.

MR: Map 53 F5

Fowlers Camp camping area

Signposted access on Fowlers Camp Road off Shark Bay Road, 22km south-east of Denham. Good beach fishing spot. Bring drinking water. Gas/fuel stove only.

MR: Map 54 G5

Whalebone Bay camping area

Located on Whalebone Road off Shark Bay Road, 25km south-east of Denham. Campsites located close to beach. Bring drinking water. Gas/fuel stove only.

MR: Map 54 G5

Goulet Bluff camping area

Signposted access on Goulet Bluff Road off Shark Bay Road, 36km south-east of Denham. Bring drinking water. Gas/fuel stove only.

MR: Map 54 G5

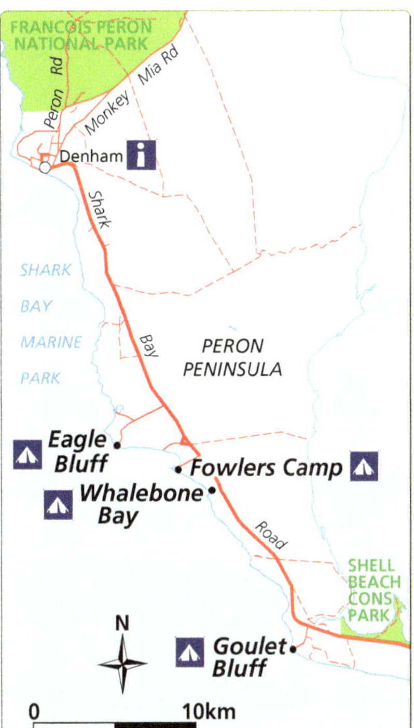

FURTHER Information

Shark Bay Discovery & Visitors Centre

Tel: 08 9948 1588. Permits are required for all sites and can be obtained by: (a) phoning number listed or (b) in person. Permits are available from Shark Bay Discovery & Visitors Centre in Knight Street, Denham during office hours which are 9am to 5pm (Monday to Friday) and 10am to 4pm (Saturday and Sunday).

Web: www.sharkbayvisit.com or www.sharkbay.wa.gov.au

Camping permits: Camping permits must be obtained the day prior to setting up camp. There are substantial fines applied to campers without a camping permit.

Maximum stay: 1 night. No consecutive night stays.

105 Dirk Hartog Island National Park

The island is the site of the first European landing on Australia's west coast. Dutch explorer Dirk Hartog set ashore here on the 25th October, 1616. The island offers excellent shore fishing with tailor, Spanish mackerel and trevally among the catches, while the surrounding Shark Bay Marine Park has wonderful snorkeling sites. The island's varied landforms provide amazing opportunities for photographers. Located 37km west of Denham in Shark Bay, the island is 11 kilometres wide and 76 kilometres wide. Access to the island is via private boat, commercial charter boat or plane. From March to October it is possible for 4WD vehicles to be taken to the island via a vehicle barge from Steep Point. All campsites on the island have limited facilities and are best suited to well set-up, self-sufficient campers.

The Block camping area

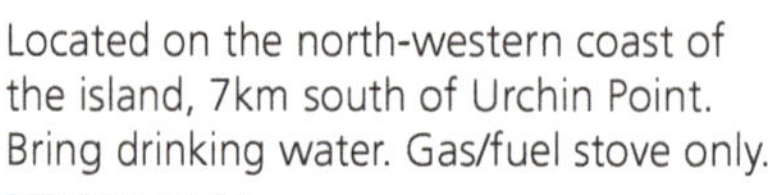

Located on the north-western coast of the island, 7km south of Urchin Point. Bring drinking water. Gas/fuel stove only.

MR: Map 53 B2

Urchin Point camping area

Located on the north-western coast of the island, 7km north of The Block and 4.1km south of Cape Inscription. Bring drinking water. Gas/fuel stove only.

MR: Map 53 B2

Withnell Point camping area

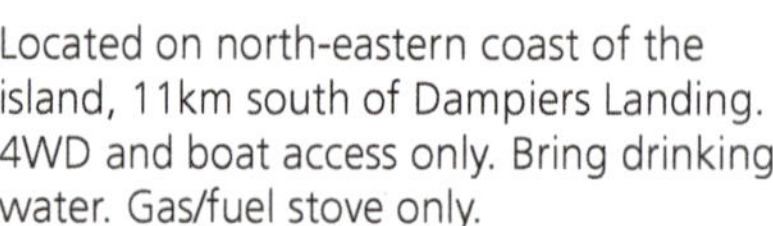

Located on north-eastern coast of the island, 11km south of Dampiers Landing. 4WD and boat access only. Bring drinking water. Gas/fuel stove only.

MR: Map 53 B2

Sandy Point camping area

Located on the east coast of the island near the Shearing Shed, 7.3km north of Louisa Bay. Bring drinking water. Gas/fuel stove only.

MR: Map 53 C3

Louisa Bay camping area

Located on the east coast of the island, 7.3km south of Sandy Point and 11km north of Herald Bay Outstation. Accessible by 4WD and boat. Bring drinking water. Gas/fuel stove only.

MR: Map 53 C3

10 Mile camp camping area

Located on the east coast of the island to the south of Quoin Bluff South. Boat access. Bring drinking water. Gas/fuel stove only.

MR: Map 53 C4

Notch Point camping area

Located on the east coast of the island to the north of Dirk Hartog Island Homestead. Boat access. Bring drinking water. Gas/fuel stove only.

MR: Map 53 D4

Jean camping area

Located on the east coast of the island to the north of Long Tom CA and situated in Blind Strait. Boat access only. Bring drinking water. Gas/fuel stove only.

MR: Map 53 D5

Long Tom camping area

Located on the east coast of the island to the south of Jean CA and situated in Blind Strait. Boat access. Bring drinking water. Gas/fuel stove only.

MR: Map 53 D5

FURTHER information

DEC Denham District Office

Tel: 08 9948 1208. Advance bookings are necessary.

Park entrance fee: $11.00 per vehicle.

Camping fees: Contact DEC Denham District Office for current camping fees.

106 Francois Peron National Park

A former sheep grazing station prior to being gazetted as a national park, the park protects various plants and shrublands, rugged coastlines and a variety of birds and wildlife. The waters surrounding the peninsula are home to dugongs, dolphins and loggerhead turtles. Located at the tip of the Peron Peninsula, access to the park is 4km north-east of Denham off the Monkey Mia Road. All roads within Francois Peron National Park are for high clearance 4WD vehicles only due to their sand base. Deflating your vehicle's tyres when venturing into the park will make driving easier.

SHARK BAY
N
0
8km
Cape Peron
Skipjack Point
Bight
Bottle Bay
Gregories
4WD Only
South Gregories
Herald Bight
SHARK BAY MARINE PARK
Broadhurst
Herald Bight
4WD Only
4WD Only
Big Lagoon
Cape Lesueur
FRANCOIS PERON NATIONAL PARK
Hopeless Reach
Cape Rose
Big Lagoon
4WD Only
DENHAM
SOUND
4WD Only
Peron
Red Cliff Bay
Monkey Mia
Peron Homestead
Rd
Mia
Monkey
Peron Rd
Dubuat Point
Little Lagoon
Peninsula
Denham
Shark Bay Rd

THE MID-WEST

Big Lagoon camping area

Signposted access off the main park road, 6km north of the park boundary. Then drive 11km in a north-westerly direction to the camping area. Allow 45 minutes to an hour travelling time. Beach boat launch. Bring drinking water. Gas/fuel stove only.

MR: Map 53 E3

South Gregories camping area

Signposted access off the main park road, 23km north of Peron Homestead. Then continue in a northerly direction for 9km to the signposted access track which leads to the coast. Allow 1 to 1.5 hours travelling time. Beach boat launch. Bring drinking water. Gas/fuel stove only.

MR: Map 53 E2

Gregories camping area

Signposted access off the main park road, 23km north of Peron Homestead. Then continue in a northerly direction to the signposted access track, which is 3km north of South Gregories access track. Allow 1 to 1.5 hours travelling time. Beach boat launch. Bring drinking water. Gas/fuel stove only.

MR: Map 53 E1

Bottle Bay camping area

Signposted access off the main park road, 23km north of Peron Homestead. Then continue in a northerly direction to the signposted access track, which is 2km north of Gregories access track. Allow 1 to 1.5 hours travelling time. Beach boat launch. Bring drinking water. Gas/fuel stove only.

MR: Map 53 E1

Herald Bight camping area

Signposted access off the main park road, 31km north of Denham. Then continue in an easterly direction to the coast. Allow 1 hours travelling time. Beach boat launch. Bring drinking water. Gas/fuel stove only.

MR: Map 53 F2

FURTHER Information

DEC Denham District Office

Tel: 08 9948 1208
Park entrance fee: $11.00 per vehicle.
Camping fees: From $7.00 per adult/night and $2.00 per child (up to 16)/night. Fees payable at self-registration station at park entrance near the Peron Homestead.

107 Geraldton Area

The Geraldton area is a popular destination for fishing, sailing, surfing, diving and snorkelling. There are a number of council camping areas in the region for travellers. Geraldton is 424km north of Perth via the Brand Highway.

Coronation Beach camping area

Located 8km west of the North West Coastal Highway on Coronation Beach Road. Coronation Beach Road is signposted off the highway, 28km north of Geraldton. Shower cubicles to hang your own shower bag. Popular beach for windsurfing and surfing. Bring drinking water. Gas/fuel stove preferred.

MR: Map 30 H4

FURTHER Information

Shire of Chapman Valley
Tel: 08 9920 5011
Web: www.chapmanvalley.wa.gov.au
Geraldton Tourist Bureau
Tel: 08 9921 3999
Web: www.geraldtontourist.com.au
Camping fees: From $15.00 per site/night. Fees payable to on-site caretaker.

Fig Tree Crossing camping area

Signposted access along Chapman Valley Road, which is signposted off the North West Coastal Highway 8km north of Geraldton. Then travel in a north-easterly direction for 5km to the camping area adjacent to the Chapman River. Bring drinking water. Gas/fuel stove preferred.

MR: Map 30 H4

FURTHER Information

Shire of Chapman Valley
Tel: 08 9920 5011
Web: www.chapmanvalley.wa.gov.au
Geraldton Tourist Bureau
Tel: 08 9921 3999
Web: www.geraldtontourist.com.au
Camping fees: From $5.50 per site/night. Fees payable at on-site honesty box.
Maximum stay: 48 hours.

Coronation Beach camping area

Ellendale Pool camping area

Located 47km east of Geraldton. From Geraldton proceed east along the Geraldton-Mt Magnet Road and at 5km turn south onto the Edward Road. Follow this in south-easterly direction to the Nangetty Walkaway Road and follow this east to the signposted Ellendale Road. Travel north along Ellendale Road for 5km to the signposted access to the camping area which is set beside a large fresh water pool on the Greenough River. Bring drinking water. Gas/fuel stove only.

MR: Map 30 I4

FURTHER Information

Geraldton Tourist Bureau
Tel: 08 9921 3999
Web: www.geraldtontourist.com.au
Camping fees: From $5.00 per vehicle/night. Fees payable at honesty box.
Maximum stay: 3 nights.

108 Hamelin Pool

Hamelin Pool protects the world's most abundant colony of marine stromatolites, or "living fossils". These unique creatures are monuments to what was life on Earth over 3500 million years ago at a time before no other complex creatures were present on the planet. Nearby is the Hamelin Pool Telegraph Station which was built in 1884. The station became an important link in the telegraph line, servicing the Perth to Roebourne line until the advent of new technology in the late 1950s saw its closure. Hamelin Pool was also an important transport hub and landing point for cargo vessels supplying surrounding stations. Access to Hamelin Pool is off the Shark Bay Road, 37km west of the North West Coastal Highway.

Hamelin Pool Caravan Park

Located on Hamelin Pool Road off Shark Bay Road, 37km west of the North West Coastal Highway. Camp kitchen, laundry facilities.

MR: Map 54 J6

FURTHER Information

Hamelin Pool Caravan Park
Tel: 08 9942 5905
Camping fees: Unpowered sites from $22.00 per site/night for 2 people. Powered sites from $27.00 per site/night for 2 people.

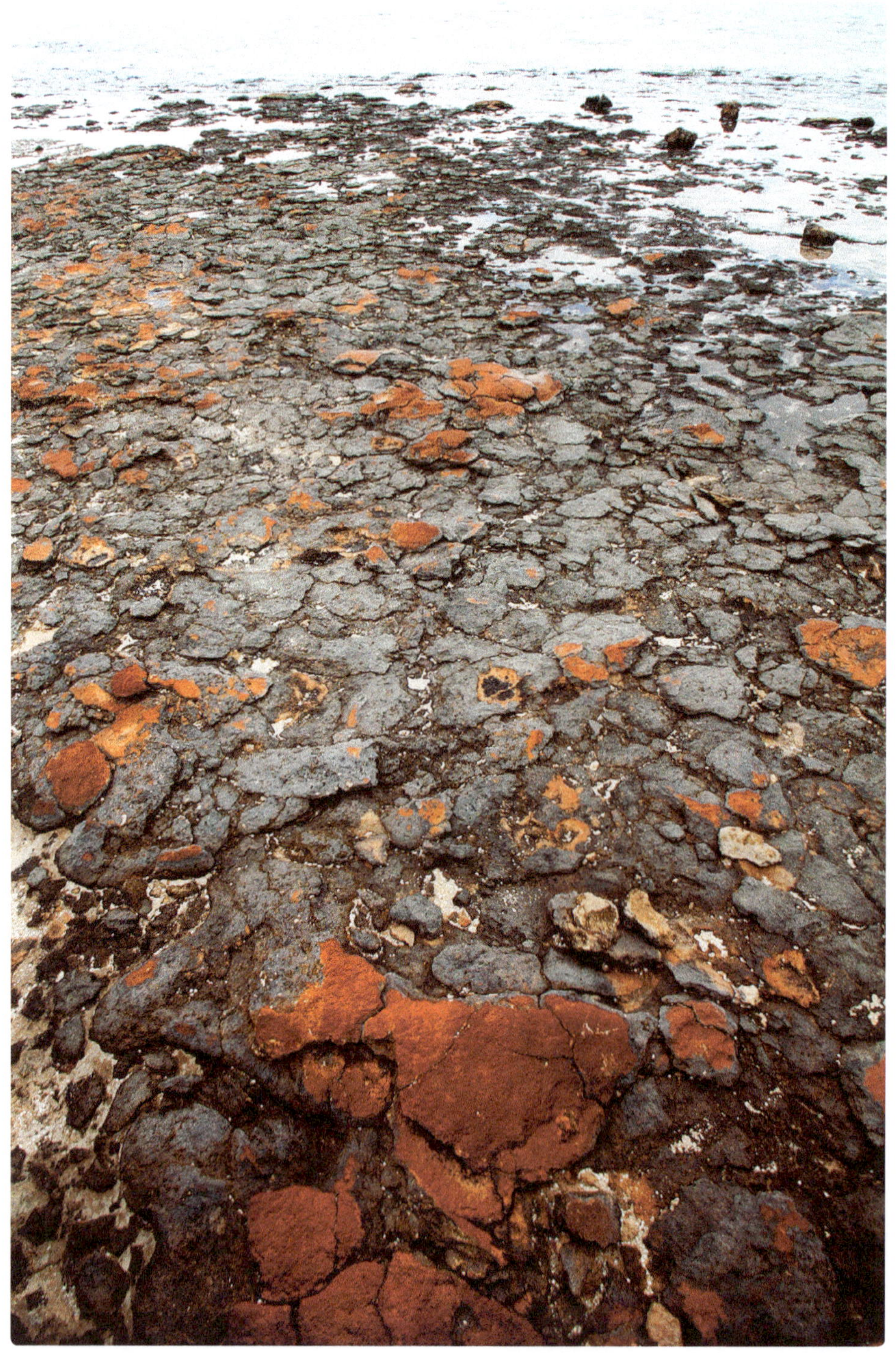

Stromatolites at Hamelin Pool, page 139

109 Lake Indoon

Lake Indoon is located 12km west of Eneabba on the Brand Highway. The lake is a popular water sports destination for swimming, canoeing, sailing and waterskiing. With over 50 bird species recorded, the area is also popular with birdwatchers. Access to Lake Indoon is from the Brand Highway via the Eneabba-Coolimba Road.

Lake Indoon camping area

Signposted access along the Eneabba-Coolimba Road, 12km west of Eneabba and 18km east of the Indian Ocean Drive. Bring drinking water. Gas/fuel stove only.

MR: Map 30 I6

FURTHER Information

Shire of Carnamah
Tel: 08 9951 7000
Camping fees: From $10.00 per adult/night and $3.00 per child/night. Fees collected by Ranger.

THE MID-WEST

110 Lake Mason Conservation Park (proposed)

Lake Mason, at just over 149,000ha, was formerly a pastoral property. Located on the property is the Lake Mason salt lake system as well as the shearers quarters and homestead which reflect its agricultural past. Lake Mason is located 56km north of Sandstone and is accessed off the Sandstone-Wiluna Road.

Lake Mason camping area

From Sandstone proceed north towards Meekathara for 27.8km to a road junction. At this junction continue in northerly direction towards the signposted Lake Mason; this is the Sandstone-Wiluna Road. Follow this road for 26.5km to the signposted road on the right to Lake Mason. This leads in 3.2km to the homestead precinct and open camping area near the homestead and shearing complex. There is little shade or wind protection here. Donkey hot water system. Bring drinking water and firewood.

GPS S:27 35.215 E:119 31.238
MR: Map 31 E1

FURTHER Information

DEC Kalgoorlie Regional Office
Tel: 08 9080 5555. Advance bookings necessary.
Camping fees: From $7.00 per adult/night and $2.00 per child (up to 16)/night. Overnight stay in homestead from $9.00 per person/night. Fees payable to DEC Kalgoorlie office.

111 Mt Elvire

Mt Elvire is located 175km west of Menzies and was once a working farm. Access to Mt Elvire from Menzies is via unsealed roads which become impassable during wet weather. Contact DEC Kalgoorlie for the latest detailed access information.

Mt Elvire Homestead camping area

From Menzies proceed west along the Evanston Menzies Road for 171km to the signposted Lake Barlee Road. Lake Barlee Road proceeds north for 42km to the homestead complex. Camping is in the vicinity of the homestead and shearer's quarters. This remote location is best for self-sufficient campers. Donkey hot water system. Bring drinking water and firewood. Gas/fuel stove preferred.

MR: Map 31 E4

FURTHER Information

DEC Kalgoorlie Regional Office
Tel: 08 9080 5555. Advance bookings necessary.
Camping fees: From $7.00 per adult/night and $2.00 per child (up to 16)/night. Fees payable to DEC Kalgoorlie office.

112 Mullewa Area

The Mullewa region is well known for its stunning wildflower displays, and in particular the wreath flower, which come into bloom from July to September. Other attractions around Mullewa include the Butteraby Gravesites and Tallering Peak and Gorge. Mullewa is located 98km north-east of Geraldton via the Geraldton-Mt Magnet Road.

Tenindewa Pioneer Well camping area

Signposted access 4km along the Yuna-Tenindewa Road, which is signposted off the Geraldton-Mt Magnet Road, 18km south-west of Mullewa. This site is best suited for self-sufficient campers. Bring drinking water and firewood. Gas/fuel stove only during fire danger period.

MR: Map 30 I4

Noondamarra Pool camping area

Signposted access 29km along the Yuna-Tenindewa Road, which is signposted off the Geraldton-Mt Magnet Road, 18km south-west of Mullewa. Bush camping area beside the Greenough River for self-sufficient campers. Bring drinking water and firewood. Gas/fuel stove only during fire danger period.

MR: Map 30 I4

FURTHER Information

Mullewa Community Resource Centre
Tel: 08 9961 1500
Web: www.mullewatourism.com.au
NB: Check with local authorities for current dates on fire danger periods prior to lighting campfires.

The Pilbara

THE PILBARA REGION IS OFTEN DESCRIBED as 'where the outback meets the ocean', and this is not hard to believe with the magnificent azure waters contrasting against the striking red escarpment. Within this region are some of the state's most popular national parks, with Cape Range and Karijini national parks offering excellent visitor facilities and stunning scenic vistas in an ancient landscape.

On the coast to the south of Exmouth is Cape Range National Park, home to beautiful white sandy beaches with crystal clear waters, while further east and in stark contrast are the striking iron red gorges of Karijini National Park with its many walking opportunities. Both parks have some great campsites for visitors to base themselves while exploring the parks.

East of Marble Bar are the remote desert plains of Karlamilyi National Park and the hidden delights of Desert Queen Baths, a secluded rock hole amongst the range. Bush camping is possible at a number of sites. This area offers a remote camping experience for well-equipped four-wheel drive tourers. Also to the east of Marble Bar is the beautiful Carawine Gorge and Running Waters.

Millstream-Chichester National Park, south of Roebourne, offers scenic campsites beside the Fortescue River. The park is an oasis contrasting with the mining operations of the nearby Hamersley Mine. Visit the information centre in the beautiful old homestead.

Other campsites are dotted along the coastal strip ranging from council reserves to camping areas on working pastoral stations.

This popular and scenic region is best enjoyed during the cooler months of the year from April through to October when it is heavily frequented by southerners escaping the cold winter weather.

BEST Campsites!

Dales camping area
Karijini National Park

Ningaloo Station camping areas
Carnarvon Area

White Gum Bore camping area
Karlamilyi (Rudall River) National Park

Mesa Camp camping area
Cape Range National Park

Murlamunyjunha Crossing Pool camping area
Millstream-Chichester National Park

THE PILBARA

113 Cape Range National Park

This coastal park abounds with magnificent coastal scenery, delightful beaches and crystal clear water along with spectacular views from Thomas Carter Lookout and Charles Knife Road. You can take a walk to explore Shothole Canyon, Mandu Mandu Gorge and to the bird and fauna hide from Mangrove Bay car park. The waters off Cape Range National Park offer top rate fishing and boating opportunities as well as great diving and snorkeling on the inshore coral reefs. Cape Range National Park is 36km south-west of Exmouth via the sealed Yardie Creek Road.

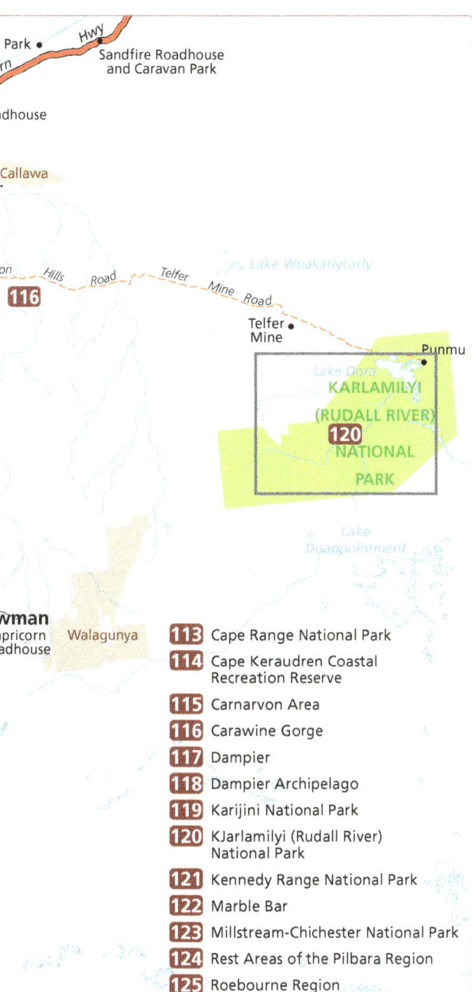

Neds Camp

Signposted access off Yardie Creek Road, 8km south of park boundary information shelter and self-registration station and 3km north of Milyering Visitor Centre. Then drive west for 600m to the camping area behind the sand dunes with 18 sites. Bring drinking water. Gas/fuel stove only.

GPS S:22 00.063 E:113 55.983

MR: Map 55 E3

Mesa Camp

Signposted access off Yardie Creek Road, 8km south of park boundary information shelter and self-registration station and 3km north of Milyering Visitor Centre. Then drive west for 1.6km to the camping area with 14 sites located close to the beach. This campsite is suitable for larger motorhomes and fifth-wheelers. Beach boat launch for small boats. Bring drinking water. Gas/fuel stove only.

GPS S:22 00.380 E:113 55.664

MR: Map 55 E3

Mesa Camp

North T Bone Camp

Signposted access off Yardie Creek Road, 11km south of park boundary information shelter and self-registration station. Turn off is at the Milyering Visitor Centre. Then drive west for 1.2km to the small camping area with three sites behind the sand dunes. Bring drinking water. Gas/fuel stove only.

GPS S:22 01.362 E:113 55.290

MR: Map 55 E3

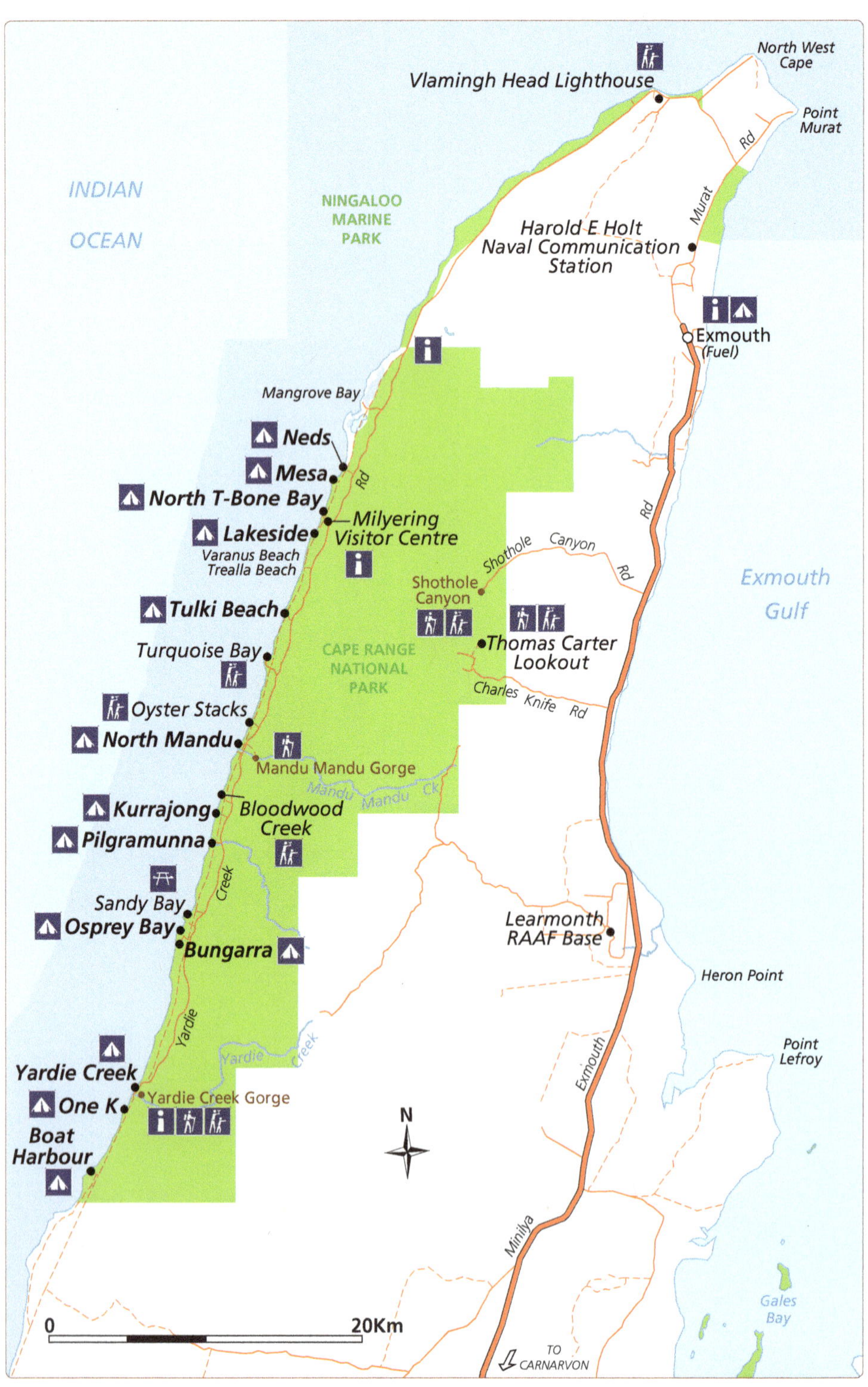
North West Cape
Vlamingh Head Lighthouse
Point Murat
Murat Rd
INDIAN OCEAN
NINGALOO MARINE PARK
Harold E Holt Naval Communication Station
Exmouth (Fuel)
Mangrove Bay
Neds
Mesa
Rd
North T-Bone Bay
Milyering Visitor Centre
Lakeside
Varanus Beach
Treala Beach
Shothole Canyon Rd
Shothole Canyon
Tulki Beach
Exmouth Gulf
Turquoise Bay
Thomas Carter Lookout
CAPE RANGE NATIONAL PARK
Charles Knife Rd
Oyster Stacks
North Mandu
Mandu Mandu Gorge
Mandu Mandu Ck
Kurrajong
Bloodwood Creek
Pilgramunna
Creek
Sandy Bay
Osprey Bay
Bungarra
Learmonth RAAF Base
Heron Point
Yardie
Yardie Creek
Point Lefroy
Yardie Creek
One K
Yardie Creek Gorge
Exmouth
Boat Harbour
N
Minilya
Gales Bay
0
20Km
TO CARNARVON

THE PILBARA

Cape Range National Park

Lakeside Camp

Signposted access off Yardie Creek Road, 11km south of park boundary information shelter and self-registration station. Turn off is at the Milyering Visitor Centre. Then drive west for 1.6km to the camping area with 7 sites. Bring drinking water. Gas/fuel stove only.

GPS S:22 02.050 E:113 54.948

MR: Map 55 E3

Tulki Camp

Signposted access off Yardie Creek Road, 6km south of Milyering Visitor Centre. Then drive west for 800m to the camping area with 11 sites, located close to the beach and adjacent to a usually dry creek. Bring drinking water. Gas/fuel stove only.

GPS S:22 04.533 E:113 53.915

MR: Map 55 D3

North Mandu Camp

Signposted access off Yardie Creek Road, 14km south of Milyering Visitor Centre. Then drive west for 400m to the camping area located behind the sand dunes with five sites. Bring drinking water. Gas/fuel stove only.

GPS S:22 08.527 E:113 52.361

MR: Map 55 D4

Kurrajong Camp

Signposted access off Yardie Creek Road, 19km south of Milyering Visitor Centre. Then drive west for 500m to the camping area with 10 sites located between sand dunes just back from the beach. Bring drinking water. Gas/fuel stove only.

GPS S:22 10.841 E:113 51.930

MR: Map 55 D4

Pilgramunna Camp

Signposted access off Yardie Creek Road, 20km south of Milyering Visitor Centre. Then drive west for 500m to the camping area with 9 unshaded sites behind the sand dunes close to the creek and beach. Bring drinking water. Gas/fuel stove only.

GPS S:22 11.633 E:113 51.383
MR: Map 55 D4

Osprey Bay Camp

Signposted access off Yardie Creek Road 26km south of Milyering Visitor Centre and 10km north of Yardie Creek CA. Then drive west for 800m to the large camping area with 15 sites, and great coastal views. Generators are permitted at sites 8 to 20, regulations apply. Beach boat launch for small boats. Bring drinking water. Gas/fuel stove only.

GPS S:22 14.338 E:113 50.308
MR: Map 55 D4

Bungarra Camp

Signposted access off Yardie Creek Road, 26km south of Milyering Visitor Centre and 9.8km north of Yardie Creek CA. Then drive west for 700m to the small camping area with five sites and no shade and set back from the beach. Bring drinking water. Gas/fuel stove only.

MR: Map 55 D4

Yardie Creek Camp

Signposted access off Yardie Creek Road, 36km south of Milyering Visitor Centre and 600m north of Yardie Creek crossing. This camping area is located back from the beach with 11 sites, with some offering shade. Bring drinking water. Gas/fuel stove only.

GPS S:22 19.240 E:113 48.863
MR: Map 55 D5

One K Camp

Signposted access off Yardie Creek Road, 1km south of Yardie Creek crossing and 4.2km north of Boat Harbour CA access track. Then drive west for 100m to the camping area with 6 sites. Yardie Creek crossing is a wide, sandy crossing (suitable for 4WD vehicles only) with water levels dependent on tides and recent rainfall. At times this crossing may be impassable. Beach boat launch for small boats. Bring drinking water. Gas/fuel stove only.

GPS S:22 19.923 E:113 48.401
MR: Map 55 D5

Boat Harbour Camp

Signposted access off Yardie Creek Road, 5.2km south of Yardie Creek crossing and 4.2km south of One K Camp access track. Then drive west for 500m to the camping area with 4 sites. Yardie Creek crossing is a wide, sandy crossing (suitable for 4WD vehicles only) with water levels dependent on tides and recent rainfall. At times this crossing may be impassable. Beach boat launch for small boats. Bring drinking water. Gas/fuel stove only.

GPS S:22 21.823 E:113 47.173

MR: Map 55 D5

FURTHER Information

Milyering Visitor Centre

Tel: 08 9949 2808. Advance bookings apply during peak season (April to October) for: Tulki Beach, Kurrajong Camp, Pilgramunna Camp, Osprey Bay and Yardie Creek camping areas.

Park entrance fee: $11.00 per vehicle.

Camping fees: From $7.00 per adult/night and $2.00 per child (up to 16)/night. Fees payable to Ranger or on-site Campground Hosts.

NB: Camping areas do change from season to season. Check with Milyering Visitor Centre for up-to-date details.

Yardie Creek

114 Cape Keraudren Coastal Recreation Reserve

Situated at the southern end of Eighty Mile Beach, Cape Keraudren is a perfect spot for beach lovers. Enjoy beautiful coastal scenery, take a stroll along the beach, fish or bird watch. Located 14km north of Pardoo and 166km north-east of Port Hedland, access is signposted off the Great Northern Highway opposite the Pardoo Roadhouse. From time to time crocodiles have been sighted in the waters off Cape Keraudren so please take care when fishing or near the water.

Cape Keraudren camping area

Signposted access off the Great Northern Highway opposite Pardoo Roadhouse, 152km north-east of Port Hedland. Then drive in a northerly direction for 14km along the unsealed road to the reserve and open camping area with dispersed bush camping along the foreshore. This is an open site with little protection from the wind. Bring drinking water and firewood.

GPS S:19 57.612 E:119 46.131

MR: Map 43 C1

FURTHER Information

Shire of East Pilbara
Tel: 08 9175 8000
Web: www.eastpilbara.wa.gov.au

Newman Tourist Bureau
Tel: 08 9175 2888
Web: www.newman-wa.org

Port Hedland Tourist Bureau
Tel: 08 9173 1711
Web: www.phvc.com.au

Park entrance fee: $10.00 per vehicle up to 4 adults.

Camping fees: From $6.50 per adult/night and $2.00 per child (6 to 15)/night. Fees payable to on-site ranger.

Cape Keraudren camping area

115 Carnarvon Area

Carnarvon is located 904km north of Perth via the North West Coastal Highway and is the confluence of Gascoyne River and the Indian Ocean. The area's main agricultural industry is tropical fruit plantations including bananas, mangos, paw paws and melons, most of which are located along the Gascoyne River. Fishing, including game fishing, is a popular past time. Carnarvon and its surrounds boast a number of historic landmarks and many natural attractions for visitors to explore.

Gladstone camping area

Signposted access off the North West Coastal Highway, 146km south of Carnarvon and 56km north of Overlander Roadhouse. Then drive in a westerly direction for 6km to the camping area. Beach boat launch, suitable for small boats. Bring drinking water and firewood.

GPS S:25 57.125 E:114 14.570

MR: Map 54 J3

New Beach camping area

Signposted access off the North West Coastal Highway, 33km south of Carnarvon. Then drive in a westerly direction for 8km to the camping area. Best for self-sufficient campers with a portable chemical toilet. Beach boat launch suitable for small boats. Bring drinking water and firewood.

GPS S:25 09.230 E:113 47.525

MR: Map 35 E5

Bush Bay camping area

Signposted access off the North West Coastal Highway, 33km south of Carnarvon. Then drive in a westerly direction for 10km. Located 7km north of New Beach camping area. Site best for self-sufficient campers with a portable chemical toilet. Beach boat launch, suitable for small boats. Bring drinking water and firewood.

GPS S:25 07.435 E:113 45.125

MR: Map 35 E5

The Blowholes camping area

From Carnarvon proceed north along the North West Coastal Highway for 25km to the signposted Blowholes Road. Then follow Blowholes Road in a northerly direction for 49km to the open camping area overlooking the coast. 4WD accessible boat ramp. Popular surfing, snorkelling and scuba diving spot. Bring drinking water and firewood.

GPS S:24 29.158 E:113 24.449

MR: Map 35 D4

FURTHER Information

Shire of Carnarvon
Tel: 08 9941 0000
Web: www.carnarvon.wa.gov.au

Carnarvon Tourist Bureau
Tel: 08 9941 1146

Camping fees: Gladstone CA and The Blowholes CA: From $5.50 per vehicle/night. Fees payable at on-site honesty box.

Quobba Station Homestead camping area

From Carnarvon proceed north along the North West Coastal Highway for 25km to the signposted Blowholes Road. Follow Blowholes road for 49km and then proceed north along Gnaraloo Road for 9km to homestead. Limited tank water available. Bring own drinking water. Firewood available for purchase. Other accommodation options available.

MR: Map 35 D4

FURTHER Information

Quobba Station
Tel: 08 9948 5098
Web: www.quobba.com.au
Camping fees: Unpowered sites from $11.00 per person/night. Powered sites from $13.50 per person/night.

Red Bluff camping area

Signposted access along Gnaraloo Road, 60km north of Quobba Station. Popular surfing spot. Caravans are advised to check road conditions first. Bring drinking water and firewood. Other accommodation options available.

MR: Map 35 D3

FURTHER Information

Red Bluff Caretakers
Tel: 08 9948 5001
Web: www.quobba.com.au/redbluff
Camping fees: From $12.00 per adult/night and $5.00 per child (5-15 years)/night.
Dog bond: A dog fee may apply – if camping with a dog, camping is in a separate area from the main camping area.

3 Mile Camp camping area

Located on Gnaraloo Station. Signposted access along Gnaraloo Road, 76km north of its turn off from Blowholes Road. Blowholes Road is signposted off the North West Coastal Highway, 25km north of Carnarvon, then drive for 49km to the signposted Gnaraloo Road. Caravan access during dry weather only. Popular surfing and windsurfing spot. Shop with basic supplies, laundry. Bring drinking water and firewood and barbecue plate or grate for your campfire. There is no fishing permitted in the lagoon.

MR: Map 35 D3

FURTHER Information

Gnaraloo Station
Tel: 08 9948 5000. Bookings recommended.
Web: www.gnaraloo.com
Camping fees: From $20.00 per adult/night and $10.00 per child (5-15 years)/night.
Dogs: $2.50 per dog/night.

Warroora Station camping areas

Located 60km south of Coral Bay and 23km west of the Minilya Exmouth Road. From the Minilya Exmouth Road take the signposted Warroora Road which is at the Lyndon Crossing Rest Area, 25km north of Minilya Roadhouse. Alternatively from Coral Bay take the signposted Warroora North Road which is signposted off the Minilya Exmouth Road, 15km south of the Coral Bay turn off. There are five camping areas located on Warroora Station (The 14 Mile area is accessible by conventional vehicles while The Lagoon, Black Moon Cliff, Elle's Beach and Steven's Surf Break are only accessible by 4WD vehicles). Surfing, diving, snorkeling are popular here. Public phone located at homestead. Best suited to self-sufficient campers with own portable chemical toilet. Bring drinking water and firewood. Other accommodation options available.

MR: Map 35 E2

FURTHER Information

Warroora Station

Tel: 08 9942 5920. Campers must call into homestead to pay fees and obtain map to camping areas.
Web: www.warroora.com
Access fee: From $7.50 per person/day. Children under 16 no charge.

9 Mile Camp camping area

Numerous bush camping sites located on Cardabia Station which is located 5km north of Coral Bay. Conventional vehicle access possible to sites, however a 4WD vehicle is recommended. There's signposted access off the Coral Bay Road, which in turn is signposted off the Minilya-Exmouth Road. Beach camping. Bring drinking water and firewood.

MR: Map 35 E1

FURTHER Information

Cardabia Station

Tel: 08 9942 5935. All campers must contact Cardabia Station, by phone or in person at homestead, prior to setting up camp.
Camping fees: From $5.00 per adult/night and $2.50 per student/night.

Ningaloo Station camping areas

Five wilderness, key access only, camping areas located on Ningaloo Station. Conventional vehicle access to some areas is possible, however a 4WD vehicle is recommended. Ningaloo homestead is located at the end of Ningaloo Road, which is signposted off the Minilya-Exmouth Road, 40km north of the Coral Bay access road. All sites have beach frontage. Suited for fully self-sufficient campers. Campers must have a portable chemical toilet, otherwise toilets are available for hire from the station office. Ground fires are prohibited at the campsites, if you wish to have a campfire bring your own portable fire bin/bucket as well as firewood. Gas/fuel stove preferred. Bring drinking water.

Homestead: **GPS** S:22 41.845 E:113 40.475
MR: Map 55 D7

FURTHER Information

Ningaloo Station

Tel: 08 9942 5936. Bookings essential. All campers must register at the homestead prior to setting up camp.
Camping fees: From $20.00 per person/week.
Car bond: $100.00 per vehicle.

Ningaloo Station camping area

116 Carawine Gorge

Located to the east of Marble Bar are Carawine Gorge and the nearby Running Waters, both situated beside picturesque waterholes on private property. The land holders are happy for campers to enjoy these beautiful waterholes as long as you leave no trace of your visit and make contact with the station prior to setting up camp. All campers must be self-sufficient. Access is off the Woodie Woodie Road, 153km east of Marble Bar via the Ripon Hills Road. Access to both sites is via 4WD vehicle only.

Carawine Gorge

Carawine Gorge

From Marble Bar proceed in an easterly direction towards Telfer Mine along the Ripon Hills Road for 162km to the junction of Ripon Hills/Woodie Woodie and Telfer Mine roads. At this junction proceed south along the Woodie Woodie Road for 8.9km to the signposted track to Carawine Gorge. This access track leads in a south-westerly direction for 22.5km to the gorge and dispersed bush camping beside the Oakover River. Best suited for self-sufficient campers. Bring drinking water and firewood.

GPS S:21 28.952 E:121 01.672

MR: Map 43 F4

Running Waters

Located to the east of the Skull Springs Road. From the Carawine Gorge access track proceed in a southerly direction along Woodie Woodie Road for 28km, then turn west onto the signposted Skull Springs Road. Follow this road in a westerly direction for 12km to the track to the east which leads a short distance to the bush camping area among paperbarks beside the Davis River. Self-sufficient campers. Bring drinking water and firewood.

GPS S:21 41.122 E:121 07.558

MR: Map 43 F4

FURTHER Information

Land holders - Mills family

Tel: 08 9176 5900

NB: As this is private property it is a courtesy to phone ahead and let the land holders know that you will be visiting their land. As well, the land holders could be working and/or mustering in the region. Please respect the landholders wishes and do not bring dogs or firearms onto their property. Take out all rubbish.

117 Dampier

Dampier for the visitor boasts Aboriginal rock engravings on Burrup Peninsula, views of the harbour from William Dampier Lookout and great swimming and picnicking at either Dampier Beach or Hearson's Cove. Dampier is situated on King Bay, 20km north-west of Karratha.

Dampier Transit Caravan Park

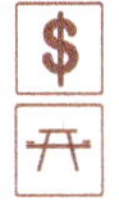         

Signposted access on The Esplanade in Dampier. Camp kitchen and laundry. Gas/fuel stove only.

MR: Map 42 I3

FURTHER Information

Dampier Transit Caravan Park

Tel: 08 9183 1109

Camping fees: Unpowered tent sites from $18.00 per site/night for 2 people. Powered tent sites from $22.00 per site/night for 2 people. Unpowered van sites from $22.00 per site/night for 2 people. Powered van sites from $28.00 per site/night for 2 people.

Maximum stay: 3 nights.

118 Dampier Archipelago

Comprising of 42 islands, the Dampier Archipelago lies in a 45km radius around Dampier. The islands within the archipelago support a diverse range of native plants and animals including numerous turtle species, snakes and reptiles, bottlenosed dolphins, humpback whales and Dugong. Visitors can view Aboriginal carvings, bird watch, go boating and sea kayaking, diving, fishing, swimming and bushwalking. Access to the islands is via boat only, with public boat ramps at Dampier and Karratha. If you don't have a boat contact the Karratha Tourist Bureau for details on local charter boat companies. For further details on camping areas and restrictions contact DEC Karratha.

Dampier Archipelago
Beach camping

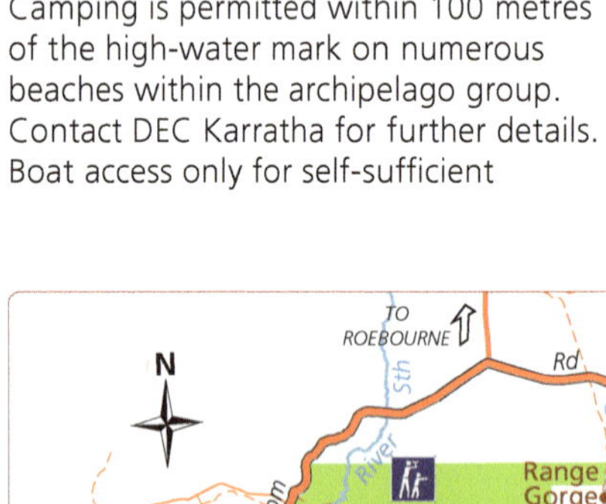

Camping is permitted within 100 metres of the high-water mark on numerous beaches within the archipelago group. Contact DEC Karratha for further details. Boat access only for self-sufficient campers. Bring drinking water. Gas/fuel stove only.

MR: Map 42 I3

FURTHER Information

DEC Pilbara Regional Office, Karratha

Tel: 08 9143 1488

Karratha Tourist Bureau

Tel: 08 9144 4600

Maximum stay: 5 nights.

THE PILBARA

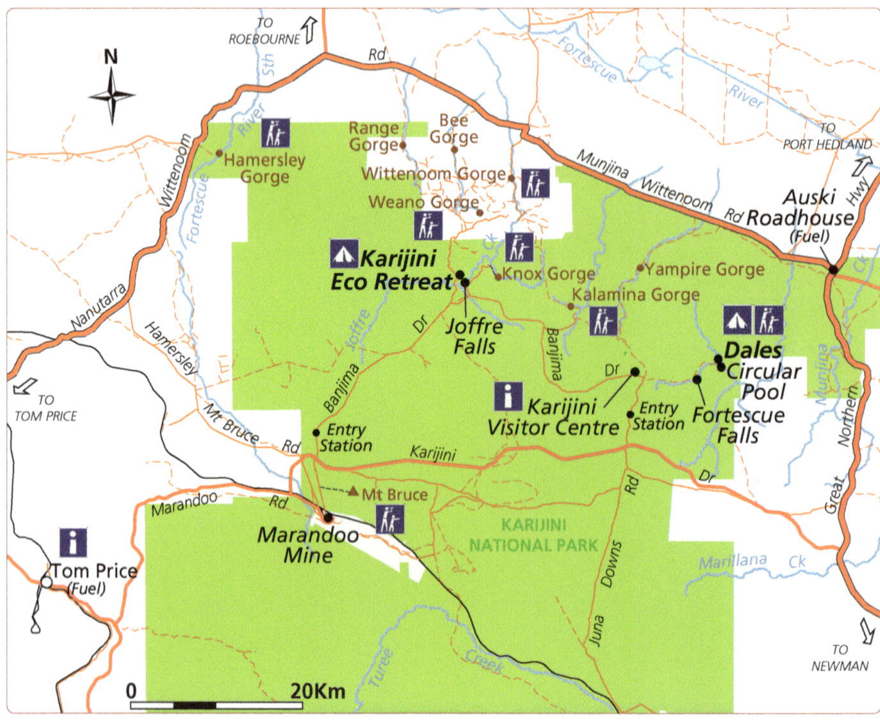

119 Karijini National Park

Straddling the majestic iron red Hamersley Range to the east of Tom Price, the park protects some of the country's oldest landscapes and is well known for its stunning gorges, prominent mountain peaks and serene watercourses cutting through canyons set deep in the ranges. Marvel at the spectacular views from one of the park's many lookouts, pull on your walking boots and take a hike along one of the many walking trails to some of the park's natural features or take a leisurely stroll through beautiful gorges, some of which boast permanent fresh water pools ideal for a refreshing dip. More sedate activities include bird watching or photography. Access to the park is along Karijini Drive which is signposted off the Great Northern Highway, 158km north-west of Newman and 50km east of Tom Price. There are two signposted entry stations into the park along Karijini Drive.

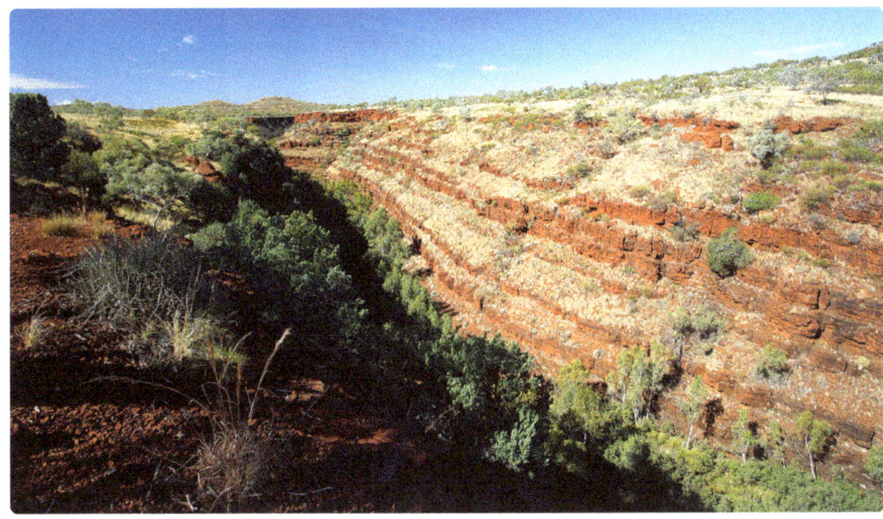

Karijini National Park

THE PILBARA

Dales Campground

From Karijini Drive take the eastern access road into the park (this is 30km west of the Great Northern Highway), and follow this north for 8.4km to the signposted access road to the east. This road leads east for 9km to the camping area entrance road. Dales is a large camping area with four separate campgrounds with total of 77 individually numbered campsites. Swimming is possible at the nearby Fortescue Falls, there are also a number of walking tracks nearby. Hot showers are located at the park's visitor centre. Bring drinking water. Gas/fuel stove only.

GPS S:22 28.352 E:118 33.049

MR: Map 43 B6

FURTHER Information

Karijini National Park Visitor Centre

Tel: 08 9189 8157

Park entrance fee: $11.00 per vehicle.

Camping fees: From $7.00 per adult/night and $2.00 per child (up to 16)/night. Fees payable at self-registration station.

Dales Campground

Karijini Eco Retreat

From Karijini Drive take the western access road into the park and follow this north for 25.8km to the signposted Banjima Drive on the right. At this junction proceed north towards Weano Gorge for 2.9km to the signposted access to the retreat. Follow this road in a westerly direction for 300m. Kiosk, restaurant/bar, camp kitchen. Bring drinking water. Gas/fuel stove only. Eco Tent accommodation is available for those without their own camping gear.

GPS S:22 23.197 E:118 15.498

MR: Map 43 A6

FURTHER Information

Karijini Eco Retreat

Tel: 08 9425 5591 or on-site number 08 9189 8013. Bookings required.

Web: www.karijiniecoretreat.com.au

Park entrance fee: $11.00 per vehicle.

Camping fees: From $30.00 per site/night for 2 adults.

THE PILBARA

120 Karlamilyi (Rudall River) National Park

Formerly known as Rudall River National Park, this vast and isolated park features an ancient landscape of stunning natural beauty. Karlamilyi has a history of Aboriginal occupation (with numerous communities still in the region), along with European exploration. In addition to the headwaters of the Rudall River, the park boasts numerous waterholes, pools and soaks. Bush camping is possible throughout the park for well equipped, self-sufficient campers. Please be aware that access to the eastern section of the park is via permit only. Contact the DEC Karratha office for access information and further details.

Access to the western section of the park is from the south via the Talawana Track. From Newman travel north along the Marble Bar Road for 56.4km to the signposted Talawana Track, then travel east for 259km to the signposted Rudall River access track. This route passes through Aboriginal reserve. A courtesy call to the Jigalong Information Centre is advised – **Tel:** 08 9175 7020.

Access from the north is from Marble Bar via Telfer Mine. From Marble Bar travel east along the Ripon Hills Road for 153km to the signposted Telfer Road. Then travel in a south-east direction for 129km, passing the Telfer Mine and then continue in a southerly direction for another 94km to the signposted access track to Desert Queen Baths.

Carry adequate supplies of drinking water, food and fuel for your stay. Due to the park's remote location visitors are advised to travel in the company of at least one other vehicle. It is also advisable when travelling to this area that you leave your travel intentions with a family member and/or friend and carry reliable long distance communication equipment such as a satellite phone or a high frequency (HF) radio.

TO MARBLE BAR
Telfer Mine Rd
Telfer Mining Centre
Great Sandy Desert
N
Lake Dora
Punmu Aboriginal Community
Coolbro Creek
Yandagooge Ck
Desert Queen Baths
Watrara Ck
Tjingkulatjatjarra Pool
Kalkan Kalkan Soak
Rooney Ck
Rudall River
KARLAMILYI (formerly RUDALL RIVER) NATIONAL PARK
Lake Blanche
Butler Ck
Cotton Creek
Mt Eva
Gibson Desert
White Gum Bore
Talawana Tk
Parnngurr Aboriginal Community
TO GREAT NORTHERN HIGHWAY
Little Sandy Desert
0 40Km

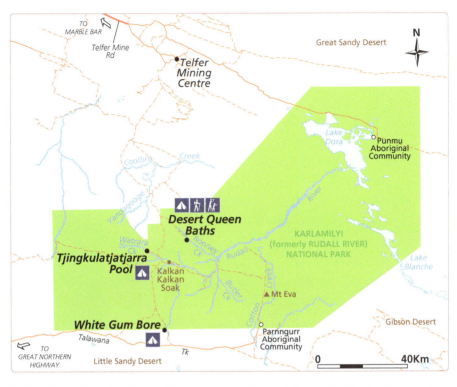

White Gum Bore bush camping

The access track to White Gum Bore is located 9km north of the Talawana Track. White Gum Bore is 100m east of the main park track. Water from hand pump bore which is advisable to boil or treat first. Bring drinking water. Gas/fuel stove only.

GPS S:22 50.250 E:122 09.252
MR: Map 44 H6

Desert Queen Baths bush camping

      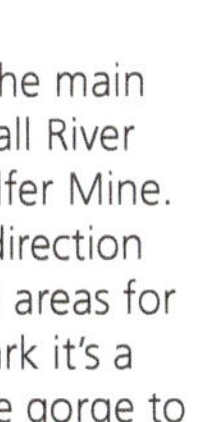

Access track is signposted off the main park track, 23km north of Rudall River crossing and 94km south of Telfer Mine. Then drive in a south-easterly direction for 18.2km to the car park and areas for bush camping. From the car park it's a 30-40 minute walk through the gorge to the main Desert Queen Baths pool. Bring drinking water. Gas/fuel stove only.

GPS S:22 27.847 E:122 15.700
MR: Map 44 I6

Tjingkulatjatjarra Pool bush camping

Access to this delightful spot is off the main park track, 38.7km north of White Gum Bore access track and 500m north of Rudall River crossing, and 21km south of Desert Queen Baths access track. Then drive in a westerly direction for 7.2km to bush camping area on the southern side of the river. Bring drinking water. Gas/fuel stove only.

GPS S:22 30.499 E:122 04.787
MR: Map 44 H6

FURTHER Information

DEC Pilbara Regional Office, Karratha
Tel: 08 9143 1488

Tjingkulatjatjarra Pool bush camping

121 Kennedy Range National Park

The impressive ramparts of the Kennedy Range loom large above the surrounding landscape, dominating the vista. Ancient sea fossils including fossilised sea shells, aboriginal rock engravings, caves and waterfalls are some of the features of this remote park. During August and September wildflowers are on display. A walk to the top of the range provides expansive vistas over the park and surrounding farmlands, providing photographers with a plethora of scenes to shoot. The park is located 60km north of Gascoyne Junction with access signposted along Ullawarra Road.

Temple Gorge camping area

From Gascoyne Junction proceed north along the signposted Ullawarra Road for 49km to the signposted access to the park. This track leads in a westerly direction for 12.9km to the open camping area at the base of the range with little shade but some protection is offered by the low scrub. Ground fires are not permitted so if you plan a campfire bring own above ground fire bin/bucket and firewood. There is one communal fireplace. Bring drinking water. Gas/fuel stove preferred.

GPS S:24 39.753 E:115 10.576

MR: Map 36 H4

FURTHER Information

DEC Carnarvon Local Office

Tel: 08 9941 3754

Road Conditions – Shire of Upper Gascoyne

Tel: 08 9943 0988

Web: www.uppergascoyne.wa.gov.au

Camping fees: From $7.00 per adult/night and $2.00 per child (up to 16)/night. Fees payable at self-registration or to on-site Campground Host.

122 Marble Bar

Marble Bar is listed in the Guinness Book of Records as being the hottest town in Australia, with recorded temperatures of 38 degrees celsius baking the remote town for 161 consecutive days. To the west of town is the Coongan River and the colourful jasper stone bar, originally mistaken for marble by early settlers from which the town is named. Marble Bar is located 153km south-east of Port Hedland.

Marble Bar Caravan Park

Located on Contest Street in Marble Bar. Signposted access along the main road in town. Located close to town with a short walk to all facilities. Grassed area. Gas/fuel stove only.

GPS S:21 10.474 E:119 44.659

MR: Map 43 D4

Marble Bar Caravan Park

FURTHER Information

Marble Bar Caravan Park

Tel: 08 9176 1569

Camping fees: Unpowered from $20.00 per site/night for 2 people. Powered from $35.00 per site/night for 2 people.

123 Millstream—Chichester National Park

With a rich and diverse history of both Aboriginal and European occupation, the area was formally a pastoral lease prior to becoming a national park in 1982. Take the scenic drive around the park, enjoy one of the many walks, swim in a permanent waterhole, canoe along the Fortescue River and check out the park's visitor centre which is housed in the former Millstream homestead which dates to the 1920s. Access to the southern section of the park is along the Millstream-Yarraloola Road, 15km west of the Roebourne-Wittenoom Road. Snake Creek camping area in the north of the park is signposted off the Roebourne-Wittenoom Road, 87km south of Roebourne. Alternative access to the park is via Pilbara Iron Access Road (first 90km sealed). A permit is required to traverse this road.

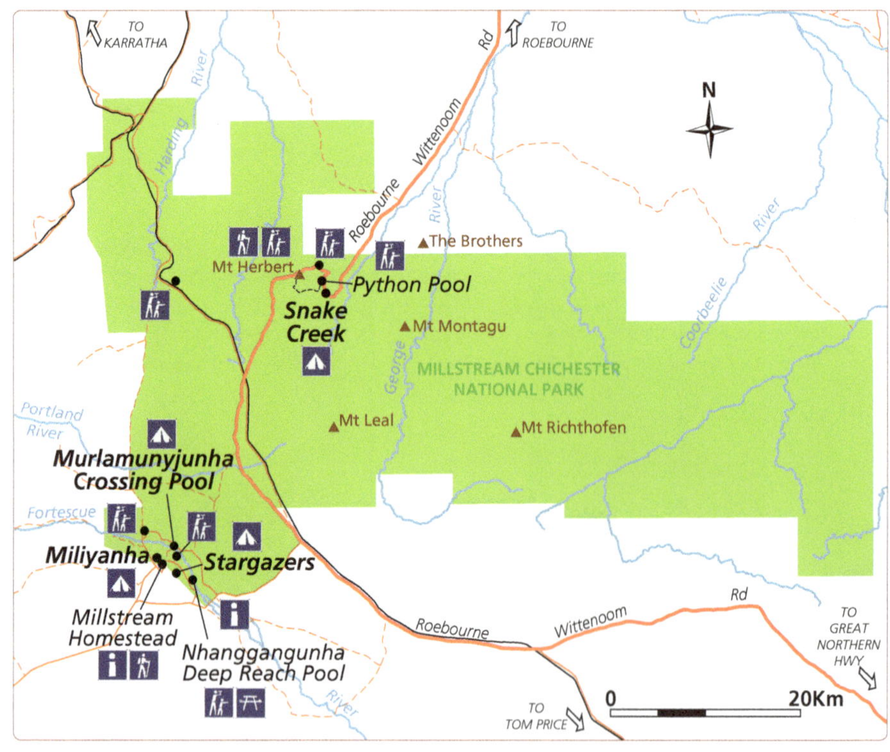

THE PILBARA

Old Millstream Homestead

Murlamunyjunha Crossing Pool camping area

Signposted access 7.9km along Snappy Gum Drive on the eastern side of the Fortescue River. Snappy Gum Drive is signposted off the Millstream-Yarraloola Road, 11.5km west of the Roebourne-Wittenoom Road. The Millstream-Yarraloola Road is signposted off the Roebourne-Wittenoom Road 98km south of the North West Coastal Highway. Bring drinking water. Gas/fuel stove only.

GPS S:21 34.631 E:117 05.224

MR: Map 58 G8

Miliyanha Campground

Camping area located opposite the visitor centre. Access is signposted 7.3km along Kanjenjie Millstream Road, which is signposted off the Millstream-Yarraloola Road, 3.2km west of Snappy Gum Drive. Camp kitchen. Boil or treat water or bring drinking water with you. Gas/fuel stove only.

GPS S:21 35.359 E:117 04.333

MR: Map 58 G8

Stargrazers Campground (seasonally opened)

Signposted access along the Kanjenjie Millstream Road north of the access track to Deep Reach Pool. Kanjenjie Millstream Road is signposted off the Millstream-Yarraloola Road, 3.2km west of Snappy Gum Drive. Bring drinking water. Gas/fuel stove only.

MR: Map 58 H8

Snake Creek camping area

Signposted access off the Roebourne-Wittenoom Road, 40km north of the Millstream-Yarraloola Road and 58km south of the North West Coastal Highway. Access track is 1.5km east of the Python Pool access track. Small open area with room for 4 to 5 campsites. Bring drinking water and firewood. Gas/fuel stove preferred.

GPS S:21 20.624 E:117 14.623

MR: Map 58 H6

FURTHER *Information*

Millstream-Chichester National Park

Tel: 08 9184 5144

Park entrance fee: $11.00 per vehicle.

Camping fees: From $7.00 per adult/night and $2.00 per child (up to 16)/night. Fees payable to patrolling ranger.

Pilbara Iron Access Road Permit: Karratha Visitor Centre

Tel: 08 9144 4600

Web: www.pilbaracoast.com

Murlamunyjunha Crossing Pool camping area

124 Rest Areas of the Pilbara Region

Main Roads WA have a number of designated 24 hour roadside rest areas located along main routes within the region. These rest areas are for an overnight stop only whilst travelling to your destination. Please remember that these designations may change from year to year, so please take note of any signage regarding overnight stays.

Lyndon River Rest Area

Signposted access along the North West Coastal Highway 49km north-east of Minilya and 109km south of Barradale RA. Bring drinking water and firewood.

GPS S:23 29.068 E:114 16.626

MR: Map 35 F2

Barradale Rest Area

Signposted access along the North West Coastal Highway 109km north of Lyndon River RA and 72km south of Nanutarra. Beside the Yannarie River. Bring drinking water and firewood.

GPS S:22 51.806 E:114 57.266

MR: Map 42 G8

Robe River Rest Area

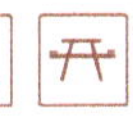
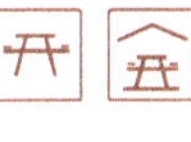

Signposted access along the North West Coastal Highway 120km north of Nanutarra and 45km south of Fortescue. Bring drinking water and firewood.

GPS S:21 36.899 E:115 55.355

MR: Map 42 H5

West Peawah Rest Area

Signposted access along the North West Coastal Highway 26km north of Whim Creek and 93km south of Port Hedland. Bring drinking water and firewood.

MR: Map 42 L3

Stanley Rest Area

Signposted access along the North West Coastal Highway 108km north of Sandfire Roadhouse and 180km south of the Great Northern Highway. Bring drinking water and firewood.

GPS S:19 02.570 E:121 39.764

MR: Map 47 B7

Home Creek Rest Area

Signposted access along the Nanutarra-Munjina Road, 59km east of the North West Coastal Highway and 211km west of Paraburdoo. Located on western side of the bridge over Home Creek. Well shaded area. Bring drinking water and firewood.

GPS S:22 27.806 E:116 02.133

MR: Map 42 I7

Beasley River Rest Area

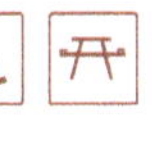

Signposted access along the Nanutarra-Munjina Road, 117km east of Home Creek RA and 94km west of Paraburdoo. Located on northern side of the road, shaded area well off the road. Grey water dumpsite. Bring drinking water and firewood.

GPS S:22 56.956 E:116 58.673
MR: Map 42 K8

Mt Robinson Rest Area

    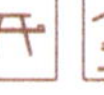   

Signposted access along the Great Northern Highway 106km north-west of Newman and 51km south-east of the junction of Karijini Road and the highway. Then drive in 740m to the rest area. Emergency phone located here. Bring drinking water and firewood.

GPS S:23 02.555 E:118 50.965
MR: Map 43 B7

Mt Robinson Rest Area

FURTHER Information

Main Roads Western Australia
Tel: 138 138
Web: www.mainroads.wa.gov.au

125 Roebourne Region

Roebourne is the oldest town in the Pilbara and has a history of gold and copper mining and grazing. The town still boasts a number of historic buildings including the Union Bank (1888), a church built in 1894 and the former gaol. Roebourne is located on the North West Coastal Highway, 33km east of Karratha.

Cleaverville Nature Based campsite

Signposted access off the North West Coastal Highway, 14km west of Roebourne. Then travel 13km north to the camping area. Campers must have their own portable chemical toilet. On-site sullage disposal point. Bring drinking water and firewood.

MR: Map 57 F2

Gnoorea Pt (40 Mile) Nature Based campsite

Signposted access off the North West Coastal Highway, 83km south-west of Roebourne. Then travel 13km north to the camping area situated on the coast. Campers must have their own portable chemical toilet. On-site sullage disposal point. Bring drinking water and firewood.

MR: Map 57 C4

FURTHER Information

Shire of Roebourne
Tel: 08 9186 8555
Web: www.roebourne.wa.gov.au/camping
Roebourne Tourist Bureau
Tel: 08 9182 1060
Web: www.pilbaracoast.com
Karratha Tourist Bureau
Tel: 08 9144 4600
Web: www.pilbaracoast.com
Camping season: 1 May to 20 September
Camping fees: From $7.00 per site/night. Fees collected by on-site caretakers.
Maximum stay: 3 months.
Off season: 1 October to 30 April
Camping fees: Fees do not apply during the off season.
Maximum stay: 3 nights per 28 days.

The Kimberley and North-West Coast

THE KIMBERLEY AND NORTH-WEST COAST covers a myriad of camping opportunities ranging from serene campsites along the coastline to the popular sites within Purnululu National Park through to the camping areas situated on large and remote cattle stations. This broad scope of destinations provides a swag of camping places in which to enjoy the Kimberley and West-Coast's unique and ancient landscapes.

North of Broome is the Dampier Peninsula where a range of bush campsites are spread along the coast. These campsites along Manari Road provide an escape from the hustle and bustle of the Kimberley's most popular tourist town, which is only a short drive away. Further north along the peninsula a number of Aboriginal communities have camping areas and offer unique cultural experiences and activities like fishing and mud crabbing.

Numerous cattle stations along the Gibb River Road offer a range of camping, while the picturesque King Leopold Ranges Conservation Park has a large camping area which is only a short drive south of the walking track to the popular Bell Gorge Falls. A detour north along the Kalumburu Road sees camping opportunities at Drysdale River Station and for the more serious 4WD traveller there's the remote Mitchell Plateau and Kalumburu Aboriginal Community.

Windjana Gorge, south of the Gibb River Road, has two large camping areas a short walk from the gorge where freshwater crocodiles can often be seen sunning themselves. Bordering the Western Australia/Northern Territory border are the unique beehive formations of Purnululu National Park while in the south-western corner is the remote Wolfe Creek Meteorite Crater.

The northern dry season from April through to October is the best time to visit this region.

BEST Campsites!

 **Punamii-unpuu (Mitchell Falls) camping area**
Ngauwudu-Mitchell Plateau

 **Walardi campsite**
Purnululu (Bungle Bungle) National Park

 **Miner's Pool camping area**
Drysdale River Station

 **Mornington Wilderness Camp**
Gibb River Road

 **Honeymoon Beach camping area**
Kalumburu

N
0
200km
INDIAN
OCEAN
Wotjalum
Bardi (One Arm Point)
127
Lombadina
127
Beagle Bay
Beagle Bay
Derby
131
Mowanjum
141
Highway
126
Roebuck
Roadhouse
Willare Bridge
Roadhouse
Broome
Loom
Great
Northern
Bidyadanga Community
126 Broome Area
127 Dampier Peninsula
128 Drysdale River National Park
129 Drysdale River Station
130 Fitzroy Crossing
131 Gibb River Road
132 Halls Creek
133 Kalumburu
134 King Leopold Ranges Conservation Park
135 Kununurra
136 Mitchell River National Park
137 Ngauwudu - Mitchell Plateau
138 Ord River
139 Parry Lagoons Nature Reserve

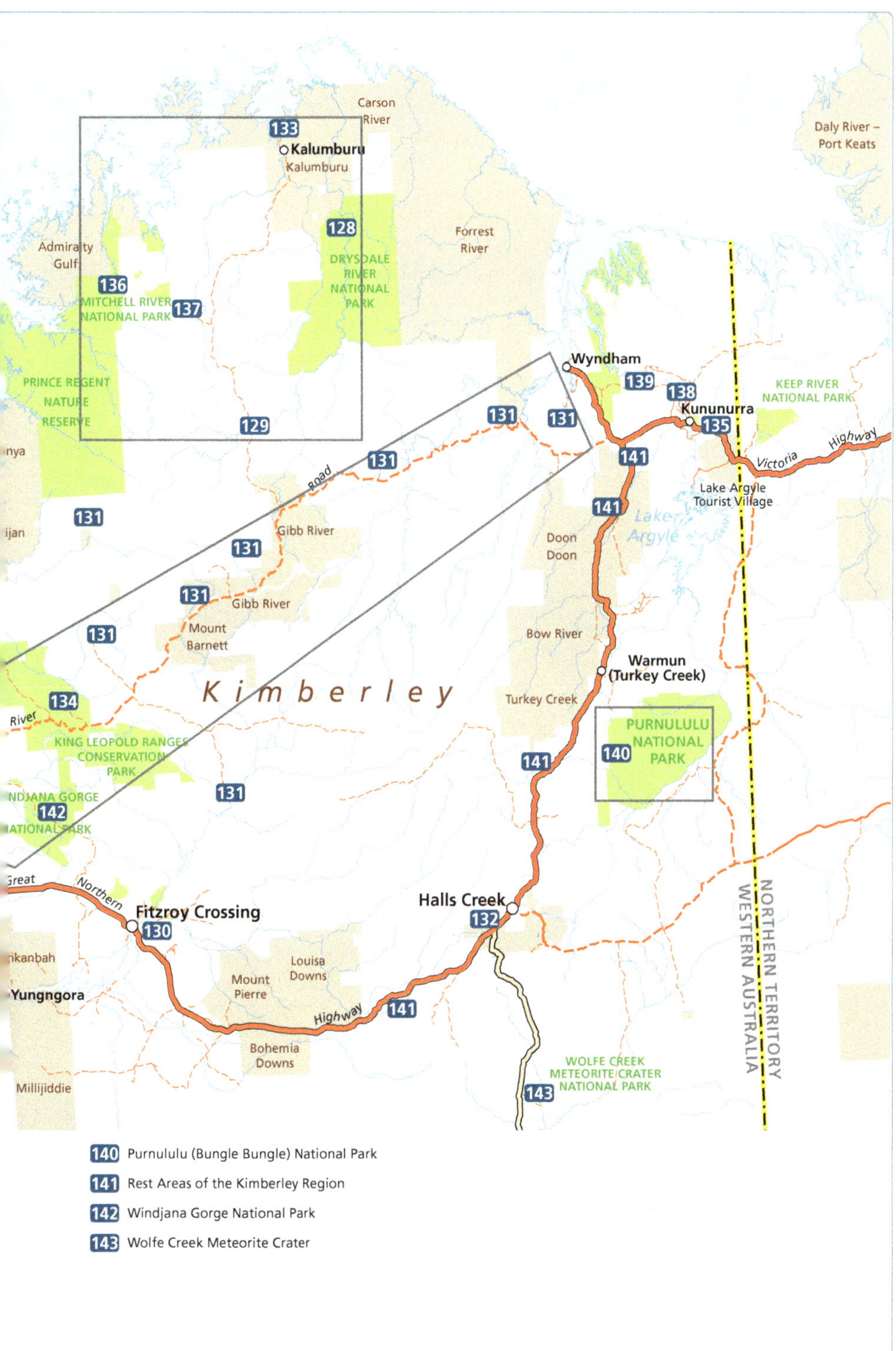

140 Purnululu (Bungle Bungle) National Park

141 Rest Areas of the Kimberley Region

142 Windjana Gorge National Park

143 Wolfe Creek Meteorite Crater

126 Broome Area

The popular tourist town of Broome is the southern gateway to the Kimberley. During June and July the region's population swells with visitors from both Australia wide and around the world as they come to enjoy the southern winter in the tropics. The town has a rich history dating back to its busy pearling years. Broome and its surrounds showcases beautiful beaches, spectacular coastline, top rate fishing, mud crabbing and boating opportunities. Located to the north of Broome along Manari Road, which is signposted off the Broome-Cape Leveque Road 15km north of Broome Road, are a number of council reserves where camping is permitted. Camping is for self-sufficient campers only as these sites have no facilities. It is recommended that all campers carry their own portable chemical toilet. Unsealed access roads can be rough and corrugated at times although they are generally suitable for conventional vehicles while if you are towing a caravan a 4WD tow vehicle is recommended. It is best to check road conditions prior to travelling if towing.

Cable Beach, Broome

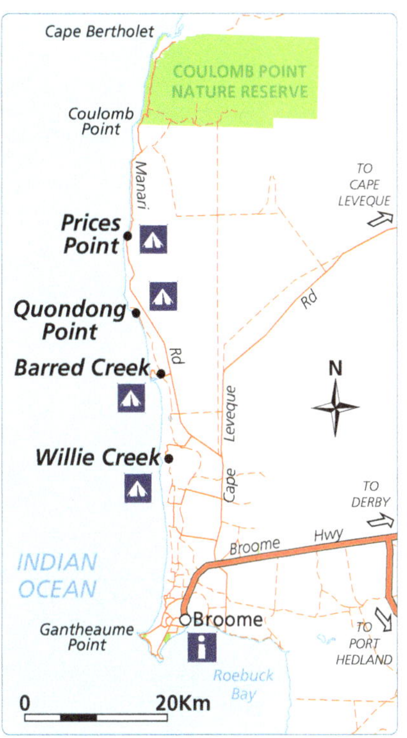

Willie Creek camping area

    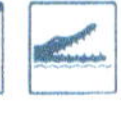  

Located 7.1km along Willie Creek Road, which is signposted 5.1km along Manari Road. Conventional vehicle access with caution. Bush camping area close to the natural boat launch. Bring drinking water. Gas/fuel stove preferred.

GPS S:17 45.550 E:122 12.649
MR: Map 47 C4

Barred Creek camping area

Access track is signposted 9.2km north of Willie Creek Road, then drive 1.2km west to a T-intersection where the road on the left leads 300m to dispersed bush camping along the banks of Barred Creek. Bring drinking water, firewood and insect repellant. Gas/fuel stove preferred.

GPS S:17 39.654 E:122 12.062
MR: Map 47 C4

Quondong Point camping area

Access track is 7.6km north of Barred Creek CA access track. Then drive west for 1.6km to the start of the camping area which has dispersed bush camping along the coast. Bring drinking water and firewood. Gas/fuel stove preferred.

GPS S:17 35.013 E:122 10.229
MR: Map 47 C4

Prices Point camping area

Access track is 13.5km north of Quondong Point CA access track. Then drive in 200m to the camping area. There's dispersed bush camping here with some sites overlooking the ocean whilst others are set back from the coast, sheltered among vegetation. 4WD vehicles are recommended as access tracks are sandy. Bring drinking water and firewood. Gas/fuel stove preferred.

GPS S:17 29.264 E:122 08.657

MR: Map 47 C4

Prices Point camping area

FURTHER Information

Broome Visitor Centre

Tel: 08 9192 2222

Web: www.broomevisitorcentre.com.au

Maximum stay: 3 nights.

NB: Fire danger periods apply. Please check with local authorities for fire ratings prior to lighting any fire.

THE KIMBERLEY AND NORTH-WEST COAST

127 Dampier Peninsula

Visit a number of the peninsula's Aboriginal communities and join in activities such as mud crab tours, fishing tours, shell collecting as well as guided walks and bush tucker walks. Beautiful white sandy beaches and spectacular coastal scenery are the norm here while the beautiful pearl shell alter in the Sacred Heart Church at Beagle Bay Community is well worth the detour. There are restricted access areas along the peninsula, so please respect the owners' wishes and keep to main access roads. The Dampier Peninsula is located to the north of Broome with the main access road to the peninsula the Broome-Cape Leveque Road. This unsealed road can be rough at times and is generally slow going with travel times of about 3.5 hours from Broome to Cape Leveque. Contact Broome Visitor Centre for road conditions prior to travel, tel: 08 9192 2222.

Banana Well Getaway

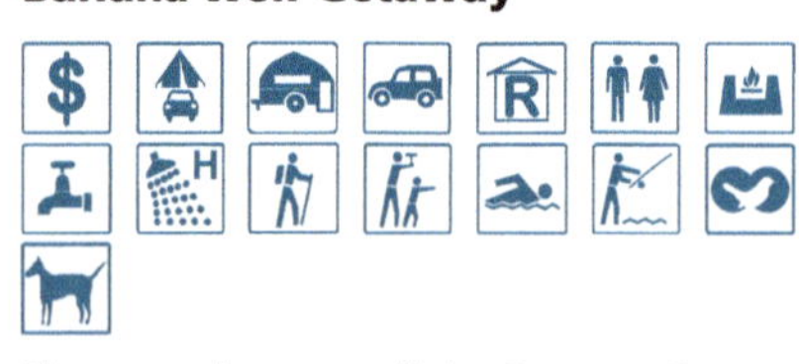

Signposted access off the Broome-Cape Leveque Road, 125km north of Broome via the Loongabid turn-off. Then drive 14km west, following all signage. Camp kitchen, laundry, tours. Other accommodation options are also available.

MR: Map 47 D2

FURTHER Information

Broome Visitor Centre

Tel: 08 9192 2222. Bookings essential.

Camping fees: Unpowered sites from $15.00 per person/night. Powered sites from $35.00 per site/night for up to 2 people.

Pets: By arrangement.

Gnylmarung Retreat camping area

Signposted access off the Broome-Cape Leveque Road, 130km north of Broome. Then drive 25km west to the retreat following all signage. Communal kitchen, laundry, tours, boat hire, firewood supplied. Other accommodation options available.

MR: Map 47 D2

FURTHER Information

Broome Visitor Centre
Tel: 08 9192 2222. Bookings essential.

Gnylmarung Aboriginal Corporation
Tel: 0429 411 241
Web: www.gnylmarung.org.au
Camping fees: Unpowered sites from $40.00 per site/night up to 2 people.

Natures Hideaway camping area

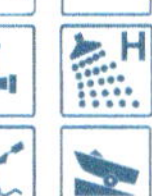

Signposted access off the Broome-Cape Leveque Road, 145km north of Broome and 22km north of the Beagle Bay access road. Then 32km west to camping area. Shop, laundry. Bring firewood. Other accommodation options available.

GPS S:16 46.431 E:122 34.572

MR: Map 47 D2

Natures Hideaway camping area

FURTHER Information

Natures Hideaway, Middle Lagoon
Tel: 08 9192 4002. Bookings essential.
Web: www.middlelagoon.com.au
Camping fees: Unpowered sites from $15.00 per person/night. Powered sites from $20.00 per person/night.

Dampier Peninsula

Goombaragin Eco Retreat

Signposted access off the Broome-Cape Leveque Road, 145km north of Broome via the Middle Lagoon Road. Then drive west for 25km following all signage. Shop/kiosk, communal kitchen, laundry. Bring firewood for wooden barbecue. Ground fires are not permitted. Other accommodation options available.

MR: Map 47 D2

FURTHER information

Goombaragin Eco Retreat
Tel: 0429 505 347. Bookings essential.
Web: www.goombaragin.com.au
Broome Visitor Centre
Tel: 08 9192 2222. Bookings can also be made through the visitor centre.
Camping fees: Unpowered sites from $30.00 per site/night for 2 people.

La Djardarr Bay Community camping area

Signposted access off the Broome-Cape Leveque Road, 149km north of Broome and 4km north of Middle Lagoon access road. Then 42km east to camping area. Some firewood supplied.

GPS S:16 52.953 E:123 09.090
MR: Map 47 E2

La Djardarr Bay Community camping area

FURTHER information

La Djardarr Bay Community
Tel: 08 9192 4891. Bookings recommended.
Camping fees: From $12.00 per person/night. Fees payable to caretaker.

Kooljaman at Cape Leveque

Located at the end of the Broome-Cape Leveque Road, 208km north of Broome. Facilities here include a store, restaurant, laundry while scenic flights and boat charters are available. Firewood supplied. Other accommodation options are available.

GPS S:16 23.767 E:122 55.649
MR: Map 47 E1

FURTHER information

Kooljaman at Cape Leveque
Tel: 08 9192 4970. Advance bookings essential.
Web: www.kooljaman.com.au
Camping fees: Unpowered sites from $18.00 per adult/night and $8.00 per child (6-16 years)/night. Power: add $5.00 per outlet/night.
Minimum stay: 2 nights.

Kooljaman at Cape Leveque

128 Drysdale River National Park

Featured within the park's 448,000 hectares are rugged cliffs and gorges, creeks and rivers and the Morgan and Solea Falls. Due to the park's remoteness and isolation there are remote bushwalking and wildlife watching opportunities. Located 100km south of Kalumburu, access can be had from the park's boundary via 4WD vehicle through Carson River Station off the Kalumburu Road. From the boundary access into the park proper is for self-sufficient, experienced walkers only. There are no designated walking trails or facilities and it is recommended that visitors to this park be experienced navigators, carry appropriate topographic maps, and carry an EPIRB. It is recommended that visitors make contact with DEC to check on conditions, ie: wildfires etc, and advise family and friends of their intentions beforehand.

Drysdale River bush camping area

Access through private property, permit required. Dispersed bush camping within the park for self-sufficient, experienced walkers. No marked walking trails in the park. No trace camping applies. Bring drinking water. Gas/fuel stove only.

MR: Map 51 F4

FURTHER Information

DEC Kununurra Regional Office
Tel: 08 9168 4200

Kalumburu Aboriginal Community
Tel: 08 9161 4300
Web: www.kalumburu.org

Department of Indigenous Affairs
Tel: 08 9235 8000
Web: www.dia.wa.gov.au/en/Entry-Permits/EP_Y_PermitForm
Permit: Permit required, a fee may apply.

Carson River Station - Bulldust Yards camping area

Located on Carson River Station at walking point access to Drysdale River National Park. Access permit and camping permit required. This area is extremely remote and isolated and is best suited to self-sufficient campers only. Bring drinking water. Gas/fuel stove preferred.

MR: Map 51 F3

FURTHER Information

Kalumburu Aboriginal Community
Tel: 08 9161 4300
Web: www.kalumburu.org

Department of Indigenous Affairs
Tel: 08 9235 8000
Web: www.dia.wa.gov.au/en/Entry-Permits/EP_Y_PermitForm
Permit: Permit required, a fee may be applicable.

129 Drysdale River Station

Consisting of a million acres, Drysdale River Station dates back to the 1800s and has a colourful and interesting history. This working cattle station is located along the Kalumburu Road, 59km north of the Gibb River Road. Kalumburu Road leaves the Gibb River Road 298km west of Kununurra and 417km north-east of Derby. 4WD vehicle access is recommended, especially if towing a camper trailer or caravan. Conventional vehicles check road conditions first.

Homestead Camp camping area

Signposted access off the Kalumburu Road, 59km north of Gibb River Road. Then 1.2km west to the homestead and camping area. Best suited to 4WD camper trailer and caravans due to varying road conditions along the Gibb River and Kalumburu roads. Store, restaurant, bar, fuel and laundry. Scenic flights over the Mitchell Plateau are also available. Some powered sites available. Limited firewood supplies so it's best to bring your own if planning a campfire.

GPS S:15 42.092 E:126 22.852
MR: Map 51 E6

Miner's Pool camping area

Signposted access off the Kalumburu Road, 2.2km north of the Drysdale River Station homestead access road. Then drive in an easterly direction for 3.2km to the large, well shaded camping area beside the Drysdale River. Best suited to 4WD camper trailer and caravans due to varying road conditions along the Gibb River and Kalumburu roads. Bring drinking water or boil from river. Limited firewood supplied.

GPS S:15 40.787 E:126 24.190
MR: Map 51 E6

FURTHER information

Drysdale River Station
Tel: 08 9161 4326
Web: www.drysdaleriver.com.au
Camping fees: Homestead Camp: From $15.00 per adult/night and $5.00 per child (5 to 15 years)/night. Miner's Pool: From $10.00 per adult/night. Check in and register and pay fees at Homestead shop between 8am to 5pm or at the Homestead bar/ reception between 5pm to 8.30pm, prior to setting up camp.

Miner's Pool camping area

130 Fitzroy Crossing

Fitzroy Crossing is located on the sealed Great Northern Highway, 391km east of Broome, 256km east of Derby and 289km west of Halls Creek. The Fitzroy River flows 1,000km to King Sound before finally emptying into the Indian Ocean.

Tarunda Caravan Park

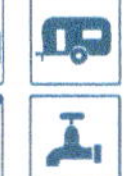

Located on Forrest Road in Fitzroy Crossing and close to all town amenities. Camp kitchen, laundry. Dogs are to be kept under strict control.

MR: Map 49 C3

FURTHER information

Tarunda Caravan Park
Tel: 08 9191 5330
Camping fees: Unpowered sites from $13.00 per person/night. Powered sites from $29.00 per site/night for 2 people.

Fitzroy River Lodge camping area

Signposted access off the Great Northern Highway, 2.3km east of Fitzroy Crossing. Restaurant, bar, camp kitchen, laundry, pool, tennis court. Firewood supplied.

GPS S:18 12.710 E:125 34.884
MR: Map 49 C3

FURTHER information

Fitzroy River Lodge
Tel: 08 9191 5141
Web: www.fitzroyriverlodge.com.au
Camping fees: Unpowered sites from $15.00 per person/night. Powered sites from $35.00 per site/night for up to 2 people.

131 Gibb River Road

The Gibb River Road is one of Australia's most popular 4WD touring road trips. Originally built to transport cattle from the surrounding stations to Derby and Wyndham for export, the road is also now a major tourist route traversed by thousands of travellers each northern dry season. The road itself stretches for 650km from Derby north-east to its junction with the Great Northern Highway, between Kununurra and Wyndham. Along its length you'll find picturesque gorges, remote wilderness areas as well as a number of national park areas. Travel is recommended during the northern dry season from May to November and while not essential, a 4WD vehicle is recommended due to varying road conditions. Travellers must ensure their vehicle is well prepared and mechanically sound. The *Gibb River & Kalumburu Roads Travellers Guide* is published yearly and is an excellent resource. It is available from tourist information centres for a small fee; contact the Derby Visitor Centre, tel: 1800 621 426 or 08 9191 1426 for further details. Bush camping is not pemitted along the Gibb River Road – camp only in designated camping areas. It is worth noting that campsite status may vary from year to year due to changed conditions after the wet season. Please be aware that you may encounter cattle along the road and the possibility of road trains.

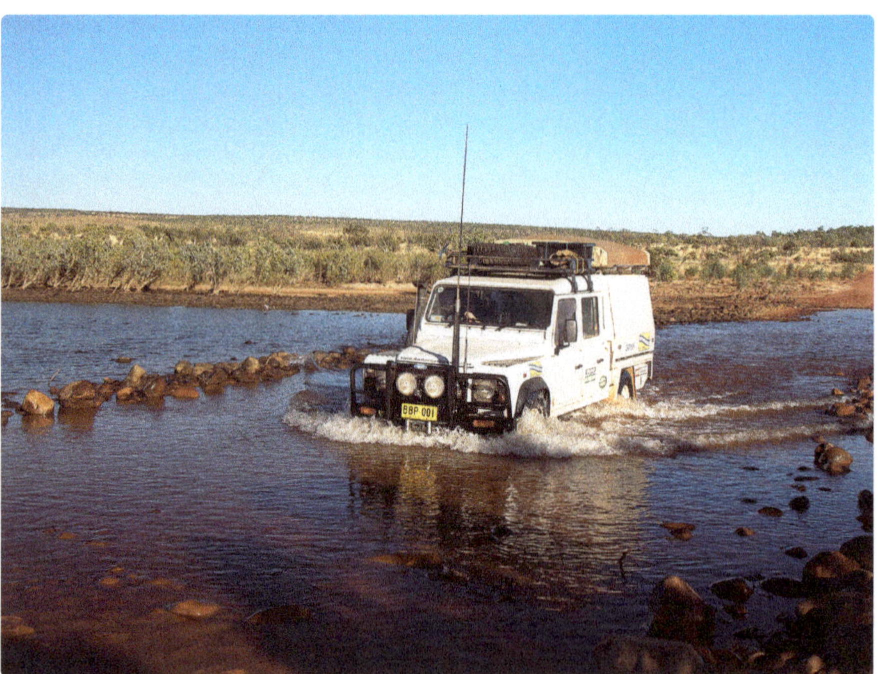

Gibb River Road

Birdwood Downs

Signposted access along the Gibb River Road, 17.6km east of Derby and 109km west of the road to Windjana Gorge. Then 1.2km north to the camping area. Restaurant, tours, horse rides. Bring gas/fuel stove. Other accommodation available.

GPS S:17 20.982 E:123 46.250
MR: Map 48 G4

FURTHER Information

Birdwood Downs
Tel: 08 9191 1275. Bookings essential.
Web: www.birdwooddowns.com.
Camping fees: From $13.00 per person/night.

Mt Hart Homestead Wilderness Lodge

Signposted access along the Gibb River Road, 65.3km east of the road to Windjana Gorge and 38km west of Imintji Store. Then drive in a northerly direction for 50km to the homestead with the camping area located nearby. Shaded campsites beside the Barker River. Restaurant, bar, laundry. Other accommodation options available. Bring firewood.

GPS S:16 49.355 E:124 54.967
MR: Map 48 H2

FURTHER Information

Mt Hart Wilderness Lodge
Tel: 08 9191 4645.
Web: www.mthart.com.au
Camping fees: From $18.00 per adult/night and $9.00 per child/night. Fees payable at the homestead.

Mornington Wilderness Camp

Signposted access along the Gibb River Road, 53.7km south-west of Mt Barnett Roadhouse and 25.5km north-east of Imintji Roadhouse. Then 95km south-east to the shaded camping area. Restaurant, bar, guided tours, canoe hire. Other accommodation options available. Gas/fuel stove only.

GPS S:17 30.799 E:126 06.624
MR: Map 48 K3

FURTHER Information

Mornington Wilderness Camp
Tel: 1800 631 946 or 08 9191 7406. Maximum numbers apply in campground, however bookings are not taken. At the start of the access road is a radio booth for visitors to call through to check on campsite availability.
Web: www.australianwildlife.org
Wildlife Sanctuary Pass: $25.00 per vehicle/per visit.
Camping fees: From $17.50 per adult/night and $8.00 per child/night.

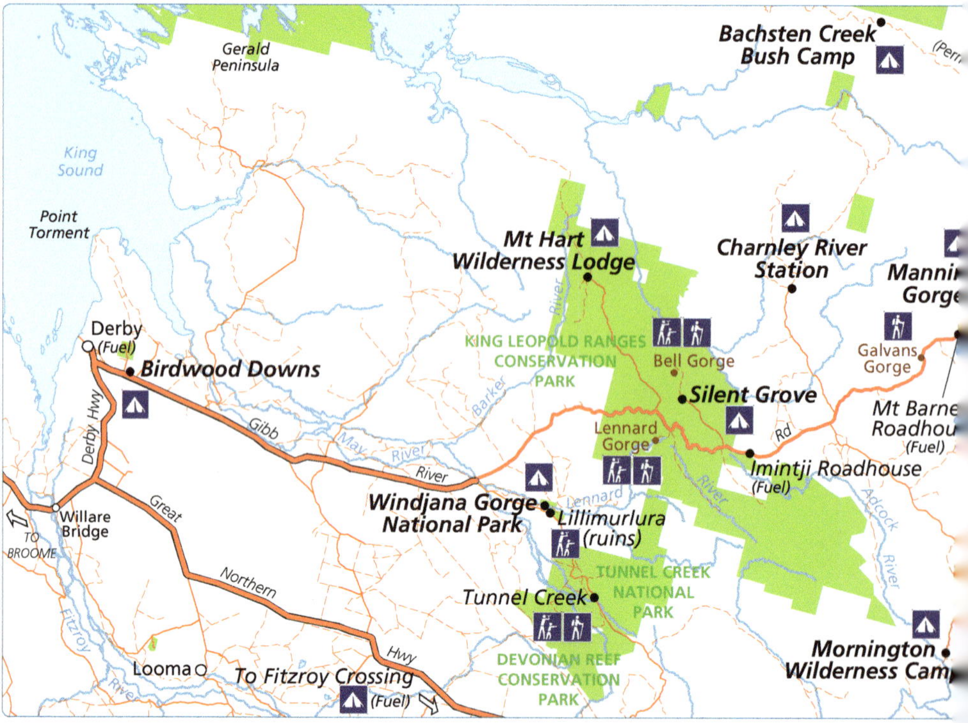

Charnley River Station

Signposted access along the Gibb River Road, 30km north-east of Imintji Roadhouse and 50km south-west of Mt Barnett Roadhouse. Then drive north for 43km to the station and camping area. Self-drive tours. Some firewood available.

GPS S:16 42.987 E:125 27.621
MR: Map 48 I2

FURTHER Information

Charnley River Station
Tel: 08 9191 4646.
Camping fees: From $15.00 per adult/night and $5.00 per child/night.

Manning Gorge camping area

Mt Barnett Roadhouse is located on the Gibb River Road, 108km south-west of the Kulumburu Road junction and 50km east of Charnley River Station access road. The camping area at Manning Gorge is located 7km north of the roadhouse. A permit is required to access the camping area. Bring drinking water and firewood.

GPS S:16 39.442 E:125 55.639
MR: Map 51 E8

FURTHER Information

Mt Barnett Roadhouse
Tel: 08 9191 7007. Permit required to camp. Must be collected from roadhouse prior to proceeding to camping area.
Camping fees: From $16.00 per adult/night. Children under 10 free.

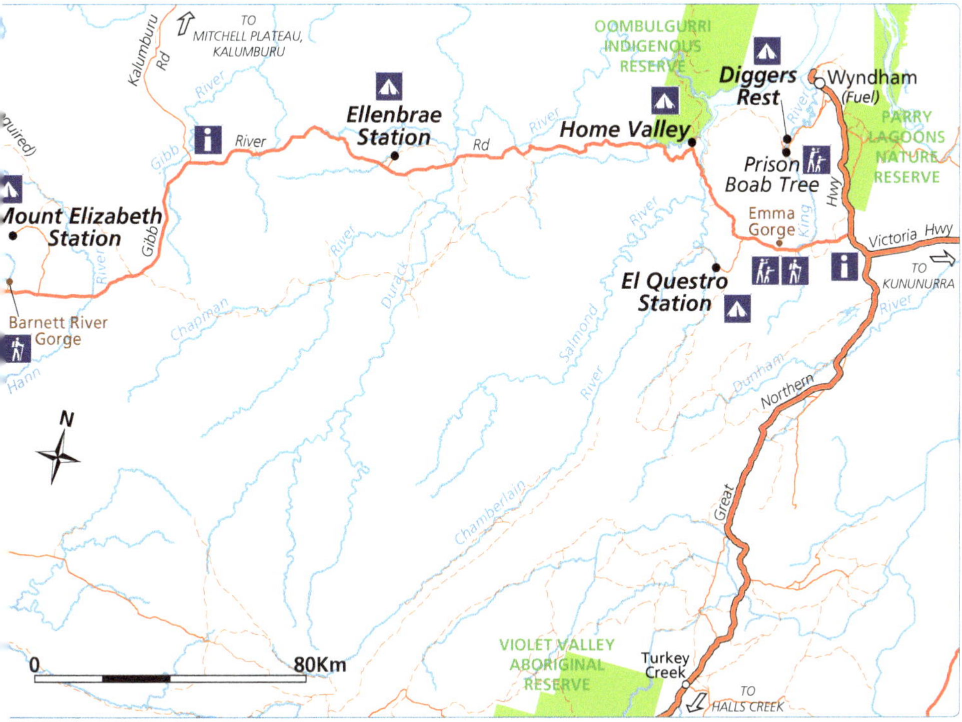

Mount Elizabeth Station

Signposted access along the Gibb River Road, 38km north-east of Mount Barnett Roadhouse and 70km south of the Kalumburu Road junction. Then drive in a north-westerly direction for 30km to the homestead and camping area. Self-drive tours to private gorges. Meals and homestead accommodation available. Some firewood supplied.

GPS S:16 25.102 E:126 06.175

MR: Map 51 E7

FURTHER Information

Mount Elizabeth Station

Tel: 08 9191 4644. Bookings essential for homestead accommodation.

Camping fees: From $15.00 per adult/night and $2.00 per child/night.

Bachsten Creek Bush Camp

Located on the southern boundary of Prince Regent Nature Reserve, 145km north-west of Mt Elizabeth Station. Access via private track. Remote bush camping for 4WD tourers with well-prepared vehicles. Camp kitchen, laundry, tours. Other accommodation options available. Some firewood supplied.

MR: Map 51 D6

FURTHER Information

Bushtrack Safaris

Tel: 08 9191 1547. Bookings essential. Permit required to access Munja Track. Open between June and September.

Web: www.bushtracksafaris.com.au

Camping fees: From $15.00 per adult/night and $2.00 per child/night.

Ellenbrae Station

Signposted access off the Gibb River Road, 69.9km east of the Kalumburu Road junction and 106.5km west of Home Valley Station access road and 115.3km west of the Pentecost River crossing. Then 4.9km north to homestead. Showers have hot water donkey. Unmarked walking trails. Some firewood supplied.

GPS S:15 57.476 E:127 03.730
MR: Map 52 G6

FURTHER Information

Ellenbrae Station
Tel: 08 9161 4325
Camping fees: Contact office for fees.

Home Valley Station

Signposted access off the Gibb River Road, 8.8km west of the Pentecost River crossing and 106.5km east of Ellenbrae Station access road. Pentecost River is 58km west of the Great Northern Highway. Conventional vehicles and caravans check road conditions first. Store, bar, laundry, swimming pool, tours, horse riding. Other accommodation available. Collect firewood near campsite.

GPS S:15 43.376 E:127 49.852
MR: Map 52 H6

FURTHER Information

Home Valley Station
Tel: 08 9161 4322
Web: www.hvstation.com.au
Camping fees: From $16.00 per person/night and $5.00 per child (2-12 years)/night.

El Questro Station - Black Cockatoo camping area

Located at El Questro Station township. Access to El Questro is signposted off the Gibb River Road, 33.7km west of the Great Northern Highway and 24km east of the Pentecost River crossing. Then 16.5km south to El Questro Station township. 4WD vehicle and off-road camper trailers and caravans recommended. Conventional vehicles and caravans check road conditions first. Store, supplies, fuel, restaurant/bar, laundry. Firewood available for collection near campsite.

Township: **GPS** S:16 00.496 E:127 58.810
MR: Map 52 I6

El Questro Station - Riverside camping

Secluded campsites along the Pentecost River. 4WD vehicle and off-road camper trailers and caravans recommended. Conventional vehicles and caravans check road conditions first. Firewood available for collection near campsite.

MR: Map 52 I6

FURTHER Information

El Questro Station
Tel: 1300 863 248 or 08 9161 4318
Web: www.elquestro.com.au
Wilderness Park Permit: From $20.00 per person (child under 15 years free) valid up to 7 days. Permits available on arrival.
Camping fees: From $20.00 per adult/night and child under 12 years free. Riverside camping areas from $25.00 per adult/night and child under 12 years free.
Tours and other accommodation available.

Diggers Rest

Signposted access along King River Road, 33.6km south-west of Wyndham and 3.9km south of the signposted Prison Boab Tree. Then 3.2km north to homestead. King River Road is signposted 5.9km south of Wyndham off the Great Northern Highway. Meals and tours available. Other accommodation options also available. Firewood supplied.

GPS S:15 38.352 E:128 04.791
MR: Map 52 I5

FURTHER Information

Kimberley Pursuits Horse Treks
Tel: 08 9161 1029
Web: www.diggersreststation.com.au
Camping fees: Bush camping beside the King River from $10.00 per person/night. Camping with facilities near the homestead from $15.00 per person/night.

GIBB RIVER ROAD Information

Derby Visitor Centre
Tel: 1800 621 426 or 08 9191 1426. **Web:** www.derbytourism.com.au
Kununurra Visitor Centre
Tel: 08 9168 1177. **Web:** www.kununurratourism.com
Wyndham Tourist Information Centre at Kimberley Motors
Tel: 08 9161 1281
Road conditions: Main Road Western Australia
24 hour Condition Report Service: Tel: 1800 013 314 or WA residents **Tel:** 138 138
Web: www.mainroads.wa.gov.au

132 Halls Creek

Halls Creek was the site of Western Australia's first gold rush in 1885. The ruins of old Halls Creek are 17km to the east of the present day Halls Creek township. Local attractions include China Wall, Caroline Pool, Old Halls Creek, Brockman's Hut, Palm Springs and Sawpit Gorge. Halls Creek is located on the Great Northern Highway, 359km south of Kununurra and 289km east of Fitzroy Crossing.

Halls Creek Caravan Park

Located on Roberta Road in Halls Creek. Swimming pool. Laundry facilities.

MR: Map 50 G3

FURTHER Information

Halls Creek Caravan Park
Tel: 08 9168 6169
Camping fees: Unpowered tent sites from $13.00 per person/night. Powered van sites from $34.00 per site/night for 2 people.
Dog bond: $25.00 refundable.

Old Halls Creek Lodge

Located on Duncan Road, 17km east of Halls Creek. Signposted access off the Great Northern Highway. Laundry. Firewood supplied.

MR: Map 50 G3

FURTHER Information

Old Halls Creek Lodge
Tel: 08 9168 8999
Camping fees: From $10.00 per person/ night.

133 Kalumburu

The Aboriginal community of Kalumburu is located 265km north of the Gibb River Road. Access to Kalumburu is via 4WD vehicle along the Kalumburu Road, which leaves the Gibb River Road 242km west of the Wyndham/Kununurra turn off and 413km east of Derby. Activities include sightseeing to places of historic interest, boating, fishing and mud crabbing. An entry fee of $50.00 per vehicle (up to 5 people) is payable to visit Kalumburu and its surrounds. Contact the Kalumburu Aboriginal Corporation, tel: 08 9161 4300 or visit www.kalumburu.org for further details. Please note that Kalumburu is a dry community and alcohol is not permitted to be consumed whilst on the reserve.

Kalumburu Mission camping area

Located in Kalumburu community. Power available. Café, camp kitchen, laundry. Firewood supplied.

GPS S:14 17.729 E:126 38.605
MR: Map 51 F3

FURTHER Information

Kalumburu Mission
Tel: 08 9161 4333
Camping fees: From $20.00 per person/ night. Power additional $12.00 per site/ night.

McGowan Island Camping Ground

Located 15km north of Kalumburu. Access is signposted 15km north of community. Beach boat launch. Firewood supplied.

GPS S:14 08.752 E:126 38.911
MR: Map 51 F3

FURTHER Information

McGowan Island Camping Ground
Tel: 08 9161 4748
Web: www.mcgowanisland.com.au
Camping fees: From $20.00 per person/ night.

Honeymoon Beach camping area

Signposted access 10.3km north of McGowan Island turn off. Beach campsites or shaded sites near homestead. Power available. Firewood supplied.

GPS S:14 06.286 E:126 40.820
MR: Map 51 F3

FURTHER Information

Honeymoon Beach – French family
Tel: 08 9161 4378.
Camping fees: From $15.00 per person/night.

Honeymoon Beach camping area

THE KIMBERLEY AND NORTH-WEST COAST

134 King Leopold Ranges Conservation Park

The rugged 560 million year old King Leopold Ranges stretch for 300km and are home to some of the Kimberley's most beautiful and picturesque gorges, as well as numerous rare plants and animals. Visitors to the park can enjoy spectacular scenery, bird and animal watching and bushwalking. Signposted access to the park is off the Gibb River Road, 230km east of Derby. The car park and walk to Bell Creek Falls is located 10km north of Silent Grove camping area.

Bell Gorge Falls, King Leopold Ranges Conservation Park

THE KIMBERLEY AND NORTH-WEST COAST

Silent Grove camping area

Signposted access off Gibb River Road, 8km west of Imintji Roadhouse. Then drive in a northerly direction for 20km to the large, open camping area. Tap water is untreated bore water, boil or treat first or bring drinking water. Some firewood supplied for cooking purposes only so best to bring you own if planning a campfire. Gas/fuel stove preferred.

GPS S:17 03.996 E:125 14.936

MR: Map 48 I2

FURTHER Information

DEC Broome Office

Tel: 08 9195 5500

Park entrance fee: $11.00 per vehicle.

Camping fees: From $11.00 per adult/night and $2.00 per child (up to 16)/night.

135 Kununurra

Kununurra is the eastern gateway to the Kimberley and located on the Victoria Highway. Visit Mirima National Park, take in the great views of the Ord Valley and Lake Kununurra from Kelly's Knob lookout, try your luck at landing a Barra at Ivanhoe Crossing or visit Diversion Dam. There are numerous tour operators in town who provide a variety of activities to visitors.

Kununurra Agricultural Society Showgrounds

Located on the corner of Ivanhoe Road and Coolabah Drive, 600m from town. Laundry. Gas/fuel stove only.

GPS S:15 46.249 E:128 43.878

MR: Map 52 J6

FURTHER Information

Kununurra Visitor Centre

Tel: 08 9168 1177

Web: www.visitkununurra.com

Camping fees: Fees payable to on-site caretaker, contact caretaker for current fees.

Dog bond: $20.00 refundable.

NB: Site closed in July each year for Agricultural Show. This site is only for travellers with pets or travellers with very large rigs. All other campers must use other town caravan parks.

Fishing at Ivanhoe Crossing

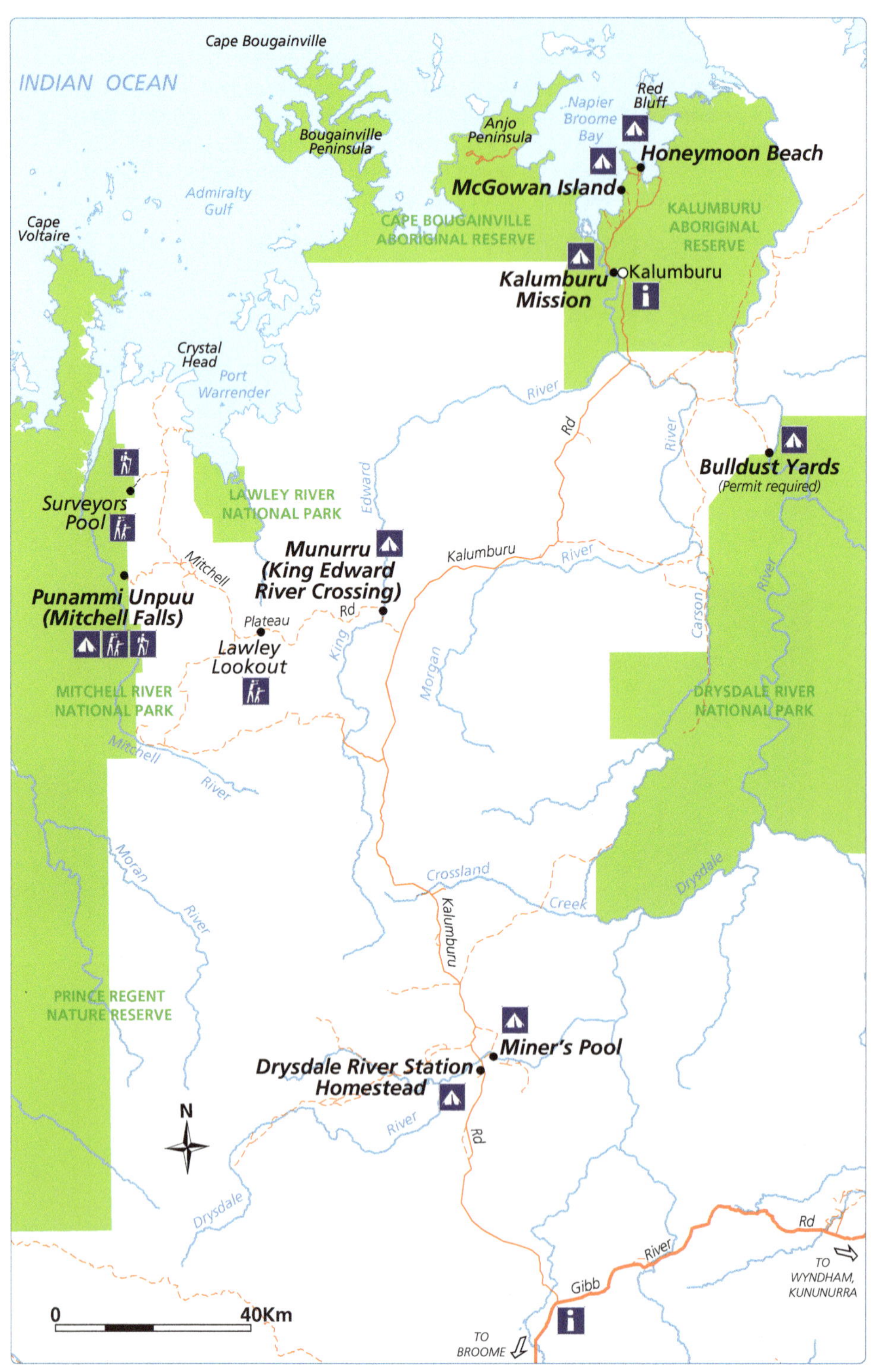
Cape Bougainville
INDIAN OCEAN
Red Bluff
Napier Broome Bay
Anjo Peninsula
Bougainville Peninsula
Honeymoon Beach
McGowan Island
Admiralty Gulf
Cape Voltaire
CAPE BOUGAINVILLE ABORIGINAL RESERVE
KALUMBURU ABORIGINAL RESERVE
Kalumburu Mission
Kalumburu
Crystal Head
Port Warrender
River
Rd
River
Bulldust Yards
(Permit required)
Surveyors Pool
LAWLEY RIVER NATIONAL PARK
Edward
Munurru (King Edward River Crossing)
Kalumburu
River
Mitchell
Punammi Unpuu (Mitchell Falls)
Plateau
Rd
Lawley Lookout
King
Morgan
Carson
River
MITCHELL RIVER NATIONAL PARK
DRYSDALE RIVER NATIONAL PARK
Mitchell
River
Moran
River
Crossland
Creek
Drysdale
Kalumburu
PRINCE REGENT NATURE RESERVE
Miner's Pool
Drysdale River Station Homestead
River
Rd
N
Drysdale
Rd
River
Gibb
TO WYNDHAM, KUNUNURRA
0
40Km
TO BROOME

136 Mitchell River National Park

This remote Kimberley park encompasses over 115,000 hectares and includes the spectacular Mitchell Falls. There is a 4.3km one-way walk to the falls with swimming possible in the upper pools. For the less energetic there are helicopter flights which leave from the camping ground to the falls. A number of Aboriginal heritage and art sites can also be visited on tours from the campground. In the north of the park is the remote Surveyors Pool. Access to the park is via the Mitchell Plateau Road which signposted off the Kalumburu Road, 172km north of the Gibb River Road and 102km north of Drysdale River Station access road. This road can be extremely rough and corrugated at times during the season and it is best to check on current road conditions prior to travel, especially if towing an off-road camper trailer.

Mitchell Falls, Mitchell River National Park

Punammi Unpuu (Mitchell Falls) camping area

Located at the western end of Mitchell Plateau Road, 88km west of Kalumburu Road. Follow signage to the park and camping area. Water from river, boil first or bring drinking water. Some firewood supplied for cooking fires. Gas/fuel stove preferred.

GPS S:14 49.212 E:125 43.104
MR: Map 51 D4

FURTHER Information

DEC Broome Office
Tel: 08 9195 5500
Park entrance fee: $11.00 per vehicle.
Camping fees: From $7.00 per adult/night and $2.00 per child (up to 16)/night. Fees payable at self-registration station.
NB: Collect firewood only from the designated signposted firewood collection zones en route to the park.

137 Ngauwudu – Mitchell Plateau

Ngauwudu is the local Wunambal Aboriginal name for Mitchell Plateau. The area is well known for the spectacular Mitchell Falls, King Edward River and Surveyor's Pool. Darngarna palms, which are native to the area, grow up to 18 metres with some as old as 280 years. There are numerous Aboriginal cave painting sites in the area. Remember that Aboriginal sites are sacred, please do not touch paintings or engravings and do not remove artefacts. Access to Mitchell Plateau is along the 4WD only Mitchell Plateau Road, which is signposted off the Kalumburu Road, 172km north of the Gibb River Road and 102km north of Drysdale River Station access road. This road can be extremely rough and corrugated at times and it is recommended to check on current road conditions prior to travel.

Rock art, Munurru (King Edward River Crossing)

Munurru (King Edward River Crossing) camping area

Located on the Mitchell Plateau Road, 8.2km west of Kalumburu Road. Large open camping area with shadey trees beside the King Edward River. Water from river, boil first. Bring drinking water. Bring firewood. Gas/fuel stove preferred.

GPS S:14 53.061 E:126 12.158

MR: Map 51 E4

FURTHER Information

DEC Broome Office

Tel: 08 9195 5500

Camping fees: From $7.00 per adult/night and $2.00 per child (up to 16)/night. Fees payable at self-registration station.

138 Ord River

The Ord River flows from Lake Argyle north into Cambridge Gulf. Located to the north of Kununurra, access can be made via the Parry Creek Road, which is signposted off the Victoria Highway west of Kununurra. Access is recommended by 4WD vehicle. Access roads may be closed during the wet season. Please note that saltwater crocodiles frequent these areas. Do not camp near the river and if travelling with a dog keep it with you at all times.

Buttons Crossing camping area

From the Victoria Highway, 16km west of Kununurra, take the signposted Parry Creek Road and follow this in a northerly direction for 18km to the signposted access track to Buttons Crossing. This track leads in an easterly direction for 800m to the bush campsites beside the river. Caravans with a 4WD tow vehicle can access this site. Check road conditions first. Campfires only in existing fireplaces. Bring drinking water and firewood.

GPS S:15 37.241 E:128 41.518
MR: Map 52 J5

Mambi Island camping area

From Buttons Crossing continue along Parry Creek Road in a north-westerly direction for 28km to track on the north side of the road which has a blue sign – it is not named. This access track, which is narrow and can have overhanging vegetation, leads in a northerly direction for 300m to grassy bush campsites stretched along the river with some shade. Access is suitable for 4WD and all-wheel drive vehicles. Caravan access with 4WD tow vehicle, check road conditions first. Campfires only in existing fireplaces. Bring drinking water and firewood.

GPS S:15 34.825 E:128 28.378
MR: Map 52 J5

Mambi Island camping area

Skull Rock camping area

Located 36.6km north of Kununurra. Access is signposted off Carlton Hill Road which is signposted off Weaber Plains Road. Weaber Plains Road is signposted off the Victoria Highway on the eastern side of Kununurra. Access is best suited for off-road camper trailers and caravans with 4WD tow vehicle. Campfires only in existing fireplaces. Bring drinking water and firewood.

MR: Map 52 J5

FURTHER information

Kununurra Visitor Centre
Tel: 08 9168 1177
Web: www.visitkununurra.com

Road conditions: Shire of Wyndham East Kimberley
Tel: 08 9168 4100
Web: www.swek.wa.gov.au

139 Parry Lagoons Nature Reserve

Popular with birdwatchers, the Parry Lagoons wetlands are used as a feeding and breeding area for numerous bird species as well as a stopover point for many migratory birds. Other areas of interest include Telegraph Hill and the Old Halls Creek Road. There is no camping in the nature reserve itself, however Parry Creek Farm is a parcel of privately owned land within the reserve which offers camping. Parry Lagoons Nature Reserve is located south of Wyndham with signposted access off the Great Northern Highway, 16km south of Wyndham.

Parry Creek Farm Tourist Resort

From the Great Northern Highway, 16km south of Wyndham, take the road to the east signposted to Parrys Lagoon. Follow this road in an easterly direction for 7km to the signposted access to the resort and camping area. This leads in 250m to the large, well grassed camping area with some shady trees. There's a restaurant, café, camp kitchen and pool. Other accommodation options are also available. Some firewood supplied.

GPS S:15 36.011 E:128 16.761

MR: Map 52 I5

FURTHER Information

Parry Creek Farm Tourist Resort

Tel: 08 9161 1139. Bookings essential for accommodation options and recommended for powered sites from June to August.

Web: www.parrycreekfarm.com.au

Camping fees: Unpowered sites from $17.00 per person/night and $5.00 per child (5 to 12 years)/night. Powered sites from $37.00 per site/night for up to 2 people.

Dog bond: May apply.

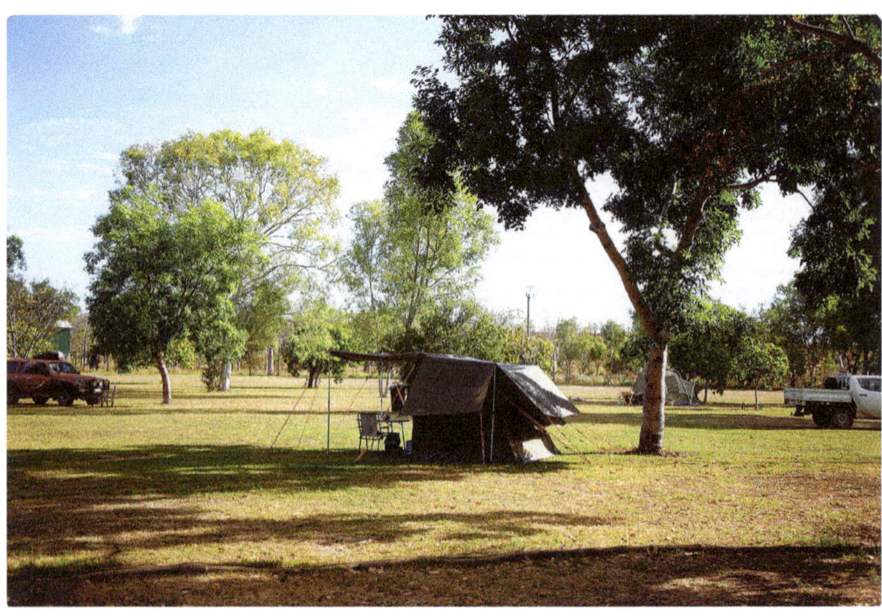

Parry Creek Farm Tourist Resort

140 Purnululu (Bungle Bungle) National Park

The striking, uniquely striped, dome-shaped sandstone towers of the Bungle Bungle Range were formed over 350 million years ago. Over time rivers and creeks have carved magnificent gorges, including Echidna Chasm, Frog Hole Gorge, Mini Palm Gorge in the north of the ranges and Cathedral Gorge in the south. Access to the gorges is by foot only or helicopter flights. The Piccaninny Gorge walk is for self-sufficient walkers and requires an overnight camp. See the visitor centre for details on all walks including length and difficulty. Signposted access to Purnululu National Park is off the Great Northern Highway, 109km north of Halls Creek and 250km south of Kununurra. The park's visitor centre is 52km east of the highway along Spring Creek Track and is suitable for 4WD vehicles only. Please not that caravan access is note permitted into the park. The park is closed to vehicle access from 1 January to 31 March.

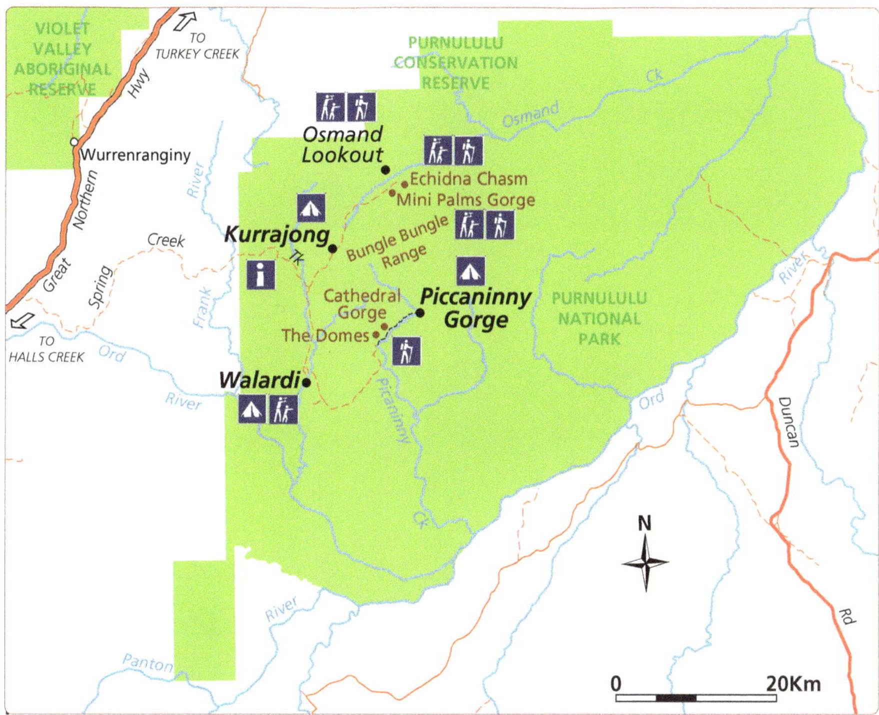

Kurrajong campsite

From the park visitor centre proceed east for 940m to a T-intersection. Turn left (north) and follow this road for 5.4km to the signposted access to the camping area. This leads in 200m to the large camping area with 106 individually numbered sites (66 of these can be pre-booked online). Some sites have shade. Tap water is untreated, boil or treat first or bring drinking water. Communal tables and fireplaces. Some firewood supplied for cooking fires. Gas/fuel stove preferred.

GPS S:17 23.227 E:128 19.818

MR: Map 50 H1

Walardi campsite

From the park visitor centre, proceed east for 940m to a T-intersection. Turn right (south) and follow this road for 11.5km to the signposted access to the camping area with 26 quite sites (18 of these can be pre-booked online) and 11 generator sites (8 of these can be pre-booked on line). Tap water is untreated, boil or treat first or bring drinking water. Communal

Purnululu (Bungle Bungle) Range

tables and fireplaces. Some firewood supplied for cooking fires. Gas/fuel stove preferred.

GPS S:17 31.298 E:128 18.029

MR: Map 50 H1

Walardi campsite

Piccaninny Gorge walking trail camping area

A 30km return walk of moderate to difficult standard. Walkers must be self-sufficient and carry drinking water. Gas/fuel stove only. All walkers must register and de-register at the park's visitor centre. Contact DEC for details on this walk.

MR: Map 50 H1

FURTHER Information

DEC Kununurra Office

Tel: 08 9168 4200

Purnululu National Park Visitor Centre

Tel: 08 9168 7300

Park entrance fee: $11.00 per vehicle.

Camping fees: From $11.00 per adult/night and $2.00 per child (up to 16)/night. Fees payable at the visitor centre.

Online bookings: www.dec.wa.gov.au/campgrounds

141 Rest Areas of the Kimberley Region

Main Roads WA has a number of designated 24 hour roadside rest areas within the region. These rest areas are for an overnight stop only whilst travelling to your destination. Please be advised that the designation of these sites may change from year to year, so please take note of any signage regarding overnight stays.

Nillibubbica Rest Area

    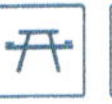 

Signposted access along the Great Northern Highway, 73km east of the Roebuck Roadhouse and72km west of the Derby turn off. Bring drinking water and firewood.

GPS S:17 39.364 E:123 07.956
MR: Map 47 E4

Ellendale Rest Area

   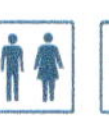   

Signposted access along the Great Northern Highway, 129km east of Derby turn off and 88km west of Fitzroy Crossing. Bring drinking water and firewood.

GPS S:17 57.669 E:124 50.130
MR: Map 49 A3

Mary Pool Rest Area

     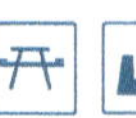 

Signposted access along the Great Northern Highway, 182km east of Fitzroy Crossing and 109km south-west of Halls Creek. Then drive in 610m to the rest area with some shaded sites. Very popular site set well off the road beside river. Bring drinking water and firewood.

GPS S:18 43.612 E:126 52.330
MR: Map 49 E4

Mary Pool Rest Area

Leycester's River Rest Area

Signposted access along the Great Northern Highway, 100km north of Halls Creek and 63km south of Warmun (Turkey Creek) Roadhouse. Bring drinking water and firewood.

GPS S:17 28.821 E:127 57.066
MR: Map 50 G1

Dunham River Rest Area

Signposted access along the Great Northern Highway, 27km north of Doon Doon Roadhouse and 33km south of the Victoria Highway junction. Bring drinking water and firewood.

GPS S:16 07.922 E:128 22.861
MR: Map 52 I6

Cockburn Rest Area

Signposted access at the junction of the Great Northern Highway and Victoria Highway 45km west of Kununurra and 55km south of Wyndham. Bring drinking water and firewood.

GPS S:15 52.116 E:128 22.275
MR: Map 52 I6

FURTHER Information

Main Roads Western Australia
Tel: 138 138
Web: www.mainroads.wa.gov.au

142 Windjana Gorge National Park

The 3.5km long, narrow Windjana Gorge was formed over millions of years by the Lennard River cutting its way through the limestone of the Napier Range. Fossils of extinct crocodiles, turtles and the giant marsupial Diprotodon have been found in the gorge and its caves. A walking track leads from the camping areas to the gorge. The gorge and its surrounds has a history of early Aboriginal occupation along with European exploration and pastoralists. The park is accessed off the Fairfield-Leopold Downs Road, which is signposted off the Gibb River Road 125km east of Derby and also signposted off the Great Northern Highway 42km north-west of Fitzroy Crossing. Access is via unsealed gravel roads suitable for conventional vehicles and caravans, however it is best to check road conditions first.

Windjana Gorge

The Generator campground

Access to the park is signposted along the Fairfield-Leopold Downs Road, 20km east of the Gibb River Road and 35km west of Tunnel Creek National Park access road. Then drive in a northerly direction for 1.2km the camping areas. Open camping area with free-form camping. Use of generators allowed in this section. Please adhere to rules regarding hours of use. Communal fireplaces with some firewood supplied. Gas/fuel stove preferred.

GPS S:17 24.792 E:124 56.46

MR: Map 49 A2

Quiet campground

Access to the park is signposted along the Fairfield-Leopold Downs Road, 20km east of the Gibb River Road and 35km west of Tunnel Creek National Park access road. Then drive in a northerly direction for 1.2km the camping areas. Large open camping area with free-form camping and some shade. Generators not allowed in this campground. Communal fireplaces with some firewood supplied. Gas/fuel stove preferred.

GPS S:17 24.848 E:124 56.604

MR: Map 49 A2

FURTHER information

DEC Broome Office

Tel: 08 9195 5500

Park entrance fee: $11.00 per vehicle.

Camping fees: From $11.00 per adult/night and $2.00 per child (up to 16)/night. Fees payable at self-registration station or to on-site campground hosts.

Quiet campground

143 Wolfe Creek Meteorite Crater

This spectacular crater measures 850 metres in circumference and was formed over 300,000 years ago when an iron meteorite, weighing thousands of tonnes, crashed to earth. Aboriginal legend believes the crater was formed by a rainbow snake when it came out of the ground to move across the land to form Sturt and Wolfe Creeks. A steep rocky climb to the rim of the crater affords good vistas into the crater and the surrounding vastness of the Tanami Desert. Access is signposted along the Tanami Road, 113km south of the Great Northern Highway. The Tanami Road leaves the Great Northern Highway 17km south of Halls Creek. Access for conventional vehicles in the dry season, check road conditions.

Wolfe Creek Meteorite Crater

Wolfe Creek Meteorite Crater camping area

Access signposted along the Tanami Road, 130km south of Halls Creek. Then drive in an easterly direction for 23km to the small camping area with little shade. Bring drinking water. Gas/fuel stove only. Conventional camper trailers and caravans check road conditions first as the access roads to this site can be rough and corrugated.

GPS S:19 10.605 E:127 47.203
MR: Map 50 G5

FURTHER information

DEC Kununurra Office
Tel: 08 9168 4200

The Outback

WESTERN AUSTRALIA'S OUTBACK REGION covers vast desert expanses, massive pastoral properties and at the same time offers some of the country's best four-wheel driving opportunities. Here you can explore historic stock routes and roads built for oil exploration, all of which provide access to a plethora of campsites in some strikingly beautiful and remote country.

The outback town of Wiluna is the start and finish point for two of the state's most famous four-wheel drive routes, the Canning Stock Route and the Gunbarrel Highway. Remote bush camping is possible along both of these routes but you will need a well set-up four-wheel drive vehicle and ample time to tackle these drives. A more leisurely route, but one still not to be undertaken lightly is the Great Central Road which has a number of camping areas located at roadhouses en-route between Laverton and Yulara in the Northern Territory.

Camping at old pastoral homesteads is at Yeo Homestead along the Anne Beadell Highway, at Goongarrie to the north of Kalgoorlie, Wanjarri located north of Leinster and Lorna Glen situated north-east of Wiluna while Rowles Lagoon Conservation Park north of Coolgardie and the remote Plumridge Lakes Nature Reserve east of Laverton are popular with birdwatchers.

In the south-west of the region is Niagara and Malcolm Dams, both built as water supplies for steam trains and now offering camping and recreational opportunities.

In the region around Kalgoorlie are the pleasant camping areas tucked away in the Goldfields Woodlands National Park as well as at nearby Burra Rock and Cave Hill nature reserves.

The northern dry season from April through to October is the best time to visit this region as summer temperatures can be furnace like at times.

BEST Campsites!

Yeo Lake Homestead camping area
Anne Beadell Highway

Durba Springs camping area
Canning Stock Route

Burra Rock camping area
Burra Rock Nature Reserve

Rowles Lagoon camping area
Rowles Lagoon Conservation Park

Camp Beadell
Gunbarrel Highway

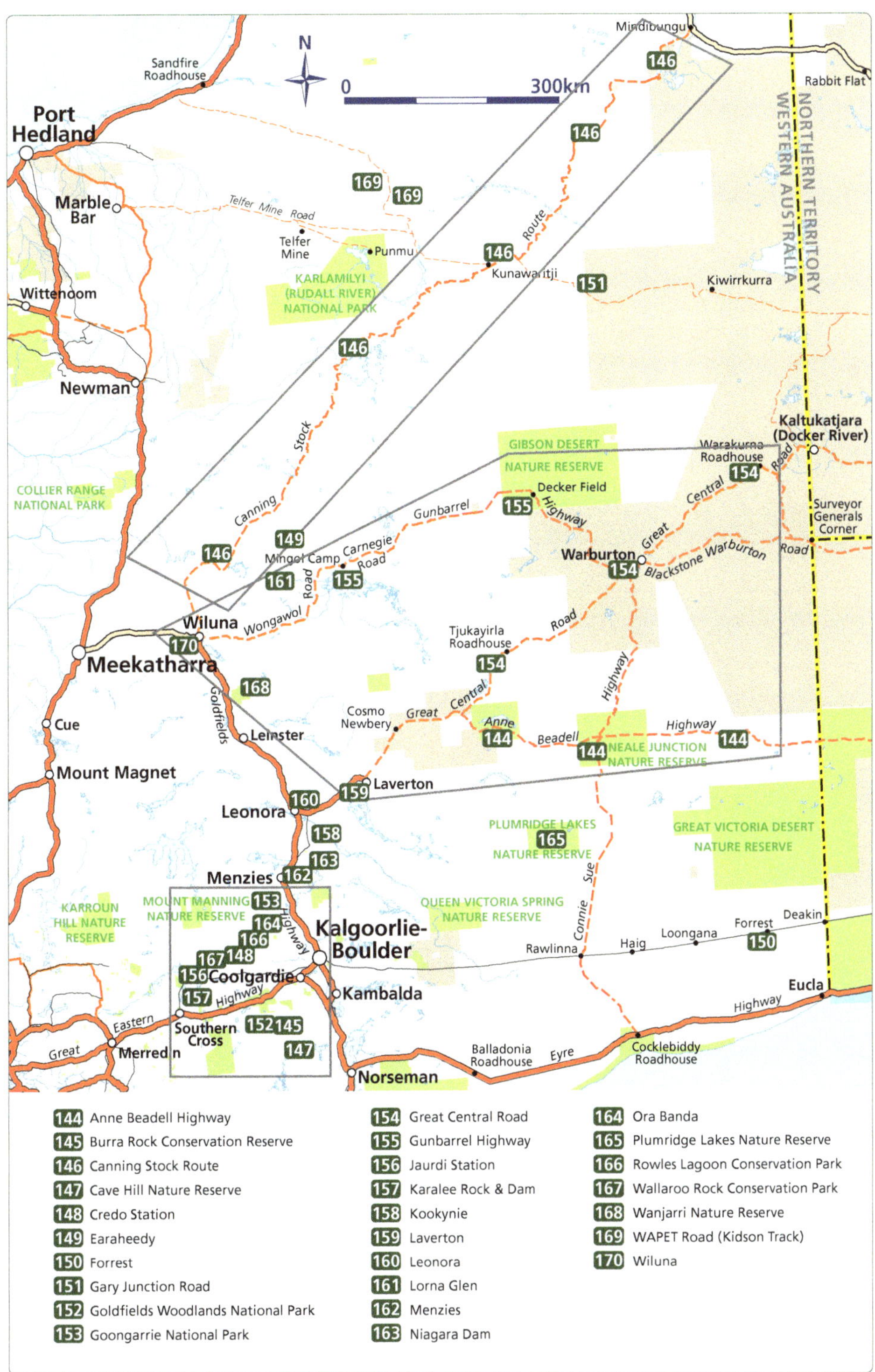
N
0
300km
Port Hedland
Sandfire Roadhouse
Marble Bar
Telfer Mine Road
Telfer Mine
Punmu
KARLAMILYI (RUDALL RIVER) NATIONAL PARK
Wittenoom
Newman
Mindibungu
Rabbit Flat
NORTHERN TERRITORY
WESTERN AUSTRALIA
Kunawarritji
Kiwirrkurra
Canning Stock Route
COLLIER RANGE NATIONAL PARK
GIBSON DESERT NATURE RESERVE
Decker Field
Warakurna Roadhouse
Kaltukatjara (Docker River)
Surveyor Generals Corner
Gunbarrel Highway
Mingol Camp
Carnegie Road
Warburton
Great Central Road
Blackstone
Warburton Road
Wiluna
Wongawol Road
Meekatharra
Goldfields Highway
Tjukayirla Roadhouse
Cosmo Newbery
Anne Beadell Highway
NEALE JUNCTION NATURE RESERVE
Cue
Leinster
Mount Magnet
Laverton
Leonora
PLUMRIDGE LAKES NATURE RESERVE
GREAT VICTORIA DESERT NATURE RESERVE
Menzies
KARROUN HILL NATURE RESERVE
MOUNT MANNING NATURE RESERVE
QUEEN VICTORIA SPRING NATURE RESERVE
Connie Sue Highway
Kalgoorlie-Boulder
Coolgardie
Rawlinna
Haig
Loongana
Forrest
Deakin
Kambalda
Great Eastern Highway
Southern Cross
Merredin
Eucla
Balladonia Roadhouse
Eyre Highway
Cocklebiddy Roadhouse
Norseman
144 Anne Beadell Highway
145 Burra Rock Conservation Reserve
146 Canning Stock Route
147 Cave Hill Nature Reserve
148 Credo Station
149 Earaheedy
150 Forrest
151 Gary Junction Road
152 Goldfields Woodlands National Park
153 Goongarrie National Park
154 Great Central Road
155 Gunbarrel Highway
156 Jaurdi Station
157 Karalee Rock & Dam
158 Kookynie
159 Laverton
160 Leonora
161 Lorna Glen
162 Menzies
163 Niagara Dam
164 Ora Banda
165 Plumridge Lakes Nature Reserve
166 Rowles Lagoon Conservation Park
167 Wallaroo Rock Conservation Park
168 Wanjarri Nature Reserve
169 WAPET Road (Kidson Track)
170 Wiluna

144 Anne Beadell Highway

Constructed in stages between 1953 and 1962, the Anne Beadell Highway stretches for 1,340km from Laverton in an easterly direction through the Great Victoria Desert to Coober Pedy in South Australia. Also known as Serpentine Lakes Road, the 'highway' is in name only – it's rugged and remote with sections of the road being narrow and twisted as well as badly corrugated and is best suited to travel by four-wheel drive vehicles only. If towing a camper trailer a well constructed 4x4 unit is required. Once leaving Laverton, the only fuel and supplies before Coober Pedy is at Ilkurlka Roadhouse, 553km east of Laverton and 785km west of Coober Pedy. To get to the start of the highway, from Laverton take the Great Central Road and drive for 1.3km to the gravel access road to White Cliffs. Turn onto the gravel road and follow this for 145km to Yamarna station ruins. At the ruins turn east along the track signposted Neale Junction - this is the Anne Beadell Highway. Travellers should be totally self-sufficient and carry adequate supplies of water, food and fuel. Permits apply to travel the Anne Beadell Highway, see page 204 for details.

Anne Beadell Highway

Yeo Lake Homestead camping

Signposted access along the Anne Beadell Highway, 212.9km north-east of Laverton, 67.6km east of Yamarna station ruins and 166.8km west of Neale Junction. Camping in vicinity of homestead. Located in Yeo Lake Nature Reserve. Limited tank water. Best to bring drinking water and firewood. There is no firewood collection within 10km of the homestead. Gas/fuel stove preferred.

GPS S:28 04.603 E:124 19.098

MR: Map 39 B7

Yeo Lake Homestead

Neale Junction camping area

Neale Junction is the intersection of the Anne Beadell and Connie Sue highways and is situated 166.8km east of Yeo Homestead and 309.5km south of the Great Central Road. The camping area is located 200m west of the junction in the Neale Junction Nature Reserve. Bring drinking water and firewood. Gas/fuel stove preferred.

GPS S:28 18.175 E:125 48.892
MR: Map 39 D7

Neale Junction Nature Reserve

Anne Beadell Highway bush camping

Bush camping is generally permitted whilst travelling the highway, sites are to be no more than 30 metres off the road. Please take note of any signage in regards to camping and access as the route travels through Aboriginal lands. Bring drinking water and firewood. Gas/fuel stove preferred. There are three established campsites located along the highway with facilities including toilets, shelters and rainwater takes. These are located at:

Site No 1. 124.1km east of Neale Junction.

GPS S:28 19.558 E:127 02.922
MR: Map 39 F7

Anne Beadell Highway bush camping

Site No 2. 107.4km east of Site No 1 and 58.5km east of Ilkurlka Roadhouse.

GPS S:28 24.491 E:128 01.562
MR: Map 40 H7

Site No 3. 100.6km east of Site No 2 and 9.9km west of the WA/SA border.

GPS S:28 31.383 E:128 54.494
MR: Map 40 J8

FURTHER Information

DEC Kalgoorlie Regional Office
Tel: 08 9080 5555
Ngaanyatjarra Council
Tel: 08 8950 1711
Web: www.ngaanyatjarra.org.au
Road conditions – Main Roads Western Australia
Tel: 138 138
Web: www.mainroads.wa.gov.au

Ilkurlka Roadhouse camping area

Camping area located on northern side of Anne Beadell Highway opposite the

Ilkurlka Roadhouse, 172.9km east of Neale Junction and 169km west of WA/SA border. The roadhouse offers basic supplies, diesel, unleaded fuel. Limited water so best to bring drinking water and firewood with you.

GPS S:28 20.979 E:127 31.014
MR: Map 40 G7

FURTHER Information

Ilkurlka Roadhouse
Tel: 08 9037 1147. Hours 8.30am to 5.00pm Monday to Friday. Saturday mornings.
Web: www.spinifex.org
Camping fees: From $20.00 per vehicle/night. Fees payable at roadhouse.

ANNE BEADELL HIGHWAY Permits

Western Australia:
Permit required to travel through Cosmo Newberry Aboriginal land (East), Reserve No. 20396, and Cosmo Newberry Aboriginal land (South), Reserve No. 25050. Permit from Aboriginal Lands Trust in Perth, tel 08 9235 8000 or visit www.dia.wa.gov.au Permit is free but allow up to four weeks for delivery.

South Australia:
Over the WA border enter Mamungari (Unnamed) Conservation Park, camping permit required, contact Maralinga Tjarutja Inc, **Tel:** 08 8674 2946.
Permit required to enter Maralinga Tjarutja Land. Contact Maralinga Tjarutja Inc, **Tel:** 08 8674 2946.
Travel permit required to travel through Woomera Prohibited Area. Contact Defence Support Centre at Woomera, **Tel:** 08 8674 3370.
Desert Parks Pass required to travel through Tallaringa Conservation Park. Contact Desert Parks Hotline, **Tel:**1800 816 078 or visit http://www.environment.sa.gov.au/parks/Park_Entry_Fees/Parks_Passes

THE OUTBACK

145 Burra Rock Conservation Reserve

Running along the base of this large granite outcrop is a long catchment wall which feeds into a dam. This was originally used to supply water to steam trains during the late 1920s when the area was used to supply wood to the nearby mines. From the summit of Burra Rock are views of the surrounding woodlands. Burra Rock is located 58km south of Coolgardie. From Coolgardie take Hunt Street and then follow signage. Conventional vehicle access is possible, however some sections of the access road may be sandy.

Burra Rock camping area

From Coolgardie follow Hunt Road in a southerly direction for 23.8km and then turn left onto the signposted road to Burra Rock and Spargoville. This road proceeds south for 34.3km to the signposted access track into Burra Rock. This leads in 300m to the shaded camping area at the base of the rock. Recommended for off-road camper trailers and caravans. Bring drinking water and firewood.

GPS S:31 23.602 E:121 12.018
MR: Map 32 H8

FURTHER Information

DEC Kalgoorlie Regional Office
Tel: 08 9080 5555

Burra Rock camping area

146 Canning Stock Route

The Canning Stock Route stretches from Wiluna in the south and runs for 1700km to Billiluna in the north. Traversing the Little Sandy Desert, the Gibson Desert, the Great Sandy Desert and the Tanami Desert, the Canning Stock Route (CSR) is the longest stock route in the world. Apart from the challenge of travelling this remote four-wheel drive touring route through beautiful desert scenery, the history of the CSR is the route's main attraction. Travellers will cross over 1100 sand dunes with sections of track containing corrugations. Travellers need to be well prepared and fully self-sufficient with 4WD vehicles that are mechanically sound. Water is available from a number of wells along the track. Please remember to always replace well lids.

To access the Canning Stock Route, travel north along Wotton Street in Wiluna for 39km to the signposted access track. Prior to the access track you will pass Well 1 and North Pool.

Canning Stock Route bush camping

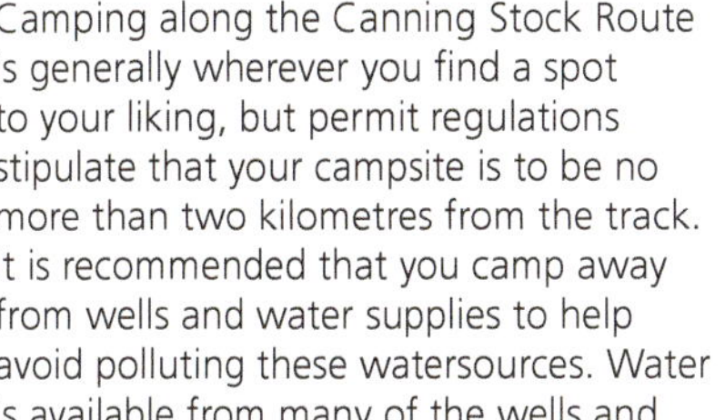

Camping along the Canning Stock Route is generally wherever you find a spot to your liking, but permit regulations stipulate that your campsite is to be no more than two kilometres from the track. It is recommended that you camp away from wells and water supplies to help avoid polluting these watersources. Water is available from many of the wells and it is recommended that water be boiled or treated before drinking. If you wish to have a campfire you will have to carry your own firewood as wood is limited along the route. Be sure to carry a gas/fuel stove. Towing a camper trailer along the CSR is not recommended. Travelling with dogs in these remote areas is also not recommended.

Wiluna **MR:** Map 37 F6
Kunawarritji **MR:** Map 45 B4
Halls Creek **MR:** Map 50 G3

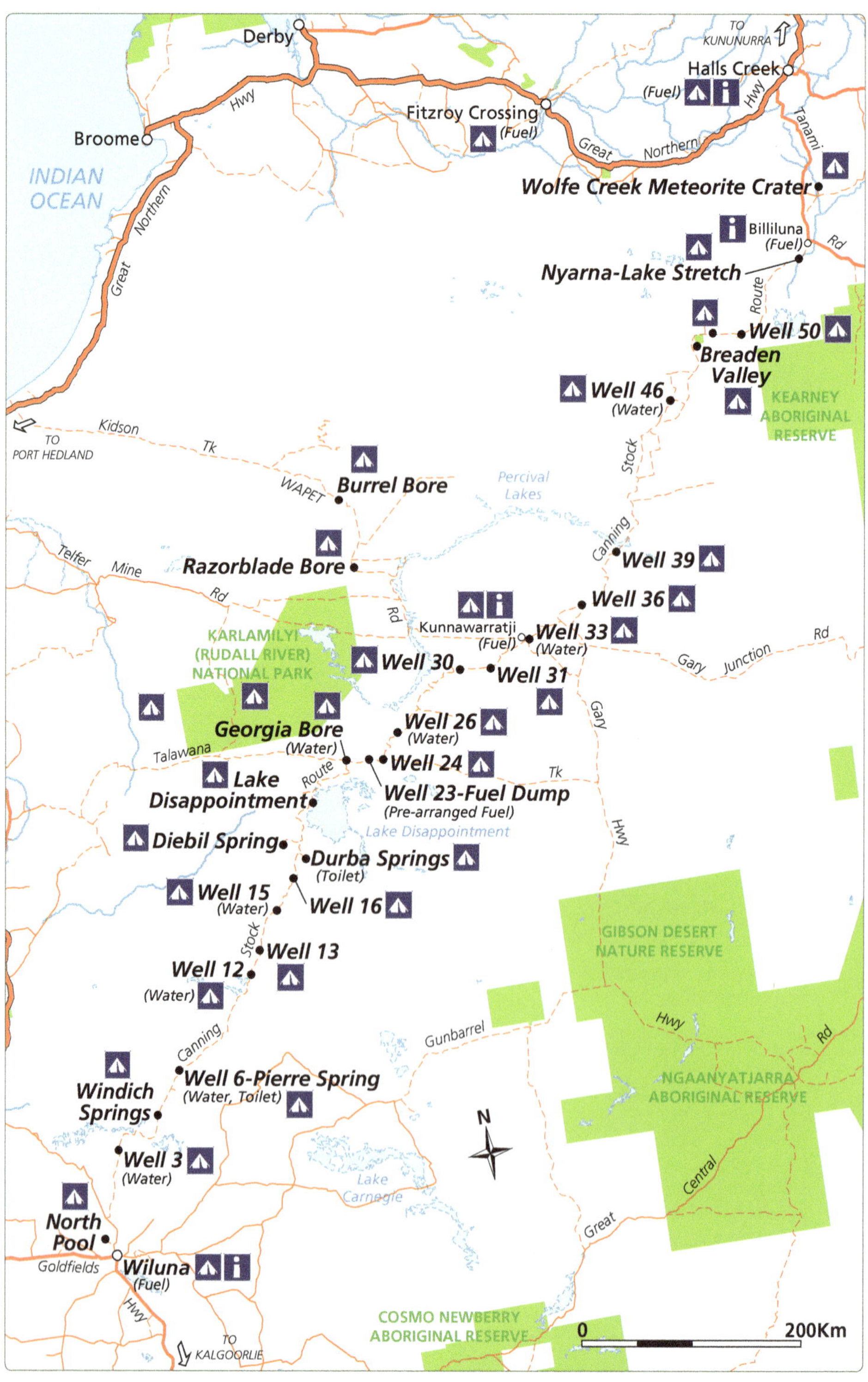
Derby
TO KUNUNURRA
Halls Creek
(Fuel)
Fitzroy Crossing
(Fuel)
Broome
Hwy
Great Northern Hwy
Tanami Rd
INDIAN OCEAN
Wolfe Creek Meteorite Crater
Billiluna (Fuel)
Nyarna-Lake Stretch
Well 50
Breaden Valley
Well 46 (Water)
KEARNEY ABORIGINAL RESERVE
TO PORT HEDLAND
Kidson Tk
WAPET
Burrel Bore
Percival Lakes
Canning Stock Route
Well 39
Telfer Mine Rd
Razorblade Bore
Well 36
Kunnawarratji (Fuel)
Well 33 (Water)
KARLAMILYI (RUDALL RIVER) NATIONAL PARK
Well 30
Well 31
Gary Junction Rd
Gary Hwy
Georgia Bore (Water)
Well 26 (Water)
Talawana Tk
Well 24
Lake Disappointment
Well 23-Fuel Dump (Pre-arranged Fuel)
Lake Disappointment
Diebil Spring
Durba Springs (Toilet)
Well 15 (Water)
Well 16
GIBSON DESERT NATURE RESERVE
Well 13
Well 12 (Water)
Gunbarrel Hwy
NGAANYATJARRA ABORIGINAL RESERVE
Windich Springs
Well 6-Pierre Spring (Water, Toilet)
N
Well 3 (Water)
Lake Carnegie
Great Central Rd
North Pool
Goldfields Hwy
Wiluna (Fuel)
TO KALGOORLIE
COSMO NEWBERRY ABORIGINAL RESERVE
0
200Km
THE OUTBACK

Canning Stock Route bush camping

Suggested campsites:

North Pool (Water 1A). Signposted access 10.4km north of Wiluna. Small site.

GPS S:26 26.772 E:120 08.868

North Pool

Well 3. Water available. Access track is 71.1km along the CSR from the turn off north of Wiluna. Well and small camping area located to the east of CSR. Please note that the CSR passes through private property north of Well 3. Camping is not permitted between Well 3 and Windich Springs.

GPS S:25 46.541 E:120 24.819

Windich Springs (No. 4A Water). Signposted access 76.6km north-east of Well 3. Camping beside large waterhole.

GPS S:25 33.432 E:120 49.541

Windich Springs

Well 6 - Pierre Spring. Water available. Located 48.1km north-east of Windich Springs. Camping in vicinity of tall river red gums.

GPS S:25 14.453 E:121 05.967

Well 12. Restored well with water available. Access track is 133.3km north-east of Well 6 and 34.7km north of Well 11 and 'Notice to Travellers' sign. Well and camping area located near shady desert oaks and is 500m west of CSR.

GPS S:24 35.651 E:121 52.361

Well 13. Signposted access 20.8km north of Well 12 access track. Well 13 and camping area is located 2.1km west of CSR. The area around the well can be boggy in wet conditions.

GPS S:24 25.318 E:121 59.294

Well 15. Water available. Access track is 42.7km north of Well 13 and 24.9km north of Well 14. Located 200m east of CSR. Open area near well.

GPS S:24 08.475 E:122 12.120

Well 16. Signposted access 38.2km north of Well 15 access track. Located 500m west of CSR. Small site.

GPS S:23 54.491 E:122 23.009

Durba Springs. Crossroads located 32km north of Well 16. Track to south-east (or straight on if coming from the south) leads 5.3km to Durba Springs. The most popular campsite on the CSR and often used by travellers for a few days break as it is roughly half way along the route. Grassy and shaded site sheltered in a pretty valley. Toilets.

GPS S:23 45.268 E:122 31.039

Durba Springs

Diebel Spring. Signposted access 20km north of crossroads to Durba Springs. Travel along Diebel Spring access track for 15.2km to track junction, then TR. After further 1.4km track junction, TR here and travel for 4.2km to campsite set among mulga trees.
GPS S:23 37.752 E:122 21.155

Lake Disappointment. A couple of bush campsites are located on the western edge of the lake. Access tracks lead to sites 3.4km north of Savory Creek crossing and 5.5km north of crossing.

Georgia Bore. Water available. Access track is 8.6km north of access track to Well 22 and 0.5km south of Talawana Track. Located 300m north of CSR.
GPS S:23 03.532 E:123 01.066

Well 24. Access track is 14km east of Well 23. Located 400m south-east of CSR.
GPS S:23 06.567 E:123 20.606.

Well 26. Water available. Located 45.2km north of Well 24 access track and 21.3km north of Well 25. Open camping area accessed along track opposite well.
GPS S:22 54.967 E:123 30.334

Well 30. Located 6.3km east of the signposted access to Nangabbittajarra Native Well. Track on north side of CSR 200m west of Well 30 leads to campsites surrounded by bloodwood trees.
GPS S:22 30.169 E:124 08.315

Well 31. Signposted access 26.2km east of Well 30. Located 4km south of CSR.
GPS S:22 31.539 E:124 24.425

Well 33. Water available. Located 3.6km north of crossroads with Jenkins Track. Road on west at crossroads leads 4km to Kunawarritji and road on east at crossroads leads to Gary Junction Road. Large open camping area.
GPS S:22 20.513 E:124 46.512

Well 33

Campsite east of Well 36. 22.2km east of Well 36 access track and 0.3km west of Well 37 access track. This is a nice campsite set among desert oaks.
GPS S:22 09.121 E:125 27.335

Campsite north of Well 39. 4km north of Well 39 and 0.4km south of Tobin Lake's southern edge. The track on the east leads to large, shady camping area among desert oaks.
GPS S:22 44.802 E:125 40.160

Well 46. Water available. Located 14.4km west of CSR. Access track is 31.6km north of Well 45 and 11.6km north of the signposted Mount Ford. Alternative access is via track to west of Well 45, which leads 26.2km to Well 46. Large camping area among shady white gums.
GPS S:20 38.510 E:126 17.258

Well 46

Breaden Valley. Access track is 24.4km north of signposted access to Well 47 and 1.3km south of access track to Well 48. Track leads 4.5km to end of Breaden Valley and car park with walk to Breaden Pool and Godfreys Tank. Here there is a small camping area in vicinity of the car park.
GPS S:20 14.793 E:126 34.169

Campsites east of 'Notice to Travellers' sign - **GPS** S:20 10.346 E:126 44.260. At 0.1km east and 0.5km east of sign are tracks which lead to the north to good bush campsites among desert oaks.

Well 50. Access track to Well 50 is 26.2km east of 'Notice to Travellers' sign and 20.2km south-west of the signposted Weriaddo Well. Access track leads 2km south to large shaded camping area, **GPS** S:20 12.531 E:126 58.079, then a further 300m to the well.

FURTHER *information*

Australian National 4WD Council, CSR Manager
Tel: 0438 853 342
Web: www.anfwdc.asn.au
Permit and fee: Permit is required to travel the CSR and a fee applies, contact CSR manager.

Newman Tourist Information Centre
Tel: 08 9175 2888
Web: www.newman-wa.org

Wiluna Police
Tel: 08 9981 7024

Halls Creek Police
Tel: 08 9168 6000

Kunawarritji Aboriginal Community camping area

Located on the Kidson Track, 4km west of the CSR, Kunawarritji is the major refuelling and resupply point along the CSR. Access from the west is via the Kidson Track from Eighty Mile Beach or from the east via the Gary Junction Road. Camper trailer access is possible from the east and west but is not recommended via the CSR. Shop, fuel, laundry. Other accommodation is available. Bring firewood.

GPS S:22 19.762 E:124 43.613
MR: Map 45 B4

FURTHER *information*

Kunawarritji Aboriginal Community
Tel: 08 9176 9040
Camping fees: Contact community office for current fee structure.

Nyarna-Lake Stretch camping area

Signposted access 19.3km south of Tanami Road and 17.3km south of Billiluna store. Located 2.4km south-east of the CSR. Camper trailer access only possible from the north off the Tanami Road. Bring drinking water. Some firewood supplied.

Access track: **GPS** S:19 40.773 E:127 33.973
MR: Map 49 F7

FURTHER *information*

Billiluna Office
Tel: 08 9168 8988. Office hours 8am to 12 noon and 2pm to 4pm Monday to Friday.

Billiluna Store
Tel: 08 9168 8076.
Camping fees: From $30.00 per vehicle for the 1st night. Campers must visit Billiluna Office to pay fees and obtain camping permit prior to setting up camp.

INFORMATION FOR CSR travellers

Fuel

Capricorn Roadhouse, Newman Tel: 08 9175 1535. Arrange for fuel dump at Well 23, arrangements to be made 4-6 weeks in advance.

Kunawarritji Aboriginal Community, Tel: 08 9176 9040. Diesel and unleaded fuel available from fuel pumps. Fuel does not need to be booked, however a phone call advising of your estimated requirements is advisable prior to commencing your trip, especially if travelling in numbers. Open Monday to Friday 10am to 11am and 4pm to 5pm. Saturday 9am to 12 noon. Closed Sundays and public holidays.

Billiluna Aboriginal Community, Tel: 08 9168 8988. Diesel and unleaded fuel available from fuel pumps. Open Monday to Friday 7am to 12 noon and 1pm to 3pm. Saturday 9am to 11am. Closed Sundays and public holidays.

Access

It is possible to access and exit the CSR at Well 5 through private property, Granite Peak Station. To do this contact Granite Peak Station, **Tel:** 08 9981 2983 prior to proceeding through the property. A fee applies, based on axle load and wear and tear of the property's access track.

147 Cave Hill Nature Reserve

The large granite outcrop of Cave Hill stretches for almost one and a half kilometres in length. Explore the large dam and catchment wall which supplied water to steam trains carrying timber to Kalgoorlie-Boulder along the 'Woodlines'. On the western side of the hill is a walking track leading to a large cave. Cave Hill Nature Reserve is located 50km west of the Coolgardie-Esperance Highway and 39km south of Burra Rock. From the east access is via a 4WD track signposted to the nature reserve 58km north of Norseman off the Coolgardie Esperance Highway. Access from the north is via Burra Rock, see page 204 for access details.

Cave Hill

Cave Hill camping area

From the Coolgardie-Esperance Highway take the signposted track to the nature reserve which is 58km north of Norseman. Then follow signage for 50.2km to the signposted access track to Cave Hill. This track leads 2.9km to the small camping area on the western side of the rock. From Burra Rock (see page 204) take the signposted 4x4 track to Cave Hill and follow the signage for 39.1km to the signposted access track to Cave Hill. Bring drinking water and firewood.

GPS S:31 40.365 E:121 14.077
MR: Map 27 D1

FURTHER information

DEC Kalgoorlie Regional Office
Tel: 08 9080 5555

148 Credo Station

This former sheep property was initially taken up in the early 1900s by the Halford family before being later purchased by the WA Government in 2007 as a conservation area to conserve the water catchment area for the neighbouring Rowles Lagoon. Access to Credo is possible via conventional vehicles, however all the station tracks are designated for four-wheel drive vehicles only.

Credo Station camping area

From Coolgardie proceed in a northerly direction along the Coolgardie Northern Road for 76km to the signposted access to the station. Camping is possible in the vicinity of the homestead or remote bush camping is possible throughout the station. Remote bush camping is best suited to self-sufficient campers. Bring drinking water and firewood. Collection of firewood in the vicinity of the homestead is not permitted. Gas/fuel stove preferred. Station stays are possible in the homestead dongers, bookings are required, contact DEC Kalgoorlie for further details.

GPS S:30 27.671 E:120 49.627
MR: Map 32 H6

FURTHER information

DEC Kalgoorlie Regional Office
Tel: 08 9080 5555
Camping fees: From $7.00 per adult/night and $2.00 per child (up to 16)/night. Fees payable at DEC Kalgoorlie office.

149 Earaheedy

This remote 321,812ha station is located 180km north-east of Wiluna. Once a cattle and sheep station, Earaheedy is now a conservation area which provides nature study and research. From Wiluna head east along the Gunbarrel Highway for 42.7km to the road signposted to Lake Violet Station. This is the Granite Peak Road which then becomes Earaheedy Road. 4WD vehicles recommended.

Earaheedy bush camping

Access is signposted along Earaheedy Road, 202km north of the Gunbarrel Highway along the Granite Peak-Lake Violet road. Remote bush camping best suited for self-sufficient campers. No facilities. Bring drinking water and firewood.

MR: Map 38 H4

FURTHER Information

DEC Kalgoorlie Regional Office
Tel: 08 9080 5555
Camping fees: From $7.00 per adult/night and $2.00 per child (up to 16)/night. Fees payable at DEC Kalgoorlie office.

THE OUTBACK

150 Forrest

Forrest is located beside the Transcontinental Railway, 639km east of Kalgoorlie and 120km north of the Eyre Highway. Used as a refuelling point by aircraft flying across the Nullarbor, Forrest has the largest bitumen airstrip outside the major airports. 4WD vehicle access via the Forrest-Mundrabilla Road off the Eyre Highway.

Forrest camping area

Situated on the Transcontinental Railway Access Road, 126km north of the Eyre Highway. 4WD access via the Forrest-Mundrabilla Road, 34km west of Mundrabilla off the Eyre Highway. Camp kitchen. Power is available. Firewood supplied.

MR: Map 34 I5

FURTHER Information

Forrest Airport
Tel: 08 9022 6403. Bookings recommended.
Web: www.forrestairport.com.au
Camping fees: Contact office for current fee structure.
NB: Use of the Transcontinental Railway Access Road is not permitted, this is a private road from Rawlinna east to Tarcoola in SA.

151 Gary Junction Road

Gary Junction Road runs east from Gary Junction (the junction of Gary Junction Rd and Gary Highway) into the Northern Territory to the Tanami Track then onto Alice Springs, a total of 1,000km. This is remote desert travel and is only suitable for well prepared and self-sufficient 4WD travellers. Permits required in WA and NT.

Jupiter Well camping area

Located on Gary Junction Road, 157km east of Gary Junction, 223km east of the CSR and 260km west of the WA/NT border. Gas/fuel stove preferred. Travelling with dogs in these remote areas is not recommended.

GPS S:22 52.613E:126 35.793
MR: Map 45 E4

FURTHER Information

Ngaanyatjarra Council
Tel: 08 8950 1711
Web: www.ngaanyatjarra.org.au

GARY JUNCTION ROAD permits

Western Australia:
Department of Indigenous Affairs
Tel: 08 9235 8000
Web: www.dia.wa.gov.au
Northern Territory:
Central Land Council
Tel: 08 8951 6320
Web: www.clc.org.au

152 Goldfields Woodlands National Park

There is plenty to see and do in this park where natural features include the large granite outcrop of Victoria Rock, eucalypt woodlands, salt lakes and freshwater swamps. Historic sites feature the remnants of the now defunct woodlines, these narrow gauge railways which carried timber to the mines at Kalgoorlie-Boulder for fuel and building supplies. The Holland Track, a popular 4WD track which follows the route cut by John Holland in the 1890s runs from Broomehill to Coolgardie and was once used by miners to travel to the goldfields. Other sites of interest include the Goldfields water pipeline which pumped water to the towns and goldfields of Kalgoorlie from Mundaring Weir, 560km to the west. The park is located to the west and south of Coolgardie.

Boondi Rock camping area

Signposted access along the Great Eastern Highway 80km west of Coolgardie and 106km east of southern Cross. Unsealed access track leads in a northerly direction for 3km to the small camping area with 7 sites situated close to the granite outcrop. Bring drinking water and firewood.

GPS S:31 12.319 E:120 17.218

MR: Map 32 G8

Victoria Rock camping area

Signposted access on Victoria Rock Road, 46km south of Coolgardie.

From Coolgardie take the signposted Gnarlbine Rock Road at the western end of town. Then travel 45km south to the signposted access track. Bring drinking water and firewood.

GPS S:31 17.256 E:120 55.678

MR: Map 32 H8

FURTHER Information

DEC Kalgoorlie Regional Office

Tel: 08 9080 5555

153 Goongarrie National Park

This easily accessible national park encompasses the old Goongarrie homestead, the salt lakes along Planto Road and 25 Mile Rock. Access is signposted along the Goldfields Highway north of Kalgoorlie.

Goongarrie Homestead camping area

Access signposted along the Goldfields Highway, 90km north of Kalgoorlie and 42km south of Menzies. Then drive in a westerly direction for 14km to the homestead with the camping area in its vicinity. Donkey hot water system for shower. Some firewood supplied, although a gas/fuel stove is preferred Bring drinking water and firewood for your campfire. The collection of firewood from the homestead vicinity is not permitted. Homestead and cottage accommodation is available for hire, contact DEC Kalgoorlie for details.

GPS S:29 58.984 E:121 02.747

MR: Map 32 H5

FURTHER Information

DEC Kalgoorlie Regional Office

Tel: 08 9080 5555

Camping fees: From $7.00 per adult/night and $2.00 per child (up to 16)/night. Fees payable at DEC Kalgoorlie office or on-site campground hosts during busy periods.

THE OUTBACK

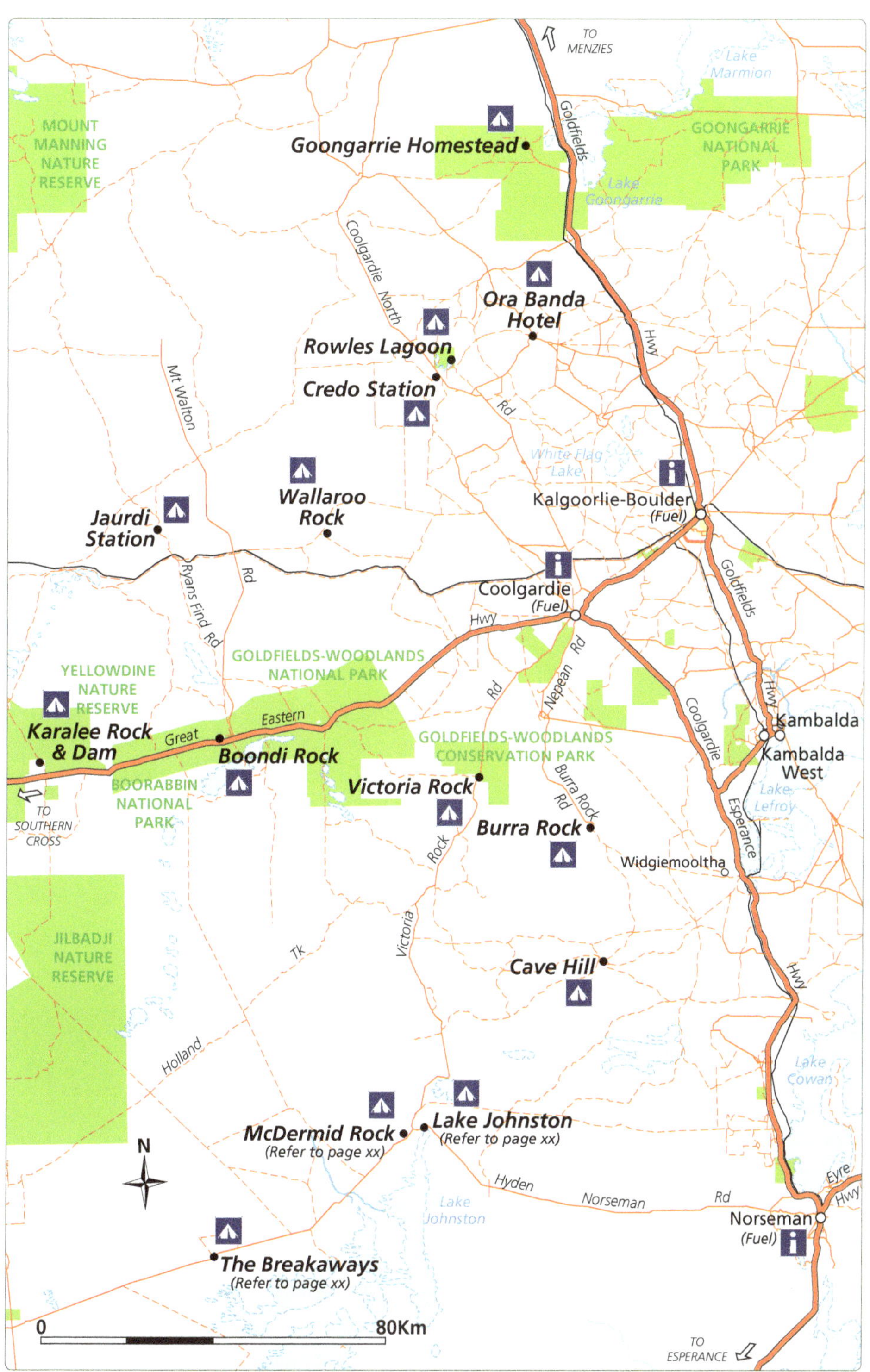
TO MENZIES
Lake Marmion
MOUNT MANNING NATURE RESERVE
Goongarrie Homestead
Goldfields
GOONGARRIE NATIONAL PARK
Lake Goongarrie
Coolgardie North
Ora Banda Hotel
Rowles Lagoon
Credo Station
Hwy
Rd
Mt Walton
White Flag Lake
Wallaroo Rock
Jaurdi Station
Kalgoorlie-Boulder (Fuel)
Ryans Find Rd
Rd
Coolgardie (Fuel)
Hwy
Goldfields
GOLDFIELDS-WOODLANDS NATIONAL PARK
YELLOWDINE NATURE RESERVE
Nepean Rd
Rd
Karalee Rock & Dam
Great
Eastern
Boondi Rock
GOLDFIELDS-WOODLANDS CONSERVATION PARK
Coolgardie
Hwy
Kambalda
Kambalda West
BOORABBIN NATIONAL PARK
Victoria Rock
Burra Rock Rd
Lake Lefroy
TO SOUTHERN CROSS
Rock
Burra Rock
Esperance
Widgiemooltha
JILBADJI NATURE RESERVE
Tk
Victoria
Cave Hill
Hwy
Holland
Lake Cowan
McDermid Rock (Refer to page xx)
Lake Johnston (Refer to page xx)
N
Hyden
Norseman
Rd
Eyre
Hwy
Lake Johnston
Norseman (Fuel)
The Breakaways (Refer to page xx)
0
80Km
TO ESPERANCE

THE OUTBACK

154 Great Central Road

The Great Central Road runs east from Laverton through to Yulara in the Nothern Territory. Travellers venturing along the Great Central Road will witness typical central Australian desert landscapes made up of red sand, spinifex and mulga. Although the road is sandy in sections it can be generally travelled by conventional vehicles in dry weather, however a 4WD is recommended. The Great Central Road passes through Aboriginal Land and transit permits are required.

Tjukayirla Roadhouse

Located 320km north-east of Laverton and 255km south-west of Warburton. Store, meals, diesel and Opal fuel, camp kitchen, laundry, wireless internet access, TV room, swimming pool. Other accommodation options also available. Firewood supplied.

GPS S:27 09.189 E:124 34.287

MR: Map 39 B5

FURTHER Information

Tjukayirla Roadhouse

Tel: 08 9037 1108. Hours Monday to Friday 8am to 5pm. Saturday and Sunday 9am to 3pm. Public holidays 9am to 12noon.

Web: www.tjukayirlaroadhouse.com.au

Camping fees: Unpowered sites from $20.00 per vehicle/night. Powered sites from $30.00 per vehicle/night.

Warburton Roadhouse camping area

THE OUTBACK

Warburton Roadhouse

Located 255km north-east of Tjukayirla Roadhouse and 231km south-east of Warakurna Roadhouse. Store, meals, diesel and Opal fuel, camp kitchen, laundry. Other accommodation options also available. Bring firewood.

GPS S:26 07.936 E:126 34.154

MR: Map 39 E3

FURTHER information

Warburton Roadhouse

Tel: 08 8956 7656. Hours Monday to Friday 8am to 5pm. Saturday and Sunday 9am to 3pm. Public holidays 9am to 12noon.

Web: www.warburtonroadhouse.com.au

Camping fees: From $12.00 per person/ night.

Warakurna Roadhouse

Located on the Great Central Road, 231km north-east of Warburton Roadhouse and 92km west of Docker River in the Northern Territory. Store, take away meals, diesel and Opal fuel, camp kitchen, laundry. Other accommodation options also available. Bring firewood.

GPS S:25 02.339 E:128 18.119

MR: Map 40 I1

FURTHER information

Warakjurna Roadhouse

Tel: 08 8956 7344. Hours Monday to Friday 8.30am to 6pm. Saturday and Sunday 9am to 3.30pm. Public holidays 8.30am to 12.30pm.

Web: www.warakurnaroadhouse.com.au

Camping fees: From $12.00 per person/ night.

GREAT CENTRAL ROAD permits

Western Australia: Department of Indigenous Affairs

Tel: 08 9235 8000. Aboriginal Lands Trust permit required.

Web: www.dia.wa.gov.au

Northern Territory: Central Land Council

Tel: 08 8951 6320. CLC permit to transit required.

Web: www.clc.org.au

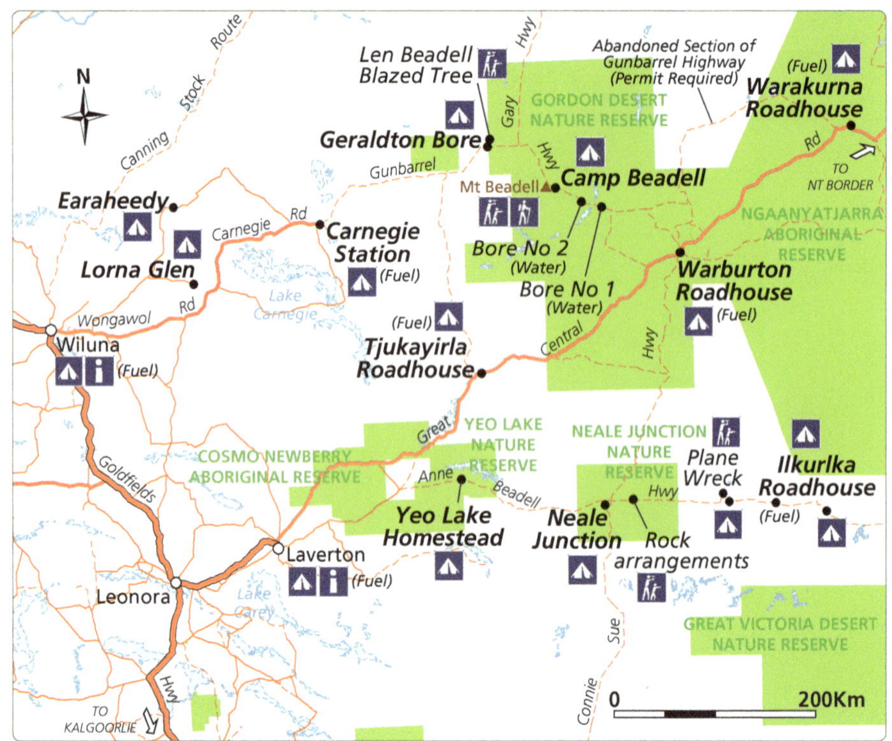

155 Gunbarrel Highway

The Gunbarrel Highway was the first major road construction by Len Beadell and the Gunbarrel Construction Party, and still today, is their best known. Stretching 1,400km from Wiluna in WA to Mt Cavenagh Station on the Stuart Highway in NT. Construction commenced in 1955 with the final section of the highway completed in 1958. Much of the original Gunbarrel Highway (known as the abandoned section) traverses Aboriginal lands, a special permit is required and restrictions apply for this section. The frequently used present day route runs from Warburton along the Great Central Road (CLC and ALT permits required, see Great Central Road, page 217) to the Heather Highway junction (ALT permit required). This track then heads in a northerly direction to the Gunbarrel Highway proper at its junction with the now abandoned section. From this junction the Gunbarrel heads in a north-west direction to Everard Junction, then south-west to Carnegie Station and onto Wiluna. The Gunbarrel Highway is only suitable for 4WD vehicles and if towing, off-road trailers or caravans. Travellers must be self-sufficient and prepared for extreme corrugations for lengthy sections of the route. Travelling with dogs in these remote areas is not recommended.

Gunbarrel Highway

Carnegie Station camping area

Signposted access along the Gunbarrel Highway, 344km north-east of Wiluna and 207km west of Geraldton Bore. Store, fuel, camp kitchen. Homestead accommodation available. Some firewood supplied.

GPS S:25 47.753 E:122 58.407
MR: Map 38 K4

FURTHER Information

Carnegie Station
Tel: 08 9981 2991.
Web: www.carnegiestation.com.au
Camping fees: From $15.00 per person/night.

Geraldton Bore bush camping area

Situated 100m south of the highway on Hunt Oil Road. Access along the Gunbarrel Highway, 207km east of Carnegie Station, 32km west of Everard Junction and 500m west of Len Beadell blazed tree. Water from bore, should be boiled or treated first. Bring drinking water and firewood. Gas/fuel stove preferred.

GPS S:25 10.480 E:124 39.825
MR: Map 39 B2

Camp Beadell bush camping area

Access along the Gunbarrel Highway, 95km east of Geraldton Bore, 62.5km east of Everard Junction, 6.3km south-east of Mt Beadell and 189km north-west of Warburton. Then drive in southerly direction for 200m to the camping area. Bore No 3 is located here. Water from bore should be boiled or treated first. Bring drinking water and firewood. Gas/fuel stove preferred.

GPS S:25 32.945 E:125 19.884
MR: Map 39 C2

Other bore pumps on the Gunbarrel Highway

Bore No 2. Located 30km south-east of Camp Beadell and just south of the highway. Water from bore should be boiled or treated first.

GPS S:25 40.620 E:125 35.162
MR: Map 39 D2

Bore No 1. Located 25km south-east of Bore No 2 and located 500m south of the highway. Access track is opposite the Len Beadell Tree and plaque. Water from bore should be boiled or treated first.

GPS S:25 43.568 E:125 46.831
MR: Map 39 D3

FURTHER information

DEC Kalgoorlie Regional Office
Tel: 08 9080 5555
NB: DEC Kalgoorlie request that if travellers find any pumps that are damaged and/or not working to contact them with details.

Ngaanyatjarra Council
Tel: 08 8950 1711
Web: www.ngaanyatjarra.org.au

Shire of Wiluna
Tel: 08 9981 8000
Web: www.wiluna.wa.gov.au

GUNBARREL HIGHWAY permits

Heather Highway: Department of Indigenous Affairs
Tel: 08 9235 8000. Aboriginal Lands Trust permit required.
Web: www.dia.wa.gov.au

Abandonded Section of Gunbarrel Highway: Ngaanyatjarra Council
Tel: 08 8950 1711
Web: www.ngaanyatjarra.org.au

Great Central Road:
See Great Central Road Permits, page 217

THE OUTBACK

156 Jaurdi Station

Jaurdi Station preserves rare flora, a large number of birds, mammals and reptiles, along with spectacular breakaway country and granite outcrops. The shearing shed along with rusting farm machinery, yards, dams and windmills are reminders of the station's pastoral history, whilst abandoned mine sites are evidence of a mining boom during the 1890s. Located 178km west of Kalgoorlie and 51km north of the Great Eastern Highway. Conventional vehicle access is possible in dry conditions, however 4WD vehicle is recommended.

Jaurdi Station Homestead camping area

Located on Ryans Find Road which is accessed off Mt Walton (Heath) Road. This road is accessed off the Great Eastern Highway, 98km east of Southern Cross and 90km west of Coolgardie. Then travel north along Mt Walton (Heath) Road for 14.8km to Ryans Find Road. Once on Ryans Find Road the track travels in a north-westerly direction for 8.3km to a signpost entrance to Jaurdi Station and for a further 27.6km to the homestead. Best suited to off-road camper trailers. Camping is in homestead vicinity where campers can use the homestead facilities. Limited drinking water so best to bring water. Bring firewood. Shearers quarters and shed available for hire, contact DEC Kalgoorlie for details.

GPS S:30 48.985 E:120 09.725
MR: Map 32 G7

FURTHER Information

DEC Kalgoorlie Regional Office
Tel: 08 9080 5555. Advance bookings and payment through DEC Kalgoorlie office.
Camping fees: From $7.00 per adult/night and $2.00 per child (under 16)/night.

157 Karalee Rock Dam

The dam was constructed between 1896 and 1897 to supply water for steam trains en route to the Kalgoorlie goldmines. An old aqueduct carrying water to the dam still stands and interpretive signs detailing the dam's history are located along a walk beside the aqueduct. Situated to the east of Southern Cross and west of Coolgardie, access is signposted along the Great Eastern Highway.

Karalee Rock & Dam picnic and camping area

Signposted along the Great Eastern Highway, 52km east of Southern Cross and 18km east of Yellowdine. Then drive in a northerly direction for 4km to the camping area. Bring drinking water and firewood.

GPS S:31 14.986 E:119 50.434
MR: Map 31 F8

FURTHER Information

Shire of Yilgarn
Tel: 08 9049 1001
Web: www.yilgarn.wa.gov.au
Maximum stay: 3 nights.

Karalee Rock Dam

158 Kookynie

Evidence of the Kookynie's early gold mining days are still visible around the town and its immediate vicinity. Once a town boasting six hotels, today The Grand Hotel is the only remaining pub. Access to Kookynie is signposted off the Goldfields Highway, 42km north of Menzies and 63km south of Leonora.

Grand Hotel

Grand Hotel camping area

Camping area behind hotel in Kookynie. Use hotel facilities. Bar, meals. Limited water, best to bring drinking water and firewood.

GPS S:29 20.167 E:121 29.447

MR: Map 32 I4

FURTHER information

Grand Hotel

Tel: 08 9031 3010

Camping fees: From $11.00 per person/ night. Fees payable at hotel.

159 Laverton

Located on the edge of the Great Victoria Desert, Laverton is the start of the Great Central Road. Visitors can walk the Mt Windarra Heritage Trail with its interpretive signs. Laverton is 124km north-east of Leonora and 361km north-east of Kalgoorlie.

Laverton Caravan Park

Located on Weld Drive in Laverton. Camp kitchen, laundry. Gas/fuel stove only.

MR: Map 32 J2

FURTHER information

Laverton Caravan Park

Tel: 08 9031 1072

Camping fees: Unpowered sites from $20.00 per site/night for 2 people. Powered sites from $35.00 per site/2 people.

160 Leonora

Leonora is located on the Goldfields Highway, 234km north of Kalgoorlie. The town, along with neighbouring Gwalia, thrived during the heady gold mining days of the early 1900s, and there are still a number of buildings from this time. Malcolm Dam, east of Leonora was built in 1902 to provide water for the railway.

Malcolm Dam camping area

From Leonora proceed in an easterly direction towards Laverton for 10.7km to the signposted access to the dam. Then drive in a northerly direction for 3.1km to the dam and open camping area with dispersed bush camping above the dam with little shade or protection. Recommended to bring portable chemical toilet. Bring drinking water and firewood.

GPS S:28 52.577 E:121 26.554

MR: Map 32 I3

FURTHER Information

Leonora Information Centre
Tel: 08 9037 7016
Shire of Leonora
Tel: 08 9037 6044
Web: www.leonora.wa.gov.au

161 Lorna Glen

Formerly a cattle and sheep property, Lorna Glen is conserved for its diverse landscapes, vegetation and wildlife and is used for field and nature study. Visitors can enjoy 4WD touring, nature study and camping in the homestead vicinity. From Wiluna head east along the Gunbarrel Highway to the road signposted to Lake Violet Station, this is the Granite Peak Road. Access is signposted along this road.

Lorna Glen Homestead camping

From the Gunbarrel Highway, 42.7km east of Wiluna, take the signposted Granite Peak Road. Follow Granite Peak Road in a northerly direction for 80km to the signposted access. Then drive in an easterly direction for 37km to the homestead precinct. Camping in the homestead vicinity. Kitchen. Donkey hot water shower. Some firewood supplied.

MR: Map 38 H5

Lorna Glen bush camping

Remote bush camping on Lorna Glen station. No facilities which is best suited for self-sufficient campers. Recommend that portable chemical toilet is carried with you if bush camping. Bring drinking water. Gas/fuel stove preferred.

MR: Map 38 H5

FURTHER Information

DEC Kalgoorlie Regional Office
Tel: 08 9080 5555. Bookings essential.
Camping fees: From $7.00 per adult/night and $2.00 per child (up to 16)/night. Fees payable at DEC Kalgoorlie office.

THE OUTBACK

162 Menzies

Gold was first discovered in the Menzies area in 1891. The town and its surrounds abounds with history and boasts some magnificent historic buildings. Located north-west of town is Lake Ballard and the Inside Australia Exhibition; a series of sculptures on a salt lake. You may like to drive the scenic Golden Quest Trail to take in more of the region's historic places. Menzies is located on the Goldfields Highway, 132km north of Kalgoorlie and 104km south of Leonora.

Menzies Caravan Park

Located on Walsh Street in town. Walsh Street is signposted off the highway. Large camping area with no shade. Playground.

GPS S:29 41.703 E:121 01.809

MR: Map 32 H5

FURTHER Information

Menzies Visitor Centre

Tel: 08 9024 2702

Web: www.menzies.wa.gov.au

Camping fees: From $20.00 per site/night for 2 people. Fees payable at visitor centre or to on-site caretaker.

163 Niagara Dam

Niagara Dam was built as a water supply for the steam trains travelling from Kalgoorlie to Leonora. During its construction around 400 camels carted the cement for the dam's wall all the way from Coolgardie. Access to the dam is signposted off the Kookynie Road, 13km east of the Goldfields Highway.

Niagara Dam camping area

From the Goldfields Highway take the signposted road on the east to Kookynie. This is 42km north of Menzies and 63km south of Leonora. Follow this road east for 15.5km to the signposted access road. This road proceeds in a southerly direction for 3.3km to the top camping area and a further 120m to the lower camping area. This is a large area with dispersed camping among trees with some sites shaded and sheltered from the elements. Bring drinking water and firewood. Please ensure dogs are kept on a lead at all times, as wild dog baiting is done in the area from time to time.

GPS S:29 24.210 E:121 25.723

MR: Map 32 H4

FURTHER Information

Menzies Visitor Centre

Tel: 08 9024 2702

Web: www.menzies.wa.gov.au

Niagara Dam camping area

164 Ora Banda

Ora Banda is another of the region's towns which traces its origins to the heady day of gold mining. Aside from a few outbuildings, the only building of significance to remain in Ora Banda is the hotel. Try your hand at some prospecting (don't forget your licence), go car touring, bird watching or walking. Ora Banda is 27km west of the Goldfields Highway with access signposted off the highway, 39km north of Kalgoorlie.

Ora Banda Hotel Caravan Park

Located behind the hotel. Bar, meals, laundry. Some firewood supplied. As the surrounding areas are baited, and baits can be carried by birds and other wildlife, it is recommended that dogs are kept on a lead at all times.

GPS S:30 22.566 E:121 03.740
MR: Map 32 H6

FURTHER Information

Ora Banda Hotel

Tel: 08 9024 2444. Open weekday 12noon to 7.30pm weekdays, and on weekends from 11am.

Camping fees: Unpowered from $15.00 per site/night for 2 people. Powered from $25.00 per site/night for 2 people.

THE OUTBACK

165 Plumridge Lakes Nature Reserve

Named in 1908 by the explorer Frank Hann whilst exploring the area, Plumridge Lakes are a popular bird watching site. Due to the remoteness of this area visitors need to be self-sufficient and well prepared. Located south-east of Laverton there is 4WD vehicle access to Plumridge Lakes Nature Reserve via the Rason Lake Road off Merolia Road. Alternatively 4WD vehicle only access can be made via the Connie Sue Highway.

Plumridge Lakes Nature Reserve bush camping

Located 85km west of the Connie Sue Highway. The access track to the reserve is 199km south of Neale Junction (see Anne Beadell Highway on page 202 for access details to Neale Junction) and 136km north of Rawlinna. Self-sufficient, no trace camping applies to this site. Recommended to carry own portable chemical toilet. Bring drinking water. Gas/ fuel stove only.

Access track on Connie Sue Highway: **GPS** S:29 50.977 E:125 40.311
MR: Map 33 C2

FURTHER Information

DEC Kalgoorlie Regional Office
Tel: 08 9080 5555
Laverton Tourist Information Centre
Tel: 08/9031 1361
Ngaanyatjarra Council
Tel: 08 8950 1711. A permit is required to travel through sections of Ngaanyatjarra land along the northern section of the Connie Sue Highway.
Web: www.ngaanyatjarra.org.au

THE OUTBACK

166 Rowles Lagoon Conservation Park

Rowles Lagoon, along with Carnage, Clear and Muddy lakes, make up Rowles Lagoon Conservation Park. Of these freshwater lakes Rowles Lagoon is the deepest and largest. The lakes are visited by a large number of birds and waterfowl each year, making the area popular with birdwatchers. The lakes are also accessible for recreational activities such as swimming, picnicking, canoeing and waterskiing. Signposted access is along Coolgardie North Road, north of Coolgardie. Access is possible for conventional vehicles in dry weather.

Rowles Lagoon camping area

Signposted access 68km north of Coolgardie along Coolgardie North Road. Then drive in a north-easterly direction for 6.5km to the camping area with individual sites among trees on the eastern shore of Rowles Lagoon. Natural beach boat launch. Bring drinking water and firewood.

GPS S:30 25.589 E:120 51.852
MR: Map 32 H6

FURTHER Information

DEC Kalgoorlie Regional Office
Tel: 08 9080 5555

Rowles Lagoon camping area

167 Wallaroo Rock Conservation Park

Wallaroo Rock is one of the region's water catchments which supplied water to the steam locomotives running along the woodlines to and from the goldfields. It is possible to drive some of the woodline tracks between Jaurdi Station and Wallaroo Rock. The park is north of the Great Eastern Highway and east of Jaurdi Station.

Wallaroo Rock camping area

Wallaroo Rock is to the north of the Great Eastern Highway with access from the Woolgangie turn off or the Mt Walton (Heath) Road, then drive north for 45km to cross the railway line. Once north of the railway continue to the signposted access. This track leads east to the base of the rock and the camping area. Bring drinking water and firewood.

MR: Map 32 G7

FURTHER information

DEC Kalgoorlie Regional Office
Tel: 08 9080 5555

168 Wanjarri Nature Reserve

This former pastoral station was established in 1920 for a sheep grazing enterprise. One of the former owners, Tom Moriarty had a greater passion for bird watching then sheep grazing, so instead of selling out to a surrounding lease holder he offered the government the property with the view to conserve the area as a nature reserve. Access to Wanjarri is off the Goldfields Highway, north of Leinster. Conventional vehicle access in dry weather.

Wanjarri Shearing Shed camping area

From Leinster proceed north along the Goldfields Highway for 58km to the signposted road on the east to Yacka. This turn off is just south of the bridge over Jones Creek. Then drive in an easterly direction through mining leases, following signage to the reserve which you will reach after 16.4km. The access road can be rough and is for use in dry weather only. Camping here is in the vicinity of the shearing shed/homestead complex. Hot water donkey for shower. Bring drinking water and firewood.

GPS S:27 24.118 E:120 38.881
MR: Map 38 G8

FURTHER information

DEC Kalgoorlie Regional Office
Tel: 08 9080 5555
Camping fees: From $7.00 per adult/night and $2.00 per child (up to 16)/night. Fees payable at DEC Kalgoorlie office.

THE OUTBACK

169 WAPET Road (Kidson Track)

The WAPET Road or Kidson Track leaves the Great Northern Highway 43.7km south of Sandfire Roadhouse and 1.4km north of the Eighty Mile Beach turn off. It then heads south-east for 617km to the Kunawarritji community which is located 4km west of the Canning Stock Route. The WAPET Road is a remote 4WD only road with no services between Sandfire and Kunawarritji. Travellers should be self-sufficient and prepared for remote desert travel. Carry plenty of water, food and fuel. The WAPET Road can have large, deep wash-outs and soft, sandy sections. It is not recommended to travel with dogs in these remote areas.

Burrel Bore camping area

Located on the WAPET Road, 329km south-east of the Great Northern Highway and 70.8km north-west of Razorblade Bore. Bore and bush camping area is 300m south-east of WAPET Rd. Bring drinking water and firewood. Gas/fuel stove preferred.

GPS S:21 01.320 E:123 20.456
MR: Map 44 J3

Razorblade Bore camping area

Located on the WAPET Road, 70.8km south of Burrel Bore and 206.5km north-west of Kunawarritji. Situated just east of the WAPET Rd. Bring drinking water and firewood. Gas/fuel stove preferred.

GPS S:21 33.198 E:123 21.666
MR: Map 44 K4

FURTHER Information

Kunawarritji Aboriginal Community
Tel: 08 9176 9040
There are emergency water supplies along the WAPET Road every 50 to 100km. These supplies are not to be used except in an emergency.

Razorblade Bore camping area

170 Wiluna

As the start/finish point for both the Canning Stock Route and the Gunbarrel Highway, Wiluna has all services required for intrepid travellers on these remote outback roads. Wiluna is situated on the Goldfields Highway, 302km north of Leonora and was first settled to service the gold discoveries in the area in 1896 and was gazetted a town in 1898.

Wiluna Caravan Park

Located on Wotton Street in Wiluna behind the Club Hotel. Laundry. Bring firewood.

GPS S:26 35.430 E:120 13.492
MR: Map 37 F6

FURTHER Information

Club Hotel
Tel: 08 9981 7012
Camping fees: Unpowered sites from $12.00 per site/night for 2 people. Powered sites from $16.00 per site/night for 2 people.

Roadside Rest Areas

REST AREA/TOWN	LOCATION	TOILET	TABLE	FIREPLACE	SHELTER/ SHADE	WATER	OVERNIGHT STAY-MAX 24 HRS	MAP
PERTH TO ALBANY VIA THE ALBANY HIGHWAY								
PERTH								4 H1
ARMADALE								4 K5
Mt Cooke Forest	44km SE of Armadale/88km NW of Williams		✓		✓			12 H6
Rest Area	82km SE of Armadale/50km NW of Williams		✓		✓			12 I7
Crossman Picnic Site	92km SE of Armadale/40km NW of Williams		✓		✓			12 J8
Extracts Arboretum	106km SE of Armadale/26km NW of Williams		✓		✓			12 J8
WILLIAMS								16 K1
Rest Area	16km SE of Williams/82km N of Kojonup		✓		✓			16 L2
Rest Area	64km SE of Williams/34km N of Kojonup		✓		✓			17 B5
Crapella Road	77km SE of Williams/21km N of Kojunup		✓	✓				17 B5
KOJONUP								17 B6
Rest Area	17km S of Kojonup/86km N of Mt Barker		✓		✓			17 C7
Tunney	37km S of Kojonup/66km N of Mt Barker		✓		✓			17 D8
Beattie Road	90km SE of Kojonup/13km N of Mt Barker		✓					21 E3
Sturdee Road	93km SE of Kojonup/10km N of Mt Barker		✓		✓			21 E3
MT BARKER								21 F3
ALBANY								22 G6
PERTH TO ESPERANCE VIA OLD COAST ROAD AND SOUTH COAST HIGHWAY								
PERTH								4 H1
Old Whittakers Mill	134km S of Perth/52km NE of Bunbury		✓	✓				15 E2
Buffalo Road	143km S of Perth/21km N of Bunbury							15 E3
BUNBURY								15 E4
DONNYBROOK								15 F6
BRIDGETOWN								16 H8
MANJIMUP								20 I2
WALPOLE								21 A6
ALBANY								22 G6
Green Range	70km NE of Albany/109km S of Jerramungup		✓					22 J3
Pallinup River	114km NE of Albany/65km S of Jerramungup		✓		✓		✓	22 K1

REST AREA/TOWN	LOCATION	TOILET	TABLE	FIREPLACE	SHELTER/ SHADE	WATER	OVERNIGHT STAY-MAX 20 HRS	MAP
PERTH TO ESPERANCE VIA OLD COAST ROAD AND SOUTH COAST HIGHWAY continued...								
JERRAMUNGUP								18 L6
Fitzgerald River	34km E of Jerramungup/81km W of Ravensthorpe		✓		✓			23 B4
RAVENSTHORPE								24 G2
Rest Area	6km E of Ravensthorpe/181km W of Esperance		✓					24 G2
Coomalbidgup	132km E of Ravensthorpe/55km W of Esperance		✓					25 B5
ESPERANCE								25 E5
PERTH TO KALGOORLIE VIA THE GREAT EASTERN HIGHWAY								
PERTH								4 H1
MIDLAND								11 E2
Greenmount	8km E of Midland/15km W of Mundaring	✓	✓	✓	✓			11 F2
MUNDARING								11 F2
Forsyth Mill	12km E of Mundaring/53km W of Northam	✓	✓	✓	✓			12 G2
Eadine Springs	48km E of Mundaring/17km W of Northam		✓	✓	✓			8 H8
NORTHAM								8 I8
Rest Area	60km E of Northam/48km W of Kellerberrin		✓		✓	✓		9 A7
Rest Area	84km E of Northam/24km W of Kellerberrin		✓		✓			9 B7
KELLERBERRIN								9 C7
MERREDIN								9 F6
SOUTHERN CROSS								10 L3
Koorarawalyee	65km E of Southern Cross/120km W of Coolgardie	✓	✓	✓	✓		✓	31 F8
Scenic Lookout	105km E of Southern Cross/80km W of Coolgardie		✓	✓	✓			32 G8
Yerdani Well	129km E of Southern Cross/56km W of Coolgardie		✓	✓				32 G7
COOLGARDIE								32 H7
KALGOORLIE								32 I7
COOLGARDIE TO ESPERANCE VIA THE COOLGARDIE-ESPERANCE HIGHWAY								
COOLGARDIE								32 H7
Mount Thirsty	143km S of Coolgardie/23km N of Norseman		✓	✓	✓			27 E1
Lake Cowan	151km S of Coolgardie/15km N of Norseman		✓	✓	✓			27 E1
NORSEMAN								27 E2
Kumarl Siding	72km S of Norseman/131km N of Esperance		✓	✓	✓			27 E3
Lions Lookout	196km S of Norseman/7km N of Esperance							25 E5
ESPERANCE								25 E5

REST AREA/TOWN	LOCATION	TOILET	TABLE	FIREPLACE	SHELTER/ SHADE	WATER	OVERNIGHT STAY-MAX 20 HRS	MAP
NORSEMAN TO EUCLA VIA THE EYRE HIGHWAY								
NORSEMAN								27 E2
Ten Mile Rocks	78km E of Norseman/112km W of Balladonia	✓	✓	✓	✓		✓	28 G1
Fraser Range	81km E of Newman/109km W of Balladonia	✓	✓	✓	✓		✓	28 G1
Newman Rocks	140km E of Norseman/50km W of Balladonia		✓	✓	✓			28 G1
Harms Lake	163km E of Norseman/27km W of Balladonia		✓	✓	✓			28 H1
BALLADONIA								28 H2
Afgan Rock	5km E of Balladonia/176km W of Caiguna		✓		✓			33 A8
Woorlba Homestead	50km E of Balladonia/131km W of Caiguna	✓	✓	✓	✓		✓	33 B8
Rest Area	92km E of Balladonia/89km W of Caiguna		✓					33 C8
Rest Area	109km E of Balladonia/72km W of Caiguna		✓					33 C8
Baxter	115km E of Balladonia/67km W of Caiguna	✓	✓		✓		✓	33 C8
Domblegabby	142km E of Balladonia/39km W of Caiguna	✓	✓		✓			33 D8
Caiguna Blowhole	176km E of Balladonia/5km W of Caiguna		✓					33 D8
CAIGUNA								33 D8
COCKLEBIDDY								33 E7
Moonera Tank	44km E of Cocklebiddy/48km W of Madura		✓	✓	✓			33 F7
Madura Lookout	91km E of Cocklebiddy/1km W of Madura		✓		✓			34 G7
MADURA								34 G7
Moondi Bluff	27km E of Madura/89km W of Mundrabilla	✓	✓	✓	✓			34 G7
Carlabeencabba Rockhole	48km E of Madura/68km W of Mundrabilla		✓		✓			34 H7
Rest Area	62km E of Madura/54km W of Mundrabilla		✓		✓			34 H7
Jilah Rockhole	106km E of Madura/10km W of Mundrabilla	✓	✓	✓	✓			34 I7
Kuthala Pass	113km E of Madura/3km W of Mundrabilla		✓	✓	✓			34 I6
MUNDRABILLA								34 I6
Najada Rockhole	30km E of Mundrabilla/36km W of Eucla		✓	✓				34 J6
EUCLA								34 J6

REST AREAS

REST AREA/TOWN	LOCATION	TOILET	TABLE	FIREPLACE	SHELTER/ SHADE	WATER	OVERNIGHT STAY-MAX 20 HRS	MAP
PERTH TO PORT HEDLAND VIA THE GREAT NORTHERN HIGHWAY								
PERTH								4 H1
Bindoon Hill	95km N of Perth/37km S of New Norcia		✓	✓	✓			
Flora Area	115km N of Perth/17km S of New Norcia		✓	✓	✓			
NEW NORCIA								7 F4
Rest Area	30km N of New Norcia/89km S of Dalwallinu		✓	✓				7 F2
Walebing	35km N of New Norcia/84km S of Dalwallinu		✓	✓				7 F2
Rest Area	42km N of New Norcia/77km S of Dalwallinu		✓	✓				7 F2
Rest Area	76km N of New Norcia/43km S of Dalwallinu		✓	✓				30 L7
DALWALLINU								30 L7
WUBIN								30 L6
Rest Area	7km N of Wubin/102km S of Paynes Find		✓		✓			30 L6
Jibberding	32km N of Wubin/77km S of Paynes Find		✓		✓			31 A6
White Wells	47km N of Wubin/62km S of Paynes Find		✓	✓	✓			31 A5
Mt Gibson	85km N of Wubin/24km S of Paynes Find	✓	✓	✓	✓			31 A5
PAYNES FIND								31 B4
Rest Area	56km N of Paynes Find/88km S of Mt Magnet		✓					31 B3
MOUNT MAGNET								31 B2
Rest Area	100km N of Mt Magnet/97km S of Meekatharra		✓					37 B8
Tuckanarra	120km N of Mt Magnet/77km S of Meekatharra		✓	✓				37 B8
Rest Area	179km N of Mt Magnet/18km S of Meekatharra		✓	✓				37 B7
MEEKATHARRA								37 C7
Middle Branch Bridge	192km N of Meekatharra/221km S of Newman		✓	✓	✓			37 D4
NEWMAN								43 D8
Mt Robinson	106km NW of Newman/303km S of the North West Coastal Hwy	✓	✓		✓		✓	43 B7
Albert Tognolini	180km NW of Newman/229km S of the North West Coastal Hwy		✓		✓			43 B6
Bea Bea	246km NW of Newman/163km S of the North West Coastal Hwy		✓					43 B5
NORTH WEST COASTAL HIGHWAY JUNCTION								43 A3
PORT HEDLAND								43 A2

REST AREA/TOWN	LOCATION	TOILET	TABLE	FIREPLACE	SHELTER/ SHADE	WATER	OVERNIGHT STAY-MAX 20 HRS	MAP
PERTH TO PORT HEDLAND VIA THE BRAND AND NORTH WEST COASTAL HIGHWAYS								
PERTH								4 H1
Regans Ford	129km N of Perth/295km S of Geraldton	✓	✓		✓			7 C5
Arrowsmith	294km N of Perth/130km S of Geraldton	✓	✓	✓	✓			30 I6
GERALDTON								30 H4
Oakabella	33km N of Geraldton/447km S of Carnarvon		✓		✓			30 H4
Galena Bridge	115km N of Geraldton/365km S of Carnarvon	✓	✓	✓	✓		✓	30 H2
Nerren Nerren	188km N of Geraldton/292 km S of Carnarvon	✓	✓	✓	✓		✓	30 G1
Edaggee	399km N of Geraldton/81km S of Carnarvon	✓	✓	✓	✓			35 F5
CARNARVON								35 E5
Yalabia	90km N of Carnarvon/278km S of Nanutarra	✓	✓	✓	✓			35 F3
Minilya	141km N of Carnarvon/227km S of Nanutarra	✓	✓	✓	✓			35 E2
Lyndon River	190km N of Carnarvon/178km S of Nanutarra	✓	✓	✓	✓		✓	35 F2
Lyndon River	32km NW of Minilya along the Minilya-Exmouth Road	✓	✓	✓	✓			35 E2
Burkett Rd info bay	258km N of Carnarvon/110km S of Nanutarra	✓	✓					41 F8
Barradale	296km N of Carnarvon/72km S of Nanutarra	✓	✓	✓	✓		✓	41 G8
Ashburton River	377km N of Carnaravon/1km S of Nanutarra	✓	✓	✓	✓		✓	42 H7
NANUTARRA								42 H7
Robe River	120km N of Nanutarra/383km S of Port Hedland	✓	✓	✓	✓		✓	42 H5
Fortescue River	165km N of Nanutarra/338km S of Port Hedland		✓		✓			42 H5
West Peawah	410km N of Nanutarra/93km S of Port Hedland	✓	✓	✓			✓	42 L3
PORT HEDLAND								43 A2
PORT HEDLAND TO KUNUNURRA VIA BROOME AND FITZROY CROSSING								
PORT HEDLAND								43 A2
DeGrey River	83km N of Port Hedland/530km S of Broome		✓	✓	✓			43 B2
Stanley	396km N of Port Hedland/217km S of Broome	✓	✓	✓	✓		✓	47 C7
Goldwire	442km N of Port Headland/171km S of Broome	✓	✓	✓	✓			47 C6
BROOME								47 C5
Nillibubbica	107km E of Broome/72km W of Derby turnoff	✓	✓		✓		✓	47 E4
DERBY turnoff								47 F4

REST AREA/TOWN	LOCATION	TOILET	TABLE	FIREPLACE	SHELTER/ SHADE	WATER	OVERNIGHT STAY-MAX 20 HRS	MAP
PORT HEDLAND TO KUNUNURRA VIA BROOME AND FITZROY CROSSING continued...								
Boab Tree	57km E of Derby turnoff/160km W of Fitzroy Crossing		✓	✓	✓			48 G4
Ellendale	129km E of Derby turnoff/88km W of Fitzroy Crossing	✓	✓	✓	✓		✓	49 A3
FITZROY CROSSING								49 C3
Ngumban Cliff	98km E of Fitzroy Crossing/193km SW of Halls Creek	✓	✓	✓	✓			48 K6
Mary Pool	182km E of Fitzroy Crossing/109km SW of Halls Creek	✓	✓	✓			✓	49 E4
HALLS CREEK								50 G3
Little Panton	45km N of Halls Creek/270km S of Victoria Highway junction		✓	✓	✓			50 G2
Leycester's Rest	100km N of Halls Creek/215km S of Victoria Highway junction	✓	✓	✓	✓		✓	50 G1
Spring Creek	109km N of Halls Creek/206km S of Victoria Highway junction	✓	✓	✓	✓			50 H1
Dunham River	282km N of Halls Creek/33km S of Victoria Highway junction	✓	✓	✓	✓		✓	52 I6
Cockburn	At Highway junction/55km S of Wyndham/45km W of Kununurra	✓	✓		✓		✓	52 I6
VICTORIA HWY junction								52 I6
Maggie Creek	23km N of Victoria Highway junction/33km S of Wyndham		✓					52 I5
WYNDHAM								52 I5
KUNUNURRA								52 J6
WA/NT border	42km E of Kununurra	✓	✓		✓			52 K6

FURTHER Information

Main Roads Western Australia

Tel: 138 138 **Web:** www.mainroads.wa.gov.au

Please note that designated 24 Hour Rest Areas may change from year to year, so please take note of any signage regarding overnight stays.

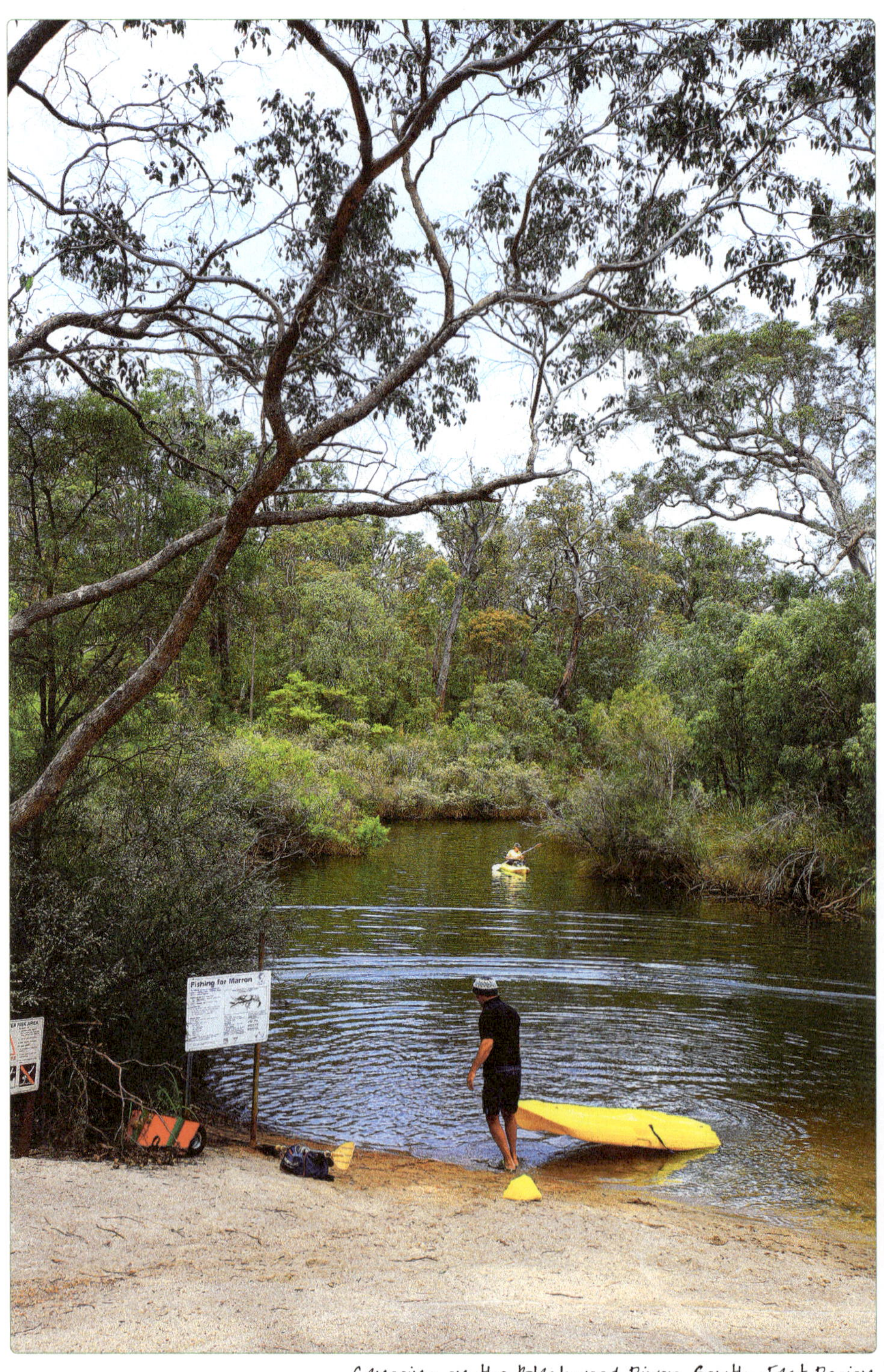

Canoeing on the Blackwood River, South-East Region

TOURING MAPS

Joins Map 7
A
B
C
D
E
F
1
2
3
4
5
6
7
8
Wreck Point
Two Rocks
Minnies Grotto
Melaleuca Cave
Yanchep Cave
The Spot
YANCHEP NATIONAL PARK
GNANGARA-MOORE RIVER STATE FOREST
Crystal Cave
Road Cave
Cauliflower Cave
Yanchep
Rose Cave
Wanneroo
Eglinton
Carabooda
Carabooda Hill
Carabooda Lake
Road
Nowergup Lake
Nowergup
Jindalee
Butler
Neerabup Lake
Merriwa
Quinns Rocks
Mindarie
Clarkson
NEERABUP NATIONAL PARK
Little Coogee Flat
Banksia Grove
CARRAMAR
TAPPING
KINROSS
Marmion
CURRAMBINE
Lake Joondalup
BURNS BEACH
JOONDALUP
LAKE JOONDALUP NATURE RESERVE
OCEAN REEF
HEATHRIDGE
Ocean Reef Boat Harbour
EDGEWATER
INDIAN OCEAN
MARMION MARINE PARK
Avenue
BELDON
MULLALOO
CRAIGIE
WOODVALE
Mitchell
Mullaloo Beach
Whitford Beach
Pinnaroo Point
HILLARYS
PADBURY
SORRENTO
DUNCRAIG
Sorrento Beach
Marmion Beach
Watermans Beach
NORTH BEACH
North Beach
CANNE
KARRINYU
TRIGG
Trigg Beach
West Coast Highway
SCARBOROUGH
Scarborough Beach
INNALOO
N
0
Scale 1:250,000
10km
Joins Map 3

TOURING MAPS

G
H
I
J
K
L
Joins Map 7
Joins Map 12
1
2
3
4
5
6
7
8
Chandala
Brand Highway
Muchea
Muchea Hill
Cockman Bluff
Lower Chittering
MOONDYNE NATURE RESERVE
Moondyne
AVON VALLEY NATIONAL PARK
Great Northern Highway
East Bullsbrook
Bullsbrook
RAAF Pearce
Woodsome Hill
Jumperkine
WALYUNGA NATIONAL PARK
Neaves Road
GNANGARA-MOORE RIVER STATE FOREST
Warbrook
Jandabup
Mount Mambup
The Vines
Upper Swan
Belhus
Gnangara
ELLENBROOK
Millendon
Baskerville
Millendon Junction
LEXIA
Gnangara Road
Gnangara Lake
Henley Brook
Mount Oakover
Thirteen Mile Flat
LANDSDALE
Herne Hill
Toodyay Road
Red Hill
Whiteman
CULLACABARDEE
ALEXANDER HEIGHTS
WEST SWAN
Middle Swan
JOHN FORREST NATIONAL PARK
Parkerville
BALLAJURA
Emu Lake
BEECHBORO
Middle Swan Road
STRATTON
Swan View
MALAGA
MIRRABOOKA
Reid Highway
NORANDA
Tonkin
LOCKRIDGE
MIDLAND
BELLEVUE
Great Eastern Highway
Nyaania
Hovea
Mahogany Creek
NOLLAMARA
MORLEY
KIARA
GUILDFORD
DIANELLA
Glen Forrest
Darlington
ZAMIA STATE FOREST
BASSENDEAN
HAZELMERE
SOUTH GUILDFORD
Charles Street
Yokine Hill
BEDFORD
BAYSWATER
ASHFIELD
Eastern
Roe
River
Helena
Avon River
Brockman River
Brook
MELTHAM
MAYLANDS
Guildford
ASCOT
PERTH AIRPORT
HIGH WYCOMBE
Pauls Valley
Maida Vale
GREENMOUNT STATE FOREST
NORTH PERTH
REDCLIFFE
Joins Map 4
TOURING MAPS

TOURING MAPS

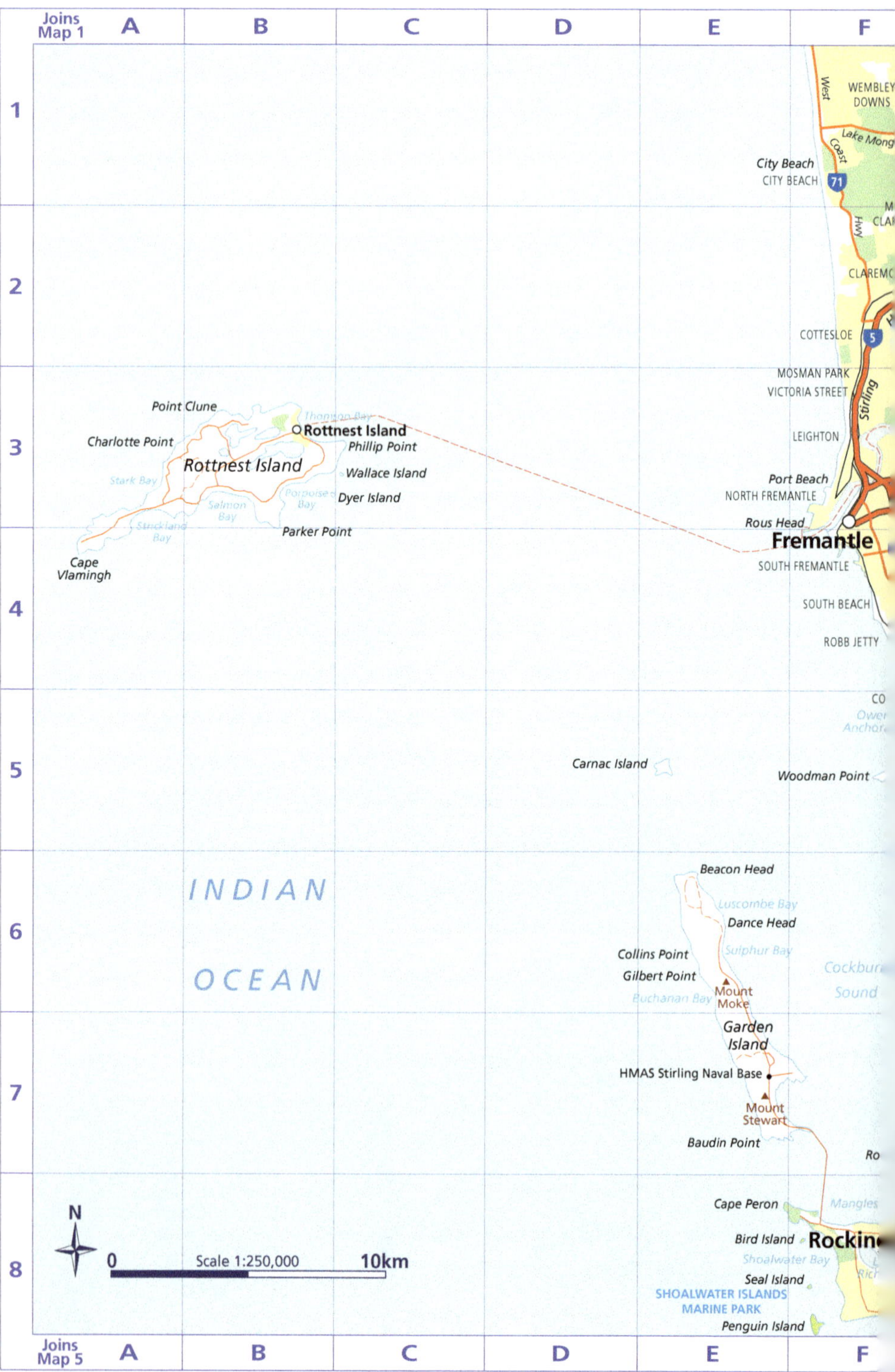

Joins Map 1
A
B
C
D
E
F
1
2
3
4
5
6
7
8
WEMBLEY DOWNS
West
Coast
Hwy
Lake Mong
City Beach
CITY BEACH
71
CLAREMO
COTTESLOE
5
MOSMAN PARK
VICTORIA STREET
Stirling
LEIGHTON
Port Beach
NORTH FREMANTLE
Rous Head
Fremantle
SOUTH FREMANTLE
SOUTH BEACH
ROBB JETTY
Point Clune
Thomson Bay
Rottnest Island
Charlotte Point
Rottnest Island
Phillip Point
Wallace Island
Stark Bay
Salmon Bay
Porpoise Bay
Dyer Island
Strickland Bay
Parker Point
Cape Vlamingh
Carnac Island
Woodman Point
INDIAN
OCEAN
Beacon Head
Luscombe Bay
Dance Head
Collins Point
Sulphur Bay
Cockburn Sound
Gilbert Point
Buchanan Bay
Mount Moke
Garden Island
HMAS Stirling Naval Base
Mount Stewart
Baudin Point
Cape Peron
Mangles
Bird Island
Rockin
Shoalwater Bay
Seal Island
SHOALWATER ISLANDS MARINE PARK
Penguin Island
N
0
Scale 1:250,000
10km
Joins Map 5

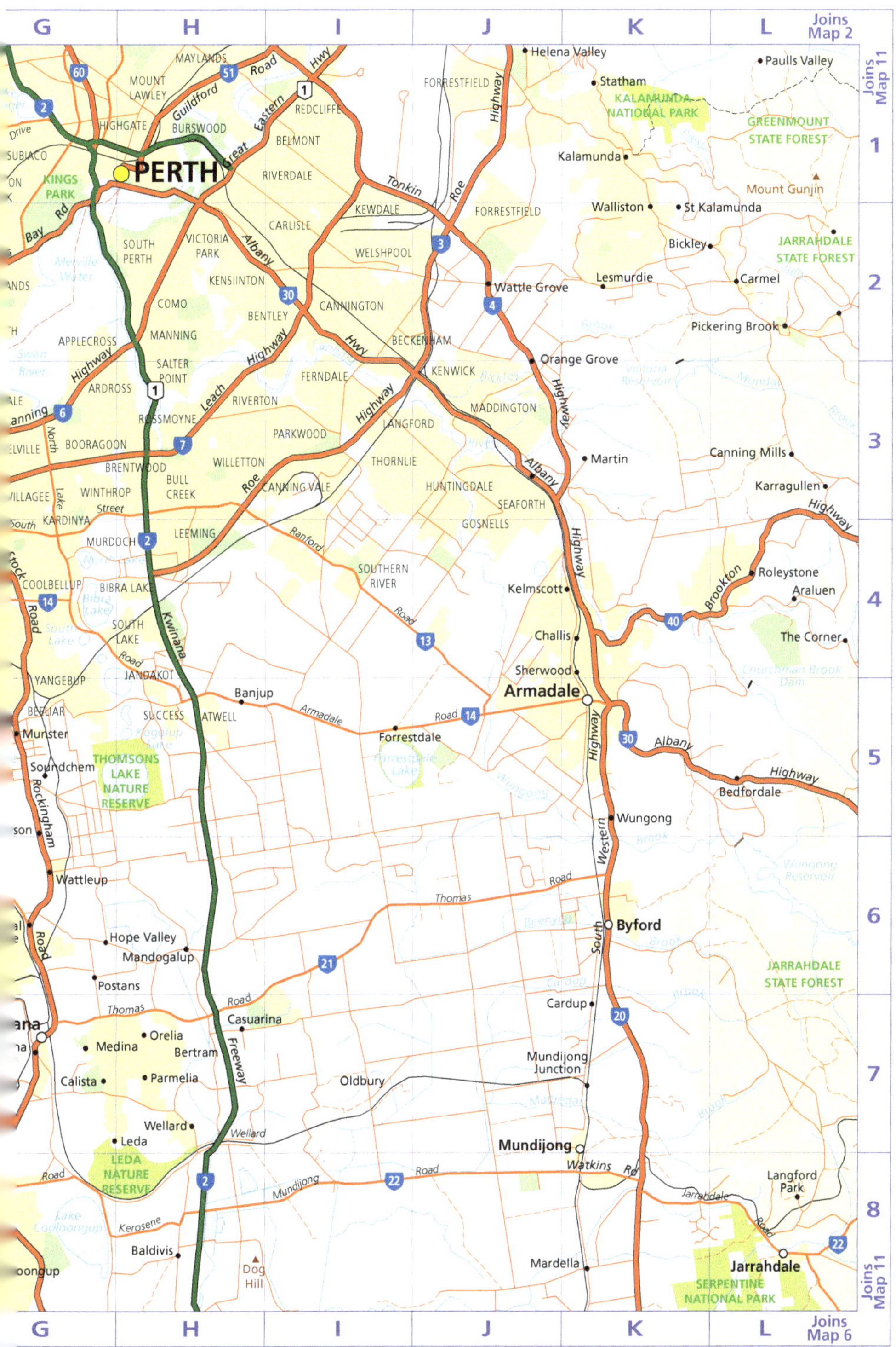
G
H
I
J
K
L
Joins Map 2
Joins Map 11
1
2
3
4
5
6
7
8
Joins Map 11
Joins Map 6
PERTH
MAYLANDS
MOUNT LAWLEY
HIGHGATE
SUBIACO
KINGS PARK
BURSWOOD
REDCLIFFE
BELMONT
RIVERDALE
FORRESTFIELD
Helena Valley
Statham
KALAMUNDA NATIONAL PARK
Paulls Valley
GREENMOUNT STATE FOREST
Kalamunda
Mount Gunjin
Walliston
St Kalamunda
Bickley
JARRAHDALE STATE FOREST
Carmel
Lesmurdie
Wattle Grove
Pickering Brook
KEWDALE
CARLISLE
WELSHPOOL
VICTORIA PARK
SOUTH PERTH
KENSIINTON
COMO
BENTLEY
CANNINGTON
BECKENHAM
KENWICK
MANNING
APPLECROSS
SALTER POINT
ARDROSS
FERNDALE
Orange Grove
MADDINGTON
RIVERTON
ROSSMOYNE
PARKWOOD
LANGFORD
BOORAGOON
BRENTWOOD
BULL CREEK
WILLETTON
THORNLIE
Martin
Canning Mills
WINTHROP
KARDINYA
CANNING VALE
HUNTINGDALE
Karragullen
SEAFORTH
GOSNELLS
MURDOCH
LEEMING
COOLBELLUP
BIBRA LAKE
SOUTHERN RIVER
Roleystone
Araluen
Kelmscott
SOUTH LAKE
Challis
The Corner
YANGEBUP
JANDAKOT
Sherwood
Banjup
Armadale
BEELIAR
SUCCESS
ATWELL
Forrestdale
Munster
Soundchem
THOMSONS LAKE NATURE RESERVE
Bedfordale
Wungong
Wattleup
Byford
Hope Valley
Mandogalup
JARRAHDALE STATE FOREST
Postans
Cardup
Casuarina
Orelia
Medina
Bertram
Calista
Parmelia
Oldbury
Mundijong Junction
Wellard
Leda
LEDA NATURE RESERVE
Mundijong
Watkins Rd
Langford Park
Baldivis
Dog Hill
Mardella
Jarrahdale
SERPENTINE NATIONAL PARK
Great Eastern Hwy
Guildford Road
Tonkin Hwy
Roe Hwy
Albany Hwy
Leach Highway
Canning Highway
Kwinana Freeway
Ranford Road
Armadale Road
Thomas Road
Mundijong Road
Kerosene
Brookton Highway
South Western Highway
Albany Highway
Rockingham Road
Jarrahdale Road
TOURING MAPS

Joins Map 3
A
B
C
D
E
F
1
2
3
4
5
6
7
8
N
0
Scale 1:250,000
10km
Shoalwater Bay
Lake Richmond
Cooloongup
Lake Cooloongup
Baldivis
Shoalwater
Safety Bay
Mersey Point
Waikiki
Safety Bay
Ennis
Avenue
Folly Pool
SHOALWATER ISLANDS MARINE PARK
Warnbro
Warnbro Sound
Lake Walyungup
Mandurah
Road
Kwinana
Freeway
Bridport Point
Becher Point
Port Kennedy
NATURE RESERVE
Stakehill Road
Secret Harbour
Kamup
Lake Amarillo
Golden Bay
Comet Bay
INDIAN
OCEAN
Madora
San Remo
Parklands
Gordon
Goegrup Lake
Greenfields
Robert Point
Blue Bay
Halls Head
Mandurah
Bypass
Black Lake
Barragup
Pinjarra
Old Coast Road
Erskine
Coodanup
Furnissdale
Murray
River
Yunderup
Falcon
Falcon Bay
Cox Bay
Placid Waters
Peel
Inlet
Avalon
Ward Point
Wannanup
Point Grey
Point Birch
AUSTIN BAY NATURE RESERVE
Austin Bay
Robert Bay
Florida
Stony Point
Dawesville
Melros
Old
Coast
Road
Tims Thickett
Point Morfitt
Park Ridge
YALGORUP NATIONAL PARK
Mealup Point
Cape Bouvard
Forrest
Highway
Joins Map 15

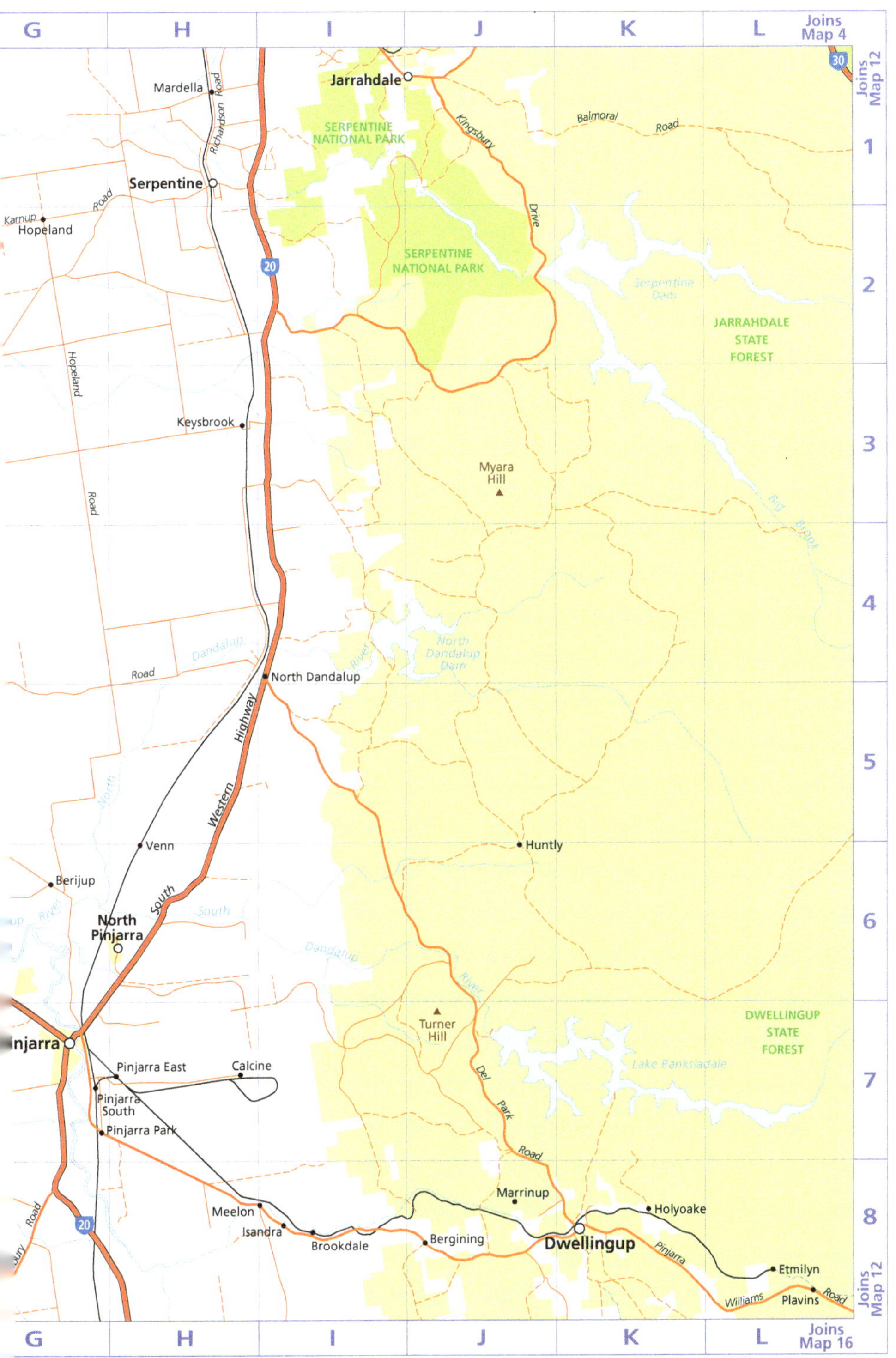

TOURING MAPS

Joins Map 30
A
B
C
D
E
F
1
2
3
4
5
6
7
8
Badgingarra
BADGINGARRA NATIONAL PARK
North West Road
Mungedar
Dunearn
Sangaree
Girraween
Cypress Hill
Obanpark
Ponda Rosa
Glen Ruff
The Midlands Road
Coomberdale
Cairn Hill
Dalaroo
Kallaroo
Berkshire Valley
Moore River
Miling
Lyons Camp
Cranmore Park
Bindi B
WONGONDERRAH NATURE RESERVE
Warra Warra
Tambrey
Chelsea
Moora
The Midlands Road
Wandena
Tuyali
Cooljarloo
Mount Misery
Dandaragan
Lupin Valley
Havelock
Barberton
Idylwild
Billinue Community
Joanna Plains
Menardie
Dambagee
Danmor
Koojan
Cataby
Caro
Brand
Yaramie
Koojan Downs
Capitela
Marry Hills
ENEMINGA NATURE RESERVE
Kilbride
Lancelin Training Area
Mimegarra
Tickeroo
Rowley Downs
Gillingarra
North River
Mundora Downs
New N
Eden Vale
Eaglehawk Flats
NAMMING NATURE RESERVE
Pindaree
Dovedale
Mogumber
Moore River East
NILGEN NATURE RESERVE
Ocean Farm
Seemore
Orange Springs
Mogumber
Northern Highway
Lancelin
Seaview
Quins Castle
MOORE RIVER NATURE RESERVE
Mindarra
Wannamal
Great
Ledge Point
Lancelin Road
Gooninong
Highway
BOONANARRING NATURE RESERVE
Beermullah
Breton Bay
Breton Bay
Moore River
Cullalla
Seabird
Redfield Park
Gingin Brook Road
Neergabby
Mooliabeenee
Gingin
Bindoon
Cape Leschenault
Woodridge
Guilderton
Wanneroo Road
Brand Highway
YEAL NATURE RESERVE
Chittering
INDIAN
Wilbinga
OCEAN
Two Rocks
The Spot
Yanchep
YANCHEP NATIONAL PARK
Chandala
Muchea
Lower Chittering
Eglinton
Carabooda
Nowergup
East Bullsbrook
For more detail see maps 1-2
1
60
116
95
Joins Map 11

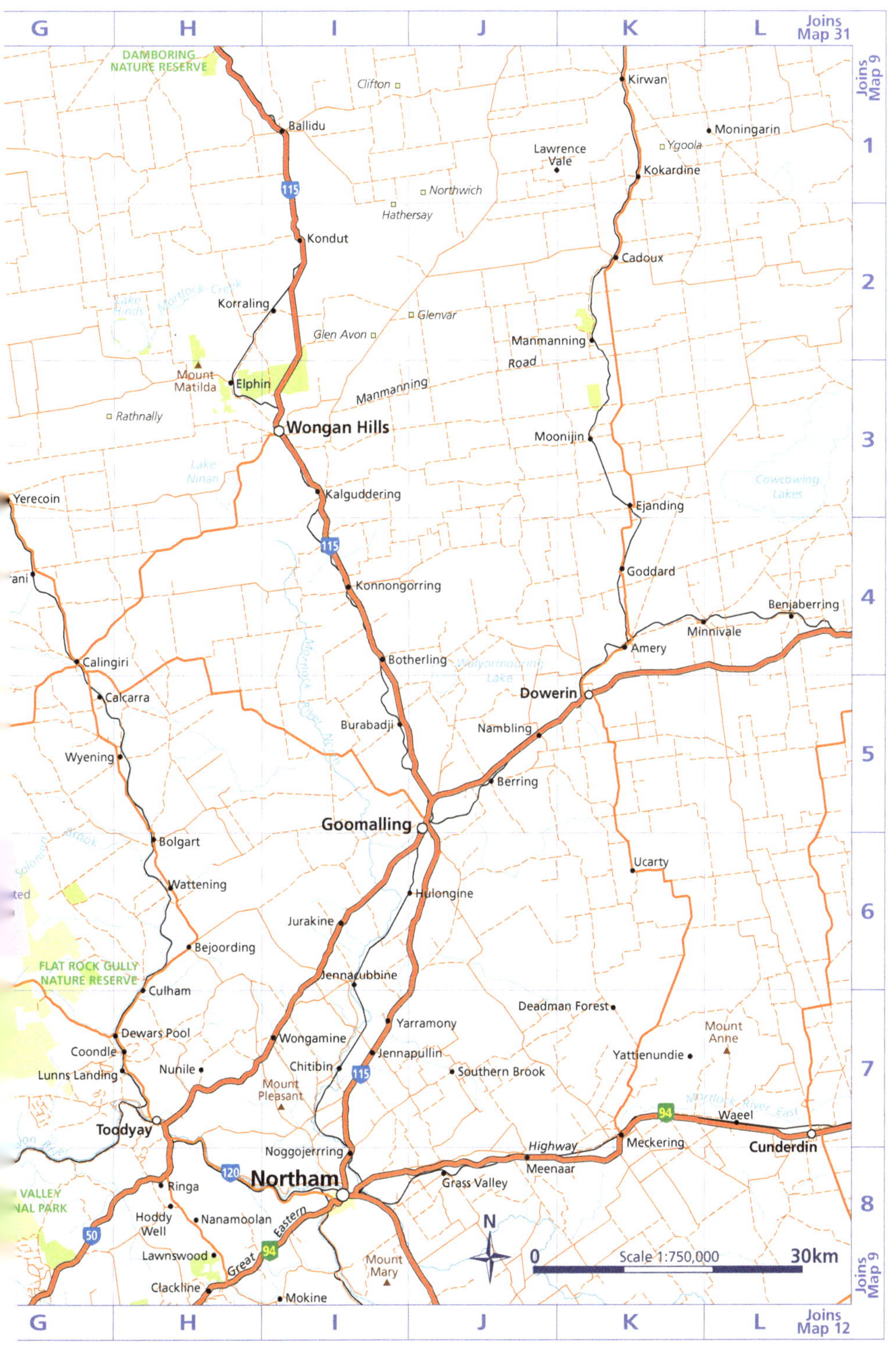
G
H
I
J
K
L
Joins Map 31
Joins Map 9
1
2
3
4
5
6
7
8
DAMBORING NATURE RESERVE
Clifton
Kirwan
Ballidu
Moningarin
Lawrence Vale
Ygoola
Kokardine
115
Northwich
Hathersay
Kondut
Cadoux
Korraling
Glenvar
Glen Avon
Manmanning
Road
Mount Matilda
Elphin
Manmanning
Rathnally
Wongan Hills
Moonijin
Lake Ninan
Kalguddering
Cowcowing Lakes
Yerecoin
Ejanding
115
Goddard
Konnongorring
Benjaberring
Minnivale
Calingiri
Amery
Botherling
Wyalyormouring Lake
Calcarra
Dowerin
Burabadji
Nambling
Wyening
Berring
Goomalling
Bolgart
Ucarty
Wattening
Hulongine
Jurakine
Bejoording
FLAT ROCK GULLY NATURE RESERVE
Jennacubbine
Culham
Deadman Forest
Yarramony
Mount Anne
Dewars Pool
Wongamine
Coondle
Jennapullin
Yattienundie
Chitibin
Lunns Landing
Nunile
Southern Brook
115
Mount Pleasant
94
Waeel
Toodyay
Highway
Meckering
Noggojerring
Cunderdin
Meenaar
120
Northam
Grass Valley
Ringa
Eastern
Hoddy Well
Nanamoolan
50
94
Great
Lawnswood
Mount Mary
N
0
Scale 1:750,000
30km
Clackline
Mokine
Joins Map 12
TOURING MAPS

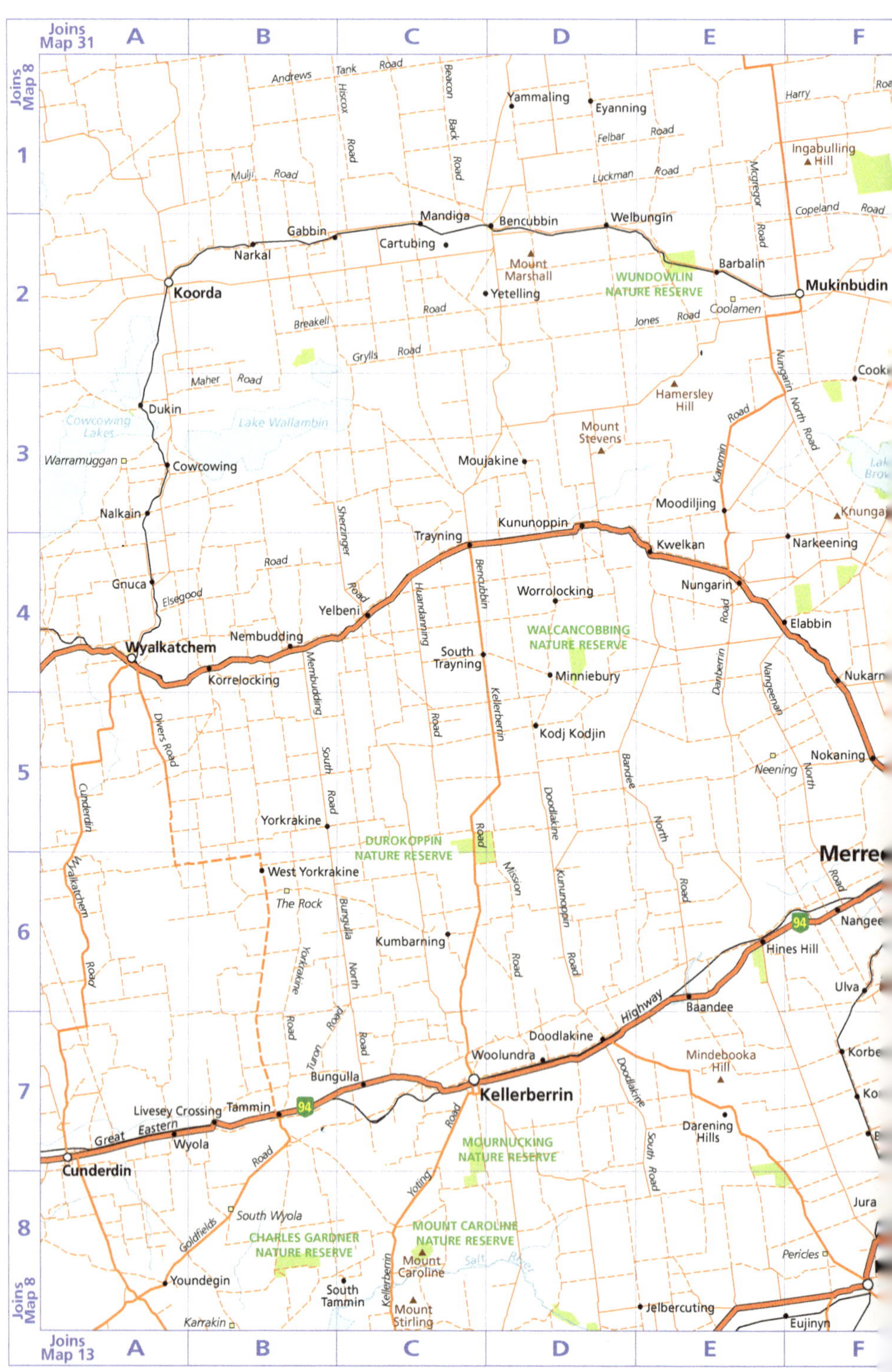

Joins Map 31
A
B
C
D
E
F
Joins Map 8
1
2
3
4
5
6
7
8
Joins Map 8
Joins Map 13
Yammaling
Eyanning
Mandiga
Gabbin
Narkal
Cartubing
Bencubbin
Welbungin
Barbalin
Mukinbudin
Koorda
Mount Marshall
Yetelling
WUNDOWLIN NATURE RESERVE
Coolamen
Ingabulling Hill
Hamersley Hill
Mount Stevens
Dukin
Cowcowing Lakes
Lake Wallambin
Warramuggan
Cowcowing
Moujakine
Nalkain
Moodiljing
Knungajin
Kununoppin
Trayning
Kwelkan
Narkeening
Gnuca
Yelbeni
Worrolocking
Nungarin
Elabbin
Wyalkatchem
Nembudding
Korrelocking
South Trayning
WALCANCOBBING NATURE RESERVE
Minniebury
Kodj Kodjin
Nokaning
Neening
Yorkrakine
DUROKOPPIN NATURE RESERVE
West Yorkrakine
The Rock
Kumbarning
Hines Hill
Nangeenan
Ulva
Baandee
Doodlakine
Woolundra
Mindebooka Hill
Bungulla
Kellerberrin
Livesey Crossing
Tammin
Wyola
Great Eastern Highway
Cunderdin
Darening Hills
MOURNUCKING NATURE RESERVE
South Wyola
CHARLES GARDNER NATURE RESERVE
MOUNT CAROLINE NATURE RESERVE
Mount Caroline
Mount Stirling
South Tammin
Youndegin
Karrakin
Jelbercuting
Eujinyn
Jura
Pericles
Merredin

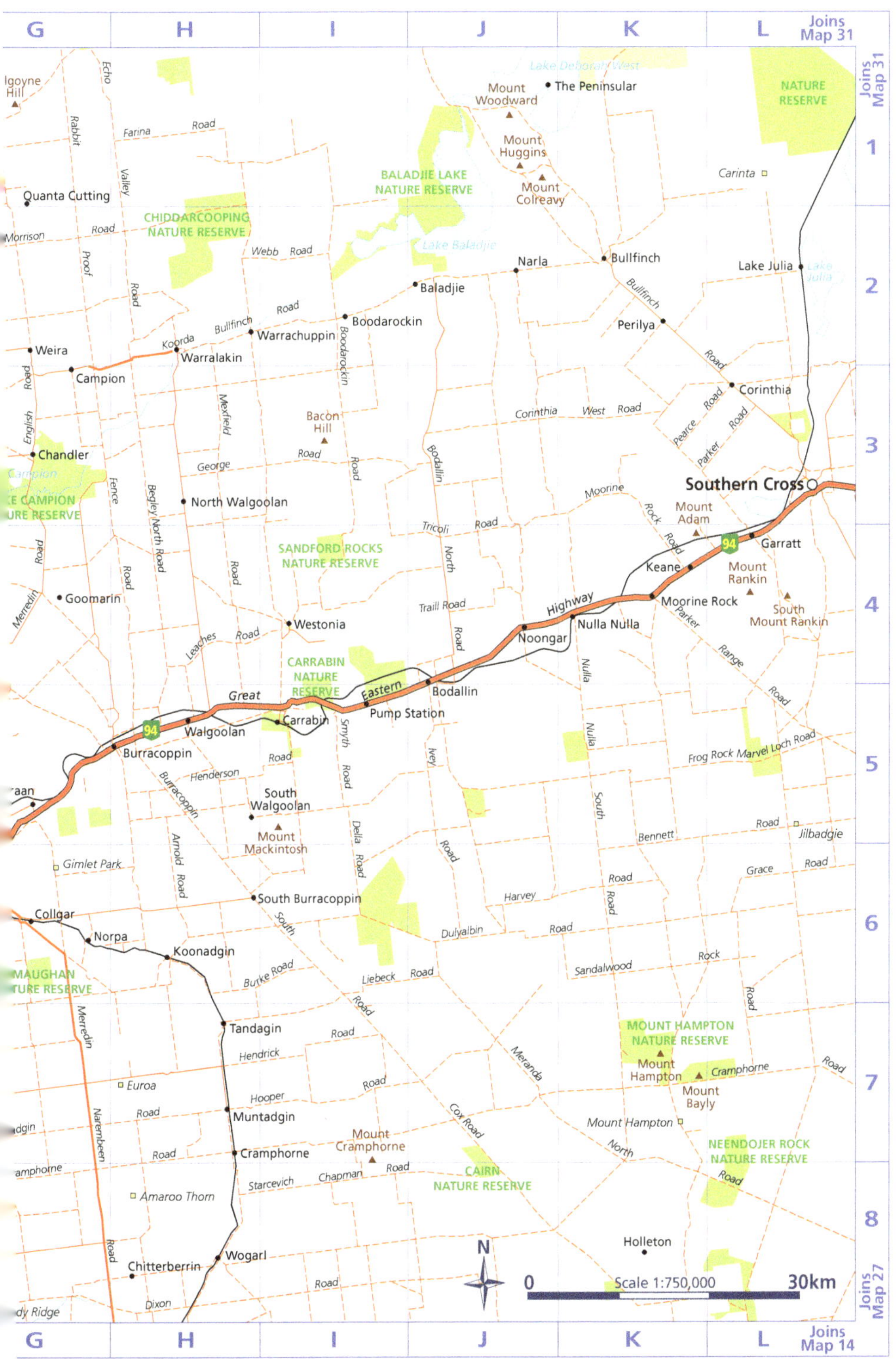

TOURING MAPS

Joins Map 7
Joins Map 15
INDIAN OCEAN
PERTH
Fremantle
Rottnest Island
Rockingham
Mandurah
Kwinana
Pinjarra
Waroona
MARMION MARINE PARK
SHOALWATER ISLANDS MARINE PARK
GNANGARA-MOORE RIVER STATE FOREST
KOOLJERRENUP NATURE RESERVE
Scale 1:750,000
0
30km
N

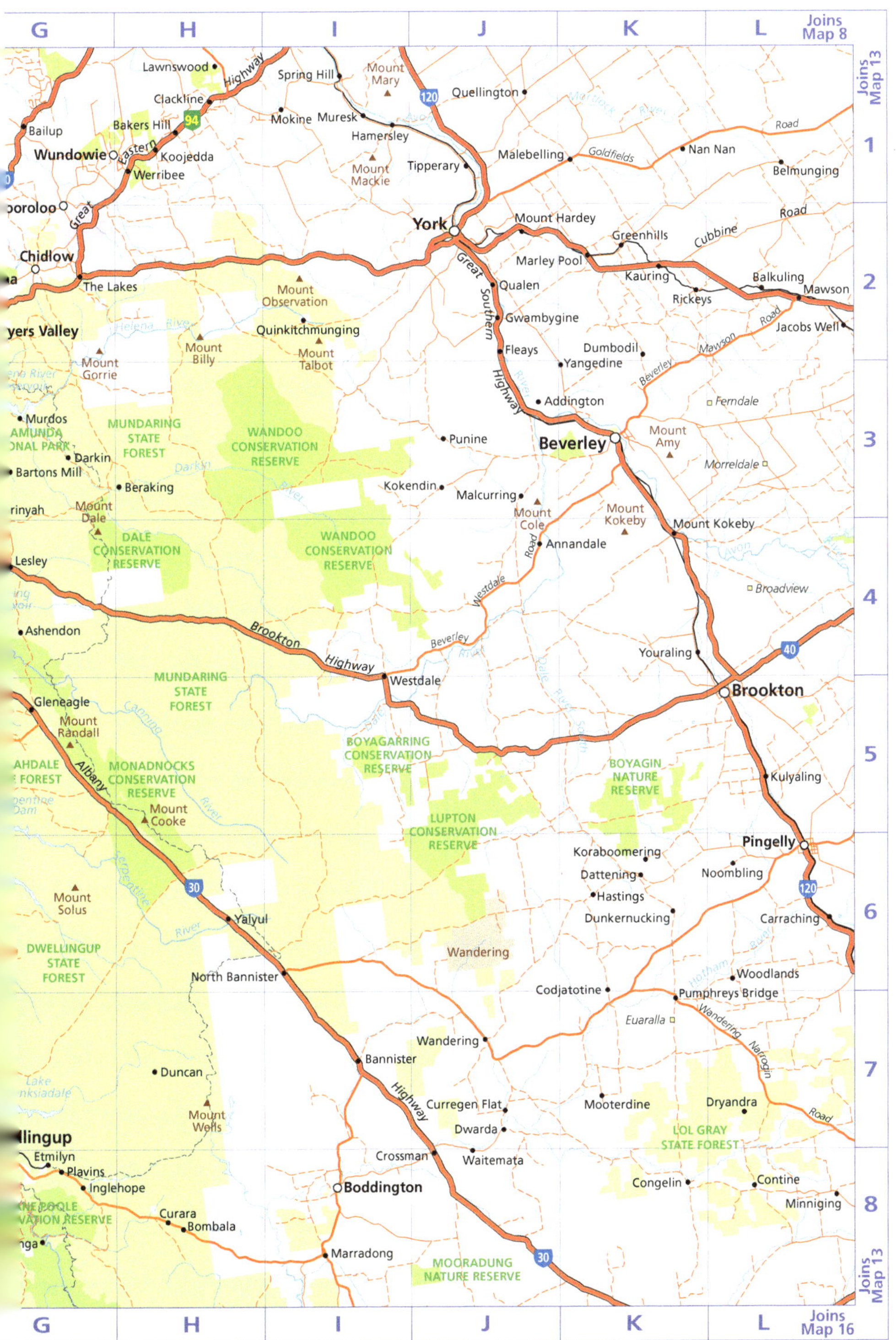

G
H
I
J
K
L
Joins Map 8
Joins Map 13
Joins Map 16
TOURING MAPS
Lawnswood
Highway
Spring Hill
Mount Mary
Quellington
Clackline
Mokine
Muresk
Hamersley
Bailup
Bakers Hill
Wundowie
Eastern
Koojedda
Werribee
Mount Mackie
Tipperary
Malebelling
Goldfields
Nan Nan
Road
Belmunging
York
Mount Hardey
Greenhills
Cubbine
Chidlow
Great
The Lakes
Marley Pool
Qualen
Kauring
Rickeys
Balkuling
Mawson
Mount Observation
Quinkitchmunging
Gwambygine
Jacobs Well
Mount Gorrie
Mount Billy
Mount Talbot
Fleays
Dumbodil
Yangedine
Mawson
Road
Helena River
Southern
Highway
Addington
Ferndale
Murdos
Darkin
Bartons Mill
MUNDARING STATE FOREST
WANDOO CONSERVATION RESERVE
Punine
Beverley
Mount Amy
Morreldale
Beraking
Kokendin
Malcurring
Mount Cole
Mount Kokeby
Mount Dale
DALE CONSERVATION RESERVE
WANDOO CONSERVATION RESERVE
Annandale
Lesley
Westdale
Road
Broadview
Ashendon
Brookton
Highway
Beverley
Westdale
Youraling
Brookton
Gleneagle
Mount Randall
MUNDARING STATE FOREST
BOYAGARRING CONSERVATION RESERVE
BOYAGIN NATURE RESERVE
MONADNOCKS CONSERVATION RESERVE
Albany
Kulyaling
Mount Cooke
LUPTON CONSERVATION RESERVE
Pingelly
Koraboomering
Dattening
Noombling
Hastings
Dunkernucking
Carraching
Mount Solus
Yalyul
DWELLINGUP STATE FOREST
Wandering
North Bannister
Woodlands
Codjatotine
Pumphreys Bridge
Euaralla
Wandering
Narrogin
Wandering
Bannister
Duncan
Curregen Flat
Mooterdine
Dryandra
Road
Mount Wells
Dwarda
LOL GRAY STATE FOREST
Etmilyn
Crossman
Waitemata
Plavins
Inglehope
Boddington
Congelin
Contine
Minniging
Curara
Bombala
Marradong
MOORADUNG NATURE RESERVE
1
2
3
4
5
6
7
8

Joins Map 9
Joins Map 12
Joins Map 17
Youndegin
South Tammin
Moordebing
Karrakin
Mount Stirling
Jelbercuting
Eujinyn
Yarding
Yalba
Jennaberring
Kwolyin
Coarin Rock
Shackleton
Erikin
MOKAMI NATURE RESERVE
Pantapin
Yoting
Yampin
Ardath
Moorak
Warra Woona
Mount Shackleton
Mawson
Quairading
Badjaling
Mulureen
Mount Bebb
Dangin
Jacobs Well
Dulbelling
Moorefield Farm
Corinya
Pekaring Hill
Babakin
Springdale
Heybrook
Navan
Peppin Park
Tamar Hills
Fennerberry
Dalmeny
Bilbarin
Brig House
Norwich Downs
Homebush
Ankuri
Glenmore
Glenmore Park
Bungaree
Nornakin
Noonam
Lake Mears
Hampton Plains
Avalon
Lake Kurrenkutten
YENYENING LAKES NATURE RESERVE
Corrigin
Bendering
Fairfield
Qualem Downs
Longview
Deloraine
Bonnie Doon
Lomos
Jubuk
Kunjin
Twin Ridges
Brookton
Dilling
Kooringal
Kweda
Aldersyde
Mears
Bulyee
Broad Acres
Barclay
Nalya
Weam
Kia Ora
Kentrevay
Glenburnie
Brooklands
Glenmore
Howland Park
Hopewell
Cloverdale
Fairhaven
Glen Morrel
Deloraine
Bullaring
Overndale
Wananing Hill
Minnawarra
Stretton
Caithness
Balmain
Newminster
Kinnaird
Red Hill
Ardeer
Pingelly
TUTANNING NATURE RESERVE
Tourello
Yealering
Llanfair
Lake Yealering
Anglefield
Glendale
Carraching
Toolang
Woolgnin
Thule Farm
Cliffordville
Logan Park
Nyamuttin
Popanyinning
Malyalling
Brambley
Malyalling East
Plainview
Erindale
Billeroy
Eastville
Yornaning
Wywurrie
Kiola
Wickepin
Traysurin Siding
Tophouse
Abunda
Ngaree
Blue Lo
Marring
Dudinin
Deadfinish
Cuballing
Glenray
Invermay
Seven Trees
Ockley
Westlands
Yilliminning
Booloo
Harrismith
Minniging
Benalta
Nomans Lake
Acadia
Kasvin
Toolibin
Narrogin
Boundain
Taarblin Lake
Wedin
Tincurrin
Clayton
Claredale
Linda Valley Park
Tara
Moonaree
BOKAN NATURE RESERVE
N
0
Scale 1:750,000
40
120
TOURING MAPS

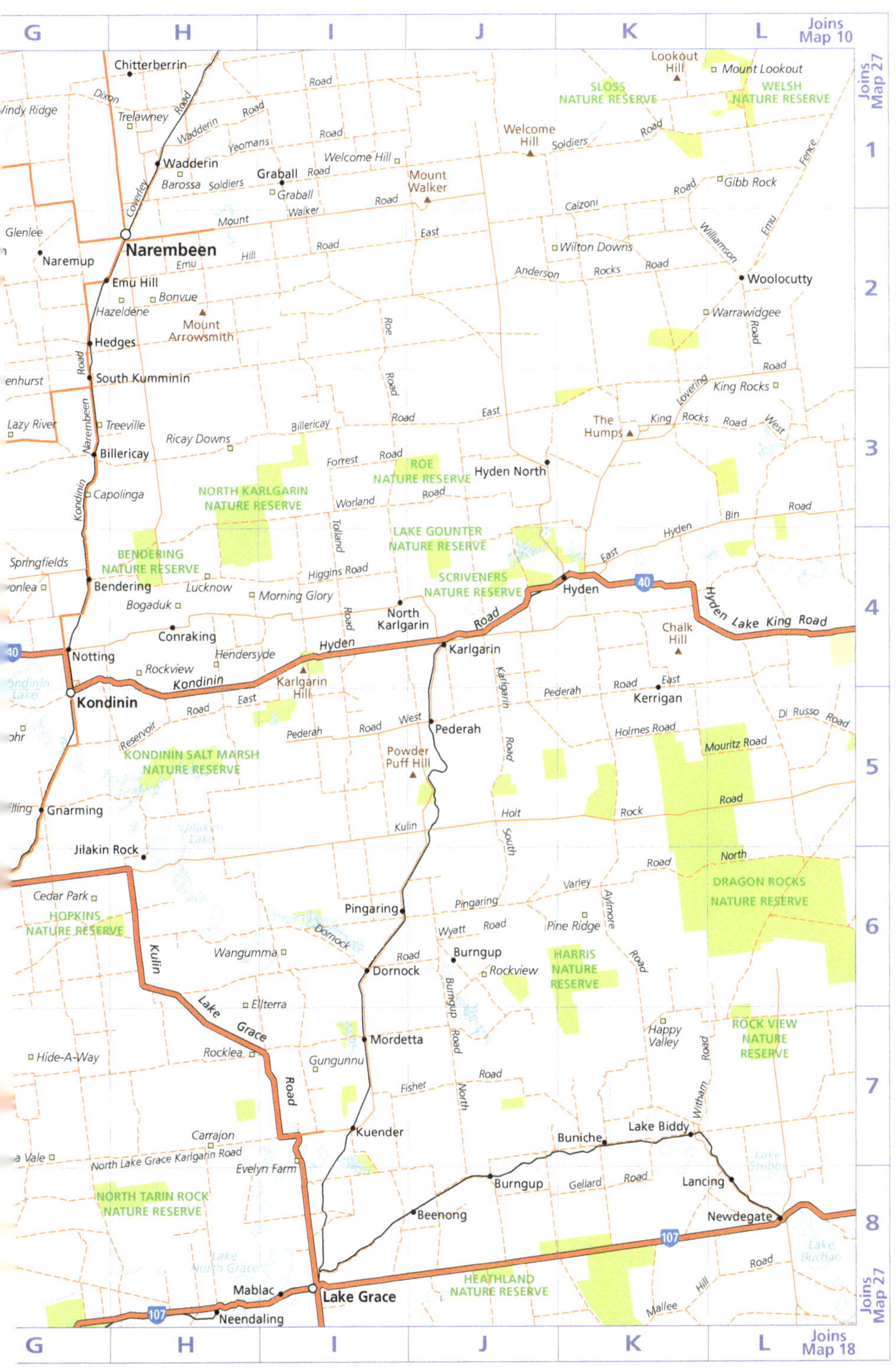

TOURING MAPS

TOURING MAPS

Joins Map 12
Joins Map 17
Joins Map 20
TOURING MAPS
Williams
Collie
Allanson
Darkan
Boyup Brook
Bridgetown
Greenbushes
Marradong
Quindanning
Daylerking
Josbury
Tarwonga
Dardadine
Hillman
Glenside
Booloading
Gibbs
James Crossing
Bowelling
Bennelaking
Cordering
Duranillin
Moodiarrup
Glenorchy
Quelarup
Eulin Crossing
Westcliffe
Cargonnup
Qualeup
Narlingup
Kulikup
Eulin
Dinninup
Asplin
Newlgalup
Condinup
Mayanup
Jayes
Growergerup
Mandalup
Winnejup
Heartlea
Nairnup
Glenlynn
Yornup
Treesville
Collie Power Station
The Cabbage Trees
Shotts
Cowcher
Muja
Cardiff
Delta
Wild Dog Flat
Mumballup
Yowungup
McAlinden
Noggerup
Goonac Siding
Goonac
Wilga
Evans
Benjinup
Yennungboonarie
Westlington
North Greenbushes
Southampton
Balingup
Grimwade
Glen Mervyn
Preston
Mungalup
Moorhead
Tallanalla
Hoffmans Mill
Hakea
Nanga
DWELLINGUP STATE FOREST
MOORADUNG NATURE RESERVE
HARRIS RIVER STATE FOREST
LANE POOLE CONSERVATION RESERVE
MUJA STATE FOREST
COLLIE STATE FOREST
WELLINGTON STATE FOREST
MUMBALLUP STATE FOREST
NOGGERUP STATE FOREST
WILGA STATE FOREST
EAST KIRUP STATE FOREST
HESTER STATE FOREST
HADDLETON NATURE RESERVE
SOUTH EAST NANNUP STATE FOREST
Albany Highway
South Western Highway
Brockman Highway
Coalfields Road

Joins Map 13
A
B
C
D
E
F
Joins Map 16
1
2
3
4
5
6
7
8
Tara
Narrogin
Torbling
Dumberning
Geeralying
BOKAN NATURE RESERVE
DONGOLOCKING NATURE RESERVE
Fence
Road
Highbury
ARTHUR RIVER NATURE RESERVE
Great
120
Southern
River
Buchanan
107
Dumbleyung
Moulyinning
Neeralin Pool
Bunkun
Coradine
Gully
Piesseville
Wishbone
Tarwonga
Golden Grove
River
Gundaring
107
Dumbleyung
Road
Nippering
Dumbleyung
Wagin
Coblinine
River
Ballaying
Dumbleyung Lake
DUMBLEYUNG LAKE NATURE RESERVE
Albany
Arthur
Wagin
30
Road
Datatine
Road
Arthur River
Arthur
Road
Warup
Mount Hugel
Lime Lake
Dumbleyung
Dellyanine
Norring Lake
Coblinine
River
East Arthur
Kylie
Boyerine
Highway
Katanning
Bellakin Hill
Mongining Hill
Beaufort
River
Woodanilling
Robinson
Road
Moojebing
COBLININE NATURE RESERVE
Badgebup
Nyabing
Coyrecup
120
Kenine Hill
Katanning
Katanning
Coyrecup Lake
Marribank
Highway
Ewlyamartup
Kibbleup
Great
Collie
30
Murdong
Greenhills
Southern
Saddleback Hill
Changerup
Holly
Three Wells
Gordon River
Cargonnup
Road
Nookanellup
Broomehill
Kojonup
Carlecatup
Coorinyup Hill
Farrar
Muradup
Road
Kojonup
Narlingup
Brook
Boyup
Peringillup
Newlands
Albany
Killeen
Rolling Acres
Rocky Creek
Jingalup
Jingalup
Road
Crosby
Road
Wyndermere
Tambellup
Dartnall
Kyramu
River
Milang
Warrenup
Glanville
Highway
JINGALUP NATURE RESERVE
Kualadale
Shamrock
Yarrawina
Road
Wancoona
Nymbup
Highway
Nymbur
Hassell
Over Ridge
Road
Tunney
Glenora
Wansbrough
N
Cliftondale
Paul Valley
Yonge
0
Scale 1:750,000
30km
120
Tone
Uannup
Road
30
Joins Map 16
Joins Map 21
A
B
C
D
E
F

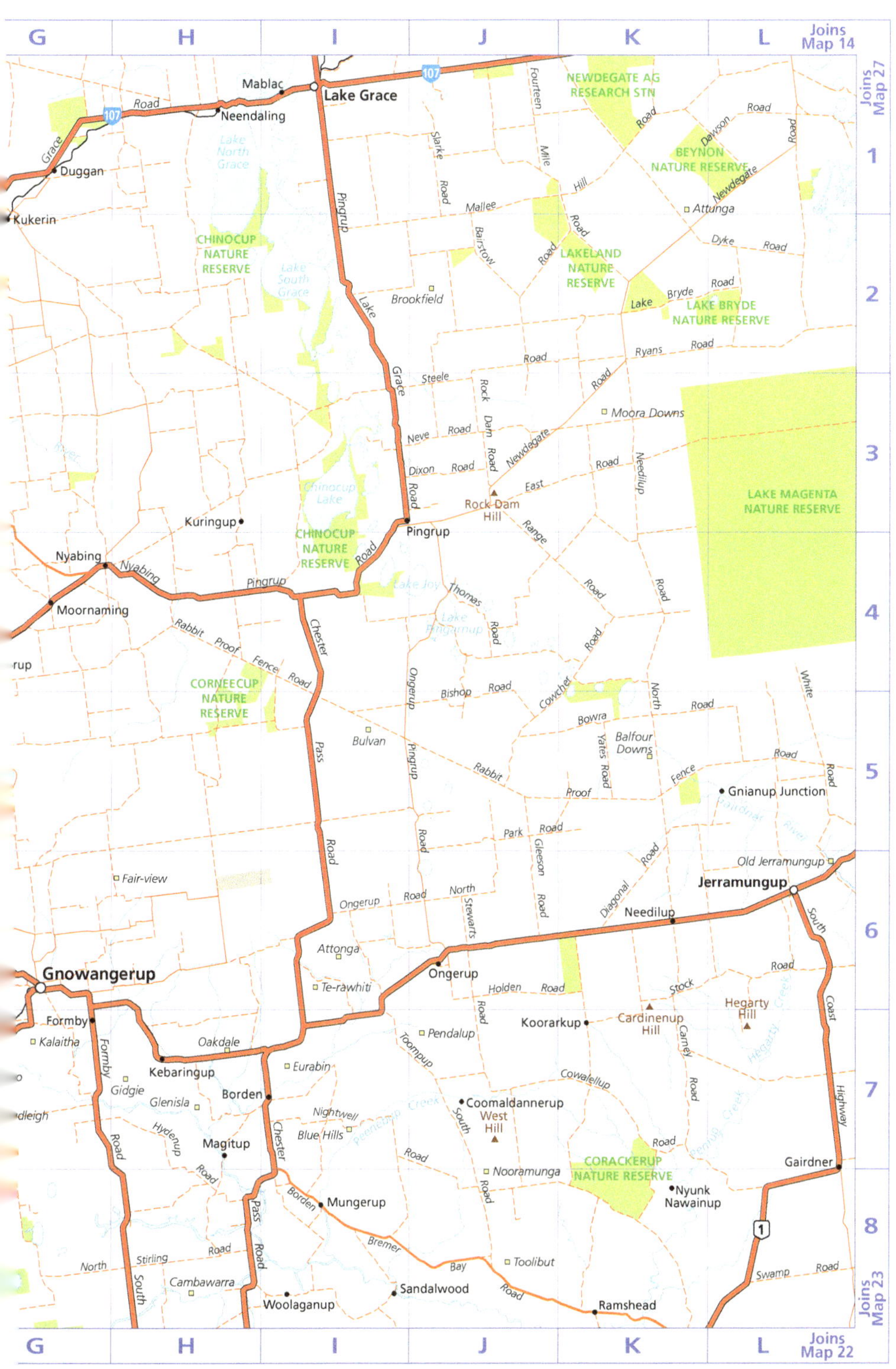

Joins Map 14
Joins Map 27
Joins Map 23
Joins Map 22
Lake Grace
Mablac
Neendaling
Duggan
Kukerin
Lake North Grace
CHINOCUP NATURE RESERVE
Lake South Grace
NEWDEGATE AG RESEARCH STN
BEYNON NATURE RESERVE
Attunga
LAKELAND NATURE RESERVE
LAKE BRYDE NATURE RESERVE
Brookfield
Moora Downs
LAKE MAGENTA NATURE RESERVE
Rock Dam Hill
Pingrup
Kuringup
Chinocup Lake
Nyabing
Moornaming
Lake Joy
Lake Pingrup
CORNEECUP NATURE RESERVE
Bulvan
Balfour Downs
Gnianup Junction
Old Jerramungup
Jerramungup
Needilup
Fair-view
Attonga
Te-rawhiti
Ongerup
Gnowangerup
Formby
Kalaitha
Oakdale
Kebaringup
Gidgie
Glenisla
Borden
Eurabin
Pendalup
Koorarkup
Cardinenup Hill
Hegarty Hill
Coomaldannerup
West Hill
Blue Hills
Magitup
CORACKERUP NATURE RESERVE
Nooramunga
Nyunk Nawainup
Gairdner
Mungerup
Toolibut
Sandalwood
Woolaganup
Cambawarra
Ramshead
TOURING MAPS

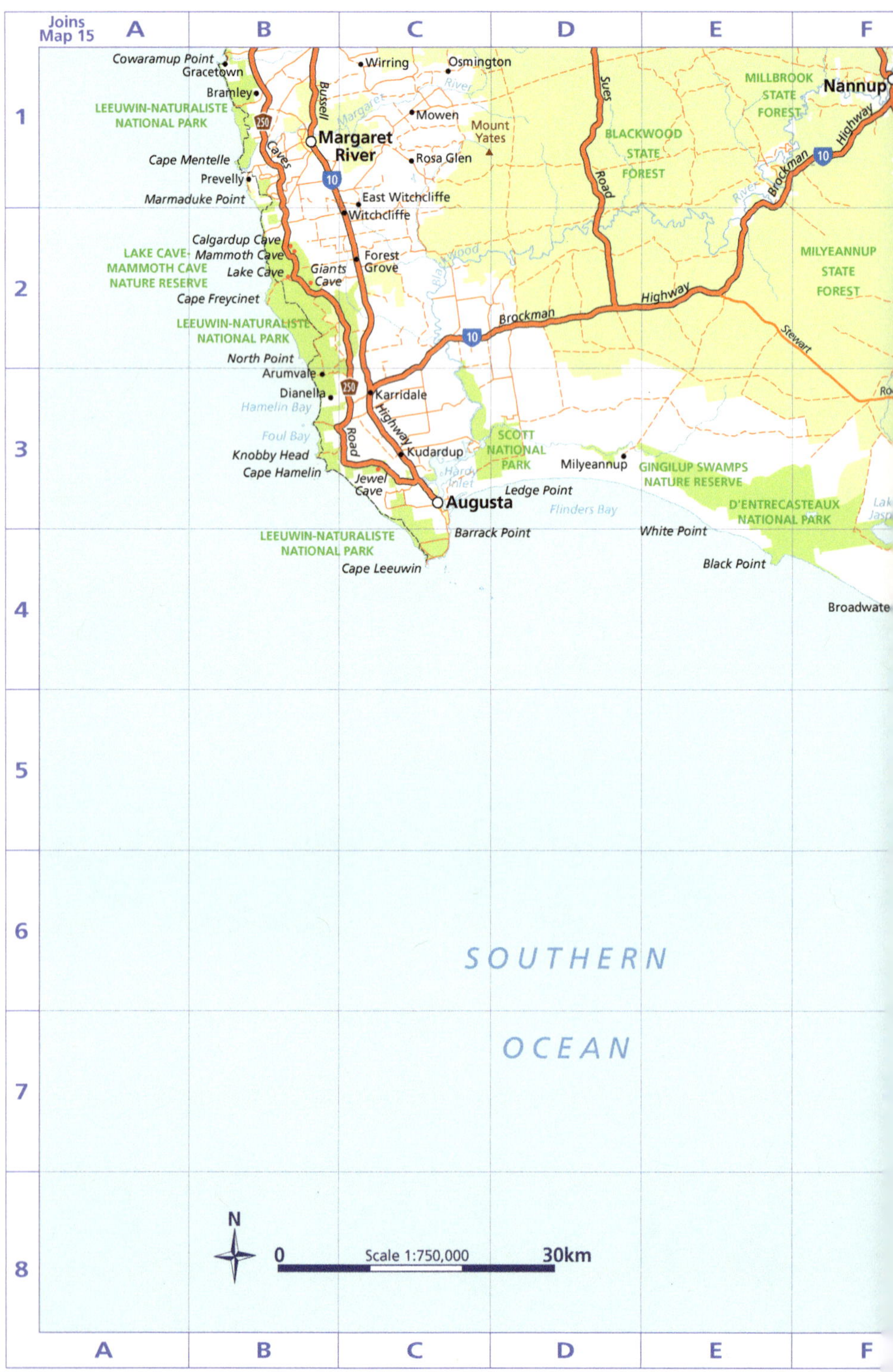
Joins Map 15
A
B
C
D
E
F
1
2
3
4
5
6
7
8
Cowaramup Point
Gracetown
Bramley
LEEUWIN-NATURALISTE NATIONAL PARK
Wirring
Osmington
Bussell
Caves
250
Margaret River
10
Mowen
Mount Yates
Rosa Glen
Cape Mentelle
Prevelly
Marmaduke Point
East Witchcliffe
Witchcliffe
Sues
Road
BLACKWOOD STATE FOREST
MILLBROOK STATE FOREST
Nannup
Brockman
Highway
Calgardup Cave
LAKE CAVE-MAMMOTH CAVE NATURE RESERVE
Mammoth Cave
Lake Cave
Giants Cave
Forest Grove
Blackwood
Cape Freycinet
LEEUWIN-NATURALISTE NATIONAL PARK
Brockman
Highway
MILYEANNUP STATE FOREST
Stewart
North Point
Arumvale
Dianella
Hamelin Bay
Karridale
Highway
Foul Bay
Road
Knobby Head
Cape Hamelin
Kudardup
SCOTT NATIONAL PARK
Milyeannup
GINGILUP SWAMPS NATURE RESERVE
Hardy Inlet
Jewel Cave
Augusta
Ledge Point
Flinders Bay
D'ENTRECASTEAUX NATIONAL PARK
LEEUWIN-NATURALISTE NATIONAL PARK
Barrack Point
White Point
Cape Leeuwin
Black Point
Broadwate
SOUTHERN
OCEAN
N
0
Scale 1:750,000
30km

Joins Map 16
Joins Map 21
Glenlynn
Yornup
Heartlea
Wilgarrup
Palgarup
Tonebridge
Balbarrup
Manjimup
Deanmill
Donnelly River
Jardee
Nyamup
Lyall
Diamond Tree
Strachan
East Brook
Pimelea
Collins
Quinninup
Pemberton
The Cascades
Brockman
Warren Bridge
Shannon
Yeagarup
Mount Burnside
Dombakup
Terry
Northcliffe
Callcup Hill
Warren Beach
Granite Peak
Mount Johnston
Mount Chudalup
Black Head
Pebbley Beach
Sandy Peak
Mount Pingerup
Point D'Entrecasteaux
Windy Harbour
Sandy Island
West Cliff Point
Sand Peak
Broke Inlet
Walpole
Crystal Springs
Cliffy Head
Chatham Island
Long Point
Point Nuyts
Mount Hopkins
Aldridge Cove
NORTH DONNELLY STATE FOREST
YORNUP STATE FOREST
PALGARUP STATE FOREST
DONNELLY STATE FOREST
BEEDELUP NATIONAL PARK
GLOUCESTER NATIONAL PARK
WARREN NATIONAL PARK
TONE STATE FOREST
UNICUP NATURE RESERVE
KODJINUP NATURE RESERVE
LAKE MUIR NATURE RESERVE
SHANNON NATIONAL PARK
LAKE MUIR STATE FOREST
WARREN STATE FOREST
GRANITE PEAKS STATE FOREST
SHANNON STATE FOREST
MOUNT FRANKLAND NATIONAL PARK
GARDNER STATE FOREST
D'ENTRECASTEAUX NATIONAL PARK
GLADSTONE STATE FOREST
WALPOLE-NORNALUP NATIONAL PARK
South Western Highway
Muirs Highway
Vasse Highway
Wheatley Coast Road
Middleton Road
Windy Harbour Road
Graphite Road
Wingebellup Road
Lake Muir
TOURING MAPS

Joins Map 17
Joins Map 20
Cranbrook
Mount Barker
Denmark
Walpole
Frankland
KULUNILUP NATURE RESERVE
QUINDINUP NATURE RESERVE
RANDELL ROAD NATURE RESERVE
TOOTANELLUP NATURE RESERVE
WAMBALLUP NATURE RESERVE
LAKE MUIR STATE FOREST
PARDELUP NATURE RESERVE
DENMARK CATCHMENT STATE FOREST
GRANITE PEAKS STATE FOREST
MT ROE-MT LINDESAY NATIONAL PARK
MOUNT FRANKLAND NATIONAL PARK
FRANKLAND STATE FOREST
WALPOLE-NORNALUP NATIONAL PARK
QUARRAM NATURE RESERVE
WILLIAM BAY NATIONAL PARK
WEST CAPE HOWE NATIONAL PARK
Scale 1:750,000
0
30km

G
H
I
J
K
L
Joins Map 18
Joins Map 23
1
2
3
4
5
6
7
8
Inglebourne
Toolibut
Cambawarra
Sandalwood
Swamp Rd
Woolaganup
Mailalup
Ramshead
Boxwood Hill
Glenelg
Arthurs Knob
Kuch
Rumbalara
Tamgaree
Chillinup
Warrungup
Isongerup Peak
Wellstead Crossing
Glen Ellen
Mount Success
Coyanarup Peak
Chester Pass
Mount Magog
Mount Hassell
Mount Gog
Hostellers Hills
Marambeena
Gnowellen
STIRLING RANGE NATIONAL PARK
Gold Holes
Wellstead
Black Head
Long Beach
Cheyne Bay
Kojaneerup
Deneryl
Blackboy Hill
Googlegong
Schooner Beach
Cape Riche
Mount Belches
Mettler
Galil
South Stirling
SOUTH STIRLING NATURE RESERVE
Kamballup
Ledge Point
Willyun Beach
Tinkelelup
HASSELL NATIONAL PARK
Haul Off Rock
Emu Bend
Warriup Hill
Kinnabulla
Boolarong
Hassell Beach
Yellanup
Kallumup
North Sister
Bluff Creek
Takenup
South Sister
Koiamip
Yarrenyungrip
Manypeaks
WAYCHINICUP NATIONAL PARK
Lookout Point
Bald Island
Mount Manypeaks
Napier
Millbrook
MOUNT MANYPEAKS NATURE RESERVE
BALD ISLAND NATURE RESERVE
Mermaid Point
Collingwood
Kalgan
Betty's Beach
North Point
Two Peoples Bay
Killarney
King River
TWO PEOPLES BAY NATURE RESERVE
Point Gardner
Mount Gardner
Nanarup
Oyster Harbour
Cape Vancouver
Herald Point
Albany
Michaelmas Island
King George Sound
Breaksea Island
Princess Royal Harbour
Little Grove
Frenchman Bay
Whaling Museum
Bald Head
Isthmus Bay
Cave Point
Peak Head
Eclipse Island
SOUTHERN OCEAN
TOURING MAPS

Joins Map 27
Joins Map 18
Joins Map 22
A
B
C
D
E
F
1
2
3
4
5
6
7
8
DUNN ROCK NATURE RESERVE
LAKE MAGENTA NATURE RESERVE
OVERSHOT HILL NATURE RESERVE
LONG CREEK NATURE RESERVE
COCANARUP TIMBER RESERVE
FITZGERALD RIVER NATIONAL PARK
Lake Lockhart
Lake Magenta
Lake Magenta Farms
Lake Cobham
Lake Morris
Ravensthorpe
Nield Rd
Aerodrome
Koomong
Bridger
Belli Road
Malkana
Thomas Road
Nooraglen
Mainnerup
Ongerup
Parwoonup
Cowderup
Fitzgerald
Wooganup
Old
Coompertup
Shackerston
Gunna Do
Jacup
Jacup South Road
Witt Road
South Coast Highway
O'Neills
North
White
Brook
Old Jerramungup
Jerramungup
Carlawillup Rd
Mount Drummond
Yarbudup
Quoin Head
Marshes Beach
Thumb Peak
Woolbernup Hill
Perkins Rock
Waijecoolallup
Bivouack Rocks
Jonacoonack
Red Peak
Twin Bays
Dempster Inlet
Fitzgerald Inlet
Point Charles
Junction Hill
Point Charles Bay
Point Ann Road
Cheadanup
Point Ann
Mount Bland
Mount Maxwell
Collets
Gairdner
West Mount Barren
Trigelow Beach
Marnigarup
East Road
Marnigarup South Road
Wirrup Hill
Devils Creek Road
Gairdner
Murray Road
Gordon Inlet
Tooregullup Beach
Whalebone Point
Point Hood
Swamp Road
Gairdner South Road
Lake Torrup
Bremer Bay
Cardiminup
Fishery Beach
Tooreburrup Hill
Black Point
Point Gordon
Point Henry
Oakdale
Warramurrup Hill
Minarup
Mount Remarkable
Stream Beach
Dillon Bay
Beaufort Inlet
Wray Bay
Reef Beach
Pallinup Beach
Mount Groper
Groper Bluff
Foster Beach
Cape Knob

TOURING MAPS

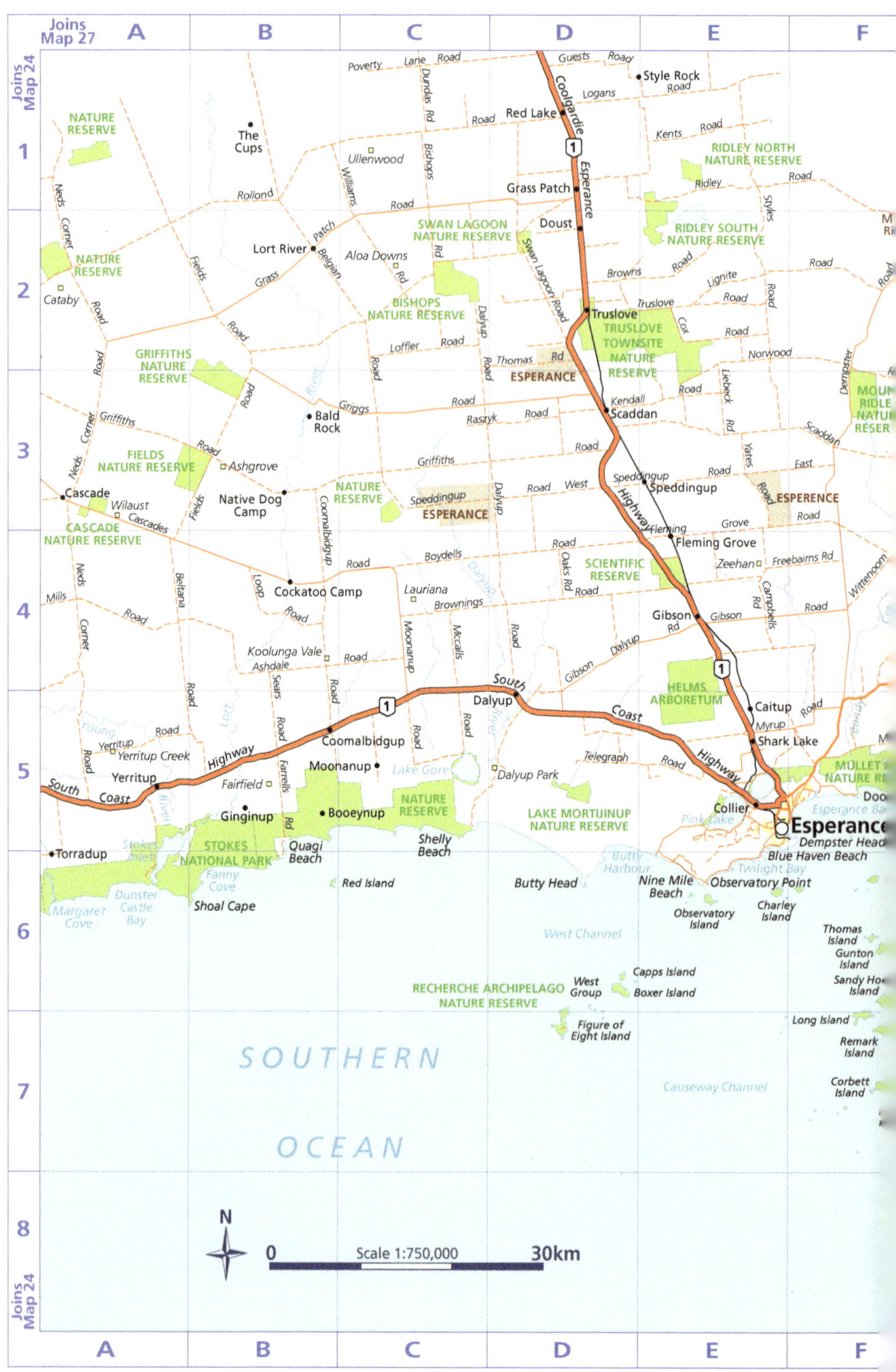
Joins Map 27
Joins Map 24
NATURE RESERVE
The Cups
Poverty Lane Road
Guests Road
Style Rock Road
Red Lake
Coolgardie Esperance
Logans
Kents Road
Ullenwood
RIDLEY NORTH NATURE RESERVE
Ridley
Rollond Road
Grass Patch
Doust
SWAN LAGOON NATURE RESERVE
RIDLEY SOUTH NATURE RESERVE
Lort River
Aloa Downs
NATURE RESERVE
Cataby
BISHOPS NATURE RESERVE
Truslove
TRUSLOVE TOWNSITE NATURE RESERVE
GRIFFITHS NATURE RESERVE
Loffler Road
Thomas Rd
ESPERANCE
Norwood
Griggs Road
Bald Rock
Kendall
Scaddan
Raszyk Road
FIELDS NATURE RESERVE
Ashgrove
Griffiths
Speddingup
Cascade
Wilaust
Native Dog Camp
NATURE RESERVE
ESPERANCE
ESPERENCE
Fleming Grove
CASCADE NATURE RESERVE
Boydells
SCIENTIFIC RESERVE
Zeehan
Freebairns Rd
Cockatoo Camp
Lauriana
Brownings
Mills
Gibson Rd
Koolunga Vale
Ashdale
HELMS ARBORETUM
Caitup
Dalyup
South Coast Highway
Myrup
Shark Lake
Yerritup Creek
Yerritup
Coomalbidgup
Moonanup
Lake Gore
Dalyup Park
Telegraph Road
MULLET NATURE RE
Fairfield
Ginginup
Booeynup
NATURE RESERVE
LAKE MORTIJINUP NATURE RESERVE
Collier
Pink Lake
Esperance
Dempster Head
Blue Haven Beach
Torradup
Stokes Inlet
STOKES NATIONAL PARK
Quagi Beach
Shelly Beach
Butty Harbour
Twilight Bay
Fanny Cove
Red Island
Butty Head
Nine Mile Beach
Observatory Point
Dunster Castle Bay
Margaret Cove
Shoal Cape
Observatory Island
Charley Island
Thomas Island
Gunton Island
West Channel
Capps Island
RECHERCHE ARCHIPELAGO NATURE RESERVE
West Group
Boxer Island
Sandy Hoo Island
Figure of Eight Island
Long Island
Remark Island
SOUTHERN
Causeway Channel
Corbett Island
OCEAN
N
0
Scale 1:750,000
30km
A B C D E F
1 2 3 4 5 6 7 8

Joins Map 28
Mount Buraminya
Sheoak Hill
CLYDE HILL NATURE RESERVE
Clyde Hill
Bonnie Hill
Fowlie Hill
Eclipse Hill
Mount Beaumont
Mount Heywood
NATURE RESERVE
BEAUMONT NATURE RESERVE
MOUNT NEY NATURE RESERVE
Mount Ney
NIBLICK NATURE RESERVE
Niblick Hill
Florabel Hill
Sparkle Hill
KAU ROCK NATURE RESERVE
BURDETT NATURE RESERVE
Witteenoom Hill
NEREDUP NATURE RESERVE
Warriup
MUNTZ NATURE RESERVE
Macsfield
BEAUMONT NATURE RESERVE
Shao Lu
Bebenorin Hill
Boyatup Hill
Boyatup
Howick Hill
Condingup
Condingup Peak
Rangitoto
Orleans Farms
Mortup Hill
ALEXANDER NATURE RESERVE
CAPE ARID NATIONAL PARK
Belinup Hill
Yokinup Bay
Tagon Bay
Tagon Point
Alexander Hill
Alexander Bay
Alexander Point
Gerbryn
Boyatup
Mount Hawes
Cornijup
Cheetup Hill
Yungarup Hill
Wharton
Mount Belches
Forrest Island
Taylor Island
Dunn Rocks
Cheyne Point
Hammer Head
RECHERCHE ARCHIPELAGO NATURE RESERVE
CAPE LE GRAND NATIONAL PARK
Rossiter Bay
Mount Le Grand
Mississippi Point
Tory Islands
York Islands
Mart Islands
North Twin Peak Island
South Twin Peak Island
Westall Island
Glennie Island
Archdeacon Island
Ram Island
Rob Island
Beaumont Island
Pasco Island
Finger Island
Hastings Island
Mondrain Island
Archipelago of the Recherche
Draper Island
MacKenzie Island
Pearson Islands
SOUTHERN OCEAN
TOURING MAPS

Joins Map 10
A
B
C
D
E
F
1
2
3
4
5
6
7
8
Joins Map 22
Marvel Loch
Jilbadgie
Tamarin
JILBADJI NATURE RESERVE
Barker Lake
Cave Hill
Mount Eaton
Higginsville
Lake Cowan
Wingarnie
Coolgardie - Esperance
Pioneer
Buldania
Eyre
Highway
Norseman
Mount Day
Lake Johnston
Mount Holland
Lake Kirk
Goodia
Dundas
Bromus
Woolocutty
North Ironcap
King Rocks
LAKE CRONIN NATURE RESERVE
Mount Gordon
Daniell
Lake Dundas
DUNDAS NATURE RESERVE
Lake Hope
Mount Glasse
Lake Gilmore
Beete
Marble Rocks
Middle Ironcap
Kumarl
Holt Rock
South Ironcap
Peak Charles
Lake Sharpe
Dowak
Gulson Downs
Varley
Mount Gibbs
FRANK HANN NATIONAL PARK
Lake Tay
PEAK CHARLES NATIONAL PARK
Salmon Gums
Mount Sheridan
Circle Valley
Lake Camm
Three Star Lake
Lake Mends
Red Lake
Murray Downs
Lake King
Pyramid Lake
Lort River
Doust
Mount Ridley
Newdegate
Karak Park
Kappi Ki
Truslove
Kilmaurs
Benelong
Bald Rock
Scaddan
Maroleigh
Burando
Cascade
Lake Magenta
Gibson
Ravensthorpe
Mayruup
Dalyup
Coomalbidgup
Esperance
LAKE MAGENTA NATURE RESERVE
Kundip
Jerdacuttup
Yerritup
Coast
Shoal Cape
Butty Head
CAPE LE GRAND NATIONAL PARK
Cape Le Grand
Fitzgerald
Cowerup
Kuliba
Powell Point
FITZGERALD RIVER NATIONAL PARK
Jacup
Hopetoun
Jerramungup
Yarbudup
For more detail see maps 25-26
Point Ann
Gairdner
Bremer River
Bremer Bay
Point Hood
Dillion Bay
Groper Bluff
Cape Knob
For more detail see maps 23-24
Cape Riche
40
107
94
1
TOURING MAPS

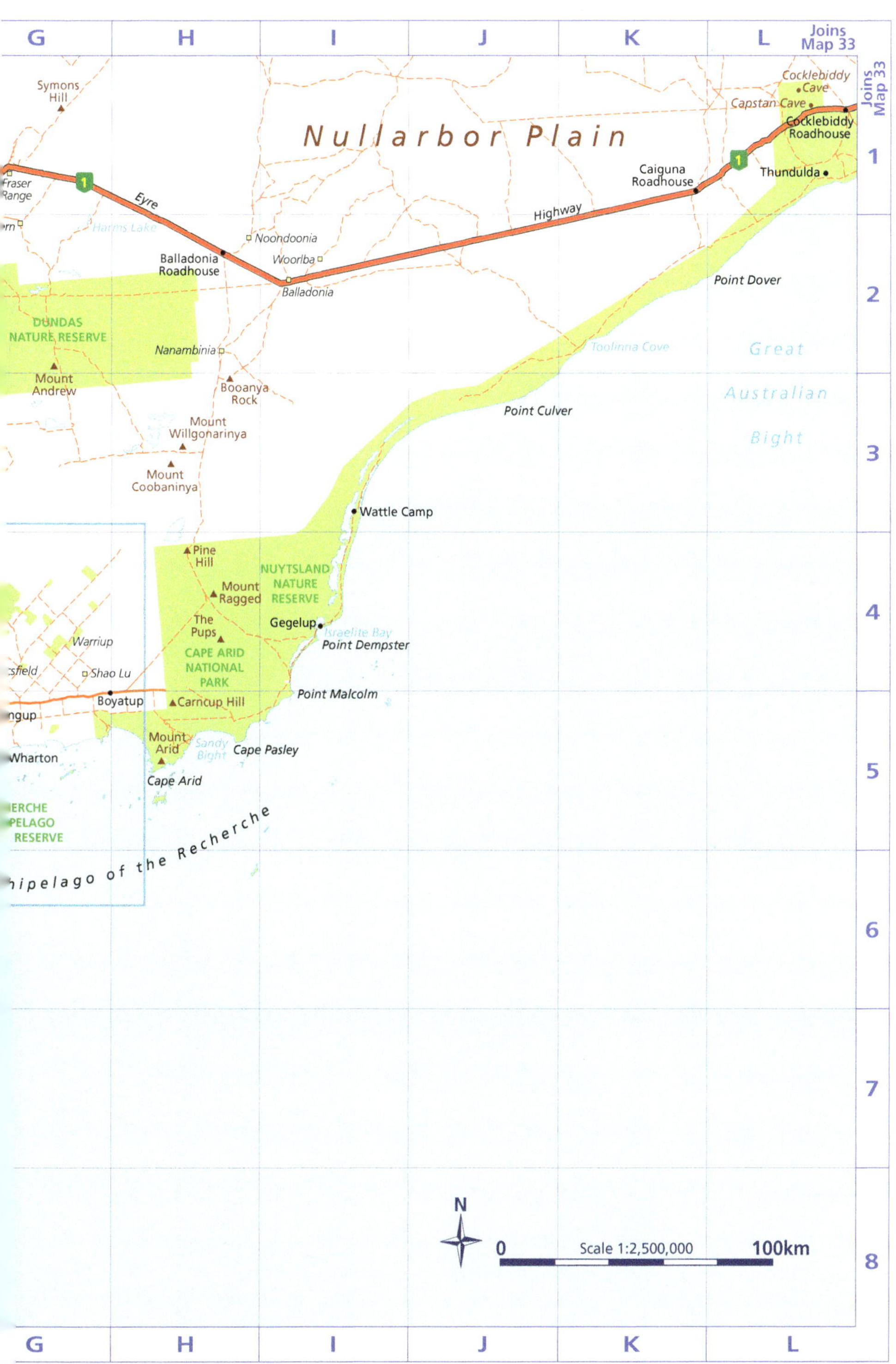

G
H
I
J
K
L
Joins Map 33
Joins Map 33
Nullarbor Plain
Symons Hill
Cocklebiddy Cave
Capstan Cave
Cocklebiddy Roadhouse
Thundulda
Caiguna Roadhouse
Fraser Range
Eyre
Highway
Harms Lake
Noondoonia
Woorlba
Balladonia Roadhouse
Balladonia
Point Dover
DUNDAS NATURE RESERVE
Mount Andrew
Nanambinia
Booanya Rock
Toolinna Cove
Great Australian Bight
Point Culver
Mount Willgonarinya
Mount Coobaninya
Wattle Camp
Pine Hill
Mount Ragged
NUYTSLAND NATURE RESERVE
The Pups
Gegelup
Israelite Bay
Point Dempster
Warriup
Shao Lu
CAPE ARID NATIONAL PARK
Boyatup
Carncup Hill
Point Malcolm
Mount Arid
Sandy Bight
Cape Pasley
Wharton
Cape Arid
Archipelago of the Recherche
N
0
Scale 1:2,500,000
100km
1
2
3
4
5
6
7
8
TOURING MAPS

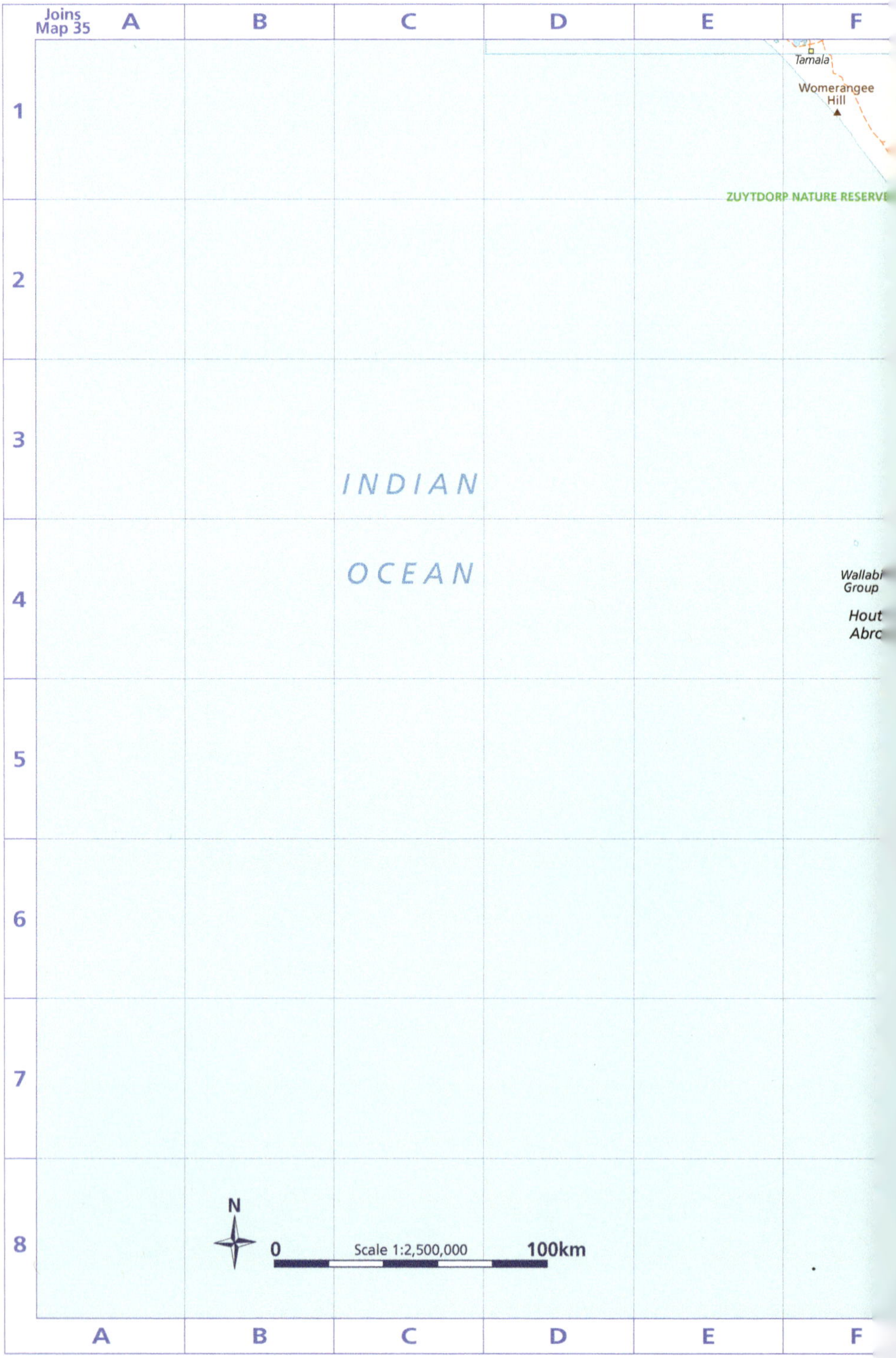

Joins Map 35

A B C D E F

1 2 3 4 5 6 7 8

Tamala

Womerangee Hill

ZUYTDORP NATURE RESERVE

INDIAN OCEAN

Wallabi Group

Hout Abro

N

0 Scale 1:2,500,000 100km

A B C D E F

TOURING MAPS

G
H
I
J
K
L
Joins Map 36
Joins Map 31
Billabong Roadhouse
TOOLONGA NATURE RESERVE
Cooloomia
North West Coastal
Nerren Nerren
Bompas Hill
Wail Outcamp
Mount Aubrey
Mount Grass
Wooleen
Pia Wadjari
Pia
Wardarbull Hill
Mount Hope
Murgoo
Meka Station
Mount Wittenoom
Nooloojoo Hill
Hump Hill
New Forest
Illimbirrie
Billabalong
Yallalong
Gie Outcamp
Drages
Malara
Muggamurra Hill
Karinwaring
Coolcalalaya
Dalgaranga
Dalgaranga Hill
Murchison River Gorge
KALBARRI NATIONAL PARK
Lake Nerramyne
Woolgorong
Wallegul
Narloo
Dudoorow
Mary Springs
Bullardoo
Jardie
Thanda
Kalbarri
354
Yarranda
Mumbawadgy
Pindathuna
Noongal
Wattle Grove
Mallee
Ajana
Dartmoor
Cooja
Yallinoka
Culgatherra
Gabyon
Carlaminda
Edah
Wileri
Binnu
WANDANA NATURE RESERVE
123
Wagga Wagga
Hutt
Yalgoo
Wolla Wolla
Weld
URAWA NATURE RESERVE
Tallering
Wurarga
Muralgarra
Gregory
Whelarra
Coonawa
Badja
Northampton
Pindar
Horrocks
Naraling
Mullewa
Barnong
Bunnawarra
Nabawa
Wilroy
Howatharra
Nanson
Indarra
Tardun
Mellenbye
Thundelarra
Ambania
Kutmia Hill
Drummond Cove
Chulaar Hill
Bringo
Geraldton
Coolangatta
Port Grey
Cape Burney
Ellendale
Kadji Kadji
Mangrove Group
Saddleworth
Pintharuka
Old Karara
Karara
Greenough
Westmine
Brand
Allanooka
Bookara
Nine Mile Beach
Mingenew
Morawa
Yongaloo
Bowgada
116
Midlands
Dongara
Leander Point
Yandanooka
Perenjori
Wanarra
Mt Adams
Arrino
White Wells
White Point
Carsons Beach
Three Springs
Prowaka
Sandasea
Bunjil
Cliff Head
Arrowsmith
Carnamah
Latham
Winchester
Knobby Head
Illawong
Yarralong
Maya
BEEKEEPERS NATURE RESERVE
Eneabba
Lombardy Farm
Coorow
Buntine
Great Northern Hwy
95
Coolimba
Mace Beach
Leeman
Judeen
Landsdale
Road
Wubin
Marchagee
Koonga
Gunyidi
Point Louise
Green Head
Highway
WATHEROO NATIONAL PARK
Dalwallinu
LESUEUER NATIONAL PARK
Radbury
Watheroo
Pithara
DROVERS CAVE NATIONAL PARK
Nylagarda
Namban
Damboring
Jurien Bay
Badgingarra
Miling
Ballidu
SOUTHERN BEEKEEPERS NATURE RESERVE
Bindi Bindi
Winja
Cervantes
Moora
Kondut
NAMBUNG NATIONAL PARK
Gabalong
Dandaragan
The Pinnacles
Elphin
115
Koojan
Wongan Hills
Cataby
Kalguddering
Lancelin Training Area
Gillingarra
New Norcia
Calingiri
Mogumber
Calcarra
Burabadji
Lancelin
Wannamal
Wyening
Joins Map 7
TOURING MAPS
1
2
3
4
5
6
7
8

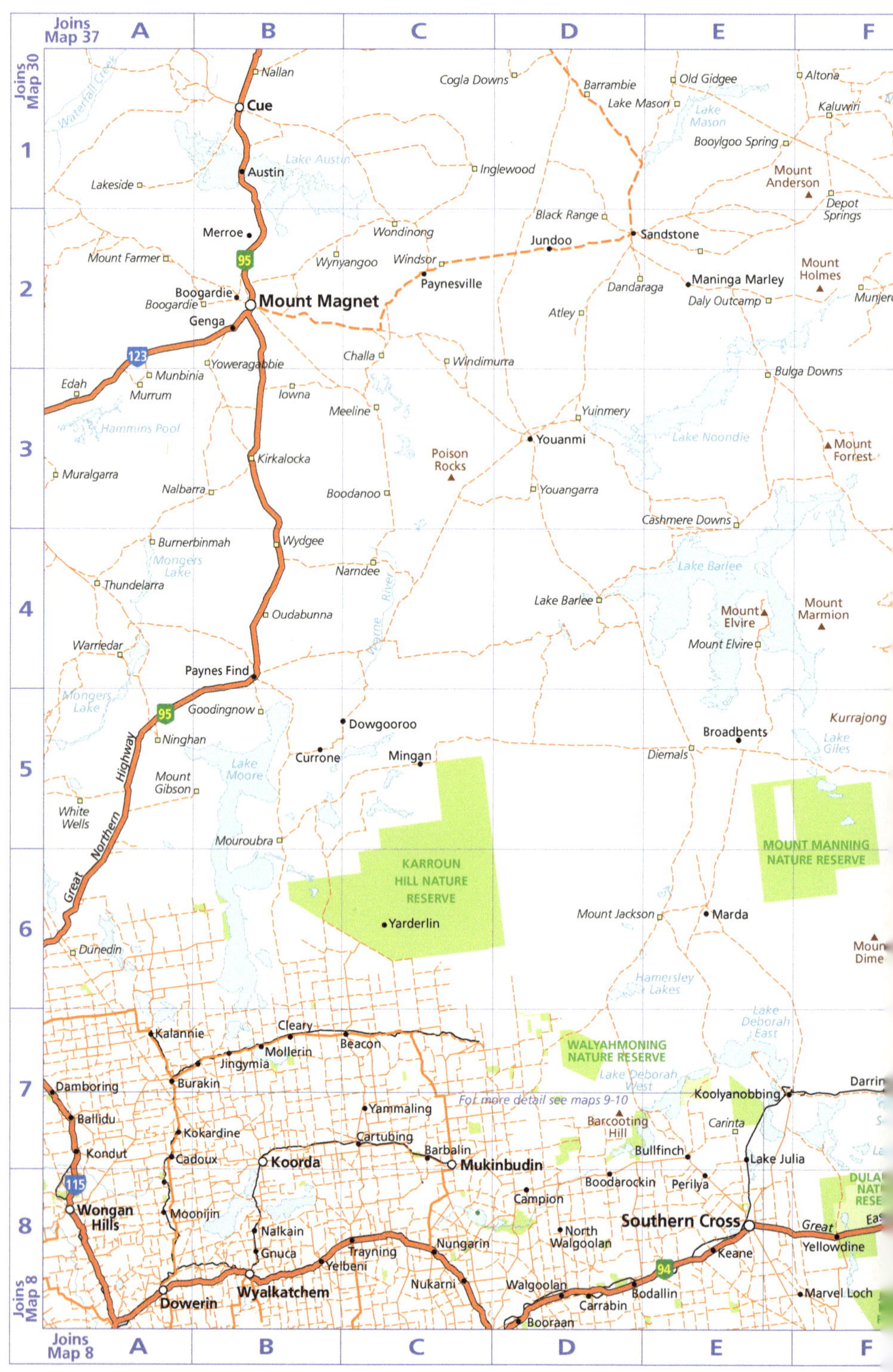

Joins Map 37
A
B
C
D
E
F
Joins Map 30
1
2
3
4
5
6
7
8
Joins Map 8
Nallan
Cue
Cogla Downs
Barrambie
Old Gidgee
Altona
Lake Mason
Kaluwiri
Lake Austin
Austin
Inglewood
Booylgoo Spring
Mount Anderson
Lakeside
Depot Springs
Black Range
Merroe
Wondinong
Sandstone
Jundoo
Mount Farmer
Wynyangoo
Windsor
Paynesville
Mount Holmes
Dandaraga
Maninga Marley
Boogardie
Mount Magnet
Daly Outcamp
Munjero
Genga
Atley
Challa
Windimurra
Yoweragabbie
Munbinia
Bulga Downs
Edah
Murrum
Iowna
Meeline
Yuinmery
Hammins Pool
Youanmi
Lake Noondie
Poison Rocks
Mount Forrest
Kirkalocka
Muralgarra
Nalbarra
Boodanoo
Youangarra
Cashmere Downs
Burnerbinmah
Wydgee
Mongers Lake
Lake Barlee
Narndee
Thundelarra
Lake Barlee
Mount Marmion
Mount Elvire
Oudabunna
Warne River
Warriedar
Paynes Find
Goodingnow
Dowgooroo
Kurrajong
Broadbents
Lake Giles
Ninghan
Currone
Mingan
Diemals
Mount Gibson
Lake Moore
Great Northern Highway
White Wells
Mouroubra
MOUNT MANNING NATURE RESERVE
KARROUN HILL NATURE RESERVE
Yarderlin
Mount Jackson
Marda
Dunedin
Hamersley Lakes
Lake Deborah East
Cleary
Kalannie
Beacon
Mollerin
WALYAHMONING NATURE RESERVE
Jingymia
Lake Deborah West
Burakin
Damboring
For more detail see maps 9-10
Koolyanobbing
Yammaling
Ballidu
Barcooting Hill
Carinta
Kokardine
Cartubing
Kondut
Barbalin
Bullfinch
Lake Julia
Cadoux
Koorda
Mukinbudin
Boodarockin
Perilya
Campion
Wongan Hills
Moonijin
North Walgoolan
Southern Cross
Great Eastern
Nalkain
Yellowdine
Nungarin
Keane
Gnuca
Trayning
Yelbeni
Nukarni
Walgoolan
Bodallin
Marvel Loch
Dowerin
Wyalkatchem
Carrabin
Booraan
Joins Map 8
95
123
115
94
TOURING MAPS

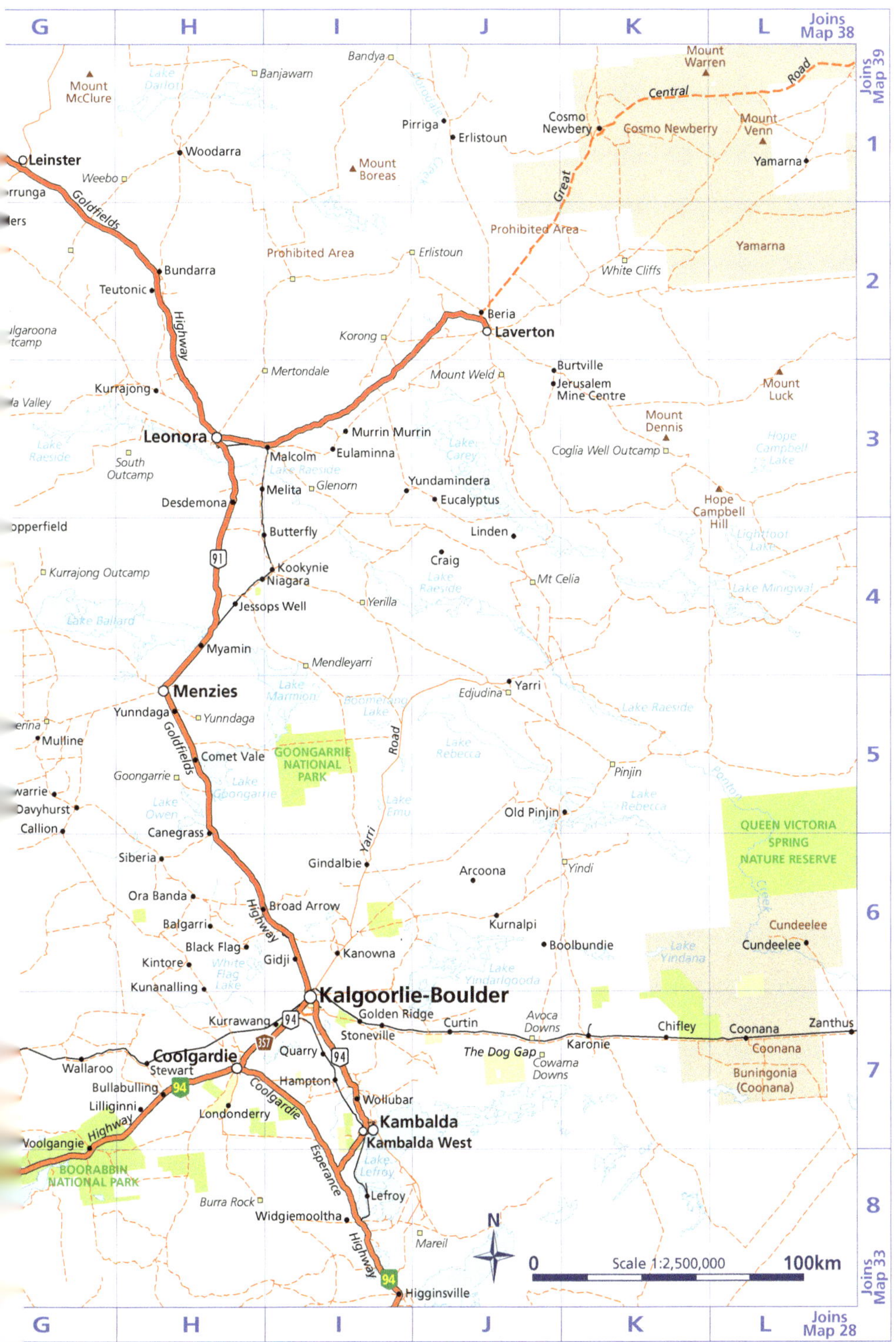
G
H
I
J
K
L
Joins Map 38
Joins Map 39
Joins Map 33
Joins Map 28
Leinster
Woodarra
Leonora
Laverton
Menzies
Kalgoorlie-Boulder
Coolgardie
Kambalda
Kambalda West
Goldfields Highway
Great Central Road
Prohibited Area
QUEEN VICTORIA SPRING NATURE RESERVE
GOONGARRIE NATIONAL PARK
BOORABBIN NATIONAL PARK
Scale 1:2,500,000
0
100km
TOURING MAPS

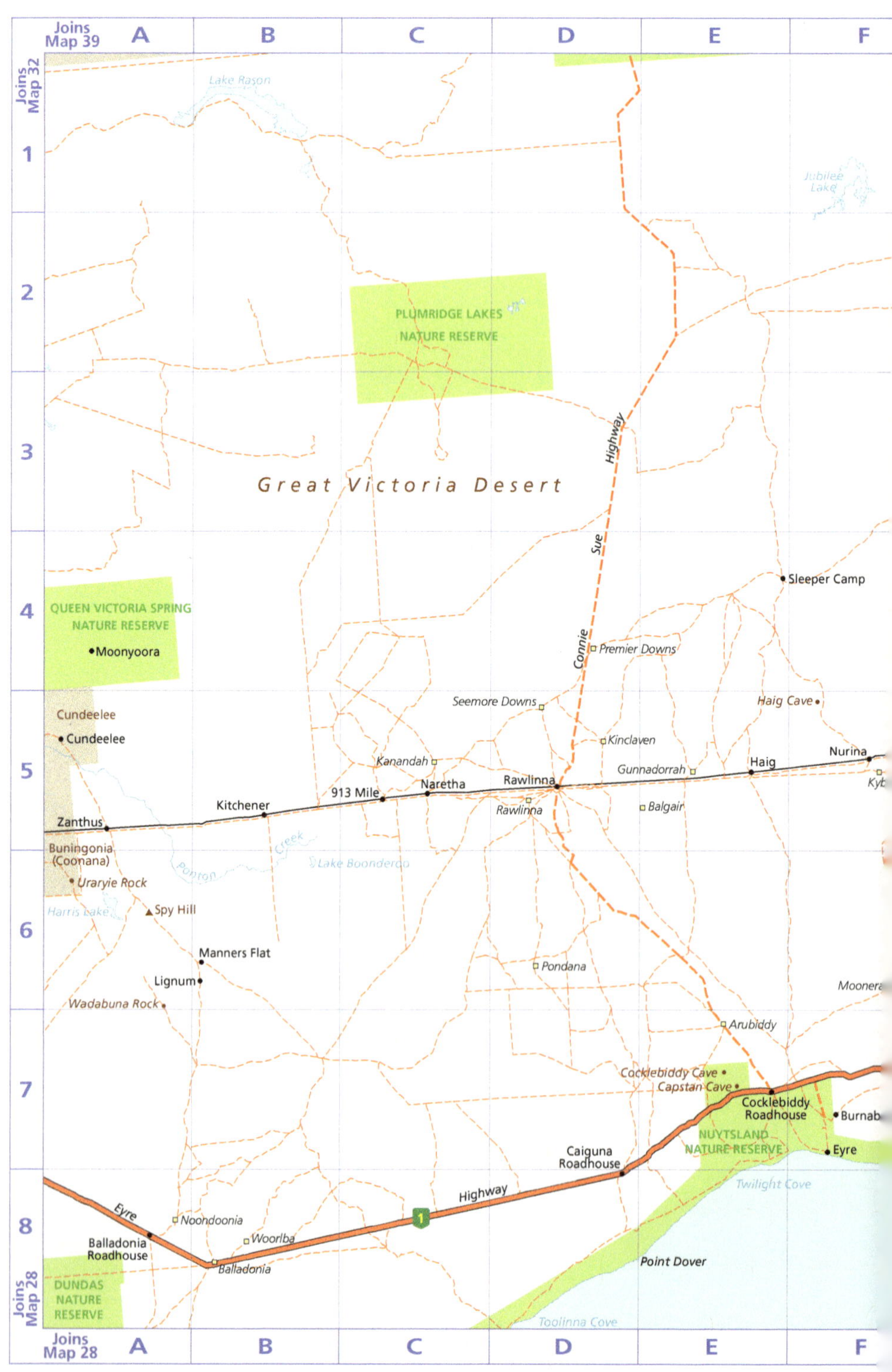

TOURING MAPS

G
H
I
J
K
L
Joins Map 40
1
2
3
4
5
6
7
8
Serpentine Lakes
Nurrari Lakes
Shell Lakes
Lake Jima
Forrest Lakes
CONSERVATION
PARK
SOUTH AUSTRALIA
Tjuntjuntjara
GREAT VICTORIA DESERT
NATURE RESERVE
Maralinga Tjarutja
Yakadunia
Yackadunyah
Decoration Cave
WESTERN AUSTRALIA
Denman
Hughes
Deakin
Reid
Forrest
Lynch Cave
NULLARBOR
REGIONAL RESERVE
Old Homestead Cave
Nullarbor Plain
NULLARBOR
NATIONAL PARK
Koonalda Cave
Eyre
Highway
Koonalda
Bunabie Blowhole
Old
Clay Dam Cave
Border Village
Highway
Eucla
GREAT AUSTRALIAN BIGHT
MARINE NATIONAL PARK
Eucla Townsite Telegraph Station
Mundrabilla Roadhouse
Webbs Cave
Firestick Cave
Mundrabilla
Madura
Eyre
Madura
Madura Cave
Noonaera
Red Rocks Point
Great Australian Bight
N
0
Scale 1:2,500,000
100km
TOURING MAPS

Joins Map 41
A
B
C
D
E
F
1
2
3
4
5
6
7
8
Jane Bay
NINGALOO MARINE PARK
Bruboodjoo Point
Cardabia
Coral Bay
Turtle Cliffs
Point Anderson
Marrilla
White Peaks
Round Knob
Milgah
Gnabbarra
North West Coastal
Pelican Point
Warroora
Marsh Hill
Cape Farquhar
Gnarraloo Bay
Gnaraloo
Minilya Roadhouse
Minilya
Gnabbarry
Manberry
Red Bluff
Lake MacLeod
Coolthan
Yalkatharra
Cape Cuvier
Boologooro
Cooralya
Quobba
Boolan Hill
Point Quobba
Boolathana
INDIAN
OCEAN
Gascoyne
Carnarvon – Mullewa
Miaboolya Beach
Cape Ronsard
Ingada Village
Meeragoolia
Carnarvon
Bernier Island
BERNIER AND DORRE ISLANDS NATURE RESERVE
Greenough Point
Callagiddy
Cape Couture
Grey Point
New Beach
Bush Bay
Shark Bay
Dorre Island
Edaggee
Cape St Cricq
Naturaliste Channel
Long Point
SHARK BAY MARINE PARK
Cape Peron North
Cape Inscription
Cape Levillain
Guichenault Point
FRANCOIS PERON NATIONAL PARK
Cape Rose
Cape Lesueur
Monkey Mia
Denham Sound
Faure
Quoin Head
Petit Po
Dirk Hartog Island
Denham
Peron Peninsula
L'Haridon Bight
SHARK BAY MARINE PARK
Dirk Hartog
Useless Loop
Steep Point
Mount Direction
Nanga Station
Thunder Bay Blowholes
Henri Freycinet Harbour
Pepper Point
Mount Dorrigo
Carrarang
Mount Elliot
For more detail see maps 53-54
Tamala
N
0
Scale 1:2,500,000
100km
Joins Map 29
TOURING MAPS

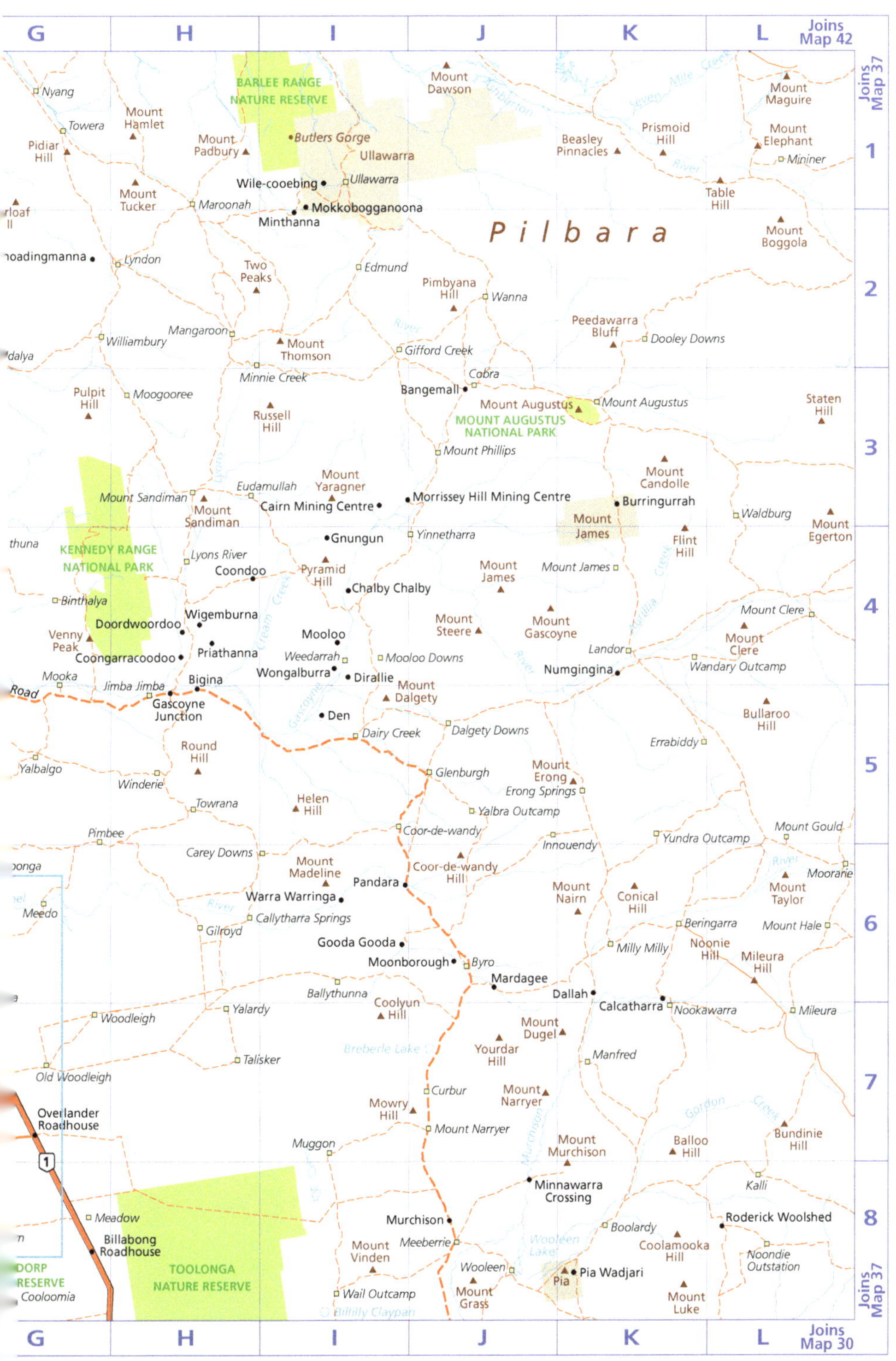
Joins Map 42
Joins Map 37
Joins Map 30
Pilbara
BARLEE RANGE NATURE RESERVE
MOUNT AUGUSTUS NATIONAL PARK
KENNEDY RANGE NATIONAL PARK
TOOLONGA NATURE RESERVE
Mount Augustus
Gascoyne Junction
Overlander Roadhouse
Billabong Roadhouse
Murchison
Meekatharra
TOURING MAPS

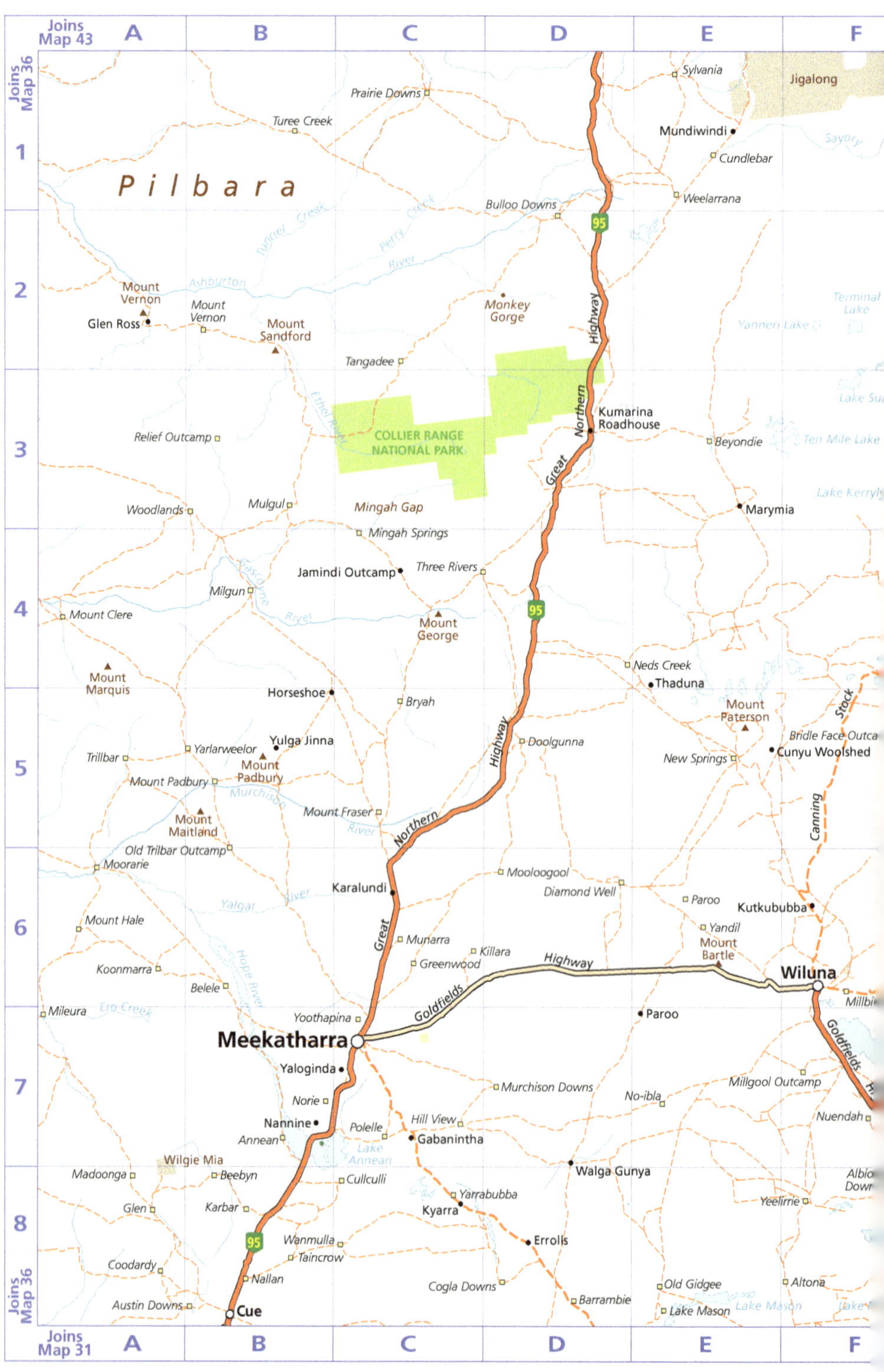
Joins Map 43
A
B
C
D
E
F
Joins Map 36
1
2
3
4
5
6
7
8
Pilbara
Prairie Downs
Turee Creek
Sylvania
Jigalong
Mundiwindi
Cundlebar
Weelarrana
Bulloo Downs
95
Mount Vernon
Glen Ross
Mount Vernon
Ashburton
River
Tunnel Creek
Perry Creek
Mount Sandford
Monkey Gorge
Great Northern Highway
Tangadee
Terminal Lake
Yanneri Lake
Kumarina Roadhouse
COLLIER RANGE NATIONAL PARK
Relief Outcamp
Beyondie
Ten Mile Lake
Woodlands
Mulgul
Mingah Gap
Mingah Springs
Marymia
Lake Kerryl
Jamindi Outcamp
Three Rivers
Milgun
Gascoyne River
Mount Clere
Mount George
Neds Creek
Thaduna
Mount Marquis
Horseshoe
Bryah
Mount Paterson
Bridle Face Outca
Cunyu Woolshed
Yulga Jinna
Doolgunna
Trillbar
Yarlarweelor
Mount Padbury
New Springs
Mount Padbury
Murchison River
Mount Fraser
Canning Stock
Mount Maitland
Old Trilbar Outcamp
Moorarie
Mooloogool
Diamond Well
Karalundi
Paroo
Kutkububba
Yalgar River
Mount Hale
Munarra
Yandil
Killara
Mount Bartle
Greenwood
Koonmarra
Highway
Wiluna
Belele
Hope River
Goldfields
Millbi
Mileura
Ero Creek
Yoothapina
Paroo
Meekatharra
Yaloginda
Goldfields
Murchison Downs
Millgool Outcamp
Norie
No-ibla
Nannine
Hill View
Nuendah
Polelle
Annean
Gabanintha
Lake Annean
Wilgie Mia
Madoonga
Beebyn
Walga Gunya
Cullculli
Albio Down
Yarrabubba
Glen
Karbar
Yeelirrie
Kyarra
Wanmulla
Errolls
Taincrow
Coodardy
Nallan
Cogla Downs
Old Gidgee
Altona
Barrambie
Austin Downs
Cue
Lake Mason
Lake Mason
Joins Map 31

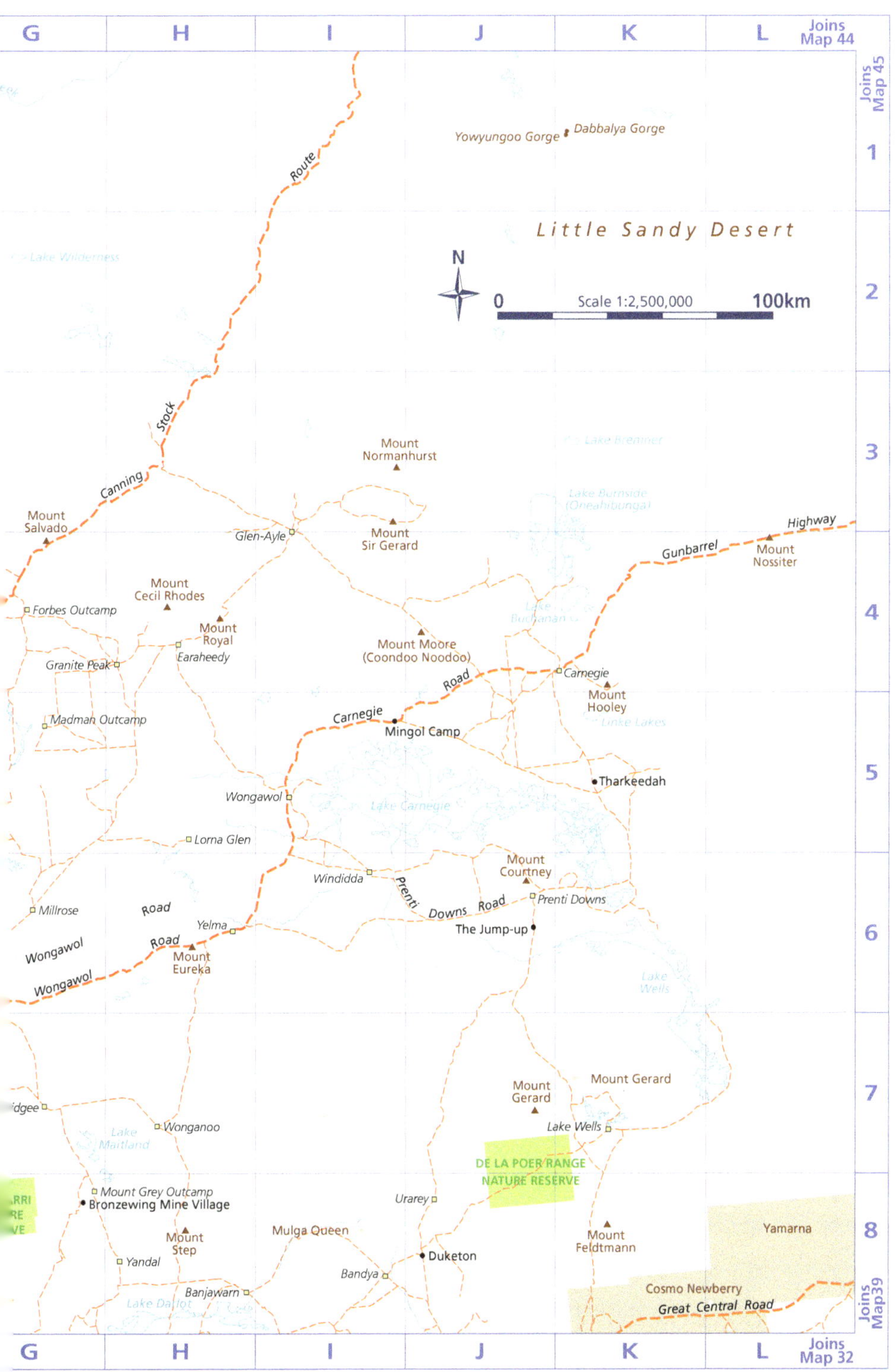

G
H
I
J
K
L
Joins Map 44
Joins Map 45
1
2
3
4
5
6
7
8
Joins Map39
Joins Map 32
Yowyungoo Gorge
Dabbalya Gorge
Canning Stock Route
Little Sandy Desert
N
0
Scale 1:2,500,000
100km
Lake Wilderness
Mount Normanhurst
Lake Breaden
Lake Burnside (Oneahibunga)
Mount Salvado
Glen-Ayle
Mount Sir Gerard
Gunbarrel Highway
Mount Nossiter
Mount Cecil Rhodes
Forbes Outcamp
Mount Royal
Earaheedy
Lake Buchanan
Granite Peak
Mount Moore (Coondoo Noodoo)
Carnegie Road
Carnegie
Mount Hooley
Linke Lakes
Madman Outcamp
Mingol Camp
Tharkeedah
Wongawol
Lake Carnegie
Lorna Glen
Mount Courtney
Windidda
Prenti Downs Road
Prenti Downs
Millrose
Wongawol Road
Yelma
The Jump-up
Mount Eureka
Lake Wells
Mount Gerard
idgee
Wonganoo
Lake Maitland
DE LA POER RANGE NATURE RESERVE
Mount Grey Outcamp
Bronzewing Mine Village
Urarey
Mount Step
Mulga Queen
Mount Feldtmann
Yamarna
Yandal
Duketon
Bandya
Banjawarn
Lake Darlot
Cosmo Newberry
Great Central Road
TOURING MAPS

Joins Map 45
Joins Map 38
Joins Map 33
Joins Map 32
GIBSON DESERT NATURE RESERVE
Len Beadell Plaque
Mount Everard
Decker Field
Mungilli
Mungilli
Mount Johnson
Mount William Lambert
MANGKILI CLAYPAN NATURE RESERVE
Gunbarrel
Highway
Mount Beadell
Thryptomene Hill
Len Beadell's Tree and plaque
Lake Breaden
Heather
Old
Mount Charles
Rururr
Gunbarrel Highway
Tjurnti
Jackie Junctio
Kurrkarturtu
Gibson Desert
Tjikrrli
Tjirrkarli
Mount Worsnop
Boyd Lagoon
Lake Gillen
Mount O'Loughlin
Warburton
Central
Pulpapur Outstatio
Blackstone
Ainslie Gorg
Beal Outstation
Warburton Ran
Highway
Great
Ngaanyatjara
Kanpa
Yapupara
MacKenzie Gorge
Baker Lake
Harkness Gorge
Waterfall Gorge
Sydney Yeo Ch
Woods Pass
Road
Breaden Bluff
Great
Central
Tjukayirla Roadhouse
Highway
Lake Throssell
Road
Great Victoria Desert
Sue
Connie
Central
Great
Yamarna
YEO LAKE NATURE RESERVE
Yeo Lake
Yalleen
Anne
Beadell
Bishop Rileys Pulpit
Disappointed Hill
Mount Brown
Highway
Yamarna
Point Salvation
Mount Fleming
Yamarna
Stony Hill
NEALE JUNCTION NATURE RESERVE
Lake Rason

TOURING MAPS

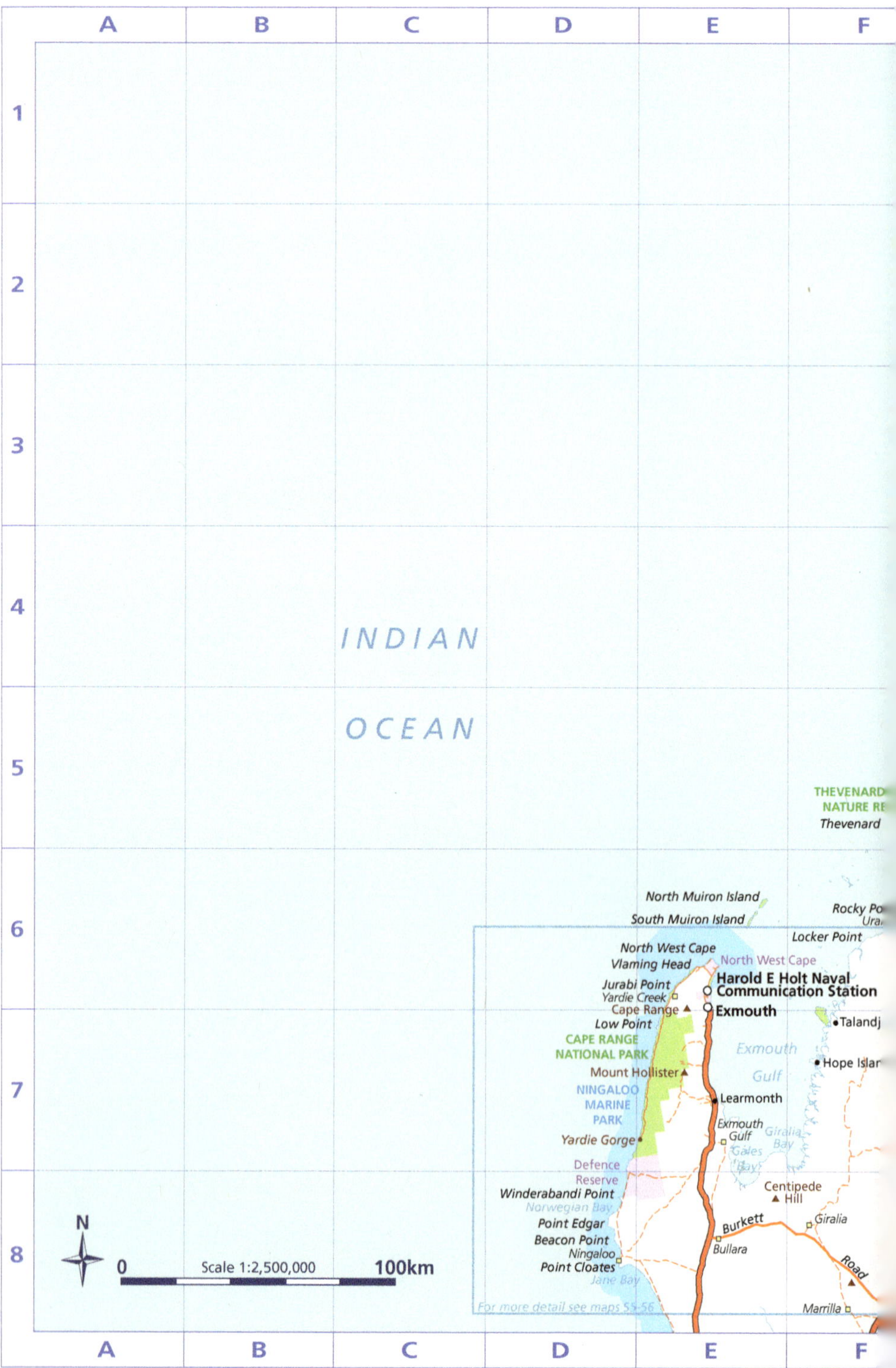
A
B
C
D
E
F
1
2
3
4
5
6
7
8
INDIAN
OCEAN
THEVENARD
NATURE RE
Thevenard
North Muiron Island
South Muiron Island
Rocky Po
Locker Point
North West Cape
Vlaming Head
North West Cape
Harold E Holt Naval
Communication Station
Jurabi Point
Yardie Creek
Cape Range
Exmouth
Talandj
Low Point
CAPE RANGE
NATIONAL PARK
Exmouth
Gulf
Mount Hollister
Hope Islar
NINGALOO
MARINE
PARK
Learmonth
Exmouth
Gulf
Giralia
Bay
Gales
Bay
Yardie Gorge
Defence
Reserve
Centipede
Hill
Winderabandi Point
Norwegian Bay
Point Edgar
Burkett
Giralia
Beacon Point
Bullara
Ningaloo
Road
Point Cloates
Jane Bay
Marrilla
For more detail see maps 55-56
N
0
Scale 1:2,500,000
100km

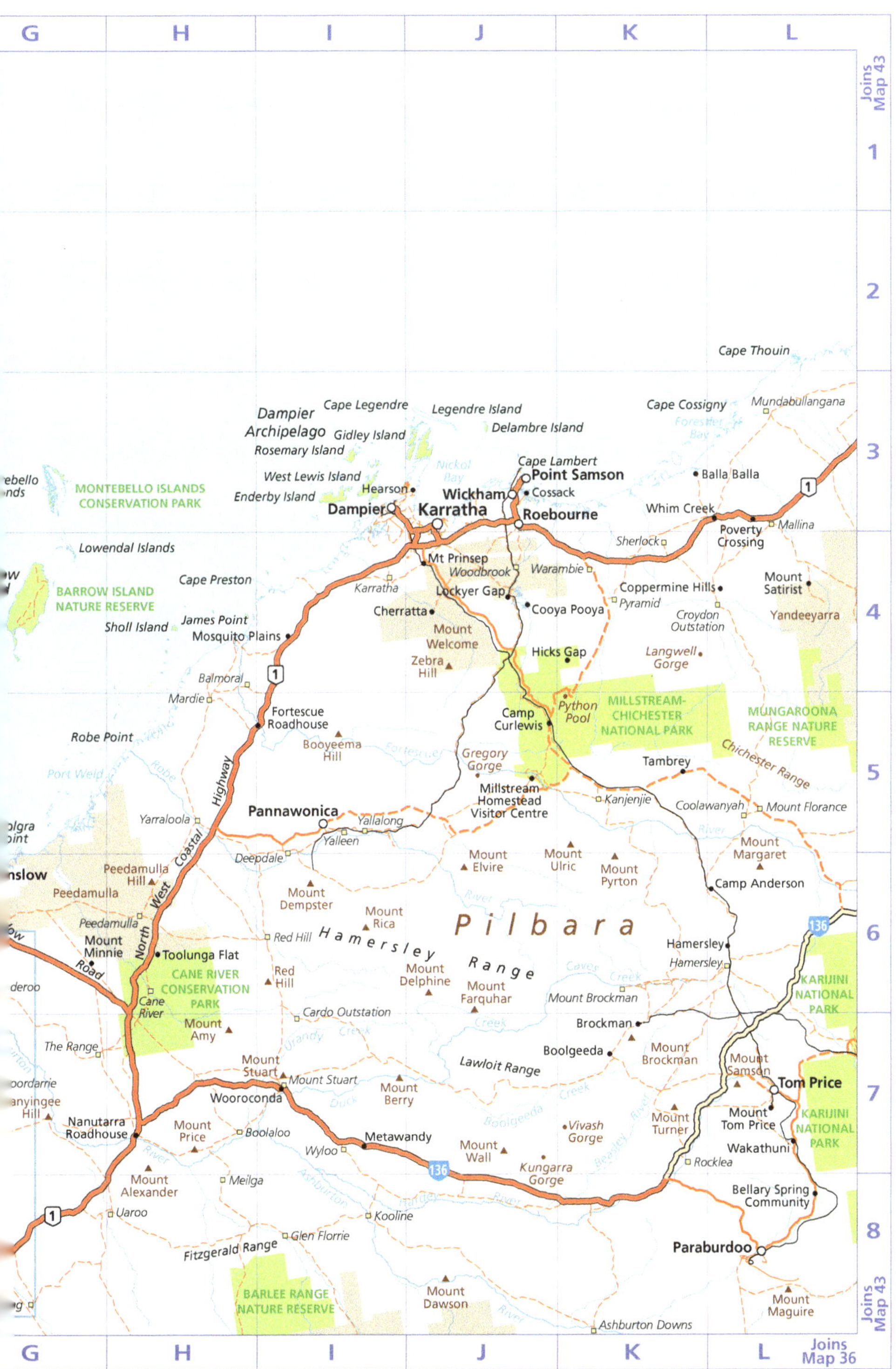

G H I J K L
Joins Map 43
Cape Thouin
Dampier Archipelago
Cape Legendre
Legendre Island
Delambre Island
Gidley Island
Rosemary Island
Cape Cossigny
Mundabullangana
Forestier Bay
West Lewis Island
Cape Lambert
Point Samson
Balla Balla
Montebello Islands
MONTEBELLO ISLANDS CONSERVATION PARK
Enderby Island
Hearson
Wickham
Cossack
Dampier
Karratha
Roebourne
Whim Creek
Mallina
Poverty Crossing
Lowendal Islands
Sherlock
Mt Prinsep
Woodbrook
Warambie
Mount Satirist
Cape Preston
BARROW ISLAND NATURE RESERVE
Karratha
Lockyer Gap
Coppermine Hills
Pyramid
Cooya Pooya
Croydon Outstation
Yandeeyarra
Sholl Island
James Point
Cherratta
Mosquito Plains
Mount Welcome
Hicks Gap
Langwell Gorge
Zebra Hill
Balmoral
Mardie
Python Pool
MILLSTREAM-CHICHESTER NATIONAL PARK
MUNGAROONA RANGE NATURE RESERVE
Fortescue Roadhouse
Camp Curlewis
Robe Point
Booyeema Hill
Gregory Gorge
Tambrey
Chichester Range
Port Weld
Millstream Homestead Visitor Centre
Pannawonica
Kanjenjie
Coolawanyah
Mount Florance
Yarraloola
Yallalong
Yalleen
Mount Margaret
Deepdale
Mount Elvire
Mount Ulric
Mount Pyrton
Peedamulla Hill
Peedamulla
Mount Dempster
Camp Anderson
Mount Rica
Pilbara
North West Coastal Highway
Peedamulla
Red Hill
Hamersley Range
Hamersley
Mount Minnie
Toolunga Flat
Mount Delphine
Hamersley
CANE RIVER CONSERVATION PARK
Red Hill
Mount Farquhar
Mount Brockman
KARIJINI NATIONAL PARK
Cane River
Cardo Outstation
Brockman
Mount Amy
The Range
Boolgeeda
Mount Brockman
Mount Stuart
Mount Stuart
Lawloit Range
Mount Samson
Tom Price
Wooroconda
Mount Berry
Mount Tom Price
Nanutarra Roadhouse
Mount Price
Boolaloo
Vivash Gorge
Mount Turner
Wyloo
Metawandy
Wakathuni
Mount Wall
Rocklea
Mount Alexander
Meilga
Kungarra Gorge
Bellary Spring Community
Uaroo
Kooline
Glen Florrie
Paraburdoo
Fitzgerald Range
BARLEE RANGE NATURE RESERVE
Mount Dawson
Mount Maguire
Ashburton Downs
Joins Map 36
TOURING MAPS

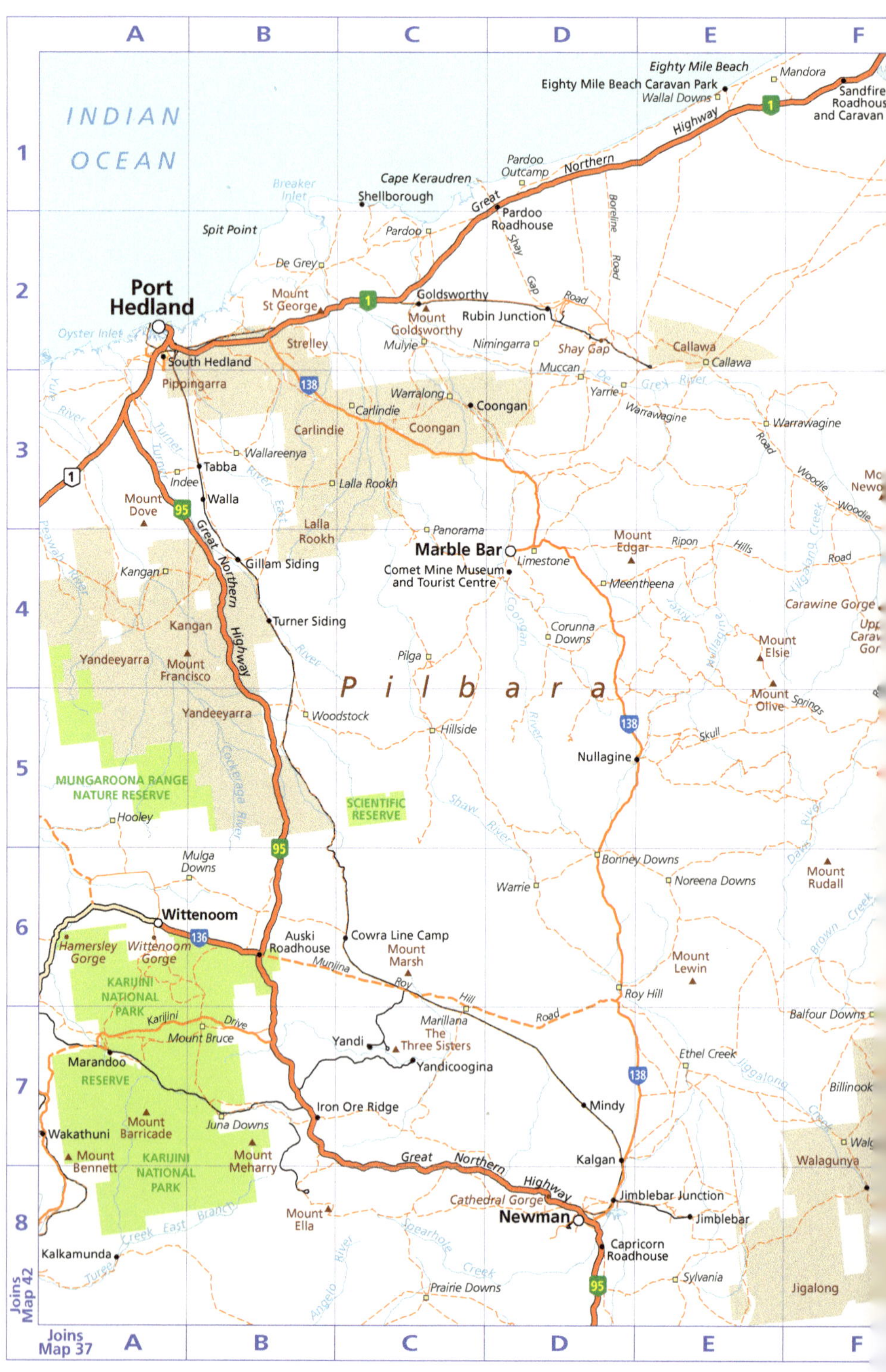
INDIAN OCEAN
Eighty Mile Beach
Eighty Mile Beach Caravan Park
Wallal Downs
Mandora
Sandfire Roadhouse and Caravan
Great Northern Highway
Pardoo Outcamp
Cape Keraudren
Shellborough
Breaker Inlet
Pardoo Roadhouse
Pardoo
Spit Point
De Grey
Port Hedland
Mount St George
Goldsworthy
Mount Goldsworthy
Rubin Junction
Shay Gap Road
Boreline Road
Oyster Inlet
Strelley
Mulyie
Nimingarra
Shay Gap
Callawa
South Hedland
Pippingarra
Muccan
Yarrie
Warralong
Carlindie
Coongan
Warrawagine
Carlindie
Coongan
Wallareenya
Tabba
Indee
Turner River
Lalla Rookh
Walla
Mount Dove
Panorama
Marble Bar
Limestone
Mount Edgar
Ripon Hills Road
Woodie Woodie
Kangan
Gillam Siding
Comet Mine Museum and Tourist Centre
Meentheena
Carawine Gorge
Kangan
Turner Siding
Corunna Downs
Mount Elsie
Yandeeyarra
Mount Francisco
Pilga
Pilbara
Mount Olive
Yandeeyarra
Woodstock
Hillside
Skull Springs
Nullagine
MUNGAROONA RANGE NATURE RESERVE
SCIENTIFIC RESERVE
Hooley
Shaw River
Mulga Downs
Bonney Downs
Noreena Downs
Mount Rudall
Warrie
Wittenoom
Hamersley Gorge
Wittenoom Gorge
Auski Roadhouse
Cowra Line Camp
Mount Marsh
Munjina Roy Hill Road
Mount Lewin
KARIJINI NATIONAL PARK
Roy Hill
Karijini Drive
Mount Bruce
Marillana
Yandi
The Three Sisters
Balfour Downs
Marandoo
Yandicoogina
Ethel Creek
Jiggalong Creek
RESERVE
Billinook
Iron Ore Ridge
Mindy
Juna Downs
Mount Barricade
Wakathuni
Mount Bennett
KARIJINI NATIONAL PARK
Mount Meharry
Great Northern Highway
Kalgan
Walagunya
Cathedral Gorge
Jimblebar Junction
Mount Ella
Newman
Jimblebar
Capricorn Roadhouse
Kalkamunda
Sylvania
Prairie Downs
Jigalong
Joins Map 42
Joins Map 37

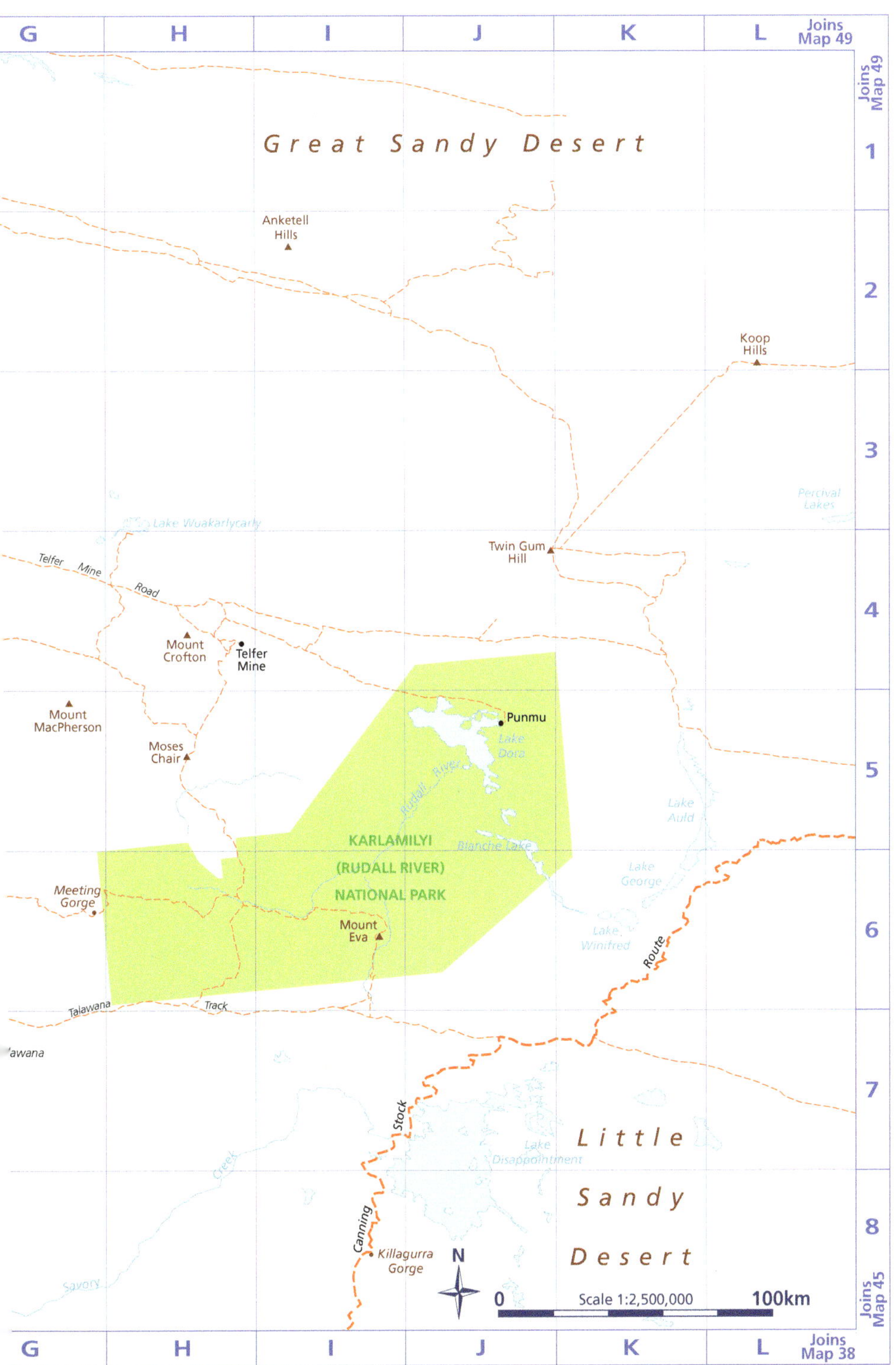

TOURING MAPS

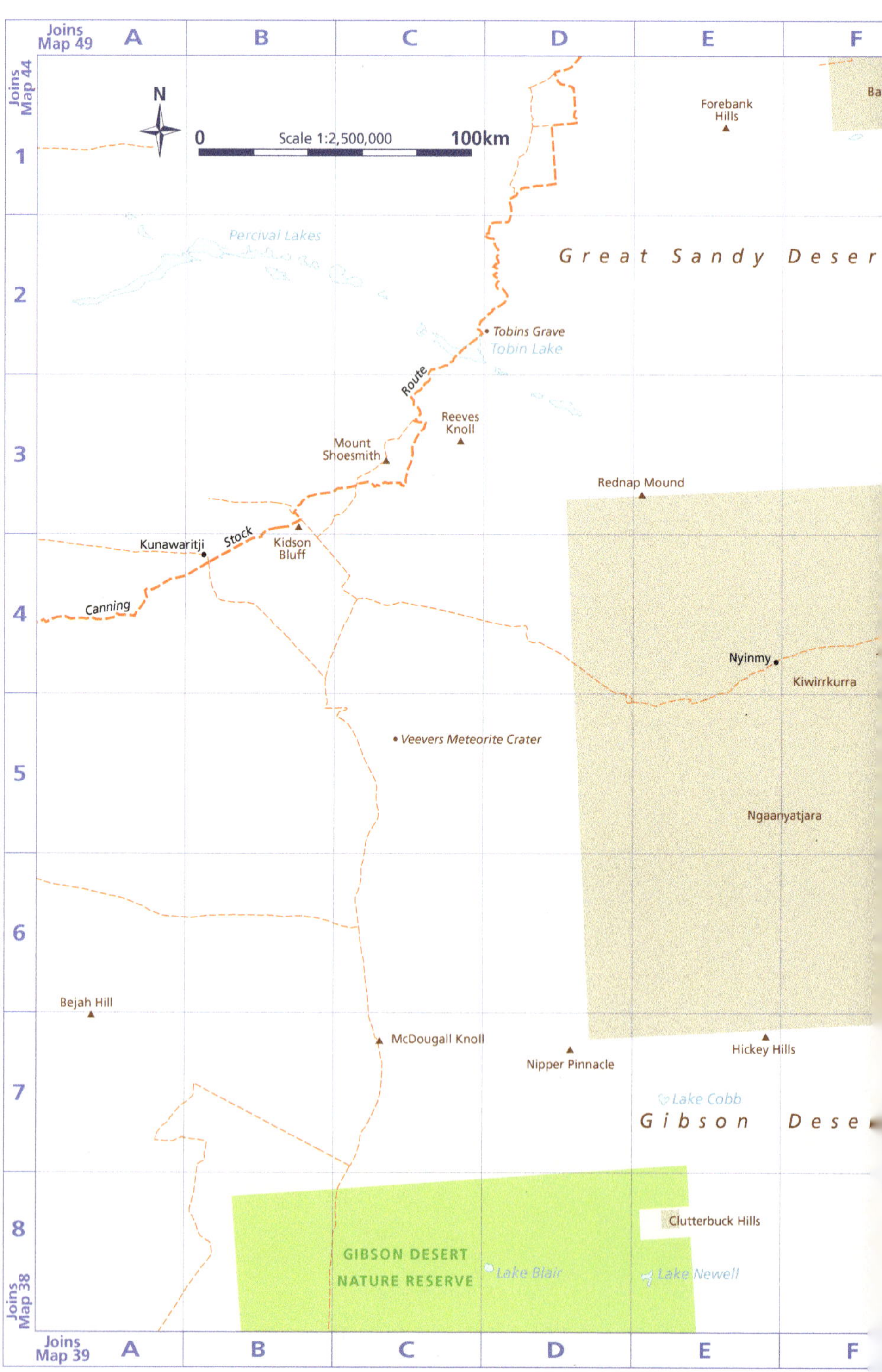
Joins Map 49
A
B
C
D
E
F
Joins Map 44
1
2
3
4
5
6
7
8
Joins Map 38
Joins Map 39
N
0
Scale 1:2,500,000
100km
Forebank Hills
Percival Lakes
Great Sandy Desert
Tobins Grave
Tobin Lake
Route
Reeves Knoll
Mount Shoesmith
Rednap Mound
Kunawaritji
Stock
Kidson Bluff
Canning
Nyinmy
Kiwirrkurra
Veevers Meteorite Crater
Ngaanyatjara
Bejah Hill
McDougall Knoll
Nipper Pinnacle
Hickey Hills
Lake Cobb
Gibson Desert
Clutterbuck Hills
GIBSON DESERT NATURE RESERVE
Lake Blair
Lake Newell

G
H
I
J
K
L
Joins Map 50
Thomas Peak
Lake White
False Mount Russell
1
Point Moody
Lamanbundah
Wilson Glen
Lake Wills
Warri Peak
Mount Russell
Waimbring Bluff
2
WESTERN AUSTRALIA
Lake Mackay
Vam Hill
Central Australia
NORTHERN TERRITORY
Ethel Creek
3
Mount Nicker
Lake Mackay
Nirrippi
Mount Carey
4
Mount Redvers
Mount Morris
Elizabeth Hills
Kiwirrkurra
Mount Webb
Ininti
Pinpirnga
Mount Russell
Corroboree Valley
Mount Greene
Tinki
Kintore
Ngutjul
Ilpili
5
Mount Lyell Brown
Mount Mein
Nguman
Yuwalki
Lake MacDonald
Johnstone Hill
Haasts Bluff
6
Lake Anec
Dinner Hill
Mount Unapproachable
Lake Hopkins
7
Lake Neale
Tjukurla
Petermann
Warburton
Mount Cowle
Hull River
Whale Hill
East Twin
Docker River
Lake Amadeus
Imbumbunna Hills
Mount Johnno
Mount Ant
8
Karrku
Walu
Yirrirra
Mount Russell
Kaltukatjara (Docker River)
Kutjurntari
Tjunti
Lapaku
Warakurna Roadhouse
Joins Map 40
TOURING MAPS

Scale 1:2,500,000
0
100km
N
INDIAN OCEAN
Buccaneer Archipelago
Cockatoo
Yampi Sound
Wotjalum
Strickland Bay
Sunday Island
Cone Bay
Cone
One Arm Point Reserve
Bardi (One Arm Point)
Thomas Bay
Lombadina
Mudnunn
Cygnet Bay
Lombadina
Willie Point
Mount
Kimbolton
Cape Borda
Djoodood
Cunningham Point
Pender Bay
Gurrbalgun
Goodenough Bay
King Sound
Emeriau Point
Neem
Embalgun
Djugarargyn
Maddarr
Lacepede Islands
North Head
Beagle Bay
Disaster Bay
Sandy Point
Beagle Bay
Beagle Bay
Low Sandy Point
Monbon
Mundud
Morard
Cape Baskerville
Carnot Bay
Nudugun
Derby
Prison Boab Tree
Munkayarra
Cape Bertholet
Country Downs
COULOMB POINT NATURE RESERVE
Fraser River
Coulomb Point
Mount Jowlaenga
Dampier Hill
James Price Point
Yeeda
Quondong Point
Northern
Highway
Cape Boileau
Kilto
Creek
Great
Kennedys Cottage
Roebuck Roadhouse
Manguel Creek
Coconut Well
Yakka Munga
Cable Beach
Broome
Gantheaume Point
Gantheaume Bay
Roebuck Bay
Roebuck Plains
Thangoo
Sandy Point
Highway
Dampier Downs Outcamp
Outpost Hill
Yardoogarra
Dampier Downs
Cape Villaret
Barn Hill Outstation
Cape Gourdon
Gourdon Bay
Yardoogara
Port Smith
Northern
Injudinah
Shamrock
Edgar Range
Geegully Creek
Goorda Tower
Lagrange Bay
Bidyadanga Community
Cape Bossut
Wanamulnyndong
Admiral Bay
Frazier Downs
Great
Brunbrunganjal
Geoffroy Bay
Cape Jaubert
Shelamar
Desault Bay
Cape Missiessy
Nita Downs
Great Sandy Desert
1
Anna Plains
McLarty
Erinbee Point
Munroe Springs
DRAGON TREE SOAK NATURE RESERVE
Highway
Woods Hills
Eighty Mile Beach
Eighty Mile Beach Caravan Park
Great
Northern
Sandfire Roadhouse and Caravan Park
Yarra Heights
Joins Map 44

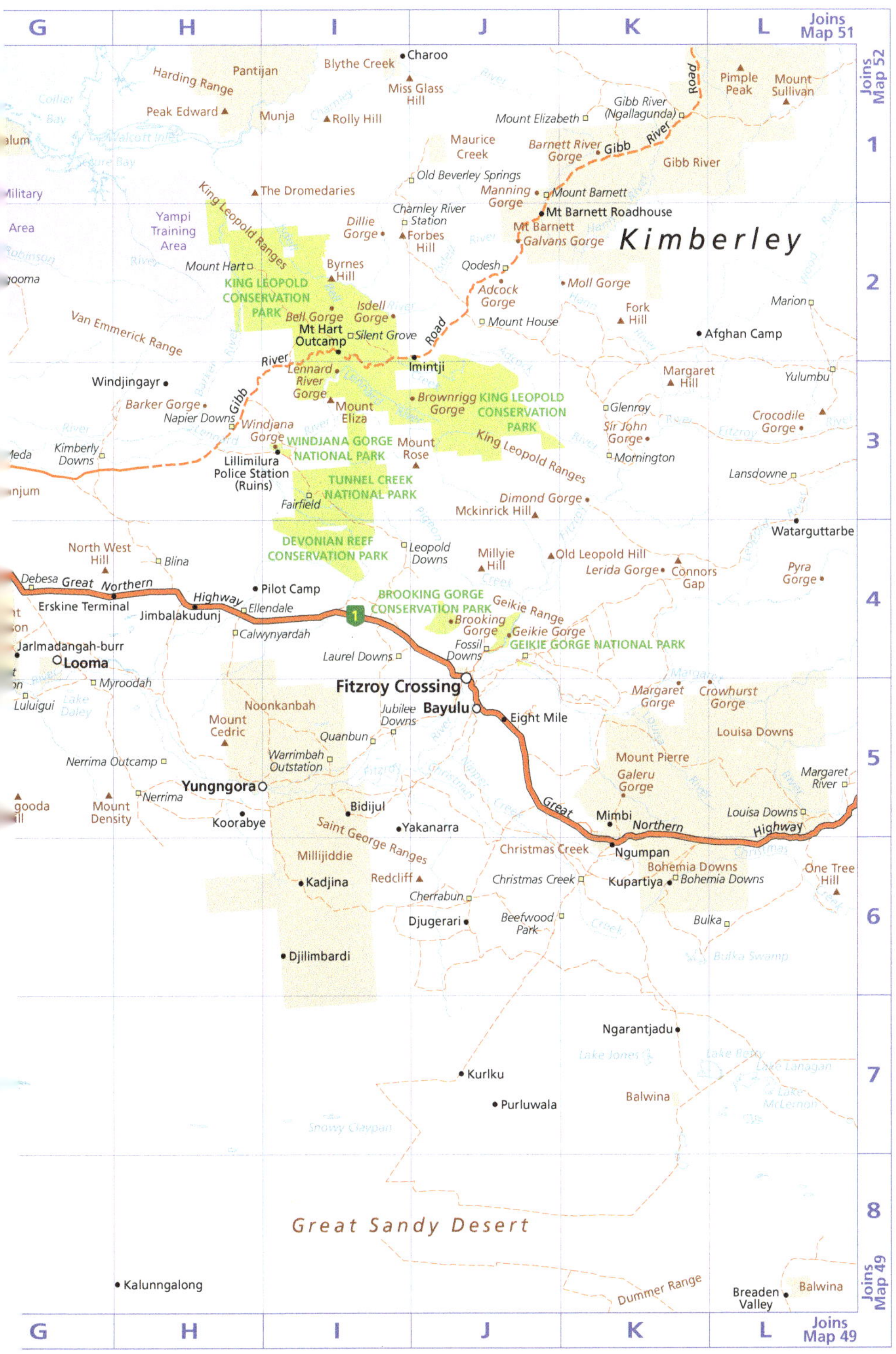

G
H
I
J
K
L
Joins Map 51
Joins Map 52
1
2
3
4
5
6
7
8
Joins Map 49
Charoo
Blythe Creek
Pantijan
Harding Range
Miss Glass Hill
Peak Edward
Munja
Rolly Hill
Mount Elizabeth
Gibb River (Ngallagunda)
Pimple Peak
Mount Sullivan
Road
River
Gibb
Maurice Creek
Barnett River Gorge
Gibb River
Old Beverley Springs
The Dromedaries
Manning Gorge
Mount Barnett
Charnley River Station
Mt Barnett Roadhouse
Yampi Training Area
Dillie Gorge
Forbes Hill
Mt Barnett
Galvans Gorge
Kimberley
King Leopold Ranges
Byrnes Hill
Qodesh
Mount Hart
KING LEOPOLD CONSERVATION PARK
Adcock Gorge
Moll Gorge
Fork Hill
Marion
Isdell Gorge
Bell Gorge
Mt Hart Outcamp
Silent Grove
Mount House
Afghan Camp
Van Emmerick Range
River
Imintji
Lennard River Gorge
Margaret Hill
Yulumbu
Windjingayr
Brownrigg Gorge
KING LEOPOLD CONSERVATION PARK
Barker Gorge
Mount Eliza
Glenroy
Napier Downs
Gibb
Sir John Gorge
Crocodile Gorge
Windjana Gorge
WINDJANA GORGE NATIONAL PARK
Mount Rose
Kimberly Downs
King Leopold Ranges
Mornington
Lillimilura Police Station (Ruins)
Lansdowne
TUNNEL CREEK NATIONAL PARK
Fairfield
Dimond Gorge
Mckinrick Hill
Watarguttarbe
DEVONIAN REEF CONSERVATION PARK
Leopold Downs
Millyie Hill
Old Leopold Hill
North West Hill
Blina
Lerida Gorge
Connors Gap
Pyra Gorge
Debesa
Great Northern Highway
Pilot Camp
BROOKING GORGE CONSERVATION PARK
Geikie Range
Erskine Terminal
Ellendale
Jimbalakudunj
Brooking Gorge
Geikie Gorge
Calwynyardah
Fossil Downs
GEIKIE GORGE NATIONAL PARK
Jarlmadangah-burr
Laurel Downs
Looma
Myroodah
Fitzroy Crossing
Margaret Gorge
Crowhurst Gorge
Luluigui
Noonkanbah
Jubilee Downs
Bayulu
Eight Mile
Mount Cedric
Quanbun
Louisa Downs
Warrimbah Outstation
Mount Pierre
Nerrima Outcamp
Galeru Gorge
Margaret River
Yungngora
Nerrima
Great
Mimbi
Louisa Downs
Mount Density
Koorabye
Bidijul
Northern
Highway
Yakanarra
Saint George Ranges
Christmas Creek
Ngumpan
Millijiddie
Bohemia Downs
One Tree Hill
Redcliff
Christmas Creek
Kupartiya
Bohemia Downs
Kadjina
Cherrabun
Djugerari
Beefwood Park
Bulka
Djilimbardi
Bulka Swamp
Ngarantjadu
Lake Jones
Lake Betty
Lake Lanagan
Kurlku
Purluwala
Balwina
Lake McLernon
Snowy Claypan
Great Sandy Desert
Dummer Range
Kalunngalong
Breaden Valley
Balwina
G
H
I
J
K
L
Joins Map 49

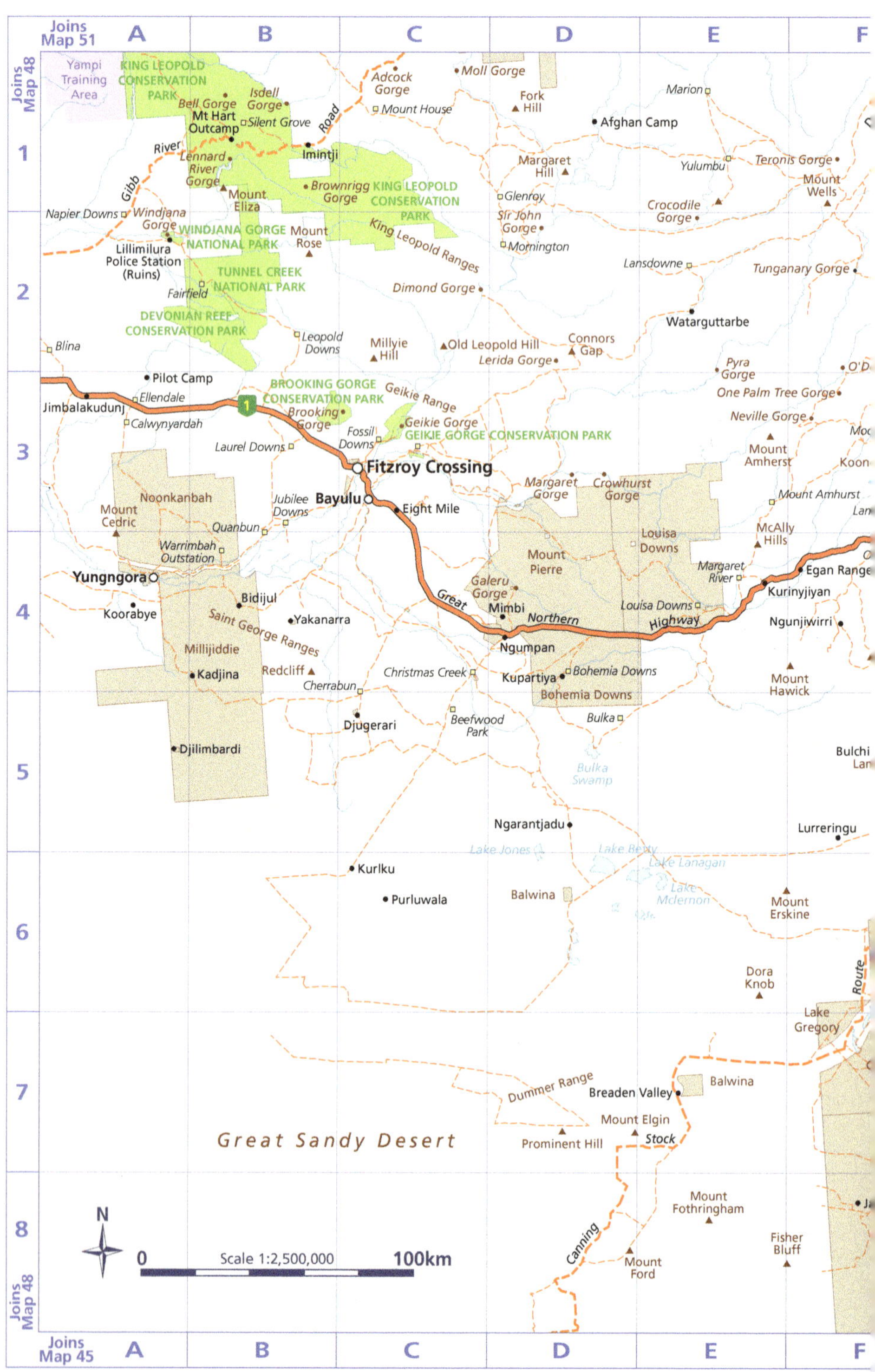

Joins Map 51
A
B
C
D
E
F
Joins Map 48
1
2
3
4
5
6
7
8
Yampi Training Area
KING LEOPOLD CONSERVATION PARK
Isdell Gorge
Bell Gorge
Mt Hart Outcamp
Silent Grove
Adcock Gorge
Mount House
Moll Gorge
Fork Hill
Marion
Afghan Camp
Road
Gibb River
Lennard River Gorge
Imintji
Margaret Hill
Yulumbu
Teronis Gorge
Mount Wells
Brownrigg Gorge
KING LEOPOLD CONSERVATION PARK
Glenroy
Mount Eliza
Crocodile Gorge
Napier Downs
Windjana Gorge
WINDJANA GORGE NATIONAL PARK
Mount Rose
Sir John Gorge
Mornington
King Leopold Ranges
Lillimilura Police Station (Ruins)
Lansdowne
Tunganary Gorge
TUNNEL CREEK NATIONAL PARK
Fairfield
Dimond Gorge
Watarguttarbe
DEVONIAN REEF CONSERVATION PARK
Blina
Leopold Downs
Millyie Hill
Old Leopold Hill
Connors Gap
Lerida Gorge
Pyra Gorge
O'D
Pilot Camp
BROOKING GORGE CONSERVATION PARK
Geikie Range
One Palm Tree Gorge
Jimbalakudunj
Ellendale
1
Brooking Gorge
Geikie Gorge
Neville Gorge
Calwynyardah
Fossil Downs
GEIKIE GORGE CONSERVATION PARK
Laurel Downs
Mount Amherst
Fitzroy Crossing
Koon
Noonkanbah
Margaret Gorge
Crowhurst Gorge
Mount Amhurst
Mount Cedric
Jubilee Downs
Bayulu
Eight Mile
Quanbun
Louisa Downs
McAlly Hills
Warrimbah Outstation
Mount Pierre
Margaret River
Egan Range
Yungngora
Galeru Gorge
Kurinyjiyan
Bidijul
Great
Mimbi
Louisa Downs
Koorabye
Northern
Highway
Ngunjiwirri
Yakanarra
Saint George Ranges
Ngumpan
Millijiddie
Mount Hawick
Redcliff
Christmas Creek
Kupartiya
Bohemia Downs
Kadjina
Cherrabun
Bohemia Downs
Beefwood Park
Bulka
Djugerari
Djilimbardi
Bulka Swamp
Bulchi Lan
Ngarantjadu
Lurreringu
Lake Jones
Lake Betty
Lake Lanagan
Kurlku
Lake Mclernon
Purluwala
Balwina
Mount Erskine
Dora Knob
Route
Lake Gregory
Balwina
Dummer Range
Breaden Valley
Mount Elgin
Great Sandy Desert
Prominent Hill
Stock
Mount Fothringham
Fisher Bluff
Canning
Mount Ford
N
0
Scale 1:2,500,000
100km
Joins Map 48
Joins Map 45
TOURING MAPS

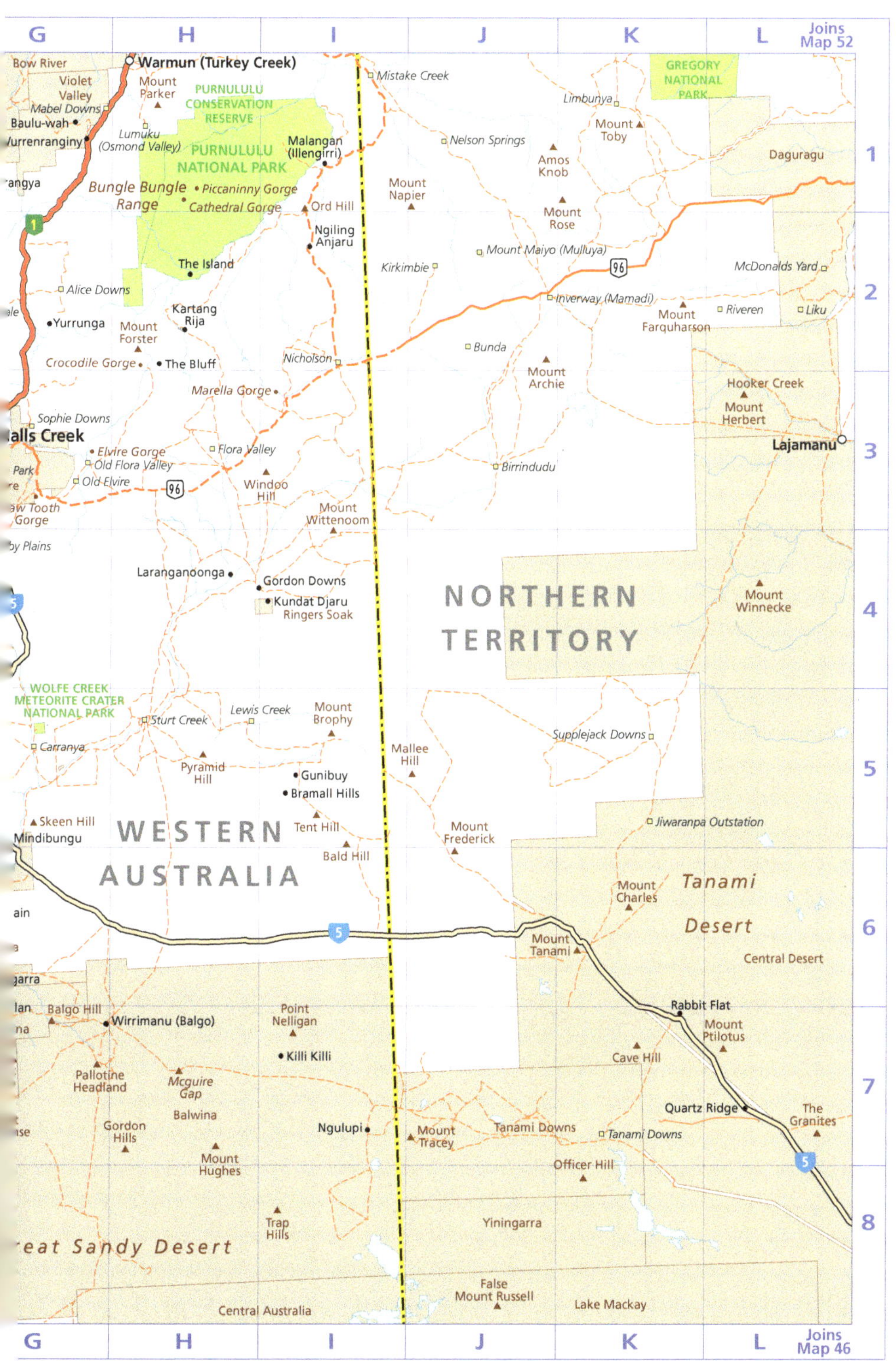

G
H
I
J
K
L
Joins Map 52
Warmun (Turkey Creek)
Bow River
Violet Valley
Mabel Downs
Baulu-wah
Mount Parker
PURNULULU CONSERVATION RESERVE
PURNULULU NATIONAL PARK
Lumuku (Osmond Valley)
Malangan (Illengirri)
Bungle Bungle Range
Piccaninny Gorge
Cathedral Gorge
Ord Hill
Ngiling Anjaru
The Island
Alice Downs
Kartang Rija
Yurrunga
Mount Forster
Crocodile Gorge
The Bluff
Nicholson
Marella Gorge
Sophie Downs
Elvire Gorge
Old Flora Valley
Old Elvire
Flora Valley
Windoo Hill
Mount Wittenoom
Laranganoonga
Gordon Downs
Kundat Djaru
Ringers Soak
Mistake Creek
Nelson Springs
Mount Napier
Kirkimbie
Limbunya
Mount Toby
Amos Knob
Mount Rose
Mount Maiyo (Mulluya)
Inverway (Mamadi)
Bunda
Mount Archie
Birrindudu
GREGORY NATIONAL PARK
Daguragu
McDonalds Yard
Mount Farquharson
Riveren
Liku
Hooker Creek
Mount Herbert
Lajamanu
NORTHERN TERRITORY
Mount Winnecke
WOLFE CREEK METEORITE CRATER NATIONAL PARK
Sturt Creek
Lewis Creek
Mount Brophy
Carranya
Pyramid Hill
Gunibuy
Bramall Hills
Skeen Hill
Mindibungu
WESTERN AUSTRALIA
Tent Hill
Bald Hill
Mallee Hill
Mount Frederick
Supplejack Downs
Jiwaranpa Outstation
Mount Charles
Tanami Desert
Mount Tanami
Central Desert
Balgo Hill
Wirrimanu (Balgo)
Point Nelligan
Killi Killi
Pallotine Headland
Mcguire Gap
Balwina
Gordon Hills
Mount Hughes
Ngulupi
Mount Tracey
Tanami Downs
Rabbit Flat
Mount Ptilotus
Cave Hill
Quartz Ridge
The Granites
Officer Hill
Trap Hills
Yiningarra
False Mount Russell
Lake Mackay
Central Australia
Joins Map 46
1
2
3
4
5
6
7
8
TOURING MAPS

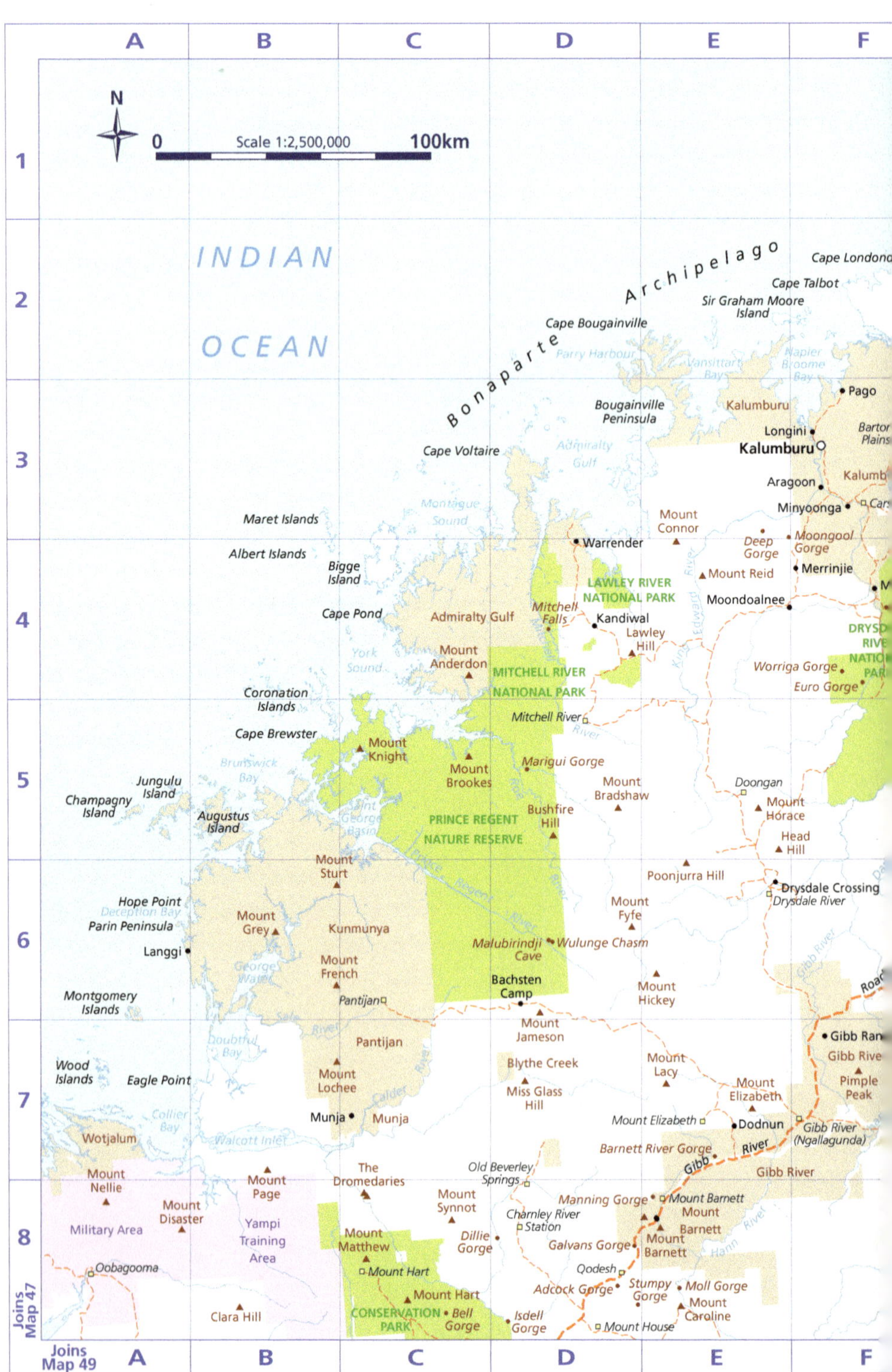

A
B
C
D
E
F
1
2
3
4
5
6
7
8
N
0
Scale 1:2,500,000
100km
INDIAN
OCEAN
Bonaparte Archipelago
Cape Londonderry
Cape Talbot
Sir Graham Moore Island
Cape Bougainville
Parry Harbour
Vansittart Bay
Napier Broome Bay
Pago
Kalumburu
Bougainville Peninsula
Longini
Kalumburu
Cape Voltaire
Admiralty Gulf
Aragoon
Minyoonga
Montague Sound
Mount Connor
Maret Islands
Warrender
Deep Gorge
Moongool Gorge
Albert Islands
Bigge Island
LAWLEY RIVER NATIONAL PARK
Mount Reid
Merrinjie
Moondoalnee
Cape Pond
Admiralty Gulf
Mitchell Falls
Kandiwal
Lawley Hill
King Edward River
York Sound
Mount Anderdon
MITCHELL RIVER NATIONAL PARK
Worriga Gorge
Euro Gorge
Coronation Islands
Mitchell River
Cape Brewster
Mount Knight
Brunswick Bay
Mount Brookes
Marigui Gorge
Mount Bradshaw
Doongan
Junngulu Island
Champagny Island
Augustus Island
St George Basin
PRINCE REGENT NATURE RESERVE
Bushfire Hill
Mount Horace
Head Hill
Mount Sturt
Prince Regent River
Poonjurra Hill
Drysdale Crossing
Drysdale River
Hope Point
Deception Bay
Parin Peninsula
Mount Grey
Kunmunya
Mount Fyfe
Langgi
George Water
Mount French
Malubirindji Cave
Wulunge Chasm
Gibb River
Bachsten Camp
Mount Hickey
Montgomery Islands
Pantijan
Road
Doubtful Bay
Pantijan
Mount Jameson
Gibb River
Blythe Creek
Mount Lacy
Gibb River
Wood Islands
Eagle Point
Mount Lochee
Miss Glass Hill
Mount Elizabeth
Pimple Peak
Collier Bay
Calder River
Munja
Munja
Mount Elizabeth
Dodnun
Gibb River (Ngallagunda)
Wotjalum
Walcott Inlet
Barnett River Gorge
Gibb River
Mount Nellie
Mount Page
The Dromedaries
Old Beverley Springs
Gibb River
Mount Disaster
Mount Synnot
Manning Gorge
Mount Barnett
Mount Barnett
Military Area
Yampi Training Area
Charnley River Station
Mount Matthew
Dillie Gorge
Galvans Gorge
Mount Barnett
Hann River
Oobagooma
Mount Hart
Qodesh
Adcock Gorge
Stumpy Gorge
Moll Gorge
Mount Hart
Mount Caroline
Clara Hill
CONSERVATION PARK
Bell Gorge
Isdell Gorge
Mount House
Joins Map 47
Joins Map 49
TOURING MAPS

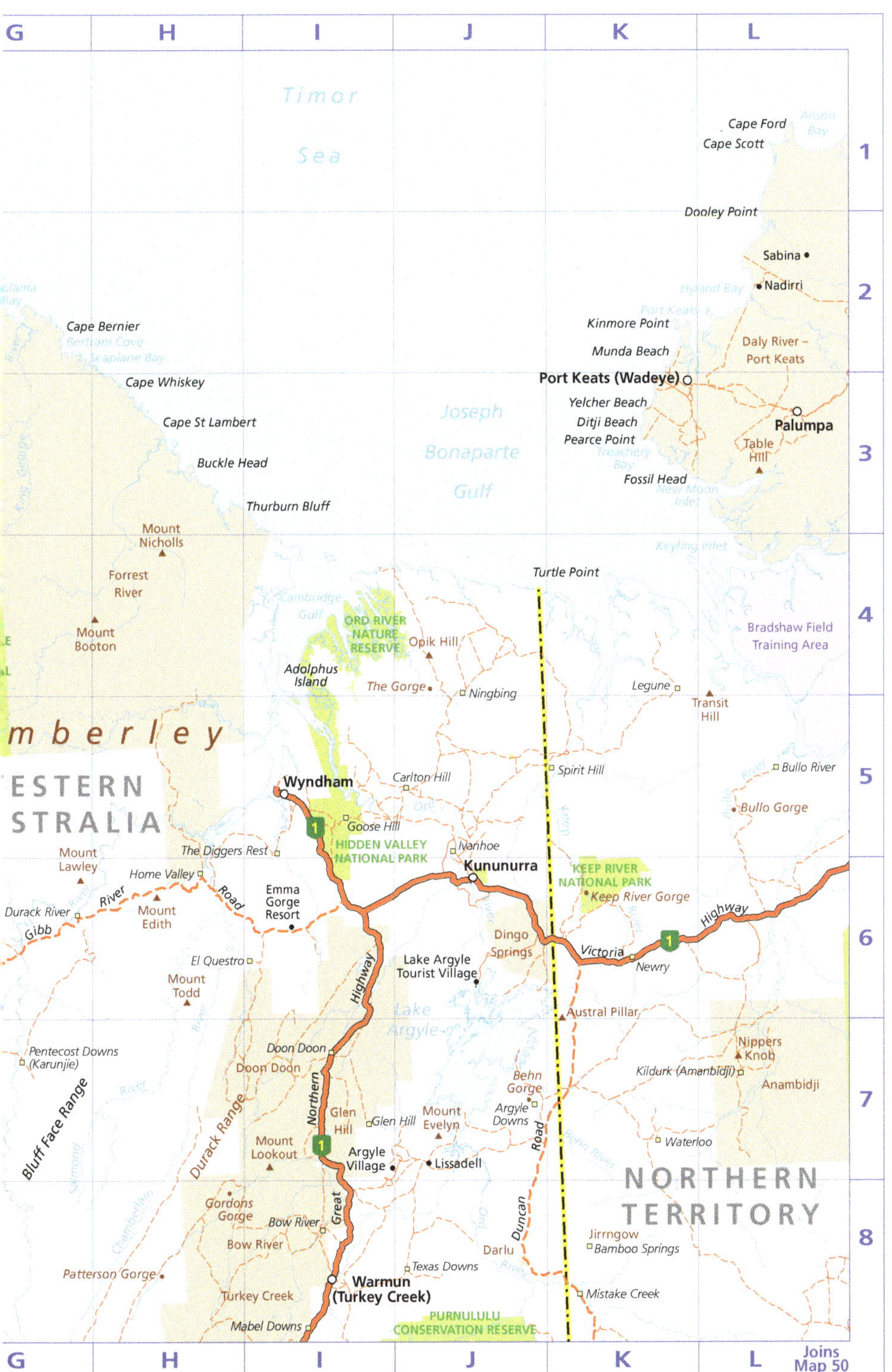

G
H
I
J
K
L
1
2
3
4
5
6
7
8
Timor
Sea
Joseph
Bonaparte
Gulf
Cape Ford
Cape Scott
Dooley Point
Sabina
Nadirri
Kinmore Point
Munda Beach
Daly River – Port Keats
Port Keats (Wadeye)
Palumpa
Yelcher Beach
Ditji Beach
Pearce Point
Table Hill
Fossil Head
Cape Bernier
Cape Whiskey
Cape St Lambert
Buckle Head
Thurburn Bluff
Mount Nicholls
Forrest River
Mount Booton
Turtle Point
ORD RIVER NATURE RESERVE
Opik Hill
Adolphus Island
The Gorge
Ningbing
Legune
Transit Hill
Bradshaw Field Training Area
mberley
ESTERN
STRALIA
Wyndham
Carlton Hill
Spirit Hill
Bullo River
Bullo Gorge
Goose Hill
HIDDEN VALLEY NATIONAL PARK
Ivanhoe
Kununurra
KEEP RIVER NATIONAL PARK
Keep River Gorge
Mount Lawley
The Diggers Rest
Home Valley
Emma Gorge Resort
Durack River
Gibb
River
Road
Mount Edith
El Questro
Mount Todd
Dingo Springs
Lake Argyle Tourist Village
Victoria
Highway
Newry
Austral Pillar
Pentecost Downs (Karunjie)
Doon Doon
Nippers Knob
Kildurk (Amanbidji)
Anambidji
Behn Gorge
Argyle Downs
Bluff Face Range
Durack Range
Northern
Glen Hill
Mount Evelyn
Waterloo
Mount Lookout
Argyle Village
Lissadell
NORTHERN
TERRITORY
Gordons Gorge
Bow River
Great
Duncan
Road
Darlu
Jirrngow
Bamboo Springs
Patterson Gorge
Texas Downs
Warmun (Turkey Creek)
Turkey Creek
Mistake Creek
Mabel Downs
PURNULULU CONSERVATION RESERVE
Joins Map 50

TOURING MAPS

A
B
C
D
E
F
1
2
3
4
5
6
7
8
Naturaliste Channel
Shark Bay
Cape Peron North
Broadhurst Bight
Bottle Beach
Gregories
Cape Inscription
Turtle Bay
Cape Levillain
Cattle Well
Herald Bight
West Point
Withnell Point
Peron Peninsula
Denham Sound
Peron Hills
Cape Lesueur
Big Lagoon
Mystery Beach
FRANCOIS PERON NATIONAL PARK
Sandy Point Outstation
Sandy Point
Middle Bluff
Peron
Louisa Bay
Quoin Head
Dirk Hartog Island
Monkey
SHARK BAY MARINE PARK
Lagoon Point
Denham
Herald Bay Outcamp
Herald Bay
Denham Channel
Notch Point
Tetrodon Loop
Cape Bellefin
Cape Heirisson
Dirk Hartog
Tumbledown Point
Bellefin Prong
Wilya Mia
Heirisson Prong
North Sand
Blind Strait
Useless Loop
Useless Inlet
Surf Point
South Passage
Steep Point
Cape Ransonnet
Shelter Bay
Useless
Mount Direction
Blind Inlet
INDIAN OCEAN
Thunder Bay
Thunder Bay Blowholes
Loop
Bibby Giddy Outcamp
Crayfish Bay
Marinus Point
Edel Land
False Entrance
Zuytdorp Point
Mount Dorrigo
Road
N
0
Scale 1:750,000
30km
TOURING MAPS

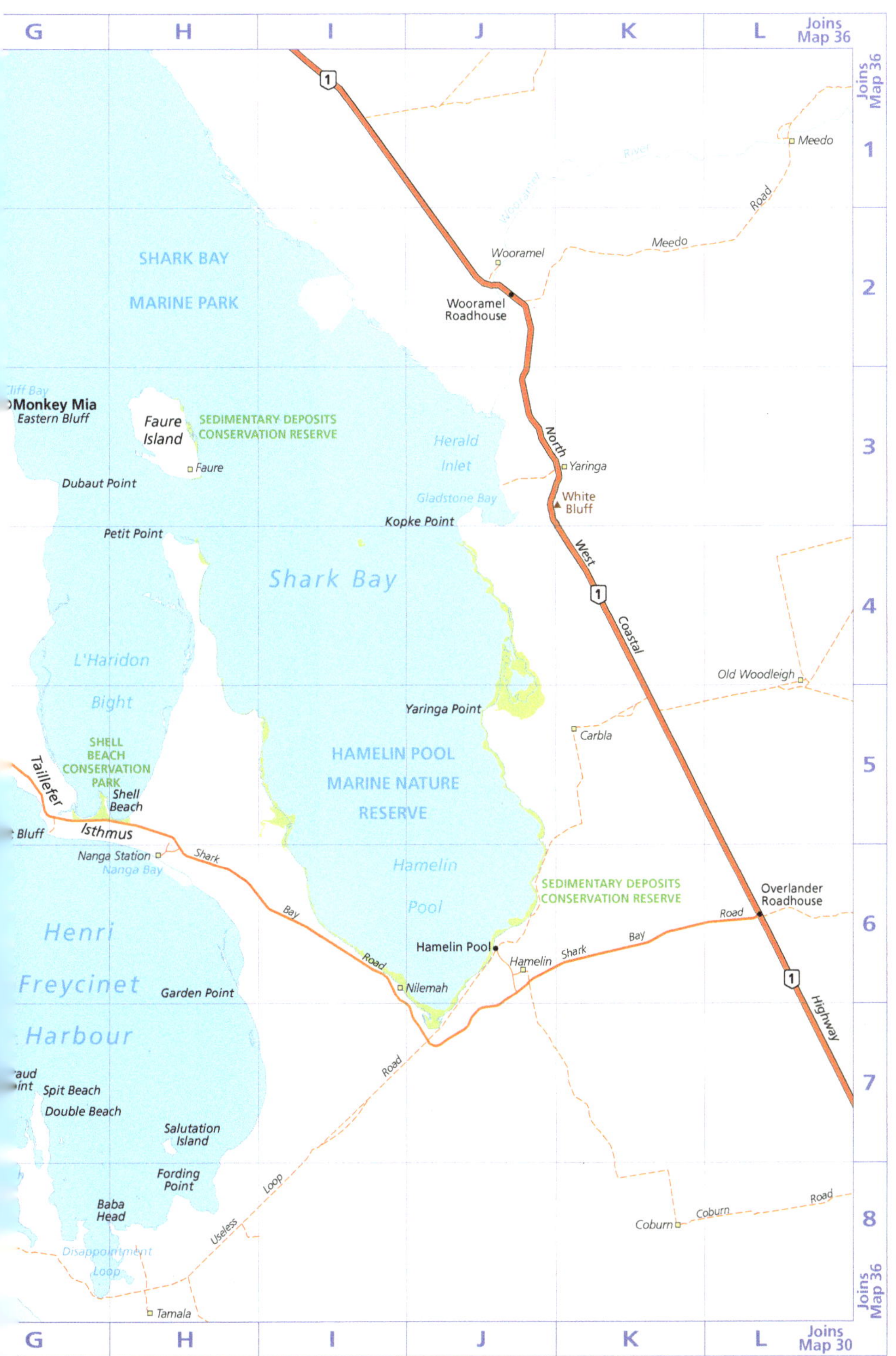

G
H
I
J
K
L
Joins Map 36
1
2
3
4
5
6
7
8
Meedo
River
Wooramel
Road
Meedo
Wooramel
Wooramel Roadhouse
SHARK BAY
MARINE PARK
Cliff Bay
Monkey Mia
Eastern Bluff
Faure Island
Faure
SEDIMENTARY DEPOSITS CONSERVATION RESERVE
Herald Inlet
Gladstone Bay
North
Yaringa
White Bluff
Dubaut Point
Petit Point
Kopke Point
Shark Bay
West
Coastal
L'Haridon Bight
Old Woodleigh
Yaringa Point
Carbla
SHELL BEACH CONSERVATION PARK
Shell Beach
Taillefer
Isthmus
Bluff
HAMELIN POOL MARINE NATURE RESERVE
Nanga Station
Nanga Bay
Shark
Bay
Road
Hamelin Pool
SEDIMENTARY DEPOSITS CONSERVATION RESERVE
Overlander Roadhouse
Henri Freycinet Harbour
Hamelin Pool
Hamelin
Shark
Bay
Road
Nilemah
Garden Point
Highway
Spit Beach
Double Beach
Salutation Island
Fording Point
Baba Head
Useless
Loop
Road
Coburn
Coburn
Road
Disappointment Loop
Tamala
Joins Map 30

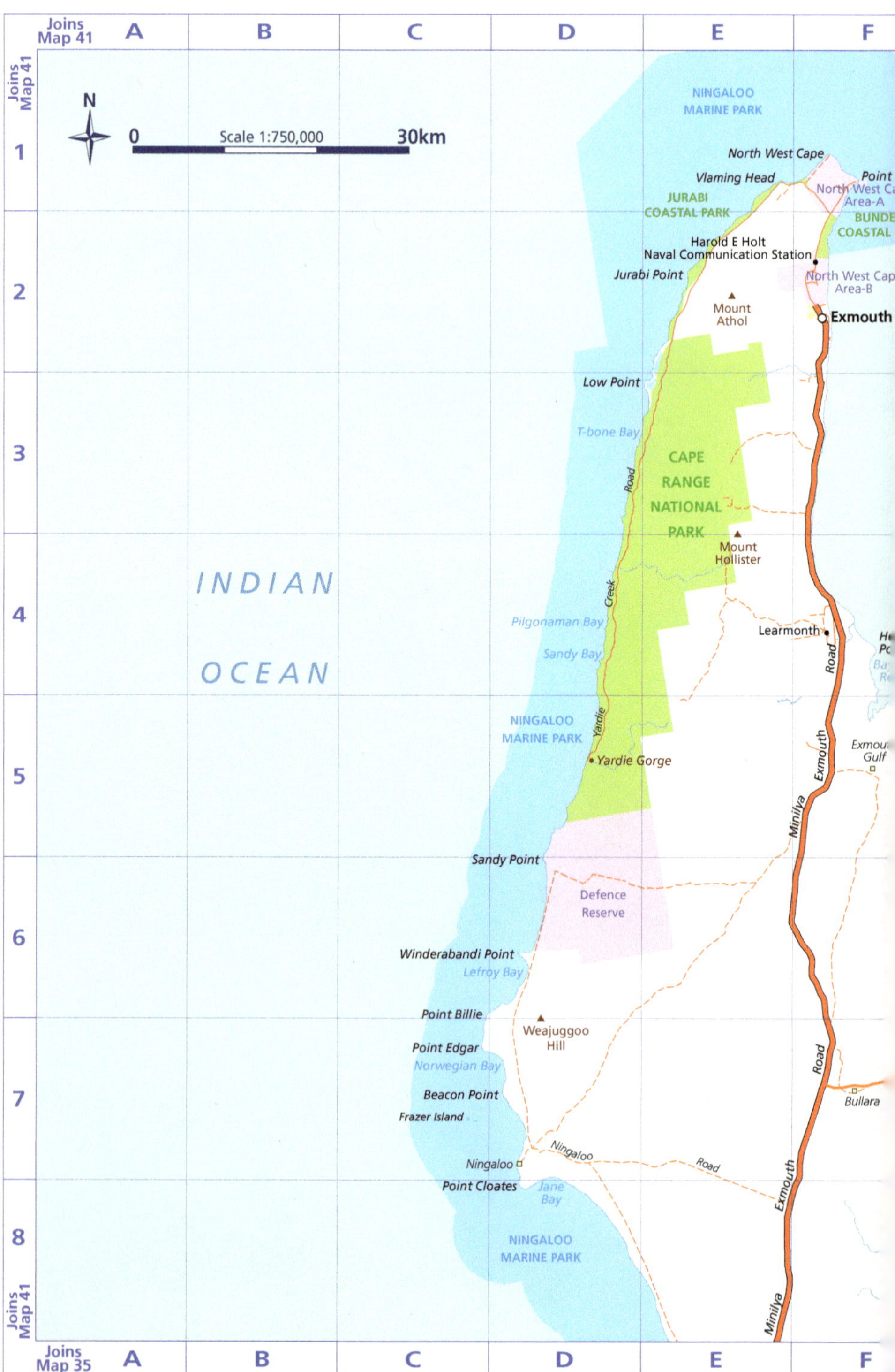

Joins Map 41
A
B
C
D
E
F
N
0
Scale 1:750,000
30km
1
2
3
4
5
6
7
8
NINGALOO MARINE PARK
North West Cape
Vlaming Head
JURABI COASTAL PARK
Harold E Holt Naval Communication Station
Jurabi Point
Mount Athol
Exmouth
Low Point
T-bone Bay
CAPE RANGE NATIONAL PARK
Mount Hollister
Road
Creek
Yardie
INDIAN
OCEAN
Pilgonaman Bay
Sandy Bay
Learmonth
NINGALOO MARINE PARK
Yardie Gorge
Exmouth
Minilya
Sandy Point
Defence Reserve
Winderabandi Point
Lefroy Bay
Point Billie
Weajuggoo Hill
Point Edgar
Norwegian Bay
Beacon Point
Frazer Island
Road
Bullara
Ningaloo
Ningaloo Road
Point Cloates
Jane Bay
Exmouth
NINGALOO MARINE PARK
Minilya
Joins Map 35

TOURING MAPS

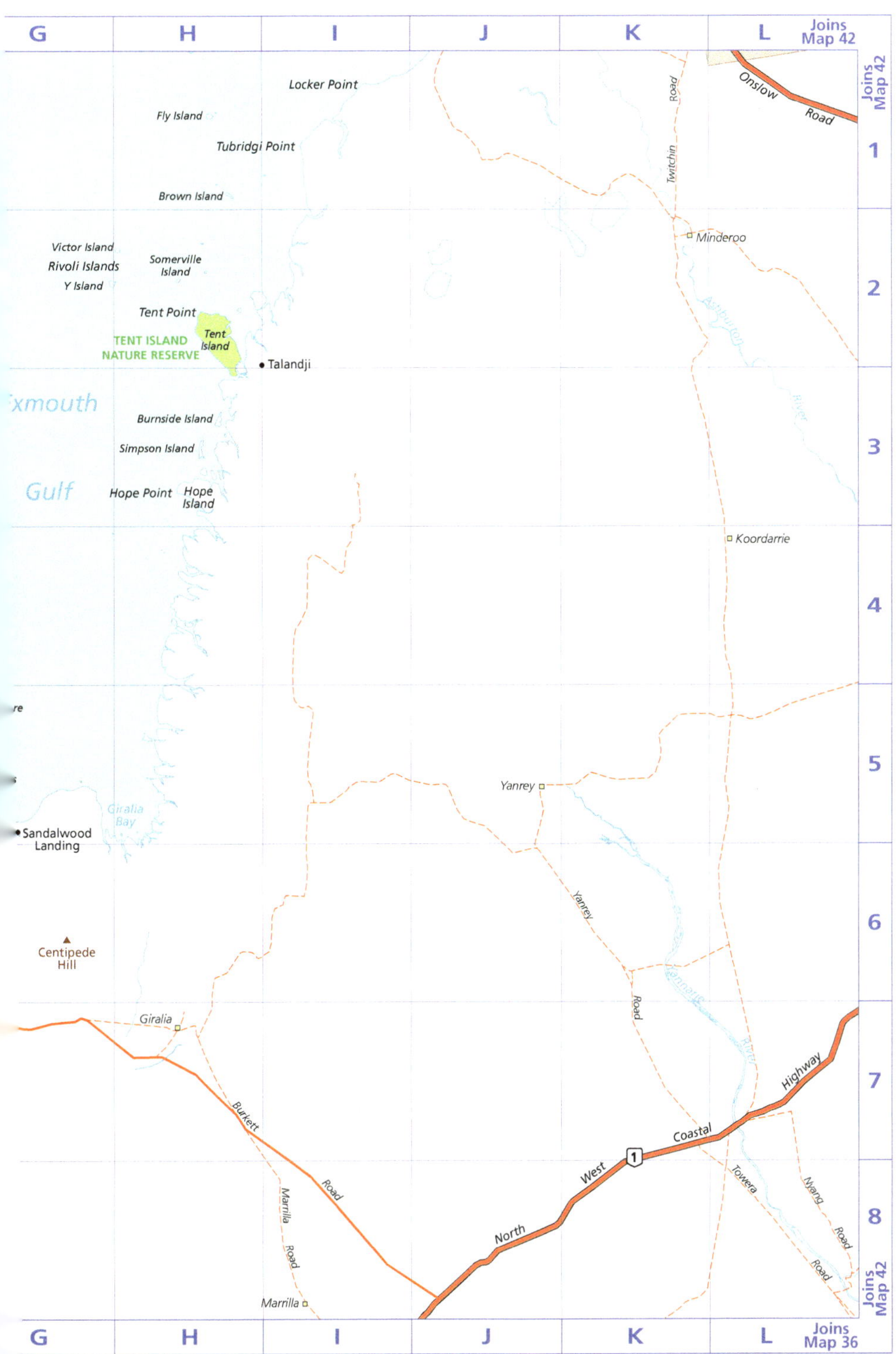

G
H
I
J
K
L
Joins Map 42
1
2
3
4
5
6
7
8
Locker Point
Fly Island
Tubridgi Point
Brown Island
Victor Island
Rivoli Islands
Y Island
Somerville Island
Tent Point
TENT ISLAND NATURE RESERVE
Tent Island
Talandji
Exmouth
Gulf
Burnside Island
Simpson Island
Hope Point
Hope Island
Giralia Bay
Sandalwood Landing
Centipede Hill
Giralia
Burkett
Road
Marrilla
Road
Marrilla
North
West
Coastal
Highway
1
Onslow
Road
Twitchin
Road
Minderoo
Ashburton
River
Koordarrie
Yanrey
Yanrey
Road
Yanarrie
River
Towera
Road
Nyang
Road
Joins Map 36

TOURING MAPS

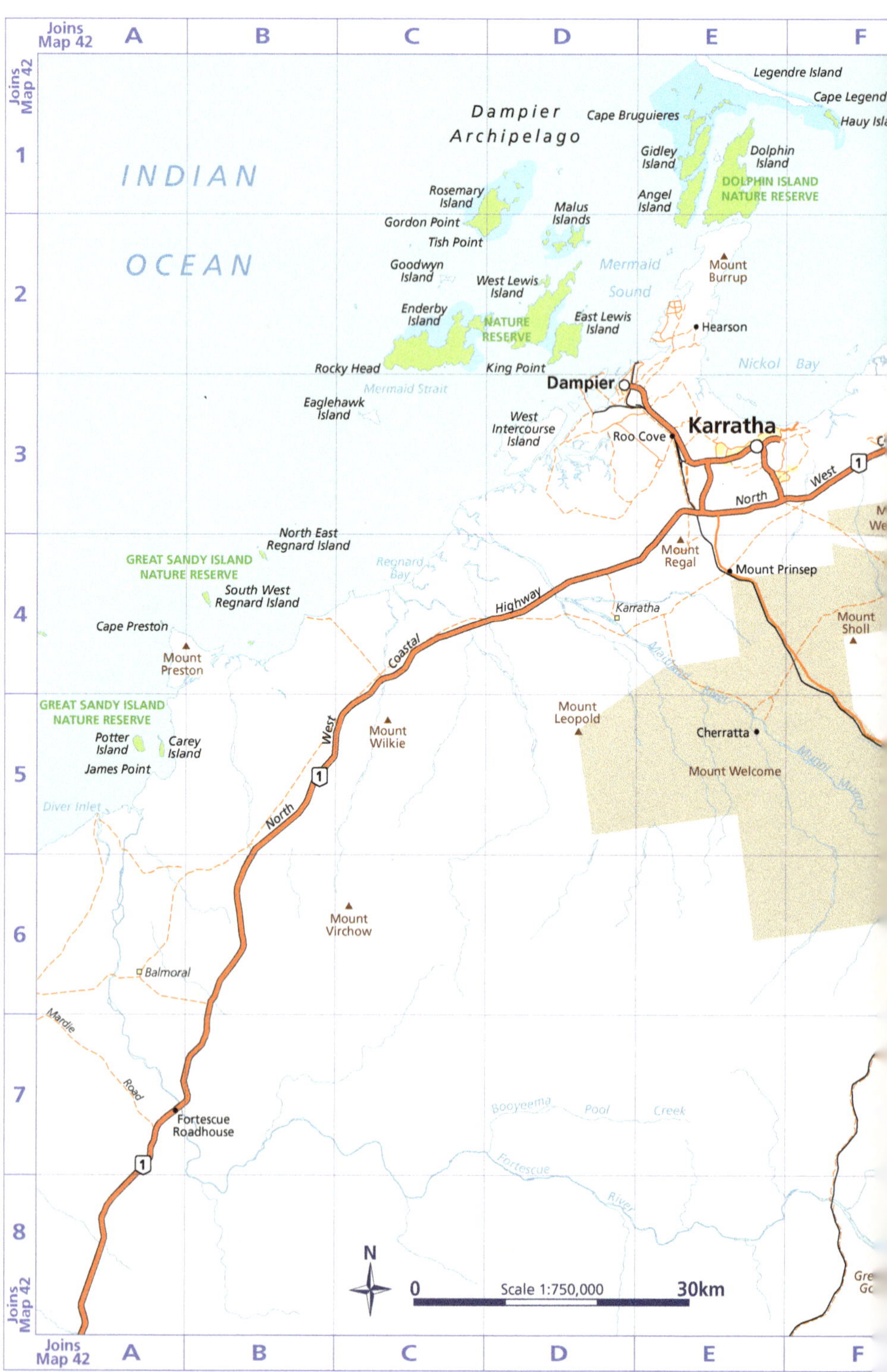
Joins Map 42
A
B
C
D
E
F
1
2
3
4
5
6
7
8
INDIAN
OCEAN
Dampier Archipelago
Legendre Island
Cape Legendr
Hauy Isla
Cape Bruguieres
Gidley Island
Dolphin Island
DOLPHIN ISLAND NATURE RESERVE
Angel Island
Rosemary Island
Malus Islands
Gordon Point
Tish Point
Goodwyn Island
West Lewis Island
Mermaid Sound
Mount Burrup
Enderby Island
NATURE RESERVE
East Lewis Island
Hearson
Rocky Head
King Point
Nickol Bay
Dampier
Mermaid Strait
Eaglehawk Island
West Intercourse Island
Roo Cove
Karratha
North West Coastal Highway
1
North East Regnard Island
GREAT SANDY ISLAND NATURE RESERVE
Regnard Bay
Mount Regal
Mount Prinsep
South West Regnard Island
Karratha
Mount Sholl
Cape Preston
Mount Preston
Maitland River
GREAT SANDY ISLAND NATURE RESERVE
Mount Leopold
Mount Wilkie
Cherratta
Potter Island
Carey Island
James Point
Mount Welcome
Diver Inlet
Mount Virchow
Balmoral
Mardie Road
Fortescue Roadhouse
Booyeema Pool Creek
Fortescue River
N
0
Scale 1:750,000
30km

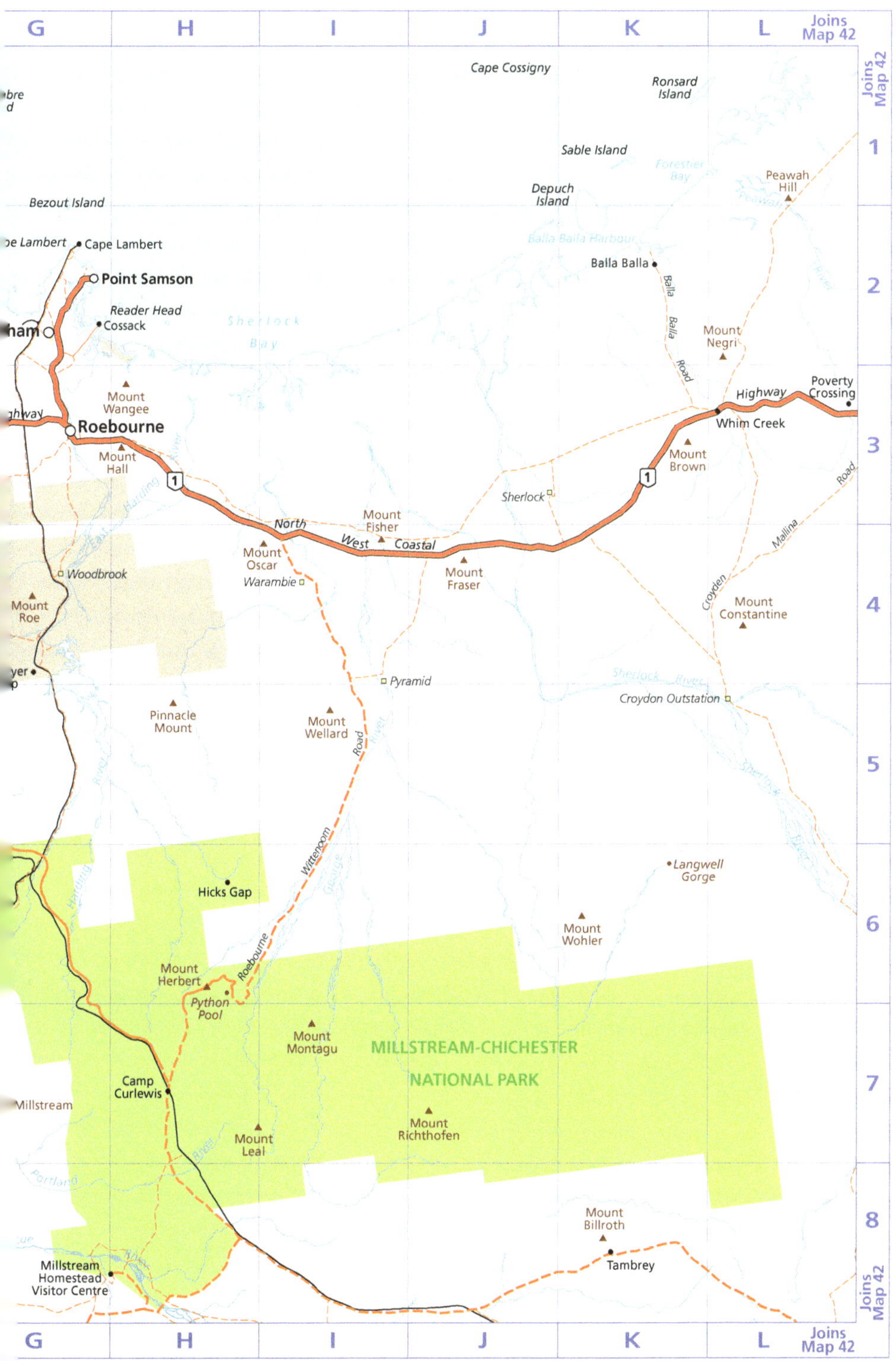

TOURING MAPS

Parks, Forests, Reserves and Campsites Index

C

D

E

L

M

*** Denotes areas with facilities (usually special access to toilets) for people with disabilities**

Campsite Index

D

E

F

G

M

N

P

Q

R

S

T

*** Denotes areas with facilities (usually special access to toilets) for people with disabilities**

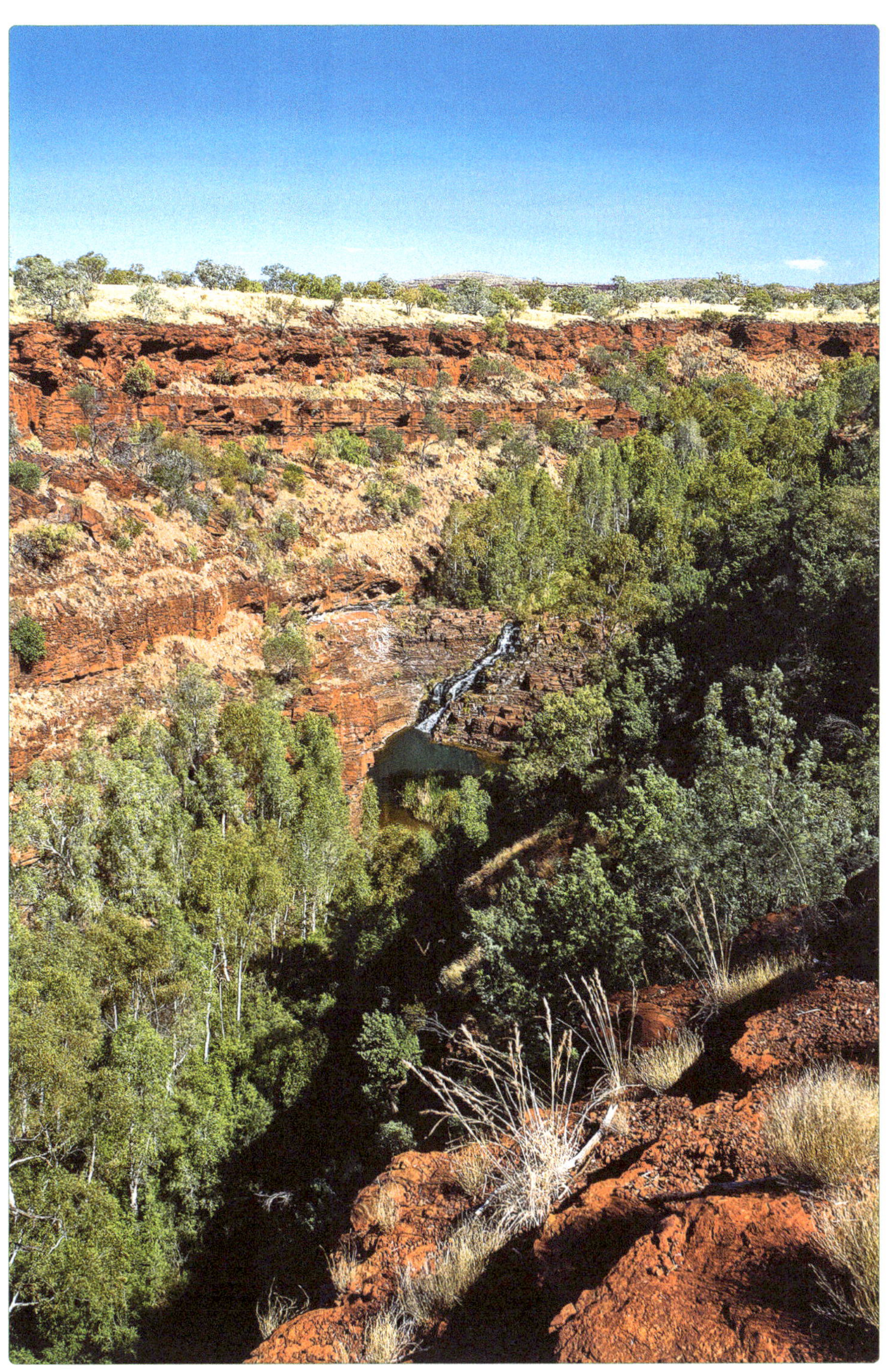

Fortesque Falls, Karijini National Park, The Pilbara Region

Boiling Billy and

This book is just one of a growing series of outdoor and souvenir guides from Boiling Billy and Woodslane Press.

Boiling Billy have been publishing guides for the Australian outdoor enthusiast for over 25 years, and details of all their titles can be found at www.boilingbilly.com.au To browse through other titles available from Woodslane Press, visit www.woodslane.com.au If your local bookshop does not have stock of a Boiling Billy or Woodslane book, they can easily order it for you. In case of difficulty please contact our customer service team on 02 8445 2300 or info@woodslane.com.au

Boiling Billy Camping Guides

Explore the best camping spots across the country with Boiling Billy's full-colour state based camping guides. Each directory contains the most comprehensive details of hundreds of campsites in national parks, state forests and reserves across the state. You'll discover places where you can pitch your tent on a mountain peak, wander along secluded riverbanks, throw in a line from your campsite, and enjoy the peace and seclusion of Australia's incredible outback.

9781921203688	Camping Guide to New South Wales	**$49.99**
9781925403879	Camping Guide to the Northern Territory	**$29.99**
9781925403862	Camping Guide to South Australia	**$34.99**
9781921874314	Camping Guide to Tasmania	**$29.99**
9781925403381	Camping Guide to Victoria	**$39.99**
9781925403954	Camping Guide to Queensland	**$39.99**

Woodslane Press

Guides for Aussie bush travellers...

If you're going bush, however you're going bush, there's a guide from Boiling Billy you'll want to take along. These new guides are illustrated with full-colour photography and packed full of helpful hints, tried and tested tips and - in two cases - delicious, easy-to-make meals.

Australian Bush Cooking
$39.99
ISBN: 9781921203930

Australian Geographic Southwest Australia
$19.99
ISBN: 9781925868067

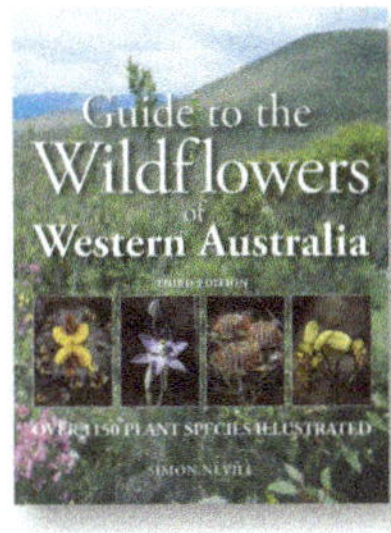

Guide to the Wildflowers of Western Australia
$34.99
ISBN: 9781925868036

Guide to the Wildlife of Perth and Australia's South West
$44.95
ISBN: 9781921683923

Australian Camp Oven Cooking

Camping or caravan trips doesn't mean you have to give up delicious, easy to make meals. Jo Clews brings many years of camp oven cooking experience to this new book featuring over 130 recipes, as well as advice on choosing and caring for equipment. This is the perfect book to take on your next camping trip.

$39.99 • ISBN: 9781925868326

Perth's Best Bush, Coast & City Walks

Perth and its environs boast a huge range of beautiful environments, making the region perfect for exploring on foot. Detailed descriptions and maps help the reader explore the region's parks, bushland, lakes, coasts and most interesting urban areas. Walking chapters include Perth Metropolitan, Coastal Walks, Swan and Canning Rivers, Wetlands, Darling Ranges.

$29.95 • ISBN: 9781925868029

All Boiling Billy and Woodslane Press books are available for bulk and custom purposes. Volume copies of this and our other titles are available at wholesale prices, and custom-jacketed and even mini-extracts are possible. Contact our Publishing Manager for further information, on +61 (0)2 8445 2300 or info@woodslane.com.au

Milton Keynes UK
Ingram Content Group UK Ltd.
UKHW052244280524
443311UK00007B/141

9 781921 606168